Intergenerational Communication Across the Life Span

LEA'S COMMUNICATION SERIES
Jennings Bryant/Dolf Zillmann, General Editors

For a complete list of titles in LEA's Communication Series, please contact Lawrence Erlbaum Associates, Publishers.

Intergenerational Communication Across the Life Span

Angie Williams
Cardiff University, Wales

Jon F. Nussbaum
The Pennsylvania State University

LEA

2001

LAWRENCE ERLBAUM ASSOCIATES, PUBLISHERS

Mahwah, New Jersey   London

Lawrence Erlbaum Associates, Inc., Publishers
10 Industrial Avenue
Mahwah, NJ 07430

Cover design by Kathryn Houghtaling Lacey

Library of Congress Cataloging-in-Publication Data

Williams, Angie.
Intergenerational communication across the life span /
    Angie Williams, Jon F. Nussbaum.

    p.   cm.

Includes bibliographical references and index.
ISBN 0-8058-2248-8 (cloth : alk. paper)
    ISBN 0-8058-2249-6 (pbk. : alk. paper)
1. Intergenerational communication. 2. Intergenerational
    relations. 3. Communication in the family. 4. Conflict of
    generations.   I. Nussbaum, Jon F.   II. Title.
HM726 .W56   2000
306.87—dc21
                                                    99-056785
                                                       CIP

Books published by Lawrence Erlbaum Associates are printed on acid-free paper, and their bindings are chosen for strength and durability.

Printed in the United States of America
10 9 8 7 6 5 4 3 2 1

To Debra, Alan, June, and John

Contents

Introduction

Effective communication is considered by many to be the number one problem in, and the number one solution for, numerous aspects of our lives. If we only communicated better, wars would not occur, lawsuits would be avoided, and all of our relationships would be more satisfying and more successful. What a wonderful world it would be if we could all communicate effectively. Sentiments such as these are accepted with so little criticism that we never question the assumption that effective communication is not difficult if people are given the right information and training. One simply needs to watch television or to enter any bookstore to see hundreds of self-help manuals and other examples of how to accomplish effective communication. The ordained wisdom of our popular culture reassures us that if we come to understand our innate bias toward behaving like true men or true women, or if we learn a few basic dating rules and behave accordingly, all our relationships will become manageable while we achieve our relational goals, and ultimately, true happiness. These popular and rather rudimentary analyses of competent communication simplify the process of effective communication and completely ignore the fact that years of academic study of these issues point us away from such simplistic solutions. N. Coupland, Giles, and Wiemann (1991) reiterated this position in their theoretical examination of miscommunication. These authors pointed out that communication is, by its very nature, ambiguous, imprecise, and inherently flawed. Furthermore, communicators are strategic and often less than honest, direct, clear, and so forth. Sometimes miscommunication itself may be the goal, at other times interactants in a conversation may not care whether they have communicated effectively or have achieved harmony because each has an entirely different agenda.

Of particular interest to us is intergenerational communication, which according to recent research, has rich potential for misunderstanding and miscommunication. This is particularly true when the chronological distance between interactants means that they lived through very different historical periods and may be operating with different communication assumptions, skills, needs, and experiences.

In recent years, interest in the social, psychological, and communication correlates of the aging process has been increasing in concert with the growth in the population of elderly individuals in Western societies. In the communication discipline itself, there has been a slow but growing recognition that populations being studied should include those who are middle-aged and old as well as young college-age individuals.[1] Beyond the inclusion of different age groups within the study of human interaction, it is becoming increasingly clear that to move to a true understanding of how humans manage to adapt and survive for such long life spans, we must explore how and why we interact with others of differing ages in diverse contexts.

We live in a world that has ambivalent feelings toward diversity—on the one hand it is celebrated and embraced, and on the other hand, discrimination and prejudice toward those who are unlike us is rife. As we move through the life span, whether we like it or not, we interact with many individuals who are very different from us, and this includes those who may not be the same age or from the same cohort. In fact, although we are accustomed to talking about communication and diversity in intercultural and other arenas of social life, we typically give little thought to the fact that we interact in a world of intergenerational communication that is rife with misunderstandings and erroneous assumptions about age. Throughout our lives we are socialized in the intergenerational contexts of our families, schooled in the intergenerational contexts of our educational institutions, placed into the intergenerational contexts of organizations, and cared for in our mature years by intergenerational teams of formal and informal caregivers. This all takes place in a world in which social psychological and communication studies indicate that we would rather strive, and indeed do strive, to interact with individuals similar to ourselves (people of similar age, attitudes, appearance, etc.). For example, despite the fact that Butler (1987) has labeled *agism* (also seen with its variant spelling, *ageism*) as the third great -ism of our time, in our society agism is still underacknowledged and underexplored.

---

[1]Throughout the book we use the terms *young, old/elderly,* and *middle-aged.* Except where specified, we assume *young* people refers to adults under age 30 (in fact usually college students in their 20s), *middle-aged* adults refers to adults age 35 to 65 years old; *old* or *elderly* adults are assumed to be those above retirement age (i.e., over 65). Broadly speaking, these categories are in line with colloquial usage and we use these terms for convenience only. We realize the dangers of categorization and labeling and in no way wish to imply that individuals in these age groups are some sort of homogeneous mass.

Although older people reflect on their lives and remember youth, young people often seem to assume that they will be forever young; they avoid thinking about their own aging, almost as if not thinking or talking about it will ensure that it will never happen. Our interactive lives, however, are forever changing as we traverse the life span, and we should be interested in these changes and what they mean for us. Indeed, if we are interested in promoting physical, social, and psychological health across the life span, we should not turn away from our futures as aging individuals (or from youth either). In fact, to understand healthy and productive aging it is going to be crucial to study institutional caregiving, or the grandparent–grandchild interaction, the changing structure of intergenerational families, and how we communicate about the life span itself.

A life-span developmental view of communication and aging, which attempts to capture the many similarities and changes that occur in our interactive lives as we age, has been promoted for some time by scholars in the communication discipline, for example, Nussbaum (1989) and N. Coupland and Nussbaum (1993). This life-span view of communication parallels a recent series of books and journal special editions examining communication and aging generally, for example, Hummert, Wiemann, and Nussbaum (1995), and Nussbaum, Pecchioni, Robinson, and Thompson (2000). These volumes have been written in a context of similar books and articles, which explore every facet of the aging process in our sister disciplines of psychology, sociology, anthropology, political science, and economics. Two recent books by Bengston and colleagues provide a demographic and structural sociological analysis of intergenerational contact. The sociological–public policy analysis inherent in these books places intergenerational contact within a macrocontext. This book, although complementary to the previous work, moves the study of intergenerational contact closer to the actual participants, to what happens within intergenerational interactions, and to how people evaluate their intergenerational experiences. In this sense, our book concentrates on the microcontext of intergenerational interaction and the cognitions, language, and relationship behaviors related to intergenerational communication across the life span.

It is important to separate the focus of this book both from intergenerational texts written by scholars with different theoretical imperatives, and also from the series of publications written exclusively about older adults. We feel that the lack of a concerted effort by scholars to concentrate on intergenerational communication as a unique aspect of our interactive world is a serious omission from the literature. Although much can be learned from the study of aging by concentrating on those older than

65 years of age, much is also lost by not presenting the lives of those who are older than 65 years of age within the context of the world in which interaction is not limited to any exclusive age category. Individuals of all ages interact with one another, and their interactions have significance throughout the entirety of their lives.

Research that is intergenerational and communicative has been scattered sporadically across a number of texts, outlets, and disciplines, and thus what we could have learned from the study of intergenerational communication per se was potentially lost in a chorus of other voices. A major purpose of this book is to bring together research from multiple disciplines concerned with intergenerational communication and framed by several unique theoretical perspectives drawn from the communication discipline. We explicitly state that our understanding of human behavior across the life span is enhanced by studying our communicative behavior during intergenerational interaction. To reach a richer understanding of intergenerational communication, we must investigate the cognitions and beliefs of individuals as they enter into and evaluate intergenerational contact. We must view language as a creative activity that we adapt to serve our purposes during intergenerational interactions. Finally, we must understand how this combination of cognitions, beliefs, language, and so forth constitutes the intergenerational relationships that are essential to our lives.

To accomplish these goals, this book is organized into three parts. Part I, Social, Psychological, and Developmental Foundations, contains seven chapters that present the theoretical perspectives that frame the book: current research concentrating on the social cognition of stereotyping, language, beliefs about language and the aging process; and finally intergenerational language strategies. A chapter about generational age identities is also included in this part. Perhaps most important are the theoretical perspectives that we feel provide a unique interpretation of intergenerational communication. As mentioned previously, we place intergenerational communication within a life-span perspective. In addition, we present intergroup theory, communication accommodation theory, the communication predicament model of aging, the stereotype activation model, and structuration theory as the frames around which we discuss intergenerational communication.

Part II is entitled Intergenerational Relationship Communication. We believe that intergenerational communication both takes place within relationships and simultaneously defines relationships. Chapters include discussions about the adult child–elderly parent relationship, the grandparent–grandchild relationship, the sandwiched generation, and several other intergenerational relationships.

The final part of this book is entitled Macrosocietal Perspectives. This part moves beyond the theoretical foundations and intergenerational relationship considerations by focusing on intergenerational conflict, societal intergenerational issues, and cultural perspectives on intergenerational communication. The epilogue summarizes our thoughts as well as points to future issues for intergenerational communication scholars.

Acknowledgments

We give our heartfelt thanks to our families and friends for supporting this project, which seemed endless to all of us at times. Debra Nussbaum, Alan Moorcroft, Melanie Williams, and June and John Sullivan have all suffered the ups and downs while the drafts were written and rewritten. Particular thanks go to Alex Giles who, in ways he will never know, contributed enormously to the production of this volume.

The authors also wish to thank colleagues. Two reviewers of the manuscript, Sandra Thompson and Jake Harwood, provided extensive and extremely helpful comments about an early draft. We would also like to thank the graduate students in the Department of Communication at the University of Oklahoma who took part in the Intergenerational Communication Seminar during the 1993–1994 session. The ideas for this book evolved and took shape during that seminar series. Subsequently, thanks go to graduate students at the same institution who read and commented about the first draft of the manuscript during the 1995–1996 session.

The authors would also like to acknowledge a number of colleagues who have contributed to the research reported in many chapters of the book. For example, portions of chapters 3, 4, and 15 appeared in Williams and Giles (1998). Portions of chapter 5 appeared in Williams (1992) and Williams and Giles (1996). Portions of chapter 12 appeared in Williams, Coupland, Folwell, and Sparks (1997). Thanks also go to colleagues around the Pacific Rim for their contributions to the work reported in chapter 14. Numerous other colleagues contributed to the material reviewed in the book and immeasurably influenced our approach to intergenerational communication. They include Howard Giles, Nikolas Coupland, Justine Coupland, Mary Lee Hummert, Ellen Ryan, Jake Harwood, and members of the Pacific Rim Intergenerational Communication Research Project.

Finally, we wish to thank Linda Bathgate and her colleagues at Lawrence Erlbaum Associates for their insight, encouragement, professionalism, and patience. Without their belief that books exploring intergenerational communication, and communication and aging in general, are important scholarly contributions to the study of human behavior, our work would remain silent.

PART I

SOCIAL, PSYCHOLOGICAL, AND DEVELOPMENTAL FOUNDATIONS

Seven chapters are included within this first part of the book. Within these chapters, we focus on the theoretical perspectives that frame the book and place intergenerational communication within a life-span perspective. These chapters include not only our theoretical orientations, but discussions on intergenerational contexts, social cognitive contributions to intergenerational communication, the importance of language and language strategies within intergenerational interaction, and generational identity. In addition, these chapters serve to focus attention on the communicative importance of intergenerational contact for all participants within this most interesting and often difficult interaction.

1

Theoretical Foundations for the Study of Intergenerational Communication

Most of the time, we strongly and unquestioningly value the modern, the technologically advanced, the new, and the youthful to the detriment of things we deem as old fashioned, outdated and worn out. There are exceptions to this rule. For example, if furniture, wine, and people last long enough, they can gain great value as they beat the odds to become antiques and octogenarians. At the same time, we often assume the naiveté and lack of wisdom of those who are young. Assumptions such as these are strongly linked to chronological age and are deeply embedded in our social collective psyches; we bring them into every interaction we have with those who are much younger or older than ourselves. Intergenerational interactions can be as routine as any other interaction, or can be markedly different from those interactions that we have with peers. For example, there may be certain topics we avoid discussing with people much older or much younger than ourselves. Why should intergenerational communication be any different from peer communication? One way of anwering this question is to look at various theories for an explanation. This is the focus of our first chapter.

The major perspectives and theories that have influenced intergenerational communication are outlined in this chapter to provide a framework for interpreting the research discussed in the following chapters. Although these are the perspectives and theories that have influenced many approaches to the study of intergenerational relations thus far, they are by no means the only way to understand intergenerational talk. Theories are important for performing a number of functions in scholarship; they help us to organize a wide variety of variables—both relationships and experiences—into an integrative whole. They provide the potential to extend knowledge as when two or more theoretical conceptions are combined to produce new predictions and hypotheses or when underlying theoretical understandings are challenged by new knowledge. In this way, then, theory should both stimulate and provide an organizing framework for future research. One of the broadest and most overarching perspectives is life-span perspective. In many ways this perspective forms the foundation for the study of intergenerational communication, and is certainly at the very core of our approach to communication and aging.

THE LIFE-SPAN PERSPECTIVE

The life-span developmental perspective provides us with an excellent orientation and frame within which to discuss intergenerational communication. During the past 30 years, the life span developmental perspective has evolved into a heuristic metaperspective, which guides much thought and research in numerous academic disciplines, including communication (see N. Coupland & Nussbaum, 1993; Nussbaum, 1989; Nussbaum, Thompson, & Robinson, 1989). Building on the early work of Erickson (1959) and others (e.g., Kolhberg, 1973), and explored at numerous life-span developmental conferences sponsored by the Department of Psychology at West Virginia University, the life-span perspective has evolved and can be summarized in five basic tenets (see Baltes, Reese, & Lipsett, 1980).

First, the potential for development extends throughout the life span; there is no ultimate end point in terms of developmental plateau (i.e., self-actualization or ego-integrity) and no prescription for, or expectation of, ultimate decline. A cursory examination of early popular developmental theories reveals a strong and lively concern with child development and what appears to be a lack of interest in adult development and aging. For example, Erickson's (1959) final stage of ego integrity versus despair is stagnant and relies almost exclusively on the alternative stereotypes of miserable and bitter old people versus the wise elder. Erickson's ultimate and ideal end point of life, development of integrity, seems to be in direct contrast to a life-span perspective because it implies an ultimate resolution to development—a position that is rejected by life-span scholars. Other stage theories, such as those of Levinson, Darrow, Klein, Levinson, and McKee (1978) and Gould (1978), are good examples of a concentration on early childhood development and have little to say about adult development. The life-span perspective views development as a life-long process.

No age period, neither the first 12 years of life nor the last 12 years of life, holds supremacy in regulating the nature of development (Baltes, Smith, & Staudinger, 1992).

The first assertion of the life-span perspective rejects commonly accepted notions of almost universal (cognitive, psychological, physical, and social) decline as we age. This perspective has yet to be fully realized when it comes to the study of communication and aging. However, it has considerable implications for the social and communicative lives of people of all ages and our lay understandings about the aging process in general. Researchers, to date, have failed to examine many of the real-life social–developmental challenges that occur across the life span. For example, the impacts of role change, becoming parents (or choosing not to), multiple marriages, grandparenthood, great-grandparenthood, job loss, job change, retirement, increased leisure time and leisure definition, or the interactive implications of death and bereavement have not been fully investigated. Researchers have often, perhaps understandably, been more concerned with the connection between age and health, which usually means declining health, and focus on the negative and problematic aspects of aging. For example, some researchers now suggest that a focus on cognitive function under laboratory conditions has inflated the notion of cognitive decline with increased age. Although health and cognitive functioning are important considerations, intense interest at this level often excludes other fruitful avenues of study, especially those involving a more social enterprise. It also implicitly discounts other developmental issues of aging, and reinforces stereotypes of aging individuals as chronically ill and in a constant state of both mental and physical decline.

Second, according to a life-span developmental perspective, development is multidirectional. "Considerable diversity and pluralism is found in the directionality of changes that constitute development. The direction of change varies by category of behavior" (Baltes, Smith, & Staudinger, 1992, p. 125). We should not expect to experience universal patterns of growth during any one period of life. Likewise, we should not expect to experience universal periods of decline. This may be especially important for communication scholars who study the simultaneous changes in the relational networks of individuals across the life span. Several of our most significant relationships may be experiencing increased intimacy while at the same time several other significant relationships experience a loss of intimacy. In addition, development may progress on a number of dimensions (intellectual, social, and physical) at different speeds. Throughout life, we have potentialities, resources, and characteristics that should not be ignored or discounted. McCandless and Evans (1973) divided the life course into three interacting components: the physical–motor, the cognitive–intellectual, and the personal–social. Although this tripartite division was derived from the study of children, it can be extended to encompass the entirety of the life span. For example, on a personal–social developmental dimension, our roles vary throughout life: We are sons and daughters who may or may not have demanding careers, may or may not become parents and grandparents, and each role change or role conflict brings its own developmental challenges and triumphs.

Third, related to the life-span developmental principle just mentioned is the notion of development as a gain–loss dynamic. The life span should not be viewed as a process of continuous growth or continuous decline. Growth and decline are joint occurrences. This point tends to emphasize the complex nature of human interactions. In any one interaction, competencies can be achieved in one communicative area while anxieties emerge in another. It is reasonable to speculate that multiple dimensions of human interaction are in play across the life span and that these different dimensions experience growth and decline simultaneously.

Fourth, there is much intra- as well as interindividual diversity as we develop across the life span. Baltes et al. (1992) suggest that the key developmental agenda for researchers is to uncover the range and limits of intraindividual plasticity and the sources of individual differences. Why is it that we can be competent communicators with another individual at Time 1 and then have a completely frustrating communicative encounter with the same person at Time 2? Why is it that we can have a very satisfying relationship with our mother but not with our father? Why is it that the level of satisfaction with our parental relationships seems to change across the life span? As students of intergenerational communication, we cannot forget the great diversity found within each individual; and we cannot forget that these individual differences will affect our interactive lives.

Finally, the life-span perspective assumes that the person and the environment are engaged in a transactional relationship, influencing and being influenced by each other. This assertion is an attempt to resolve the debate between those who would place emphasis on nature and genetic considerations and those who would emphasize nurture or the role of the environment. Instead, the transactional approach suggests that relationships, rather than objects or elements, are of central importance. Life-span developmentalists recognize that living organisms are inherently and spontaneously active in organizing their environments, that environments have reciprocal influences on organisms, and that the confluence of the two is of most interest. In addition, each individual is situated in a sociocultural–historical context that influences all human development. It matters where and when someone is living. To understand human development, one must have a complete grasp of the many economic, political, social, and physical conditions in which the development is occurring.

Applying the life-span perspective to intergenerational communication suggests that communication between people who are of very different ages may be special and interesting to discuss in its own right. Communication between people who are developing quite differently in terms of their physical, cognitive, or psychosocial selves, and who have experienced quite different life events in unique historical contexts presents a rather large interactive challenge. In some senses, perhaps, we could even go as far as to suggest that many individuals belong to different developmental cultures and that some features of intergenerational communication can be likened to intercultural communication (N. Coupland & Nussbaum, 1993; Giles & Coupland, 1991).

The life-span perspective does not specify which theories of social behavior are the best explanations of development. Thinking of intergenerational communication as a life-span challenge, within which interpersonal relationships need to be negotiated in an historical context, opens up the possibility of drawing from intercultural theory to enhance our understanding of the particular ways that people from different generations manage their interactions. We are now in the position to consider older and younger people as members of different social–generational groups who may identify themselves within a particular generation. In fact, the development of individual identity has for many years been a lively topic for debate and theorizing among life-span and developmental theorists. However, we not only develop a sense of *personal identity* (who we are as a unique individual), but we also can be expected to develop a sense of *social identity* (our awareness of our membership in particular social groups or categories, combined with our feelings about such membership). Intergroup theory is a social–psychological theory that places a central importance on social identity and accounts for the way that people behave as members of different social groups. In recent years, intergroup theory has had a strong influence on intergenerational communication research, an influence that is shown in almost every chapter in this book.

INTERGROUP THEORY

The term *intergroup theory* encompasses a cluster of theories originating in European social psychology, many of which focus on interethnic behavior such as nationalism and racial prejudice. One of the fundamental aspects of intergroup theory is the notion that identity can be either personal or social. Personal identity, according to Turner (1982), refers to self-definitions in terms of particular personality attributes and behavioral characteristics, whereas social identity is a definition of self in terms of a social category or of group membership. We may have a number of social identifications, of which some are more important than others. Context and timing also play important roles in the development and expression of social identity. For example, some situations call attention to individuals' group memberships (their social identities) rather than to their personal identities, and both may develop throughout the life span. Different groups and social categories may have differential meaning to us depending on our life stage, social circumstances, and so on. For example, being a woman or a member of a minority ethnic group may be more salient and important at some times of life, and in some circumstances, than others. In this book, we are mainly concerned with peoples' social identities as members of age categories or generational groups.

Tajfel (1978, 1981) argued that we have inherent tendencies to divide our social world into groups and social categories, and that we are aware of our own and other's membership of particular social groups. To demonstrate this inherent tendency, Tajfel's seminal experimental studies showed that merely categorizing people as belonging to two arbitrarily chosen different groups was enough for them to show ingroup favoritism in the allocation of rewards (Tajfel, Billig, Bundy, & Flament, 1971). In other words, as soon as we see ourselves and others as belonging to different groups, no matter how trivial the divisions, we tend to favor our own group. This tendency can be observed in many real-life situations in which group membership is the focus—nationality differences, gender differences, support of different teams in sports events, and so forth.

This means that we categorize ourselves as ingroup members, and sometimes behave as stereotypical ingroup members, emphasizing the attributes that we believe portray who we are and where we belong. There are many ways to signal group membership and to behave in stereotypical ingroup ways. For example, individuals may communicate group membership by the way they dress. Members of youth subcultures and gangs often have an unwritten dress code, and everyone who can read the code knows who belongs to which group.

Besides categorizing ourselves, we also categorize others as group members. More often than not we use ready-made information to do this, such as demographic characteristics (age, gender, race etc.), objective characteristics (hair, skin color), or salient characteristics, and we often do this regardless of whether people subjectively feel that they are members of such groups. First impressions are important: It is then that we are most likely both to categorize and to be categorized, and this may set the tone for the first conversation, for further communication, and for the future of the relationship. Once categorization occurs, we ascribe certain attributes to group members and generalize them to all group members, downplaying any given individual's idiosyncratic or unique personality characteristics. For example, one might meet an older woman, think "she's a typical grandma," and assume that she is kindly and bakes good cookies. On the other hand, consider an older person who, on the basis of a youth's disheveled appearance, categorizes that person as a degenerate regardless of whether he or she is or not. The older person might go one step further and assume that the youth is aggressive and takes drugs. These two examples demonstrate the process of stereotyping, which can ultimately lead to bias, unfair discrimination, and even prejudicial behavior toward outgroup members (see Turner, Hogg, Oakes, Reicher, & Wetherell, 1987).

When thinking of ourselves as group members, we are also likely to attempt to assess our group standing relative to others through the process of social comparison. As a result of these comparisons, it is important that we gain distinctiveness and positive outcomes for our ingroup in relation to relevant outgroups, showing ingroup favoritism and outgroup denigration (Turner et al., 1987). According to Tajfel and Turner (1979), the main motivation for social comparison and the desire for positive distinctiveness is to gain self-esteem as group members. Other motivations may be present too, such as the desire for coherent self-conceptions and the desire to make oneself and one's experiences meaningful (Hogg & Abrams, 1988). Ultimately, however, we want to feel good about ourselves and our groups; we want our groups to be on top; and we want to be the good guys and the winners. One of the ways we acheive this is to establish that other groups are not as smart, are not on top and are losers rather than winners. When the context is perceived as intergroup, and we have classified ourselves and our conversational partners as members of different groups, this suggests that we may strive—even in subtle ways—to reassure ourselves that our group is best.

This means that whether or not an encounter is seen as interindividual or intergroup is important for tracking the course of the encounter. Interindividual and intergroup foci may be two crucial dimensions of encounters between people (Tajfel, 1978). In an interindividually salient encounter, particular individual qualities of the participants are salient and are attended to (see also Fiske & Neuberg, 1990). Intergroup encounters occur when people categorize each other as group members, and in this case individual characteristics become relatively less important, and interactants respond to each other in terms of their social identities. More often than not, this results in treatment of individuals in terms of the stereotypes associated with their particular social groups, and can lead to negative evaluations, misunderstandings, and conflict. For example, the intergroup nature of intergenerational interactions may be particularly predominant when the interactants have minimal personal information about each other and when their age-identities are salient. Under these conditions, there is little information for people to access, and group categorization, social comparisons, and stereotyping may be the result. Moreover, a strong sense of allegiance to a particular social group might be more meaningful to some group members than to others. For example, some young people may have a more heightened sense of being members of the younger generation than others, and this may be indicated by their preferences for certain kinds of music, movies, lifestyles, and so on. This sense of age-identity may work as a preinteractional tendency to be more aware of age differences, which may be further triggered by certain contexts, such as those in which a much older person is encountered (see Williams, Giles, Coupland, Dalby, & Manasse, 1990). A relatively strong sense of identification with a particular social group would also be expected to influence communication with outgroup members.

Many similarities can be drawn between social aspects of aging, ethnic, intercultural, and intergroup phenomena. From a social-psychological perspective, perhaps the strongest and most useful parallels between age groups and cultural or ethnic groups derive from shared sociopsychological processes such as (group-based) categorization, social comparison, self- and other- stereotyping, prejudice, and discrimination. Thus, age can be a fundamental categorization device; we assign people to categories based on years lived, and tend to downplay their individual or idiosyncratic characteristics. By doing so, we maximize the perceptual differences between age groups and minimize differences between individuals within groups (Tajfel, 1978; Tajfel & Wilkes, 1963). It has been persuasively argued that many intergenerational interactions are intergroup in their nature and consequences, and are thereby subject to all of the previously discussed processes (Harwood, Giles, & Ryan, 1995).

In reality however, age is also a unique social category because the boundaries between generational groups are constantly in transition. Younger people will one day be members of the out group, whereas older people will have once been in-group members and both parties may be aware of this. Each generation is arguably uniquely placed in time because the particular historical period in which it matured has unique characteristics that interact with development. Thus, different generations are likely to be exposed to different sets of developmental experiences (Schaie & Strother, 1968). The fuzzy nature of the intergroup boundaries is what makes age-categorization a unique and interesting intergroup phenomenon. Intergroup theorists commonly consider that groups who are alike in some ways experience an increased desire to differentiate from each other. We feel a greater sense of threat from outgroup members when group boundaries are unclear and may go to extra lengths to shore up those boundaries by emphasizing difference. Many younger people feel very threatened by the thought of their own aging and try to avoid confronting the fact that they too may one day belong to the outgroup. This could be why some young people actively avoid interacting with older people and even experience a form of extreme aversion to older people known as *gerontophobia* (Levin & Levin, 1980).

Not only has intergroup theory provided a driving force at the heart of many recent studies of intergenerational interaction, it is also at the heart of many current theories that focus on communication and aging. Intergroup theory is not a communication theory: although it helps us understand how people might identify and act as group members, it does not tell us what kind of communication to expect when persons of very different groups meet and interact. It does suggest that under certain conditions, such as when group membership is valued and is salient, people might choose to be competitive, seeking to enhance their own self-esteem at the expense of that of other people. Of course, an alternative is communicative cooperation and seeking common ground. By extending intergroup theory to examine the way individuals behaving as group members communicate with each other, communication accommodation theory (CAT) bridges the gap between intergroup theory and communication. As demonstrated throughout the rest of this book, CAT has made an important contribution to the understanding of intergenerational communication.

COMMUNICATION ACCOMMODATION THEORY

CAT was developed by Giles and colleagues to describe and explain aspects of the way people modify their speech according to situational, personal or even interactional variables (for recent reviews, see Giles, Coupland, & Coupland, 1991; Gallois, Giles, Jones, Cargile, & Ota, 1995). For example, when we wish to signal ingroup solidarity or to express personal affiliation, we may converge our speech towards others', but when we wish to indicate outgroup membership and to distance ourselves personally or both, we would more likely diverge our speech patterns away from others. *Convergence* occurs when we make our speech and communication patterns more like that of our partners, and it is typical of many cooperative interpersonal encounters. In general terms, convergence is responded to favorably. *Divergence* occurs when people communicatively emphasize the difference between themselves and their partners; it is characteristic of many intergroup encounters in which identity is salient and is often negatively attributed and evaluated by recipients. In addition, *speech maintenance* refers to a style that is supposedly *cross-situationally constant* (i.e., neither convergent nor divergent). In many circumstances, *maintenance* is subjectively perceived by recipients as somewhat socially divergent.

These three strategies—convergence, divergence, and maintenance—have been entitled *approximation strategies* (N. Coupland, Coupland, Giles, & Henwood, 1988). *Approximation* is said to occur when interactants focus their attention on their partners' speech styles. Most importantly, approximation occurs in response to perceptions or expectations about the other person's speech style. For example, in an age context there are some lexical and stylistic features that can distinguish one generational group from another. Consider, for example, the sociolinguistic exclusion of older people with the use of youth slang such as "veging," "bummer," and "way cool," or the dating effect of outmoded words or expressions such as "fortnight," "presently," and 1960s expressions such as "groovy" and "far out man."

A second possible focus of attention is on the other person's *interpretive competence*, which is his or her ability to decode, or the ability to figure out what is being said. This focus can lead to *interpretability strategies* used to modify speech in order to make what is said more clear. Changes in vocabulary, modifications of pitch and tone, placing emphasis on certain keywords, or staying within certain easy-to-understand topic areas are examples of this. To place this in a more specific context, consider a situation in which a younger person may feel the need to explain to an older conversational partner that in youth slang "bad" is positive. If the older person was already fully aware of this, then the younger person could be characterized as overaccommodating in terms of interpretability.

A third focus of attention may be the other person's *conversational needs* and this focus is said to lead to *discourse management* strategies (e.g., topic switching). Discourse management may be further divided into three subcategories: field, tenor, and mode. *Field* refers to the ideational or referential content of talk. For example, in an aging context, older people may choose topics that they think will be relevant for younger partners, such as talk about modern music. When talking to a younger person about latest trends in music, an older individual might be said to be focusing on the younger person's conversational needs and managing the discourse to meet those needs. The second subcategory, *tenor*, concerns the management of interpersonal positions, roles, and positive and negative faces. To take the example further, the younger person may wish to protect the older person's negative face and may avoid pointing out that he or she is 20 years out of touch with the youth music scene. In this case, the younger person is managing the discourse to save the older person embarassment. The third subcategory, *mode*, refers to the procedural and textual dimensions or both, that structure talk (N. Coupland, Coupland, Giles, Henwood, & Wiemann, 1988). If, in the previous example, the older person realizes that he or she knows little about modern music he or she might begin to question the younger person repeatedly and at length to gain information. In this case, the older person is managing the discourse by using a mode of interrogation.

Finally, a fourth focus of attention may be on the *role relations* operating in the interaction. This focus of attention may lead to interactants using various *control* strategies that are designed to manage perceived discrepancies in power. Control strategies can be used to gain command of the interaction (e.g., interruptions). An older person's authoritarian stance toward a younger partner would be a good example of a control strategy.

All of the previous strategies (i.e., approximation, interpretability, discourse management, and control) have together been entitled *attuning* strategies (Gallois, Franklyn-Stokes, Giles, & Coupland, 1988). High attuning along these dimensions, it is argued, can attenuate sociolinguistic differences, bring the other person psychologically closer, accentuate shared group memberships, indicate empathy, enhance conversational effectiveness, and so on. Of course, the converse can be achieved by means of counterattuning.

Under- or overattuning occurs when one or other of the participants deems the interactional strategies of his or her partner to have been under- or overplayed. For example, in the case of interactions with older people, overattuning may be characteristic of demeaning or patronizing talk, which, although well intentioned, may be negatively evaluated. Caporeal and colleagues (Caporeal, 1981; Caporael, Lucaszewski, & Culbertson, 1983) have described secondary baby talk to institutionalized older persons in which excessive concern is paid to vocal clarity, amplitude, message simplification, and repetition. Alternatively, excessively authoritarian or dismissive styles are examples of underattuning along dimensions of control and discourse management, respectively. In general, we expect recipients of such strategies to feel dissatisfied. However, evidence is emerging that different groups of people place different evaluations on accommodation strategies depending on their sociolinguistic needs. For example, experiments by Ryan and colleagues (e.g., see Ryan & Cole, 1990) demonstrated that older people, who are institutionalized and are less healthy than their counterparts living in the community, evaluate overaccommodation more positively.

As indicated in the previous discussion, CAT's focus has thus far been essentially cognitive and its strategies, largely derived from studies of discourse, have not explored affective components of communication accommodation. Nevertheless, even intuitively, the communication goals and outcomes concerned with CAT (e.g., cooperation, affiliation and identity, involve affect). Recently, it was proposed that another focus might center around attending to another person's affective orientation (Williams, 1994). The links between communication strategies and affect are not only an interesting and relatively unexplored avenue of research, but may also open up a broad program of research elucidating the affective reasons why people avoid some interactions or interactional strategies and not others.

The potential long-term effects of intergroup categorization, stereotyping, and overaccommodation are all important components of the next theory to be discussed—the communication predicament model of Aging (CPM; Ryan, Giles, Bartolucci, & Henwood, 1986).

Communication accommodation has a central role at the heart of the next two theories to be discussed. In the CPM, overaccommodation by younger people to an older partner is proposed to be at the heart of communication predicaments for young and elderly interactants, and overaccommodation can lead to various identity and developmental predicaments for elderly persons. The stereotype activation model proposes that negative stereotypes of older people prompt age-adaptive speech adjustments. This model is also particularly concerned with overaccommodation as one form of age-adapted speech. Positive stereotypes of older people are thought to be less likely to prompt such adjustments.

THE COMMUNICATION PREDICAMENT
MODEL OF AGING

The CPM (illustrated in Fig. 1.1) has been presented as an attempt to summarize the kinds of communication problems and dilemmas facing old and young interactants. Ryan, Giles, Bartolucci, and Henwood (1986) first sug-

gested this conceptualization to explain how stereotypes may lead to problematic speech, which may ultimately affect the health of older people
(Harwood, Giles, Fox, Ryan, & Williams, 1993; Williams et al., 1990).

This perspective has focused mainly on problematic intergenerational
speech, particularly forms of patronizing speech directed from young people
to the elderly, and on the potential socioemotional consequences of this.
According to the CPM, when a younger and an older person meet, certain
physical cues (e.g., grey hair, dress style) may trigger intergroup categorization and associated age stereotypes. Such stereotypes then invoke certain
types of speech behavior from the younger to the older person that are
stereotypically consistent. Therefore, if the stereotype of older people is
that they are cognitively challenged or are suffering certain sensory deficits,
speech patterns may include overaccommodation, topic selection or re-
striction, increased used of questions, and so forth (see Harwood, Giles, &
Ryan, 1995), but may especially include patronizing speech.

As a result of such speech patterns in the microsituation—as well as over
time and across contexts—the CPM suggests detrimental consequences for
the older person. Drawing on the work of Rodin and Langer (1980), the

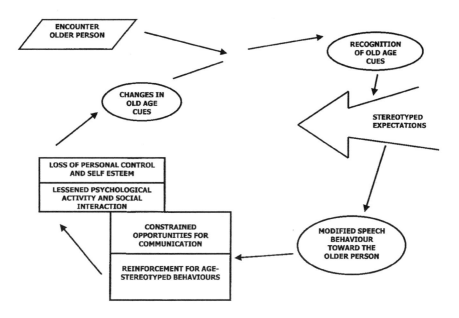

FIG. 1.1.   The communication predicament model of intergenerational communication. From
"Psycholinguistic and Social Psychological Components of Communication By and With the Elderly," by E. Ryan, H. Giles, G. Bartolucci, and K. Henwood, 1986, *Language and Communication*, 6, 1–2. Copyright ©1986 by Elsevier Science. Reprinted with permission.

CPM emphasized the loss of control and self-determination that can be associated with patronizing speech to the elderly, and the gradual and eventual loss of control for the older person over time as exposure to such patterns becomes routine. Ultimately and in line with the notion of a self-fulfilling prophesy (see Snyder, 1981), the model suggests that the person may begin to self-stereotype and to act in role. Losses of control combined with self-stereotyping may lead to learned helplessness, and may eventuate over the long term in social, physical, and emotional decline. This process is cyclical in that the stereotypical assumptions that hypothetically triggered the speech behavior in the first place may become part of the person's behavioral repertoire, and they are thereby confirmed. Through several revisions, the CPM has attempted to represent the roles of both young and elderly speakers (N. Coupland, Coupland, Giles, & Henwood, 1988), and the potential for certain responses (e.g., elder assertion) to young patronization to interrupt the cycle (Harwood et al., 1993).

THE STEREOTYPE ACTIVATION MODEL
OF COMMUNICATION IN OLDER ADULTHOOD

Like the CPM, Hummert's (1994) stereotype activation model focuses on the initial activation of stereotypes of the elderly individual in an interaction and how this can lead to problematic speech directed toward elderly adults (see Fig. 1.2). However, rather than focusing on negative stereotypes per se, this model stresses the role of both positive and negative stereotypes of the elderly and the effects that different stereotypes may have on speech behavior. This model suggests that the younger interactant's speech and communication vary according to the particular elder stereotype activated.

This model is highly cognitive in its approach to intergenerational communication, hence the emphasis on activation of cognitive schemas and stereotypes. The exact stereotype that is activated is partly related to certain perceiver characteristics—the *self-system*. This includes age, frequency, and quality of contact with the elderly as well as cognitive complexity. Middle-aged and older people seem to have more complex schemas of older people than do young people, and are also more likely to identify positive traits of older people. Younger people may be more likely to rely on various stereotypes of older people. Not surprisingly, of the three age groups, older people have the most complex and positive schemas of the elderly.

The model also suggests that cognitive complexity is related to the activation of stereotypes. According to the research of Burleson (1987) and colleagues, persons who are cognitively complex have more sophisticated and detailed schemas for judging other people, and are able to produce sophisticated messages that are specifically adapted to the needs of a conversational partner—in other words, they could be characterized as more sensitively accommodative or attuned. Therefore, it is suggested that those people who have more complex cognitive schemas in general, would be less likely to rely on fairly rigid and simplistic stereotypes of older people.

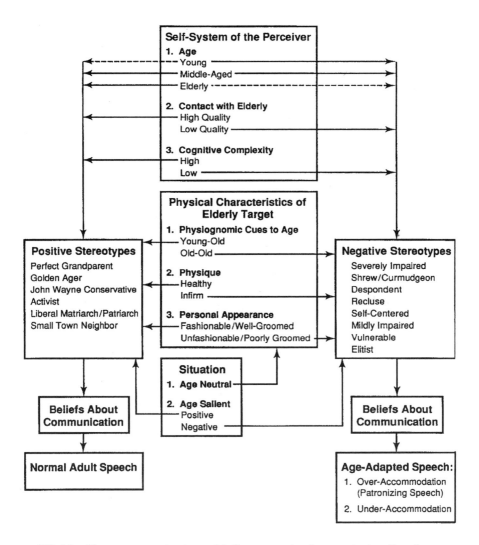

FIG. 1.2.   The stereotype activation model of intergenerational communication. From *Interpersonal Communication in Older Adulthood* (p. 172), by M. L. Hummert, J. M. Wiemann, and J. F. Nussbaum (Eds.), 1994, Thousand Oaks, CA: Sage. Copyright ©1994 by Sage. Reprinted with permission of Sage Publications.

A third variable that relates to the perceiver's self-system is the amount and quality of contact with older adults, an issue that is discussed in more detail in chapter 2. Presumably, younger people who have opportunities for frequent contact with the elderly are able to form more complex schemas. In addition, if that contact is positive rather than negative, they would be likely to form richer and more positive schemas about older people and aging. Putting these three aspects of the perceiver's self-system together, the model predicts that young people with low levels of cognitive complexity who experience low-quality contact will be more likely to negatively stereotype an older person.

Of course, the activation of a particular stereotype is also related to certain characteristics of the older individual. Among the important cues that prompt a stereotype are the older person's physical characteristics. These include obvious physical characteristics such as grey hair and wrinkles, or evidence of infirmity such as a walking stick. Stereotypes can also be activated by more subtle cues in a person's appearance such as outmoded and old-fashioned clothes. In addition, the context of the intergenerational contact provides cues that may elicit either negative or positive stereotypes. Some situations, such as nursing homes for the elderly, are negatively age salient and the model suggests that older people in such contexts are more likely to be negatively stereotyped.

Like the communication predicament of aging model, the stereotype-activation model is designed to explain intergenerational communication. The model predicts that if the net result of the perceiver's self-system, of characteristics of the older person, combined with a negatively age salient context, is negative stereotyping, then the younger person's speech and communication behavior will align with the activated stereotype, which is labeled *age-adapted speech*. This is likely to occur regardless of the older individual's particular characteristics or communication needs or both. One example of age-adapted speech is patronizing speech directed toward the elderly.

This conceptualization stresses that positive stereotypes of elderly people are also part of our cognitive repertoires. Following the predictions of the model suggests that the activation of positive stereotypes may be more likely given the following conditions; perceiver is middle aged or elderly; perceiver has high-quality contact with older people; perceiver has high cognitive complexity; the older person is young–old, healthy, fashionable, or well groomed; and if the situation is positively age salient. In this case positive stereotype activation is followed with speech that is not age adapted and is termed normal adult speech.

The final theory discussed here has not been applied to intergenerational communication, but it has the potential to be an overarching and organizing theory that can bring many seemingly disparate research findings under one rubric and explain how various perspectives can work together. This theory is attractive because it can operate at different levels of analysis: interindividual, community, and society, and also because it is comprehensive because it aids understanding of the interplay between interpersonal communication and macrosocial structures and macroprocesses. So, for example, it helps us view the processes described in the CPM as both influenced by, and also as constitutive of, the larger social picture.

Writing in *Communication Yearbook*, Banks and Riley (1993) argue for a structuration theory view of communication. Within the communication discipline, structuration theory has been used with impressive insight in the study of small-group decision making (see Poole, Seibold, & McPhee, 1985), and promises to provide a similar set of insights into the study of intergenerational communication. Throughout the ensuing chapters we discuss various components of intergenerational communication and relationships in our society. In our epilogue, we bring these various viewpoints together to argue that structuration theory provides a holistic and macroview that allows us to integrate a multiplicity of different research findings and theories.

STRUCTURATION THEORY

Structuration theory is a macrotheory that has evolved from the prolific writings of sociologist Anthony Giddens (e.g., 1976, 1984, 1990). The theory of structuration examines the fourfold link between the individual and society, and social stability versus social change.

A crucial tenet of Gidden's theory is the *duality of structure*. This refers to the process whereby individuals in everyday social interaction employ readily available rules and resources provided by a social system, and in so doing actively reproduce that social system. Giddens (1984) maintains that: "... human social activities are recursive. In and through their activities, agents reproduce the conditions that make these activities possible" (p. 2).

In structuration theory, the dualism of individual and society are reconceptualized as the duality of agency and structure. *Structure*, in Giddens' sense, consists of social rules and resources. *Rules* are similar to action schema or norms operating in various social contexts. Rules are not proscribed as such, but are more like habitual procedures, they often constitute knowledge that is shared by persons in given situations. *Resources* are the ability of social actors to command authority over the social and material conditions of others (social, authoritative, and allocative resources). *Agents* can use rules and draw on resources to carry out social action.

Agency refers to action by people. Of course, one important agency is social interaction–communication, and this is where the primary interest of the book lies. Action is governed by *intentionality*; thus we reflect on and think about our actions as group members or as individuals and think about the consequences of such (reflexive monitoring). Partly through reflexive monitoring we are able to explain our actions and discursively account for them as a continuous stream of reasoned action (*discursive consciousness*). Communication researchers draw on participant's reflexive monitoring and discursive consciousness when they distribute questionnaires and conduct interviews to collect self-report data.

Discursive consciousness is distinguished from *practical consciousness*, which includes automatic day-to-day routines, taken-for-granted behavior, and so forth, that is not readily available to our consciousness and is thus relatively non accountable. Researchers also attempt to discover people's practical consciousnesses and to use different methodologies to do so. For example, by analysing discourse, researchers may find evidence of underlying processes that participants are not necessarily consciously aware of, but are using in talk. These underlying routines, assumptions, and so forth may be crucial for communicatively structuring relatonships throughout the life span.

Action is governed by the fact that we are *rational*; we do not simply account for our behavior, we also plan future behavior and make adjustments in order to fulfill our goals. Of course, action is motivated, but often the motivation for our actions is not consciously available to us and is often motivated by unacknowledged conditions. Again, communication researchers seek to reveal the unacknowledged but socially shared conditions that govern communication.

Communication researchers can focus on communication as action to reveal underlying rules and resources, and to examine the ways in which rules and resources actively structure their relationships between individuals, groups, communities, and societies. Society does not necessarily influence communication in a top-down fashion. One of the most useful aspects of Giddens' theory is that it demonstrates that society and our social institutions are as much bottom-up as they are top-down. In other words, it is people, using available rules and resources for action, who structure society as a whole.

Action is also contextually bound or situated in time and space, and is subject to a number of enablements and constraints. According to structuration theory, the first action constraint is *temporality*. Action is located in a temporal flow and is constrained by historical precedents, including the sociocultural rules and resources as well as structure created earlier by the agent or others. In terms of intergenerational relationships, chapter 2 seeks to uncover some of these features by taking temporal and spatial look at the contexts of intergenerational interaction.

Action is constrained by the differential distribution of knowledge and resources, and may feed back into the system and eventuate in *unintended consequences*, which were not anticipated or intended by the original action.

Structuration theory recognizes that structuration occurs in interaction that involves the interplay of three major modalities or dimensions of structure. These are: (a) interpreting or understanding—the production of interaction is meaningful, (b) a sense of morality or proper conduct—we judge and take part in a moral order, and (c) a sense of power in action—relations of power are operating in interaction. Every act draws on these three modalities to some extent and the modalities call on three institutional orders found in historical systems: *signification* (language and other meaningful codes), *domination* (resource allocation and authorization), and *legitimation* (religion, ethics, and the law).

The structural properties of social systems are said to be both enabling and constraining. The social structure provides both constraints for behavior and resources for social action. Because social norms may be used creatively in microinteractions, they may be transformed by actors. This relates to the intricate connection between structure and systems, and emphasizes that it is people who create and structure social systems by their social actions (see Poole, Seibold, & McPhee, 1985).

The final aspect of structuration theory discussed in this chapter is the notion of contradictions, which are fundamental to change in social structures. Contradictions exist when fundamental characteristics of the structuring processes that reproduce a system oppose each other. Contradictions arise because of the integration of the different elements in a system, and they supply fault lines along which change can occur. If the contradictions are recognized, the fault lines can open up, conflict can occur, and the system can change. According to Poole, Seibold, and McPhee (1985), when analyzing the contradictions in a system we must look for:

> fundamental structuring principles: (1) in opposition to each other; (2) organized around the structuration of the practice in question; (3) implicated in the reproduction of the system; (4) giving rise to consequences that may cause conflicts, or at least, spur group activities to hide, repair, or repress reactions to the consequences; and (5) serving as a nexus and generative principle of multiple empirical contradictions. (p. 94)

Contradictions may, but need not necessarily, lead to conflict and system change. According to Giddens (1984), there are three limiting conditions that govern the emergence of conflict: the *opacity of action* (i.e., actors' lack of knowledge, similar to the notion of false consciousness); *dispersion of contradictions* (i.e., many contradictions prevent focus on any one contradiction); and *direct repression* (i.e., China's repression of the Tiannamen Square Rebellion).

The power of structuration theory lies not so much in its predictive potential, but in its unifying and clarifying potential. It allows us an ontological template with which to understand, using one framework, how the entirety of a particular phenomenon may work together to produce (and to reproduce) certain effects. To our knowledge, structuration theory has not been applied to age relations in modern society. However, within the communication discipline, it has been used with considerable success to explain small-group decision making (Poole, Seibold, & McPhee, 1985).

Therefore, by examining intergenerational interactions we should gain insight into wider social relationships between younger and older people, and into practices that may be long established and continually reproduced in our society. For example, according to structuration theory, the rules and resources employed by younger and older people in their interactions reproduce the very conditions that brought them about in the first place. Our tasks in the following chapters are to explore and outline exactly what those rules and resources are, and to explore the processes by which not only reproduction occurs, but also to uncover some of the contradictions that reinforce the status quo as well as to consider the very problematic questions of how and along what lines change can occur.

OVERVIEW OF CHAPTERS

Chapter 2 begins our discussion by placing age relationships in a space and time context, providing essential sociohistorical background of age relations in modern society. Chapter 2 describes some of the constraints of intergenerational interaction by discussing how the notion of age groups and age-group boundaries has been instantiated and legitimated through recent history. Points of contact for younger and older people in our society are examined, as are the typical community contexts in which younger and older people usually meet and interact. This raises important questions such as: Do our social institutions promote or reduce these points of contact, and what are the consequences of this? The vexed question of whether or not programs promoting contact between the very young and the very old have their intended effects is considered again in chapter 11. Chapter 2 finishes by discussing the degree and influence of mediated-intergenerational contact.

Apart from social structure and institutional organization of young and old people, what are the rules and resources that young and old people draw on when they interact? In other words, what are our attitudes, beliefs, and stereotypes about age and older people, and what is the nature of our stereotypes of old age and youth? What are the social norms that provide resources for interacting in, and accounting for, intergenerational communication? These concerns begin to be addressed in chapter 3, which examines perceptions, beliefs, and stereotypes of older people, as well as the limited information we have regarding beliefs and stereotypes of younger people. This discussion continues into chapter 4, which focuses on beliefs about language and communication and how these emerge in action—such as when evaluating older and younger speakers. Having provided the essential foundation for understanding the nature of perceptions and evaluations of intergenerational communication in earlier chapters, chapter 4 considers language and communication development in older adulthood, describing a range of language and communication resources—skills and abilities—and how these change and develop as we age. This sets the stage for chapter 5, which continues and develops the themes of stereotyping, perceptions, and expectations to examine the links between stereotypes, evaluations, and language and communication as action. This chapter is the first of two that discuss certain speech modifications typical of intergenerational communication. Patterns of intergenerational-communication accommodation, particularly under- and overaccommodation, are central to these two chapters. These chapters also attempt to elucidate the constraints and enablements of such communication in various contexts and also examine the unintended consequences in producing and reproducing intergenerational relationships.

Identity, particularly age identity, becomes the specific focus for chapter 7, in which life-span perspectives are used to examine identity development through aging, and how age identity may be realized through discourse. Here we consider younger and older people's self-categorizations as old or young, and the ways in which people may defend against negative categorizations and identities. Again then, at various levels of analysis, this chapter tries to reveal how people use rules and resources in everyday communication, to examine some of the contraints and enablements of this, as well as to examine how such action feeds back to influence both intended and unintended consequences.

Chapter 8 signals a switch of focus because we begin here to consider relationships more explicitly. Much research about intergenerational communication and language strategies has focused on strangers, and we begin here to ask whether or not the theory and research findings discussed in the first part of the book can be generalized to conversations between people who have longer term relationships, particularly familial relationships.

Chapter 8 turns to the relationships between adult children and their elderly parents, relationships that have been the focus of a great deal of recent interest from the general public, as well as from researchers. As demographic and social changes make their mark on our society, relationships and role negotiations between adult children and elderly parents have also demanded adjustment and change, and we discuss the ramifications of this in this chapter. Recent research and theory concerned with gender, power, and caring in the context of this relationship suggests that communication researchers' theoretical perspectives, such as those outlined in chapter 1 have significant contributions to make to relational research in the future. Chapter 9 considers grandparents and grandchildren, relationships that are perhaps undergoing some major changes concurrent with changes in life expectancy, health, and activity of older people. Among other things, this chapter discusses different types of grandparenting and the resources that grandparents may command and provide in family systems. Again, the chapter makes connections with the theory outlined in chapter 1.

Chapter 10 reviews research about the so-called "sandwich generation"—those (mostly middle-aged) people who can be construed as brokers positioned between older adults and younger generations. This is thought to place a number of demands on the sandwich generation, as for example, some middle-aged adults are simultaneously adjusting to their own aging, coping with the ill-health of aging parents, and supervising the growth and development of their own children. In this regard, the communication predicament model comes into focus and the precursers, range, and consequences of age-adapted speech in families across the lifespan is considered.

Chapter 11 returns to the burgeoning research interest in older people and intergenerational relationships in community contexts, and discusses intergerational contexts in medicine, education, adult day care, and intergenerational friendships. Again then, the applicability and explanatory power of the theoretical perspectives is considered.

The last three chapters begin to take a more macro–social view. Both inter-individual, intergenerational conflict and then intergenerational conflict as reflected through media representations are considered in chapter 12. This continues in chapter 13 with discussion of political issues, particularly intergenerational competition for economic resources. Crucially, chapter 13 describes the way that macroissues are channeled through the media and find their way into public-mediated, as well as interindividual and private, discourse. Then, chapter 14 signals another change of direction as it turns to examine perspectives on age and intergenerational communication in other cultures, with a focus on Eastern contexts. Research designed to explore perceptions of age and intergenerational communication in Eastern nations is reviewed. The Epilogue pulls together the main themes of the book for an overall summary of our perspective about intergenerational communication and points to some major avenues for further research. Having our perspective in overview, the Epilogue draws on a combination of social identity and structuration theory to explore evidence and possibilities for social change.

2

Intergenerational Contexts and Contact

The majority of the chapters in this book are concerned with intergenerational communication in various social and relational contexts. Of primary interest is what happens when people of vastly different ages and with diverse life experiences meet and talk. Accordingly, some chapters focus at a microlevel to examine, for example, particular conversational strategies characteristic of intergenerational talk. Other chapters, such as this one, focus more at macro-levels to look at the wider contexts in which such microinteractions take place. In the spirit of Giddens' theory of structuration, the issues and questions we consider include historical precedent, as a backdrop to the changing structure and patterns of intergenerational contact, in modern societies across time and space.

In very crucial ways, these patterns are integral to what actually takes place when younger and older people come into contact with each other and talk, and there may be less opportunity for this to happen than we first think. In Giddens' (1984) words: "a person's daily routine activities ... can be charted as a path through time-space ... social interaction from this point of view can be understood as the coupling of paths in social encounters" (p. 180). One of the aims of this chapter is to explore the points at which the paths of younger and older people cross.

Beside the sheer reality of social opportunities for contact, it is people's perceptions of the structure and pattern of modern intergenerational contact that comprise, in Gidden's terminology, rules and resources for conversations both about and with people of different generations. Attitudes and beliefs are influenced by perceptions and not necessarily by any objective reality. Thus, common-sense notions, such as the generation gap, may preinteractionally influence people's perceptions of what can possibly be achieved during intergenerational interactions, as do a variety of other lay beliefs, which are rarely questioned in our society. For example, an often-expressed and unquestioned assumption is that people are better off when socializing with those who are their own age, and we also assume that people gain the most pleasure from peer interactions. How did these taken-for-granted assumptions evolve, and what are their consequences, unintended or otherwise? How do they shape and form communication across generations?

This chapter aims to trace the development of such beliefs by discussing the historical development of ages as social categories and how the boundaries around age and different life stages have become sharpened and reinforced throughout recent history. It seems that the notion that people of very different ages—the young and the old—form different cultures or communities (as discussed in chapter 1) may be related to the development of particular social trends that can be traced back into the last 2 centuries. What effect have social trends had on the frequency and quality of social contact between the generations?

Research investigating the frequency of intergenerational contact, both between family members and in the wider community, shows some interesting trends, which intersect at various points with assumptions we might make about the solitary life experience of many contemporary older people. Perhaps partly in response to these assumptions about the lifestyles of older people, there has been a fairly recent growth in more formal programs designed to foster intergenerational contact. Intergenerational contact in family, community, and organized contexts is discussed here (see also chapter 13). The chapter finishes by considering the mass media as contact between generations, and begins to examine how the amount and type of media portrayals of aging and intergenerational communication reflect and construct wider social issues.

A discussion about contact between members of different social groups, be it ethnic, religious, age related, or comprised of any other social group might begin with a number of related questions. How do we know about people? How do we know about intergenerational interactions and about people much older or younger than ourselves? One answer to such questions is provided by uncertainty reduction theory (Berger & Bradac, 1982). According to this theory there are three means (passive, active, and interactive) by which we learn about others and reduce uncertainty in social situations. Even though active and interactive strategies might seem, at face value, to be the most important, we should not discount *passive strategies*, which derive from Bandura's theory of social learning, and suggest that we learn through watching and observing others (e.g., through media portrayals). Each of these strategies for uncertainty reduction can be conceptualized in terms of levels of contact.

Referring to relational communication, Andersen (1993) suggested a number of sources of social information, which can be adapted for intergenerational knowledge, and which relate quite well both to the structuration perspective that was discussed in the previous chapter (see Giddens, 1984), and to uncertainty reduction. First, we both gain information from and follow norms in our society or culture. Second, we learn by observing others both passively and actively; for example, we can observe friends and others in the community interacting with older and younger people and we can gather information through mass-media portrayals. Third, we gain information actively as well as incidentally from third parties such as friends and family (e.g., when we discuss elderly people with our same-age peers). Fourth, we gain information directly through our first-hand-intergenerational interactions. Finally, as a result of our own intraindividual communication—that is, our ongoing conversation with ourselves—through our cognitive work and reflexive activity, our knowledge can feed back into our future interactions.

Considering direct interpersonal contact in terms of its frequency, intergenerational contact has become something of a contentious issue in the academic, particularly sociological, literature. There tend to be two opposing positions, which are bandied back and forth. The first position suggests that modern society is obsessed with the age divide, is obsessed with chronological age as an influential factor dictating what and when people can achieve, as well as with whom they should appropriately mix. Because of this, intergenerational integration and contact across generations is in decline. Relatedly, *modernization theory* (Cowgill & Holmes, 1972; Parsons, 1944) suggests that in the largely rural and agricultural society of the past, older people were venerated and admired. According to this view, structural changes such as urbanization, industrialization and technologization in the 20th century (modernization) are linked to a decline in status of older people and devaluation of wisdom and skills associated with old age. Essentially, this view suggests that a decline in elders' status also coincides with a decline in intergenerational contact. Further, it suggests that as old age has become devalued, older people can be seen as useless, and modern society has effectively abandoned and disengaged them. Populist views conjure up stereotypes of abandoned grannies and uncaring adult children. Thus, families may become unconcerned about older people, confining their elderly relatives to institutions and nursing homes, not visiting them, and showing no concern with their welfare. It is suggested that this has come about because life expectancy has increased, the extended family unit has broken down, and family members suffer enormous time pressures and need to be highly mobile in search of work. Furthermore, women's employment outside the family home has rendered them unavailable as caretakers of elderly relatives.

The second position suggests that, in spite of demographic and social changes, perceptions that intergenerational contact is in decline are at worst incorrect and are at best overstated. Increases in mobility and advances in technology can counteract other changes and families can find innovative ways of maintaining contact and intergenerational support. According to this position, research should show no decline in the estimated amount of contact between older and younger generations of the family (see, e.g., Hareven, 1982). One of the tasks of this chapter is to reconcile these two different positions.

The debate concerning the circumstances of contact between younger and older people in modern society is much more important and complex than either one of the two positions in this debate reveal. Perhaps most obviously, there is no guarantee that frequent contact aligns with positive contact, and this assumption often appears to be underacknowledged. Highly frequent contact that is of poor quality can be very damaging. As shall be demonstrated, many measures of intergenerational contact do not typically assess contact quality in the ways that communication scholars would expect—that is, in terms of communication satisfaction and support. Also of importance is the issue of what exactly we are referring to when we use the term *intergenerational?* When discussing family dynamics intergenerational talk usually refers to that talk occurring among grandparents, parents, and children. Some developmentalists have suggested a 10-year age gap as marking out different generations. Is a 10-year age gap enough to suggest that a conversation is intergenerational? Clearly this can not be universally so, but we all work with implicit meanings about what intergenerational boundaries are; we talk of children, adolescents, middle-aged people, and the elderly. How did these understandings come about?

THE HISTORICAL DEVELOPMENT OF AGE CATEGORIES

Increased consciousness of age categorizations based on chronological age and age segregation are thought to be relatively recent social developments emerging from social changes in Western industrial societies throughout the 19th and 20th centuries (Chudacoff, 1989; Coleman, 1974). Changes have emerged from a complex of events including responses to socio- structural needs such as those of industrialization and the growth of social programs designed to protect more vulnerable members of society (e.g., the very young as well as the very old). Added to this, there have been vast changes in family structure, and in the pattern of work, health, and life expectancy. These changes have been matched and reified by the development of social practices such as pensioned retirement, and by age-associated rituals such as coming of age at 21. Scholars have also pointed out how the work of early social academicians contributed to what some have called the social construction of aging; that is, differences in chronological age may be more strongly constituted by the meanings with which we infuse them than by any objective characteristics (Karp & Yoels, 1982). A historical perspective on the development of age segregation allows us to judge whether or not an alleged trend toward age segregation is indeed occurring, and thereafter to consider what the consequences of this might be.

Social historians (e.g., Shorter, 1977) have documented the process by which boundaries between age categories have been marked out and reinforced by social and economic changes throughout history. Of particular significance are the life stages we know as childhood, adolescence, youth, middle age, and old age (see Karp & Yoels, 1982). Current social perceptions of the life stages known as childhood, adolescence, and youth evolved from historical developments, especially developments throughout the 20th century, and in part, such life stages can be characterized as social constructions (Coleman, 1974; Karp & Yoels, 1982).

For example, there have been vast historical changes in the perceptions of children. According to Aries (1962) and to Karp and Yoels (1982), in the Middle Ages (i.e., about 600–1450 A.D.) children were essentially considered as no different from adults. These writers and others suggest that evidence of this is apparent in portrait paintings in which babies and young children were painted with adult features—as miniature adults (Aries, 1962). The tendency to view children as small adults is also apparent in other social practices. For example, until the 17th century, it was fairly common practice to require children to work in the fields and mines as if they were adults, without special considerations for their welfare. Gradually this perception of children changed, and they were considered as quite different from adults with special needs for physical, social, and emotional development. These were recognized, for example, in the need for play. The notion of a distinct childhood became commonplace to such an extent that in the late 20th century we have witnessed the development and growth of the child-centered society.

These changes in the perception of children are not independent from societal needs. The development of a distinct life stage, now known as childhood leading to adolescence, has been linked with the need for extended periods of schooling in order to provide a more skilled workforce for job specializations due to industrialization (Coleman, 1974). On the other hand, to view children as no different from adults is a convenience, perhaps linked to an economic need to send children to work as productive, not dependent, members of the family and society.

In a similar fashion, with the increase of industrialization, adolescence was gradually recognized as a stage of life that resulted in complete independence from the family as the person grew into young adulthood and then married. According to Karp and Yoels (1982; see also Coleman, 1974) the boundaries around this age group were partly marked out by late-19th and early-20th century social movements in the United States. Such movements campaigned for compulsory education, child labor legislation, and specific legal procedures for the treatment of juveniles (Bakan, 1971). Other writers (e.g., Heaven, 1994) earmark the advent of adolescence as being associated with scholarly writings such as these by G. S. Hall (1904), which, for the first time, identified adolescence as a particular stage of life with its own unique developmental characteristics—one of which was a need to develop a distinct identity apart from the family of origin. According to Heaven (1994), it was chiefly the writings of Hall (1904) who, borrowing from previous writers, helped popularize and establish the belief that adolescence is a time of storm and stress. This coincided with opinions of a number of other writers and social commentators, who linked the adolescent's developmental need to establish a unique personal identity to social-psychological turmoil (see also Mead & Wofenstein, 1955). In effect, such writing created an age group, adolescence, and defined its characteristics. There is a great deal of popular folklore about adolescence and what we can expect from people at this stage of life, and this has helped fuel and sustain (both positive and negative) stereotypes of young people (Heaven, 1994).

The concept of middle age is largely a post-war construction. Before the 20th century, middle age was not thought of as a distinct period of the life span (Chudacoff, 1989). Middle age, too, has its stereotypical characteristics. Particularly prominent in popular literature is the notion of the middle-age life crisis (e.g., see Sheehy, 1976). This is purported to be a time of life when the adult realizes that youth may be lost and struggles to reformulate who he or she is. Popular lore posits the familiar notion of older men suddenly developing a taste for fast cars and young women in a desperate bid to reclaim fading youth. As for the life stages called childhood and adolescence, demographic and social shifts led scholars and academics to focus on middle age as distinct and interesting in its own right. In due course, their work found its way into popular culture. Thus, the writings of Erickson (1959), Havinghurst (1956, 1972), and Levinson and his colleagues (Levinson, Darrow, Klein, Levinson, & McKee, 1973), along with the popularization of such work by lay writers such as Gail Sheehy (1976) combine with changes in life expectancy, feminism, the changing pattern of the family, and so forth to influence the development of middle age as a distinct period of life in popular consciousness.

The following pages present much discussion about old age as a distinct life phase and older people as a conceptually distinct group. Definitions of when old age begins have been linked to the advent of pensions and retirement (Chudacoff, 1989; Karp & Yoels, 1982). Definitions of what is old have been changing in recent decades. Rather than years lived per se, it is perhaps social, economic, and health factors that have a strong influence in marking out this period of life. Increases in life expectancy and gains in medicine, health care, and social welfare mean that people now live far longer and healthier lives. What was defined as old age in the 19th century is chronologically distinct from what we now define as old age. One of the consequences is that we have recently witnessed the need to distinguish further stages of life in old age, as the young old, the old old and the oldest old. This seems to have come about because of the need to identify and target populations who might be in the greatest need of health and welfare services, but it is does not come without other social consequences, such as the danger of labeling and marginalizing the oldest-old (person) as the neediest and most socially draining old.

Chudacoff (1989) outlined four factors that he suggests strongly influence the importance of chronological age in modern society. First, age is a convenient objective indicator. Modern industrial societies need a skilled workforce, and thus need to develop expectations about skills potential and learning abilities. Chronological age provides an objective index of when certain skills and achievements can be expected from a potential workforce. Second, age grading has also provided the organizing principle for social control because it enables a standardization for administering services and institutions such as education, health care, and so forth. Third, age grading moves us away from kinship-based traditions (such as in hiring and job promotions) and the dangers of organizational nepotism. Chronological age, rather than family and informal ties, can be used to determine whether people are ready to take on senior responsibilities. Finally, according to Chudacoff, expectations based on chronological age have provided a more objective index of when people can be expected to make transitions between roles and responsibilities. In summary, Chudacoff suggests that the use of chronological age marks an attempt to use objective indices for regulating and controlling modern societies. Again, this trend is not without enablements and constraints. It also has unintended consequences, as Giddens would predict, and these are discussed in later chapters relating to agism. Before leaving this issue, we might also mention the self-esteem consequences if ability, rather than chronological age, was used as the criterion for retirement. After all, a customary- or mandatory-retirement age may provide a degree of dignity and be more face-saving than being obliged to retire because one is no longer competent to perform one's duties.

THE CHANGING STRUCTURE OF THE FAMILY

As the boundaries between the various stages of adulthood, adolescence, and childhood were strengthened perceptually in popular social consciousness and in social practice, it became almost natural to segregate children and adults into same-age peer groupings. This process has been well documented by Chudacoff (1989), who provides ample evidence of the fairly recent emergence of a peer society. The segregation of children away from both adults and older and younger peers was due, in part, to changes within family structure. For example, during this century, family size has decreased considerably. Twelve children was not an unusual size for a typical Victorian family and it was not unusual, therefore, for a young person to have siblings who were 5 and even 10 years older or younger. Furthermore, multigenerational age groupings were more common, not just within the family, but within the workplace (mostly agricultural), and it was not unusual that a peer group was made up of those aged from 12 to 25 years old. Modern families have far fewer dependent children, a demographic trend, which, when combined with increasing life expectancy, means that our demographic structure has changed from being bottom heavy, with many young children and few older adults, to being more top heavy with increasing numbers of older people in the population. Far from causing some sort of economic crisis, as is reported from time to time in the newspapers (Coombes & Holladay, 1995), researchers point out that this means there are now actually fewer dependent persons per worker in the United States than a century ago (Bond & Coleman, 1990; Cowgill, 1984).

Another change in family structure has been that of increasing mobility, particularly since World War II. In modern society, people do not typically live in the area where they were born and grew up; often adult children live long distances from their parents (Abrams, 1978). At the same time, air travel has become easier and cheaper, and the widespread use of telephones and other technological devices allows families to keep in contact across very large distances. Also, increasing use of E-mail and the Internet allows increased opportunities for family members to maintain contact through an ever-expanding computer network. In fact, as Giddens (1984) suggests, in the latter part of this century, developments such as these have effectively redefined time and space. Technological innovations such as the development of the videophone and the growth of the internet contributes to this redefinition in considerable ways.

The changes that have been occurring in demographic structure this century have been of particular interest to sociologists in their efforts to describe and predict the effects of such changes on intergenerational, particularly familial relationships (e.g., see Bengston, Harootyan, & Contributors, 1994; Bengston, Schaie, & Burton, 1994). For example, increasing participation of women in the work force means they are less available to care for aging parents. High rates of divorce have led to increases in single-parent families often headed by women.

Bengston, Harootyan, et al. (1994) note that a shift from a high-mortality and high-fertility society to a low-mortality and low-fertility society may have profound effects on intergenerational contact and relationships both within the family and within elements of society at large. Bengston, Rosenthal, and Burton (1990) suggest that imminent family-structure changes due to a remarkable decline in fertility, combined with increased longevity, could be likened to a beanpole—the image of a long, thin structure with few branches. Because of increased life expectancy, future families would be made up of a number of generations up and down the beanpole, but because of decreased fertility there would be fewer people at each generational level. Typically, it was predicted that families could be composed of up to six generations at one time. A recent study by Farkas and Hogan (1995) shows that more than 90% of the people in their seven-nation (Australia, West Germany, Great Britian, Austria, Hungary, Italy, and the United States) cross-sectional survey had someone either above or below them on the generational beanpole, however only 1% reported five-generational families. Almost 30% of middle-aged people in this study reported three-adult generations. This leads to more cross-generational contact and less peer contact within families (for further discussion of multigenerational communication, see chapter 10, this volume).

INTERGENERATIONAL CONTACT–FAMILIAL CONTACT

Cross-generational contact between family members is an important feature of the demographic changes previously mentioned, and the issue of declining contact, resulting in relative isolation of the nuclear family away from elder relatives, has been a focus of debate for many years. According to DeWit and Frankel (1988), researchers have generally reached consensus that increases in geographic distance due to modern mobility tend to nega- tively affect intergenerational contact, but that contact does continue in spite of distance. More recent evidence from a cross-national study by Farkas and Hogan (1995), indicates that Americans have more contact with more generations than do members of many other Western nations (Australia, West Germany, Great Britian, Austria, Hungary, and Italy). However, findings of self-reported contact may need to be treated with some caution because they are susceptible to demand characteristics (DeWit & Frankel, 1988; Treas, 1995). Also, we must keep in mind that knowing the reported quantity of contact tells us very little about the com- munication or quality of contact or both (see also DeWit & Frankel, 1988). Summarizing Farkas and Hogan's (1995) intergenerational contact find- ings, Treas (1995) suggests that their data show that "having surviving gen- erations within the lineage does encourage a preference for kin assistance and that overall, contact is greater for the never married, better educated and for women" (p. 28).

Recent survey research by Lawton, Silverstein, and Bengston (1994) found no evidence that familial intergenerational contact was in decline. In their very large cross-national (U.S.A.) sample they found that most adult–parent pairs lived near each other, had frequent contact, were self-re- portedly emotionally close, and believed they had similar opinions. There was also ample evidence of reciprocal helping behavior. In summary, their find- ings indicated that 69% of adult children reported at least weekly contact with mothers (around 60% if both parents are included), whereas 20% re- ported daily contact (12% for fathers only). Parents reported comparable fre- quencies of contact with their eldest children. This research also indicated that women play a central role in family solidarity, mothers were more likely than fathers to share a home, to live nearby, to have contact, to have a close relationship, and to give and receive help. Intact marriages were associated with closer ties between adult children and fathers, whereas people with higher levels of education were more likely to be mobile and this affected fam- ily solidarity. Finally, there was more solidarity between African Americans and their grandparents and parents (more discussion of these familial intergenerational relationship can be found in chapters 8, 9, and 10).

Thus, considerable research by social scientists, such as that outlined previously, shows that there are what Bengston, Harootyan, et al. (1994) call hidden connections in Western society. Some might suggest, however, that there are hidden disconnections too. In other words, how can we square these findings with claims of increasing intergenerational segregation, perceptions that older people are isolated, and self-reports of very infrequent intergenerational contact outside family contexts? Can we dismiss such claims and perceptions? Is there any evidence of age segregation as suggested by Chudacoff, and if so, what is the nature of it?

INTERGENERATIONAL CONTACT OUTSIDE THE FAMILY: COMMUNITY CONTACT

Compared to the amount of research conducted into intergenerational contact among families, there is little available information concerning the amount of intergenerational contact between persons who are not bound together with family ties, such as contact among strangers, acquaintances, and friends. Some contexts of intergenerational contact that we do know of are networks of volunteers who provide instrumental help and social support; mentoring programs; education, employment, church, and religious groups; programs such as adopt a grandparent; day centers; medical and care institutions; community services, such as meals on wheels; and community contacts in shops, banks, restaurants, and so forth.

Several writers suggest that a move toward a peer-centered society means that there is increasingly minimal contact (in terms of both quantity and quality) between younger and older generations in our society (e.g., see Chudacoff, 1989; Coleman, 1974). Younger and older people often seem to inhabit different, if adjacent, geographical and social areas within society. Of particular concern is the possibility that younger and older people inhabit and move in different, rarely intersecting, social–psychological cultures.

Apart from the usual family visits (in some cases, in spite of), there appears to be very little sustained or meaningful overlap between these cultures. Writers such as Chudacoff illustrate how such cultures are institutionalized, as for example, younger people are segregated into schools and graded by age in class groups. Around the age of 18, many young people (in the United States particularly) leave home to spend 4 or more years on a college campus. Even though they may interact with older people from time to time during school holidays or while at work off campus, the majority of their time is spent with peers. Senior citizens may choose to take up residence in retirement communities, to join age-specific clubs (e.g., exercise for people over 60) and to express a preference to take holidays with same-age peers (e.g., SAGA; see Ylänne-McEwen, 1997). Young holidays are a comparable example (e.g., Club Med; 18–25). Such developments may be cited as indications of increasing age segregation and an increasing bias in favor of peer interaction (see Chudacoff, 1989), as can the growth of retirement communities, protected housing, institutions, clubs, and organizations that effectively cordon off younger and older people. From this perspective, we can understand concerns that increases in intergenerational segregation are potentially divisive. The young people who come into contact with elders, on any regular basis, in many such contexts do so in defined roles—as institutional employees, housekeepers, waiters, gardeners, and caretakers, teachers, and bosses and clients. (Chapter 11 discusses intergenerational relationships in professional contexts.) Apart from the fact that many such interactions are often so ritualized that interactants may not actually "see" each other, such role relations typically limit the possibilities for relational development within the boundaries of the roles. In fact, relatively little is known about the frequency and nature of intergenerational contact in nonfamilial contexts, although some data collected from college students, which suggest that contact between this group of young people and elders is minimal in every sense (Williams & Giles, 1996), is now discussed.

Young College Adults' Contact With Older Adults

A recent study conducted with students on a California college campus, althoguh not claimed as representative of American society as a whole, throws a small glimmer of light on some aspects of intergenerational contact outside the family (Williams, 1992). The average time that college students who took part in the study estimated that they spent with young adults (defined as under 35 years of age) was estimated at 84.7%, middle-aged (over 45 years old) 13%, and old (over 65 years old) 4.5%. For college students, therefore, self-reported contact with people over 65 years old is probably very infrequent indeed. In this same study, respondents described conversations they had with older people (approximately age 70) who were not family. These results are discussed in more depth in later chapters (see, especially, chapter 5, this volume); however, some of the characteristics of intergenerational contact as reported in this study are worth discussing here.

Respondents were asked to provide a description of who the conversational partners were, their frequency of contact, the location and topic(s) of the conversation, and their relationship with their partner. Results revealed that 62% of reported conversations were with older women. The level of personal knowledge of older conversational partners was actually very low because they were most frequently strangers (38.02%) or an acquaintance known through a third party (36.97%), and were less frequently a coworker, neighbor, church member, or club member (7.09%). Accordingly, when asked, "How long have you known your partner?" 40.57% had met their partner for the first time. Many young people had known their conversational partner for less than 1 year (i.e., a few weeks or months; 17.69%), some partners were known between 1 and 5 years (18.85%), for 5 to 10 years (10.82%), and for life (12.07%). Respondents were also asked about frequency of interaction, and more than one third of reported conversations were once-only encounters (35.35%). Almost one third (28.04%) of the respondents saw their partners regularly, but only for a few minutes of casual conversation or polite exchange. Finally, there were a number of people who reported seeing their partners only occasionally, once or twice a year or every few months (30.94%).

The kinds of locations where these intergenerational conversations took place were typically at the family home or at the home of the older partner (36.45%), at a place of work (e.g., restaurant or shop), at school or college (29.96%), or in a recreational setting such as a restaurant, club, or sports facility (20.64%). Other places of contact were on public transport (6.55%) and in institutional-care settings (e.g., hospitals) (4.92%). The range of topics of these conversations was very wide (but only very few conversations could be described as having depth); they included talk about life plans, relationships, education, information giving or advice, death, instrumental or task oriented topics, politics, sports, hobbies, reminiscing, health or illness, travel, and the youth of today. In satisfying conversations, the young person's schooling and hopes and dreams for the future were often topics for conversation (20.5%). When conversation was dissatisfying, the most frequent topics were task oriented, usually associated with the young person's failure in various ways (25.6%). Other topics included sports (7.0%), health and illness (5.2%), youth today (4.0%), hobbies (3.0%), and reminiscing (3.7%). Although the percentages are fairly small, hobbies and reminiscing were more frequently mentioned when respondents reported satisfying conversations, whereas health and illness and youth today were more often mentioned for dissatisfying conversations.

Participants were also asked to describe their relationships with their partners. About 10% of the partners in satisfying conversations were reported to be like family (usually grandmother or grandfather). Other descriptions were: family friend (6.02%), friend (6.44%), acquaintance (19.30%), but stranger was the largest category (34.2%). When the conversation was reportedly dissatisfying, respondents were more likely to note that their partner had a higher status, perhaps because many were relationships between customers or clients (usually the older partner), and waiters or shop assistants (usually the young respondent).

In summary then, although the data indicate considerable variability, some generalized profiles of nonfamily-intergenerational contact for this sample of college students can be extracted. One characterization involves strangers who meet once and then never meet again. They meet each other in a variety of settings: at the home of either partner (most likely the older person is associated with the younger person's family or friends), at a place of business (usually where the young person is employed), or in a recreational setting. If the conversation is satisfying, the topic might be life in general, with a good portion of this being the young person talking about his or her education and career plans; whereas if the conversation is dissatisfying, the topic is more probably task oriented, although relational talk and talk about educational goals featured in dissatisfying conversations, too. The other characterization involves partners who are likely to be known to each other through family or friends; they have known each other anywhere from a couple of years to the whole of the young person's life (in which case they are often mentors), and they meet fairly regularly, particularly when the young person is at home with family in school vacations. Topics of conversation with these partners can be very wide-ranging, but mostly concern family, relationships, school, and the young person's plans for the future.

If these findings are taken together, they suggest the possibility that intergenerational contact between some age groups, particularly nonfamilial contact between the very young and the elderly, is very low indeed and that research investigating familial contact obscures this to a certain extent. There is no doubt that we implicitly perceive such contact as very infrequent and also as problematic as we demonstrate in following chapters. The degree and nature of community-based nonfamilial contact between other age groups (i.e., as grossly characterized earlier) and seniors has not been systematically studied. We simply do not know if the minimal contact reported by college students is representative of others in the community. It seems probable that adults at different life stages, such as those engaged in full-time employment, involved in community activities, and raising their own families in the community probably experience much more intergenerational contact, but as yet, we do not know any details about the nature of such contact. A useful means of examining community contact of seniors might be through looking at the number and nature of network connections between seniors and other community members (for a description of network analysis, see Albrecht, Adelman, & Associates, 1987).

Certainly there is a general perception that contact between elders and younger people is limited, as evidenced by the growth of organized intergenerational contact programs. A very wide range of contact programs have been instituted (for a review, see Fox & Giles, 1993). Some such as adopt a grandparent, are long-term, but many involve short-term interventions. For example, Steichen and Arguitt (1975) arranged for college students to share college dorms with retired adults aged 55–58. Usually the aim of such programs is to foster intergenerational understandings in the belief that contact itself will achieve such goals (e.g., Allen, Allen, & Weekley, 1986; Chapman & Neal, 1990). Contact programs are very wide-ranging; some are very informal, involving contact with grandparents telling stories to adolescents, whereas others are much more formal, involving taught segments and visits to nursing homes designed for trainees in the helping professions. Educational interventions for medical and social-work students are introduced to promote increased knowledge about the social, psychological, and developmental aspects of aging, social health, and welfare services. Of course, the ultimate aim of such programs is to promote goodwill and understanding among the different age groups. Many programs explicitly set out to tackle negative intergenerational attitudes and attempt to measure some sort of post-hoc attitude changes. (These issues are discussed further in chapter 13, this volume.)

MEDIATED INTERGENERATIONAL CONTACT

Up to this point, the development of social norms and understandings regarding age groups and boundaries, direct interpersonal exchange between old and young family members, and interaction in community settings and organized programs, all of which promote direct personal interaction, have been discussed. At the outset of this chapter, we suggested that social information was also derived both actively and passively from more indirect sources involving third parties or was mediated or both. Mediated-contact situations are an important means of gaining information about other age groups. For many younger and older people alike, television is an important resource, and is even a primary source of contact with people of vastly different ages who are not family members. Thus, for both young and old people, the media can be an indirect site of intergenerational contact. For example, a study by Harwood (1992) indicated that, for at least a sample of college students, the mediated contact they have with the characters of the television show *The Golden Girls* far exceeds the level of interactive contact they have with older adults in general. Furthermore, television portrayals of interpersonal interactions between younger and older people can be modeled by younger people in intergenerational interactions who, given a lack of experience, view these interactions as appropriate and acceptable (Huston et al., 1992).

A similar situation prevails if we look at older people's interactions with the mass media. Bleise (1982) outlined 10 ways in which the elderly interact with the media, including uses that can influence intergenerational communication quite directly, such as: to substitute for interpersonal relations; to gather content for interpersonal interactions; to form and or reinforce self-perceptions of, and to gather information about, social perceptions of various groups of people; to learn appropriate behaviors (including age-appropriate behaviors); and to network and obtain social support. In fact, Mares and Cantor (1992) have suggested that elderly people may use the media to alter their moods. According to this perspective, people have a preference for television programs in which they can compare themselves to characters who are of a similar age and social group. Mares and Cantor found that elders who were lonely or unhappy or both, preferred programs in which they could make a positive social comparison between themselves and characters whom they saw as worse off. Congruently, programs that prompt relatively negative social comparisons of self to similar others were avoided.

Even mediated-intergenerational contact is relatively infrequent according to research from the 1970s and 1980s reviewed by Robinson and Skill (1995). Older people are one of the least represented groups on the television, although they are probably the highest consumers. Older males are far more frequently represented than older females—at about a three-to-one ratio (note that this does not reflect the demographic distribution of these genders in wider society). A recent content analysis of commercials undertaken by Roy and Harwood (1997) indicates that the picture painted by Robinson and Skill has not changed very much. Older people, especially older women, were still underrepresented in television commercials. When commercials were shown, they were more likely to be associated with advertising for financial services and retail chains, and less likely to be associated with advertising for automobiles and travel services. As Roy and Harwood point out, this general underrepresentation is curious, especially given the fact that older people make up a market that one would suppose advertisers would be falling over themselves to capture. Presumably the selective underrepresentation is related to the goods and services that advertisers think will be relevant and of interest to an older population. In addition to general media underrepresentation of the elderly, evidence is emerging that suggests that both older and younger people are motivated to select media that represents their own age group as opposed to other age groups (Harwood, 1997). This self-selection is another means by which contact between the young and the old is minimized.

No discussion of intergenerational contact is complete without considering the evaluative aspects of the contact, whether as preinteractional expectations or as evaluative outcomes. Expectations, beliefs, and attitudes are topics that form the central focus of both the next chapter and following chapters. Of course, the evaluative nature of mediated contact is important too—the nature of the representation is as important as the amount of representation.

A considerable amount of research has shown that when older people do appear on television, they have minor roles and are often portrayed negatively. As Robinson and Skill (1995) point out, however, we need to exercise some caution in extrapolating these findings into the 1990s where (in Britain at least), we have seen an increase of shows featuring the elderly, especially sitcom shows—*The Golden Girls* was one of the first (a sitcom featuring an all-elderly cast of women who are physically and sexually active and are engaged in society) that made the transatlantic crossing from the United States to the United Kingdom. More recently, shows such as *Waiting for God, One Foot in the Grave,* and *My Good Friend* are representative of British-made sitcoms that feature elderly characters in lead roles. Occasionally, we see older people on the dating game show, *Blind Date,* in which their appearances seem at best to be evaluatively ambiguous (and the same goes for many of the elderly characters in these sitcoms). However, thus far such casual observations of the increase in elderly lead characters are not reflected in research findings.

Robinson and Skill's (1995) content analysis of the U.S. prime-time television season found that overall very little had changed during the last few decades. They concluded that the elderly are still rarely represented on television, and that when they are, they are portrayed in lead roles at about half the rate of all other age groups. Roy and Harwood's (1997) study of commercials shows that older adults were frequently presented in a positive light (active, happy, and strong). However, Roy and Harwood (1997) also note the extreme nature of this positivity and note that, among other things, it may violate expectations about elderly characters, or may tap into positive stereotypes of elders (discussed in chapter 3). Presumably, negative images of elders would probably not sell products and services.

Some research was concerned with the role of mediated contact in promoting and reinforcing negative views of elders. At least one major study demonstrated that television portrayals have direct correlates in the beliefs of heavy television viewers, those who have a tendency to view elderly individuals as less healthy, less sexually active, and in worse financial situations (Gerbner, Gross, Signorielli, & Morgan, 1980; see, however, Wober & Gunther, 1982). As pointed out by Robinson and Skill (1995), "the way groups are portrayed on television is not so much an indication of how that group is viewed by society as it is an indication of how the writers believe the target audience views that group" (p. 366). Robinson and Skill (1993) have suggested that peripheral characters are more likely to be generalized or stereotypically portrayed. Because of this, examination of peripheral character portrayals on successful shows might provide insights into the attitudes and stereotypes of the target audience. To date, we know of very little research about this aspect of media portrayals of elderly people except that of Harwood (1997).

Television's negative representation and underrepresentation (Bishop & Krause, 1984; Davis & Kubey, 1982; Robinson, 1989) of the elderly conveys a message of marginalization to both younger and older people. Even media supposedly designed to enhance the image of elderly people (e.g., the Senior Olympics) can be interpreted as actually reproducing and sustaining agist views that may interfere with face-to-face intergenerational encounters. An example is provided by Harwood and Giles (1992), who examined the text of *The Golden Girls* (see Bell, 1992) and found that themes of age are inextricably tied up with the humorous interpersonal dynamics that made the show so popular. However, the incessantly humorous tone of comments about (often serious) problems that face the elderly can be seen as having a discounting and trivializing effect on any suggestion that these are serious problems (Nahemow, McCluskey-Fawcett, & McGhee, 1986). Therefore, although the mediated-intergroup contact exemplified by shows such as *The Golden Girls* is qualitatively different from face-to-face interpersonal contact, we would, nonetheless, claim that such contact plays an important role in wider contact networks. Television and print-media portrayals of older people and intergenerational relationships can invariably affect how we think about aging, and subsequently how we communicate these beliefs interpersonally both to ourselves and to others.

SUMMARY

This chapter aims to lay some of the groundwork for subsequent chapters. Beginning with a discussion of the variety of ways in which we gather information about other people, some of these were taken up more explicitly and considered in terms of intergenerational contact. In order to achieve this, it was necessary to first examine the way we conceptualize and talk about people as members of different generational groups. The historical and social development of age groups as social categories, which are constructed, or structurated, as much or more than they exist in any real sense, was briefly outlined.

Using Giddens' structuration perspective, this chapter begins to set out some of the rules and resources of social action, and also outlines some of the enablements and constraints arising from contact in various intergenerational contexts. Action is governed by historical precedent—the historical development of age categories and boundaries was an essential precondition for the way we perceive age relations in modern society. We cannot conceive of, and talk about, relationships among groups if we do not have a handy mental image of group characteristics and categorizations of group membership. Age categories largely derived from the growth of human developmental sciences provide those categories. This means that the very act of identifying, refining, and targeting developmental needs also inadvertently defined the conditions for categorization, and even for subsequent discriminatory intergroup behavior.

The social forces that promoted healthy development of children organized into age-stage peer groupings implicitly discouraged both intergenerational interaction and intergenerational understanding. These constraints then found their way into a belief system that reinforced them; as the well-worn adage urges: Choose someone your own age. Often enough those who do not are suspected of malevolent intent, or are considered to be social misfits, at the wrong stage of development. The discussion of intergroup theory suggested in chapter 1, that once groups are constructed and the boundaries between them established, the way is open for a host of other social consequences, some intended and others not. Consequences include establishing norms of life-span development, the emergence of a peer-oriented society, age stereotyping, and age identity. These social consequences are discussed throughout the rest of this book.

This chapter largely focuses on what could be characterized as logistical and structural constraints in the system. For example, changes in family structure and working environments, which mean that contact across generations is less likely, structurate intergenerational relationships. Varying lifestyles of the generations can place them in minimally overlapping contexts. However, within the family we find, that, in spite of demographic and social changes that are purported to break-down family life, there is fairly frequent intergenerational contact and helping. This contact and helping has adapted to modernity, with families finding new and creative ways to maintain contact and provide support across the generations.

The picture for community contact between older and younger people is much more hazy. Self-reported contact is minimal both in terms of frequency and depth. Personal preferences, social norms, and institutional practices may fuel this minimal contact. If we accept social norms and believe that older and younger people have little to gain from cross-generational linkages (even if only in the form of social interaction, let alone in sustained cross-generational friendships) then we are unlikely to seek such opportunities. If we are aware of and value our own social identities as age-group members, we may even actively avoid such interaction unless it is encouraged in a familial system of intergenerational support and helping.

Finally, we suggested that mediated-intergenerational contact is an important source of information about people of different ages. However, elders (particularly women) are typically underrepresented in the media, and when they are shown they tend to be negatively portrayed or are agistly comical. Although, in television commercials, older people appear to be extremely positively portrayed, which may be a function of the need to present attractive commercials to sell products and services. It seems that the media place constraints on intergenerational contact also.

3

Social Cognitive Contributions: Intergenerational Attitudes and Stereotypes

Chapter 2, beginning with a historical look at how age categories have been created, legitimized, and institutionalized, discussed intergenerational contact and its frequency and nature in various contexts. This chapter takes the next step and examines how, once age categories are established, they become associated with particular traits and stereotypes, which can lead to discrimination—agism (for recent reviews of agism, see Pasupathi, Carstensen, & Tsai, 1995; Williams & Giles, 1998). Recall from chapter 1 that stereotyping and age prejudice are fundamental inputs to the communication predicament and the stereotype activation models, as well as components of intergroup behavior and potential precursers to some of the communication adjustments discussed by CAT.

Researchers interested in social cognition argue that, while being cognitively and socially efficient in some ways; the way we think about people, social groups, and social behavior may, in other ways, lead us to make social-judgment errors (see Fiske & Taylor, 1991). For example, as was discussed in chapter 1, the notion that we engage in stereotyping has some very negative connotations, but is actually a very cognitively efficient method for initializing and carrying on interactions in social settings where there is little other information available. Stereotypes can act as rules of thumb that work for us much of the time. When we first meet someone, we may have very little knowledge of him or her, and uncertainty may be high (Berger & Bradac, 1982). We may instantly try to reduce some of this uncertainty by categorizing him or her into some social group, which in very general terms increases predictability and comfort. We can use a variety of cues to do this. Some immediate visual cues include skin color, hair color (e.g., gray hair), wrinkles and other facial characteristics, or clothing style (see Hummert, 1994). We use these features as clues for behaving toward somebody, what we should talk about, and so on. We might also begin to engage in interactive uncertainty reduction strategies (see Berger & Bradac, 1982); for example we might ask the person what he or she does for a living, where he or she was born, or other information that allows us to categorize. In this way, certain stereotypes might be invoked, we feel that our uncertainty is reduced, and we have some clues about how to behave. There is nothing inherently wrong, or even politically incorrect, about this process. Problems almost inevitably arise, however, when we get it wrong or take it too far. Then we might upset and irritate people by instantly acting upon mistaken assumptions. For example, we might make mistaken assumptions when encountering a young man clad in leather motorcycling gear, with long, streaky hair and a ring through his nose. If we meet such a person in a dark alley, we might be unnecessarily fearful.

Broadly speaking, this chapter sets out a social-cognitive approach to communication because it examines attitudes and beliefs about age with a special emphasis given to research concerned with age stereotyping. First, category labels and traits typically applied to older people are examined, which leads to a discussion of how groups of traits can be put together to make up more complex person perceptions or stereotypes. Taking this one step further leads to a discussion of how stereotypes can lead to agism and prejudice toward older people. This chapter also considers stereotypes and agism toward young people, a hitherto-neglected dimension of agism, and one not formalized in theoretical models of intergenerational talk. The material in this chapter is an important basis for what is to come in the remainder of the book.

Among scholars interested in social gerontology, the social psychology of aging and so on, there has been a fairly extensive research interest in age stereotyping (for the most part, in Western contexts) and in very general terms, this has resulted in an emerging picture of negative stereotypes of older people. As discussed in chapter 1, self- and other stereotyping is a major consequence of categorizing oneself and others as members of particular social groups, in this case, the young or the elderly. Chapter 2 traced the historical development of age categories and distinct life stages, which over time have been given labels (e.g., middle age), and accordingly people have fairly well-developed expectations about what should happen at these distinct life stages. An inevitable consequence of the identification and labeling of distinct developmental stages or phases of life (young, middle aged, or elderly) is that we become more and more inclined to associate a set of typical characteristics with such labels, and oftentimes we expect ourselves and others to behave accordingly.

LABELING AND STEREOTYPING

Labels can function as sociolinguistic triggers of stereotypes (see Hamilton & Trolier, 1986). For example, when talked about, older people quite frequently suffer the indignity of having numerous agist adjectives such as biddy and codger levied against them (Nuessel, 1993). Palmore (1990) lists the following colloquialisms for elders: coot, crone, geezer, hag, old buzzard, old crock, old duffer, old fogey, old maid, old fangled, old fashioned, and over the hill.

According to a historical analysis conducted by Covey (1988), words relating to old age have changed their meanings over time. For example, the word *old* itself was originally associated with very positive meanings including skill and wisdom. More recently it has taken on a very negative flavor, being associated with derogatory terms as illustrated by old bag and old fogey. Covey classified his findings as follows: Different words were used to describe older men and older women; the terms were often inherently ambiguous; older people were subjected to less pejorative and negative terms in the past than they were at the time the research was conducted; and terms used to describe older people were frequently negative and focused on decline and disability. Covey claims that contemporary older people do not like to be called old, and thus seek to distance themselves from the negative associations reflecting the decline in the status of the old. Nuessel (1982) points to a vast lexicon of agist words, which are used routinely in everyday language, and indeed, the examples cited by Palmore lend weight to this argument. Even in these so-called enlightened times when racist and sexist language is proscribed, agist language is still an inherent feature of everyday talk, general literary work (Berman & Sobkowska-Ashcroft, 1986), as well as in social–scientific writing (Schaie, 1993). Typically we let such language and derogatory terms pass in conversation, and often we use them either to tease or for a humorous effect; they are not challenged as we might challenge derogatory terms for women or ethnic minorities. For example, in 1995, a British newspaper reported a dispute between the English rugby captain and the executive board of what was then English Rugby Union. At one point, the captain referred to the latter as old farts. Much discussion revolved around the competencies of the management and the legitimacy of the captain's public statement, but no attention was ever afforded the agist rhetoric itself. Nuessel (1982) pointed out that there are few positive age-specific terms used to refer to the elderly. Nuessel and other writers (e.g., Oyer & Oyer, 1976; Schaie, 1993) have argued for a new vocabulary to eliminate agism from language, but unfortunately it is doubtful if changing the words themselves will help to completely eradicate agist sentiment. Comparatively, attempts to reduce and reform sexist language have produced rather mixed results (Prentice, 1995; Rubin, Greene, & Schneider, 1994).

What labels do people prefer? A survey of people age 17 to 65, grouped into three age categories, was conducted by Barbato and Feezel (1987). The people were asked for their evaluations of 10 words that referred to older people. Results showed that all age groups basically agreed that the terms *Mature American, Senior Citizen,* and *Retired Person* were more positive and were rated as active, strong, and progressive; whereas *Aged, Elderly,* and nouns using *old* were considered more negative.

Of course, age labels and age-specific language reflect and create a wide range of social meanings. A review of the literature by N. Coupland and J. Coupland (1990) maintained that much current research about elderly language and communication is *age-decremental* in orientation; that is, elderly people are documented as having deficient communicative and sociolinguistic competences. Gerontology itself has been criticized for an agist focus on decrements such as linguistic competence (Estes & Binney, 1979). Psycholinguistic experiments have documented a litany of relative deficits such as a decline in working memory, making it harder for older people to understand and use more complex linguistic structures (Kemper, Kynette, & Norman, 1992). In addition, older people are typified as talking slower (Stewart & Ryan, 1982), using their grammar in a less sophisticated way (Emry, 1986), being verbose (Gold, Arbuckle, & Andres, 1994), and being overly concerned with their ages and painful life events (N. Coupland, Coupland, & Giles, 1991). Academia does not stand outside society. Scientists, gerontologists, and the like draw upon available images, understandings, and stereotypes to formulate questions, to design studies, and to weave interpretations around a framework of assumptions, which feed back into lay interpretations of this work (see Giddens, 1984). This is not to say that this is malevolent in intent or that older people are passive victims—in fact, certain older people unwittingly collude in promoting dependence (J. Coupland, Robinson, & Coupland, 1994; N. Coupland, 1997). Of course, some developmental changes are associated with age (such as losses in eyesight and hearing), and these almost certainly accumulate to make late old age a very challenging time. One of the criticisms of research into language and old age is that there has been an overemphasis on deficit. In fact, some of the seeming catalogue of age-associated deficits uncovered by research can be interpreted and understood in more functionally advantagous ways for older people. For example, recently, positive aspects of eldertalk have been reported (e.g., Kemper, Kynette, & Norman, 1992).

Beyond the labels discussed previously, there is a considerable research tradition that looks at traits and characteristics associated with older people. The following sections outline some of this research and then further develop the discussion to describe a number of distinct stereotypes of older people.

Beliefs About the Characteristics of Older People

Stereotypes are made up of a set of typical characteristics that we associate with a group of people, but rather than being simplistic, stereotypes and trait attributions of older people are quite wide-ranging. There is a considerable body of research that describes negative perceptions of elders. For example, beliefs that elders are irritable, nagging, grouchy, weak, verbose, and cognitively deficient are not uncommon (Braithwaite, 1986; Branco & Williamson, 1982; Nuessel, 1982). To confront and refute many common stereotypes of old age, Palmore (1990) studied age stereotyping in considerable detail and developed a "Facts on Aging Questionnaire" as well as workshop exercises designed to dispel some of the myths of aging. He lists nine characteristics that are typically associated with older people. They are: ill health and illness, asexuality and impotency, ugliness or unattractiveness, cognitive and mental decline, uselessness, isolation, and loneliness, poverty, and depression. Each of these is examined in more detail before discussing specific stereotypes.

According to Palmore (1990), at least 50% of Americans believe that people over 65 years old have serious health problems (Harris, 1981, cited in Palmore). Moreover, elders are not considered to be sexually active; in fact, sexual elders are frequently considered to be disgusting or comical (Cameron, 1970; Golde & Kogan, 1959). Moreover, in a media context, preliminary evidence suggests that young people may consider romantic elders as unwatchable (Harwood, 1997). Palmore suggests that older people share this aversion and often feel guilty and embarrassed about their own sexuality (Williamson, Evans, & Nunley, 1980). In Britian, we need only turn on the television to watch an episode of the popular dating game *Blind Date* for an illustration. Occasionally, the blind dates are arranged between senior citizens rather than as is more usual, among those in their 20s and to a lesser extent, 30s. These episodes, the presentation of age in a dating context, audience reaction to the older couples, and their subsequent accounts of dates, are well worth the attention of researchers. Romance and graciousness between these older participants seem to be regarded with kindliness, whereas any hint of sexuality or passion raises considerable mirth among the audience.

Many people, older and younger alike, believe that increasing age is associated with loss of attractiveness, and this is communicated by the visual images of age we see portrayed in the media. By way of illustration, consider the number of older women, movie stars as well as others, who are willing to undergo painful surgery in order to stave off the effects of time by having their wrinkles removed or their tummies tucked and so forth. As a demonstration of the link between older age and unattractiveness, Palmore cites a study of attractive and unattractive faces that found that both younger (under 30 years old) and older people (over 56 years old) believed that the unattractive faces were more likely to be older (Wernick & Manaster, 1984).

Another striking example comes from a British magazine for women. Recently, this publication ran a Levi Strauss Jeans Company advertisement that portrayed an aged couple sitting on a park bench in swimwear. Considerable trouble seems to have been taken to make the photograph (a two-page spread) as strikingly unattractive as possible. There is no color in the picture except for a tiny red Levi tag at the edge of the page; the couple are each overweight and their sagging flesh is accentuated by their swimwear, which is the same shade of gray. The woman has her hair in an old-fashioned bun and is engrossed in her knitting. The man leaning forward with his elbow resting on his knee has a mug of hot drink hanging slightly in his hand. He has a decidedly dejected expression on his face as he gazes at the grass. The caption reads, "Age doesn't improve everything."

Palmore (1988) argues that what is attractive or unattractive is culturally created and that there is nothing inherently ugly about old age. It seems to us that such a stereotype of old age is going to be very hard to dispel. Commenting on images of the aging body, Hepworth (1995) pointed out that youth is strongly associated with beauty. Although our societal obsession with appearance is actually relatively modern, its roots and negative perceptions of the aging body can be traced back to early Greek civilization (Hepworth, 1995). Interested readers should refer to Featherstone and Hepworth (1994) for a very interesting account of "images of aging" (p. 250).

Another common belief is that we lose many of our cognitive faculties as we age, especially our memories and ability to learn and integrate new information (Palmore, 1988). People believe that such losses and declines are inevitable as we age, and that decline begins as early as middle age. According to Poon (1987), cited in Palmore (1988), when other factors such as illness, motivation, learning style, lack of practice, and amount of education are taken into account, the connection between chronological age and learning ability declines. The aged are also thought to suffer mental illness and senility. In 1988, Palmore found that two thirds of those he surveyed believed that elders have more mental impairments than younger people. What seems particularly worrysome is the belief that mental illness among the elderly is inevitable and untreatable. When these beliefs are shared across various sections of society, not just the general public or young people, and are believed by elders and the health professionals who care for them, it is particularly invidious.

Palmore (1990) discusses a pervasive image of older people as having nothing to do and nothing productive to contribute to society, and this links to a belief that older people disengage from society as they make their ways to death. From this viewpoint, older peoples' physical and health challenges conspire with mental and cognitive decline to render them less and less useful and more and more dependent as members of society. This belief is not reserved for those who are increasingly being identified as the *old-old,* those in their 90s or even those in their 70s and 80s, but in some cases, has been applied to those in middle age. For example, in Britain, there is still no age-discrimination legislation and it is not uncommon for job advertisements to stipulate that only persons less than 30 need apply because people over 30 are assumed to be past their best and are unlikely to have the energy, motivation, and cognitive capability that the job requires. During the recent climate of economic recession and stalemate in the United Kingdom, many companies have been implementing compulsory redundancies for employees over 50 and are not abashed to admit on national television that this practice is born from their beliefs that such people are not as mentally agile and productive as younger workers.

Palmore's (1988) research was conducted in the late 1980s; some recent images of age promoted by popular media lead us to question whether or not some of these beliefs are undergoing change. For example, the issue of whether or not we believe that many or most older people are living in poverty has been complicated by recent images of wealthy elders, and to concurrent changes in the economy, pensions and so on during the last few decades. In the 1990s, there are probably at least two versions of old age in relation to wealth. One characterization is of very poor elders living on subsistence in very bad housing conditions. Alternatively, there is the view of very rich elders enjoying life and spending their children's inheritances (as the bumper sticker reads). In 1988, Palmore found that half of his respondents believed that the majority of older people live below the poverty line, but in recent years there has been much discussion in the United States about Medicare and social security, and some news media have portrayed elders as getting more than their share of public funds (Coombes & Holladay, 1995). This illustrates how images are often mixed or are even contradictory—an issue we discuss more in later sections.

The final stereotype identified by Palmore (1988) is that elders are relatively miserable and unsatisfied with their lives. Research by Palmore found that one third to one half of his respondents thought that the majority of older people were isolated and lonely, and two thirds of people over 65 believed that loneliness is a very serious problem for most people over 65 (Harris, 1981). However, other research challenges these views by suggesting that younger people experience more boredom, depression, and restlessness than do older people (Gerstein & Tesser, 1987). Note that it would probably be more accurate to characterize Palmore's list as typical trait attributions and salient features that may trigger certain stereotypes of older people. Stereotypes tend to be more complex cognitive packages of such characteristics put together in certain combinations, as we discuss in more detail.

The previous chapter mentioned that some theorists suggest that our attitudes toward older people have become more negative in the 20th century with the advent of modernity. Addressing this issue, Featherstone and Hepworth (1990) provide a historical perspective on attitudes toward aging, pointing out that our lay beliefs about the status of age often hold up the past as an example of a golden era for the aged, during which elders enjoyed levels of respect and care in preindustrial societies that they have not experienced since. We often point to industrialization as being responsible for the decline in status for those who are old. Industrialization and the technological revolution of society have essentially made elders redundant and superfluous to our needs, as was discussed in chapter 2. However, Featherstone and Hepworth (1990) argue that we have always had rather ambivalent attitudes towards the aged. In support of this viewpoint, they cite a study of 19th-century British children's stories, songs, and games that revealed three predominant stereotypes of older people. The first is a rather passive but wise and moral individual who is not actively involved in life but provides approving and friendly moral support to the young. This characterization is rather positive in that it is the one "most approved of by children's didactic literature" (p. 264). The second characterization is of older people who do not act their age. These are sometimes men but are more often women who make futile and pitiful attempts to seem younger than they are and who refuse to fit into an approved age stereotype. The third characterization is of those who are suffering the physical declines and indignities of old age. These people are the subject of taunts and humor; they are not portrayed as morally good or bad, but they are simply the decrepit elderly.

The news is not all bad, because our characterizations of older people and of old age, although being predominantly negative, are more complex than this. As Featherstone and Hepworth (1990) argue, our attitudes toward old age are full of ambivalence. This means that alongside negative perceptions, we feel benevolently toward elders, sometimes kindly and sympathetic, sometimes patronizing. Consider, for example, the image of the sweet and well-meaning, if rather ineffectual, little old lady and how we would typically respond to such a person. Related to this, Kite and Johnson (1988) have argued that traits typically associated with older people are not all negative and actually include some positive traits such as sociability (see also Braithwaite, Lynd-Stevenson, & Pigram, 1993).

Brewer, Dull, and Lui (1981) proposed that traits could be grouped to form several different stereotypes of elderly people. They outlined three predominant subtypes; *grandmother* (a nurturing, family-oriented woman), *elder statesman* (a distinguished conservative man), and *senior citizen* (an inactive isolated person of either sex). More recently, a range of other positive stereotypes has been identified and labeled as part of our cognitive repertoire of aged stereotypes. Such characterizations include images of older people as wise and benevolent. Hummert and colleagues (Hummert, 1990, 1994; Hummert, Garstka, Shaner, & Strahm, 1994) used trait generation and trait-sorting tasks, and through a number of studies have investigated both positive and negative stereotypes of older people. This research identified four predominantly negative and three positive, stereotypes of older people held by young, middle-aged and older persons (see Tables 3.1 & 3.2). Negative stereotypes of older people are: Severely Impaired, Despondent, Shrew/Curmudgeon, and Recluse. The traits associated with these stereotypes are listed in Table 3.1.

The three positive stereotypical subcategories of older people are labeled: Perfect Grandparent, Golden Ager, and John Wayne Conservative and their associated traits are listed in Table 3.2.

Moreover, experimental studies by Hummert et al. (e.g., Hummert, Garstka, & Shaner, 1995) indicate that unfavorable evaluations of older targets follow activation of negative stereotypes, and accordingly, positive-stereotype activation stimulates correspondingly positive evaluations. These studies are discussed in more detail in following chapters.

To some extent, the nature of evaluations of older and younger people can be tied to study design and focus: Within-subjects manipulations of target age and a focus on generalized-older and younger targets tend to yield more nega-

TABLE 3.1
Four Negative Stereotypes and Associated Traits of Older People

Severely Impaired	Recluse	Shrew/Curmudgeon	Despondent
slow-thinking	quiet	complaining	depressed
incompetent	timid	ill-tempered	sad
feeble	naive	bitter	hopeless
incoherent		prejudiced	afraid
inarticulate		demanding	neglected
senile		inflexible	lonely
		selfish	
		jealous	
		stubborn	
		nosy	

tive evaluations of older targets than younger ones, whereas between-subjects manipulations of age and a focus on specific-old versus young targets find either no age effects or evaluations that favor older targets as often as younger ones (Crockett & Hummert, 1987; Kite & Johnson, 1988; Kogan, 1979). However, methodological choices alone cannot account for the mixed positive and negative evaluations of older people. Even when within-subjects designs or generalized targets are employed, elderly persons are sometimes judged positively in absolute scale values, or as no different from young targets, or more positively than young targets on some dimensions (e.g., Braithwaite, 1986; Harris, 1975; Ryan & Capadano, 1978; Schwalb & Sedlacek, 1990). Likewise when between-subjects designs have compared perceptions of individualized old and young targets, old targets have sometimes been judged more negatively than young ones on certain dimensions (e.g., O'Connell & Rotter, 1979; Perry & Varney, 1978; Ryan & Laurie, 1990; Stewart & Ryan, 1982).

Agism

The identification of so-called positive stereotypes should not make us complacent about agist attitudes. Negative attitudes toward, and prejudice against, those who are old—*agism*—has been identified as a pervasive prob-

TABLE 3.2
Three Positive Stereotypes and Associated Traits of Elderly People

Perfect Grandparent	John Wayne Conservative	Golden Ager
kind	patriotic	lively
loving	religious	adventurous
family oriented	nostalgic	alert
generous	reminiscent	active
grateful	retired	sociable
supportive	conservative	witty
understanding	emotional	independent
trustworthy	mellow	skilled
intelligent	determined	productive
wise	proud	successful
knowledgeable		capable
		volunteer
		well traveled
		future oriented
		fun loving
		happy
		curious
		healthy/health conscious
		sexual
		self-accepting
		courageous
		interesting
		well informed

lem in Western societies (Butler, 1987; Palmore, 1990), and is often likened to sexism and racism. Palmore identified agism as the third great "*ism*" of our century, defining it as "prejudice or discrimination against or in favor of an age group" (p. 4). Butler (1987) defined agism as:

a process of systematic stereotyping of and discrimination against people because they are old just as racism and sexism accomplish this for skin color and gender. Old people are categorized as senile in thought and manner, old fashioned in morality and skills. ... Ageism allows the younger generations to see older people as different from themselves thus they subtly cease to identify with their elders as human beings. (p. 22)

Bytheway and Johnson (1990) claim that this definition has been a crucial determinant, not only of the scope of gerontological inquiry but also of political policies. In their analysis of the definition, Johnson and Bytheway (1993) point out that Butler clearly delimits agism to those who belong to a group marked as "old," inherently assuming that there is such a social group. Furthermore, those who are young, middle aged, and so forth are excluded from this definition (see Itzin, 1986). Agism toward young people will be discussed later, but for the most part, research in recent years has been concerned with agism directed toward older people (usually those over 65 years old).

There are a number of permutations of old-age stereotyping and its consequences. For example, very negative stereotypes elicit extremely negative responses to elders, such as avoidance, abuse, and disgust, known as *gerontophobia* (Levin & Levin, 1980). Alternatively, responses can be benevolent and compassionate, but none-the-less the underlying attitude and beliefs about elders may still be very negative. In this vein, Kalish (1979) argues that a form of new agism exists whereby benevolent practitioners and the public alike respond with caring to a perception of older people who are weak, incompetent, poor, ineffectual, and in need of help. For example, a study of physicians' attitudes toward their older patients (Revenson, 1989) showed that although negative age stereotypes were less prevalent than expected, there was evidence that physicians who treat elderly patients draw upon compassionate stereotypes. Of course, this may be an important aspect of good care, but it may also reinforce assumptions that older people are a homogenous group of needy persons and may mask the heterogeneity of the older population (for discussion of intergenerational communication in professional, medical contexts, see chapter 11). This tendency may not be restricted to physicians and those working within a medical or caring context or both. Thus, rather than outrightly agist and negative attitudes toward elders, many people may feel positively disposed to elders, based on sympathy or compassion (Scheier, Carver, Schulz, Glass, & Katz, 1978). This too can be misdirected, oppressive, and agist, and is undoubtedly strongly connected to communication, especially patronizing speech directed toward older people (see Hummert, Garstka, & Shaner, 1995).

Yet another conceptually ill-defined position exists when older people are given an overly and thus unrealistic positive gloss as in the sweet little old lady who is cute and who is benevolent toward those who are younger. The consequences of being categorized as such and being expected to behave in the sweet old lady role may be no less damaging (and perhaps are even more pernicious) than is outright denigration. Notice the similarities of this general characterization with Hummert's Perfect Grandparent stereotype. Sontag (1978) has argued that such benevolent attitudes toward older women can be characterized as a mask for oppression, especially so because women suffer the double jeopardy of sexism and agism.

Making comparisons between societal "isms" such as racism, sexism, and agism alerts us to the possibility that even positive stereotypes may sometimes be potentially socially debilitating for older people if they are infrequently individuated or are not afforded rights and roles beyond their social-group membership, that is, beyond the stereotype. In other words, an important practical goal should be to treat older people as individuals rather than as positive or negative representatives of a social group, as pointed out by Ryan, Meredith, MacLean, and Orange (1995).

Chapter 2 suggested that, in very general terms, older people are underrepresented in the media and when they are portrayed it is in line with expected stereotypes. We now briefly return to this discussion, to further examine the portrayals of older people in media contexts. Overall, it has been estimated that as much as 80% of U.S. media portrayals of older people conform to stereotypical images. A recent analysis argued that even the supposedly antiagist television program, *The Golden Girls*, rather than dispelling agist assumptions, could be perpetuating them (Harwood & Giles, 1992). Shaner (1995) has alerted us to the fact that older men and women may often be portrayed very differently in motion pictures. Her comparative analysis of the motion pictures *Grumpy Old Men* and *Widow's Peak* revealed that older adults of both sexes were portrayed as busybodies in these movies, but that the women were portrayed as overwhelmingly more nosy than the men. The men also were much more active and healthy, both physically and mentally, and were also portrayed as sexual. Although this research is exploratory and preliminary because it draws on only two movies, it may well be worthwhile to turn our attention to the issues underlined here—the interaction between agism and sexism. Indeed, other evidence also suggests that there seems to be a double standard with which women are negatively stereotyped at a younger age than are men (Hummert, Garstka, Shaner, & Strahm, 1994). As Robinson and Skill (1995) have argued, there is a pressing need for updated analyses of images of age and elderliness in the contemporary media.

Stereotyping and Agism Toward the Young

Older people are not the only group who suffer discrimination on grounds of their chronological age. Young people, too, are subject to many similar linguistic and communicative stigmatizations. For example, in earlier sections we briefly considered derogatory terms used to describe older people. Can we recognize similar themes when we examine terms used to describe the young? The proportion of derogatory terms for the young compared to those for the old may reflect the relative balance of social power, and especially a shared social perception that being young is a preferred state, but there are a few other considerations to discuss. As a starting point, we could suggest that negative stereotypes of young people tend to rely on images of inexperience, eagerness to impress, irresponsibility, and laziness. For example, many terms for the young refer in a derogatory way to immaturity and naiveté, including the terms whippersnapper, babe-in-arms, babysnatching, young rake, and the denigration intended in referring to a person as a child when he or she is not.

We do not have to look too far to provide a more specific example. In the U.S. media particularly, there has been a vast amount of recent press concerned with the current generation of young people (i.e., those born anywhere between 1961 and 1981). The labels for the generation, some of which are positive and others negative, are worth considering. For example, a popular label for this generation, "X," (taken from a popular novel by Douglas Coupland, 1991) has been used to represent the facelessness and aimlessness of a generation, the members of which have no distinct identities, causes, ambitions, or so forth. *Time* magazine is credited with the first use of a more positive label: "twentysomethings" (Ladd, 1993, p. 37), and Strauss, Howe, and Williams (1993) coined the term: "The thirteenth generation."

On their own, these labels sound relatively neutral, but many media reports have also included some very negative trait characterizations of the generation characterizing them as losers, slackers, whingers and whiners, who are dependent on their parents. In fact, a close examination of popular press reports shows that negative characterizations of the generation are ubiquitous and are lined up against younger people's attempts to debunk them. This is evident by the negative redefinitions given to the labels themselves; for example, the term twentysomething has often been rephrased as twentynothing. A 1994 article in *Newsweek* magazine cites the following: *Advertising Age* as referring to the generation as "that cynical, purple-haired blob watching TV"; a *Washington Post* headline declaring "the boring twenties: Grow up, crybabies, you're America's luckiest generation." Along the same lines, *New Republic* columnist Michael Kinsley writes: "These kids to-day, they're soft. They don't know how good they have it. Not only did they never have to fight a war ... they never had to dodge one." Of course, self-claimed representatives of Generation X argue that it is the outgroup (i.e., Baby Boomers) who perpetuate such images, which are often cast in contrast to notions of Baby-Boomer demographic vitality, economic secu-rity, and generational imperialism (Williams, Coupland, Folwell, & Sparks, 1997). Some young people, perhaps in an effort to differentiate themselves from their parent's generation, may actually collaborate in creating and sus-taining counter-status quo identities for themselves and their peer groups. These issues, their interpretation in terms of intergroup theory, and their implications are discussed more in chapter 12. At present, there is little re-search concerned with agist attitudes toward young people and youth sub-culture, but this may prove to be an important and interesting direction for future research.

Just as with effects of agism toward the old, the effects of agism toward the young can be observed through all our social institutions including edu-cation, law, and health care. No less so in government, for example, early at-tempts to undermine the first Clinton administration may have involved raising public fears by expressing doubts about a young presidency, and young people inappropriately taking over the corridors of power. Readers will perhaps remember media references to kids in the White House who listened to rock and roll on their boomboxes, presumably between policy meetings. Writing in *The New Republic* in July 1994, Ruth Shalit acknowl-edged that "social critics have denounced the Clinton youth corps as a brood of ill-mannered bumblers" (p. 23). According to this article, Oliver North had "declared war on an administration replete with 'twentysomething staffers with an earring and an axe to grind.'"

As the previous examples demonstrate, there is agism toward the young, although it has not received as much attention as that directed at older peo-ple. It probably does, however, affect some young peoples lives in very signif-icant and, as yet, under-researched ways. Age-stereotyped traits associated with young people in their teens and early 20s can take several forms (see Giles & Williams, 1994). When older people treat young people negatively, young people believe that older people view them as immature, naive, un-wise and unworldly, irresponsible, disrespectful, lazy, self-centered, noisy, disruptive, and delinquent (Williams, 1992).

Hummert et al's. studies of positive and negative stereotypes of people of different age groups revealed a number of stereotypes of young people too.

This research revealed nine negative stereotypes and four positive stereotypes of younger people (see Tables 3.3 & 3.4).

Negative stereotypes of younger people were labeled as Red Neck, Country Clubber, Nosy Neighbor, Loner, Member of Underclass, Homeless, Invalid, Small-Town Homebody, and Mentally Handicapped. Positive stereotypes of young people were identified as: Activist, Mature Young Professional, Athlete/Extrovert, and Perfect Friend. Other research revealed stereotypes that adolescents have of their ingroup crowds (Brown, Mory, & Kinney, 1994) with labels such as Preppies, Normals, Brains, Dirtballs, Outcasts, Jocks, Populars, Loners, Druggies, Nerds, Punkers, Hippies, and Headbangers. This research was conducted with high-school adolescents, and may not be generalizable to perceptions that older people have of young people, but some of these labels do seem to coincide with some of Hummert's, such as Loner with Loner, Jocks with Athlete/Extrovert, Preppies with Mature Young Professional, and Populars with Perfect Friend. Further research is needed to reveal general, succinct, and valid stereotypes of young people as well as older people's own perceptions and expectations of their interactions with different types of young people.

Most probably, young people are particularly prone to age stereotyping and agisms when they are in positions that do not correspond to some sort of age-associated role or occupation. This can be a problem for those who serve, or are served by them, in the public sphere. For example, young parents (especially mothers) may be seen as incompetent and even somewhat feckless, and this may lead unwarranted suspicions of child neglect or even of abuse. The public may not have confidence in young-looking policemen and doctors (service providers) and they may not receive credit for being able to help. The same goes for young lawyers and young politicians or any young person in a professional sphere, some of whom may go to considerable lengths to look and self-present as older. As is pointed out by the Stereotype Activation model, the way you look can trigger stereotypes and have a very far-reaching effect on your life. An interesting example is provided by research on the so-called "baby faced" phenomenon, which has shown that when a person looks young he or she is typically rated as physically weak, submissive, honest, and naive (Berry & McArthur, 1985; McArthur & Apatow, 1983–1984). Further experimental research by Berry and McArthur (1988) showed that baby-faced defendants in law courts were more often found guilty of negligent actions, but were less often perceived to be guilty of intentional criminal action than were more mature-

TABLE 3.3
Nine Negative Stereotypes and Associated Traits of Young People

Labels:	Redneck	Country Clubber	Nosy Neighbor	Loner	Member of Underclass	Homeless	Invalid	Small Town Homebody	Mentally Handicapped
Trait ratings	greedy	distinguished looking	conservative	emotionless	lives on fixed income	lonely	forgetful	live in past	dependent
	selfish	wealthy	frugal	humorless	poor	sad	slow thinking	tells stories about the past	rambling of speech
	prejudiced	demanding	busy-body	bored	dirty	miserable	sedentary	old-fashioned	grateful for any aid
	annoying	snobbish		unable to communicate	poor posture	neglected	needs nursing care		
	bitter			naive	unattractive	victim of crime	physically handicapped		
	ill-tempered			quiet	burden to society		sick		
	set in ways				incapable of handling a job		waiting to die		
	complaining				useless		slow moving		
	easily upset						fragile		
	miserly						sexually inactive		
							arouse pity		

TABLE 3.4

Four Positive Stereotypes and Associated Traits of Young People

Activist	Mature Young Professional	Athlete/Extrovert	Perfect Friend
concern for future	intelligent	happy	loving
liberal	knows a great deal	healthy	understanding
patriotic	wise	active	generous
mellow	interesting	alert	good support to others
	comes to terms with their life	enjoys life	volunteer
	courageous		family oriented
	capable		
	useful		likes to be around young

faced defendants. Moreover, baby-faced defendants who were perceived to be guilty of negligent behavior were given lighter sentences than comparatively more mature-looking defendants.

It is a mistake to assume that only elderly people are affected by agism. Stereotypes and expectations associated with age and agism affect all age groups in a variety of ways. Stereotypes and agism toward young people have not been studied as systematically as those directed towards older adults, but may warrant more attention in the future because they too can have far-reaching effects. No doubt, as research continues, researchers will find that they need to reinterpret theories and models of the process of intergenerational communication. For example, we could speculate about the effects of two-way stereotyping (old-to-young and young-to-old) on the communication predicaments of aging described in chapter 1.

SUMMARY

This chapter sketchs a picture of age stereotyping and agism beginning with a look at the language and labels of age and agism. Early studies of trait characteristics and stereotypes of older people can be traced to more sophisticated positive as well as negative characterizations of elders. Recent studies outline a variety of different substereotypes of elders, and these substereotypes can be associated with different levels of societal agism. In addition, this chapter attempts to widen the discussion of age stereotypes and agism to include young people—a neglected dimension in age-stereotyping research. Distinct negative and positive traits and stereotypes are often associated with young people, and this may affect their lives in important yet underresearched ways. Stereotypes of young people are not considered in theoretical models of stereotyping and aging process, either. It seems that it is this very transactional nature of age stereotyping that can further frustrate attempts to improve intergenerational relationships both without and within family contexts and particularly intergenerational relationships at the community level.

Returning now to the theoretical perspectives outlined in chapter 1, this chapter illustrates intergroup and social-identity theory at work in intergenerational relationships. When people perceive themselves and others as members of distinct age groupings, for example, youth and the elderly, they have a tendency to atttribute particular sets of traits to those group members. Those traits can be grouped into sub-stereotypes, which, when used as rules to initiate and sustain social interaction, can set constraints on that interaction. Eventually, such processes lead to discrimination against outgroup members, as the discussion of agism demonstrates. Although there is no doubt that some agisms are intended as hostile intergroup moves and divergences, there is a great deal of well-intentioned agism. Again, looking at this from a structuration perspective allows us the insight that this often occurs as an unintended consequence that has its roots in the history of age categorizations discussed in chapter 2. If, in Giddens' terms, there are contradictions in this system, such as the juxtaposition of positive and negative substerotypes of elders, or the inevitability of joining a denigrated outgroup (with all the associated self-esteem implications) if you live long enough, it seems that these contradictions do not yet threaten the system. Perhaps this is partly because of what Giddens terms "the opacity of action" fueled by our inherent ability to explain away and distance ourselves (i.e., avoid reflexive consideration) from contradictions. Perhaps because of these and other inherent contradictions, agism, unlike sexism and racism, still falls on the acceptable side of political correctness.

4

Language, Cognition, and Age

As the last chapter demonstrated, research about social attitudes toward older people reveals that age stereotypes, especially negative stereotypes, are quite widespread in our society, and are constituted and manifest in various aspects of communication, including interpersonal (peer and intergenerational) and mass communication. Communication scholars interested in aging have argued that there is a transactional relationship between age stereotypes and language and communication behavior (Harwood, Giles, & Ryan, 1995; Hummert, 1994). For the most part, research interest has centered on how attitudes, stereotypes, and communication-related beliefs influence perceptions of, and communication with, older people (see Hummert, Garstka, & Shaner, 1995, for an extended review of this literature). There is also some interest in how stereotypes may be produced as post hoc accounts for communication problems, and miscommunication (e.g., Giles, Henwood, Coupland, Harriman, & Coupland, 1992; Williams, 1996).

Although chapter 3 focused on the components and nature of age stereotypes as well as the prevalence and thrust of agism, this chapter looks at language issues. Two strands of language and adulthood are woven together here. One explores language in older adulthood as it relates to stereotypes, expectations, and perceptions of age, the other explores some of the gerontological and psycholinguistic research into language development and communication abilities as they change across the life span and into old age.

There is little doubt that language and cognitive-processing skills are important factors in successful interpersonal communication. However, communication is a complex social accomplishment, the success of which depends on a number of factors—cognitive, sensory, interpersonal, and social—that interact in any given situation. Ryan and colleagues (Ryan, Giles, Bartolucci, & Henwood, 1986; Ryan, Kwong See, Meneer, & Trovato, 1992a) argued that psycholinguistic and clinical research, some of which is discussed in this chapter, have largely ignored this. As Orange and Ryan (1995) point out, language is a complex system composed of cognition (e.g., attention, perception, and memory) as well as production, but it is not simply a mechanical physiological process, it is highly social, and thus is modified by social as much as it is by physiological and cognitive factors. In order to achieve a more holistic view of these factors, Ryan, Meredith, MacLean, and Orange (1995) schematize the multiple influences that contribute to conversational success during later life as illustrated in Fig. 4.1.

Importantly, this schematic model points out that language and communication competence as evidenced by language performance on any particular occasion is affected by a number of other influences besides some sort of objective or life-stage developmental ability (knowledge, information-processing strategy, etc.). The individual's life history and environment influence competence. For example, we might predict that those who achieved a high educational level, or who are middle class or perhaps privileged in other ways,

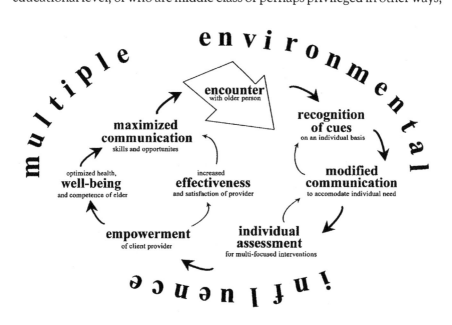

FIG. 4.1.   The communication enhancement model. From "Changing the Way We Talk With Elders: Promoting Health Using the Communication Enhancement Model," by E. B. Ryan, S. D. Meredith, M. J. MacLean, and J. B. Orange, 1995, *International Journal of Aging and Human Development, 41*, p. 91. Copyright ©1995 by Baywood Publishing. Reprinted with permission.

may be broadly classified as more competent than those who do not have such a background. More explicitly, people with more education would perhaps be expected to command a wider vocabulary than those with less.

Language performance would also be affected by situational or context features. Ryan, Meredith, et al. (1995) highlight task demands and interpersonal factors. Circumstances of high task demand would be expected to have a deleterious effect on language and communication processing and skills. Thus, older people who participate in laboratory-based research, clinical situations, or other situations wherein task demands may be high, such as noisy and busy social situations and telephone conversations, may perform less well than when demands are lower. Also, different task situations have different criteria by which success is measured, as well as having different perceived levels of task relevance. For example, many older people may be skeptical of a range of research tasks, especially those that appear highly abstract, structured and clinical, and are more likely than young people to question the real life applicability of this kind of research. If older people perceive research as having relatively low relevance and importance, they may not invest as much energy into completing the tasks as do college-age individuals who are acclimatized to testing situations and who often do not question the tasks they are asked to perform.

As Fig. 4.1 illustrates, interpersonal factors operating in various task situations are crucial and include expectations and attitudes (both self- and other), communication behavior of both self and others and emotional factors. These factors are expanded in much more detail when issues such as under- and overaccommodation, age identity and others are discussed in later chapters. For present purposes, the groundwork laid in chapter 3 is expanded now to discuss beliefs and expectations about the language and communication abilities of old and young communicators and about how communication behavior is interpreted in terms of age expectations. It is important to realize that such beliefs and expectations play important roles in the theoretical schematic models (i.e., social identity and intergroup theory, communication accommodation, the communication predicament and the stereotype activation models) discussed in chapter 1.

BELIEFS ABOUT OLDER PEOPLE'S LANGUAGE AND COMMUNICATION

Ryan and Kwong See (1993) showed that adult's predictions about their own and others' memory performance at different ages showed that they expected significant decline from young adulthood through middle age to older adulthood: Older adults' negative beliefs and expectations about their own hearing, memory, and language processing and production may affect their communication experiences, eventually their self-esteem, and even their social psychological and physical health in important ways (Ryan, Giles, Bartolucci, & Henwood, 1986).

A number of recent studies have used the *Language in Adulthood Scale* (*LIA*) (Ryan, Kwong See, Meneer, & Travato, 1992a, 1992b), to investigate perceptions about older adults' receptive and expressive language and communication abilities. The LIA is composed of a number of items designed to assess language performance (e.g., "... its hard to understand when noisy" and "I often lose track of a topic in conversation") and conversational skill (e.g., the ability to tell interesting stories). Some items tap into beliefs about age-related decline in conversational performance, whereas others focus on age-related language skills including sincerity (Ryan & Heaven, 1988), size of vocabulary (Salthouse, 1988), and storytelling skills (Kemper, Rash, Kynette, & Norman, 1990).

In an initial study, Ryan, Kwong See, Meneer, and Trovato (1992a) asked a group of young (mean age 26.4) and elderly (mean age 72.9) adults to provide assessments of their own language abilities as well as those of either a typical 25-year-old or a typical 75-year-old. The study made comparisons between self-perceptions and age-based social perceptions for two groups of typical others (25- and 75-year-olds) from two groups of respondents (younger and older).

As expected, for self-perceptions of receptive skills, younger people reported fewer problems with hearing, memory, and also (unexpectedly) with vocabulary than did older people. For self-perceptions of expressive skills, younger people reported fewer problems with memory-related factors (e.g., tip of the tongue) than did older people. Younger people were also more likely than older people to report talking most, a finding which was interpreted as reflecting young self-confidence and conversational dominance. Even items thought to favor older adults failed to do so; older respondents rated themselves more poorly than did young adults across domains of conversation skills, memory, and hearing.

For social perceptions of typical others' receptive skills, results showed more positive expectations for typical young versus typical older adults, even for vocabulary. The young were also perceived to perform better with expressive skills, whereas older people were thought to be more skilled at telling enjoyable stories and were thought to be more sincere than young people. In general, and following the results of self-perceptions, typical 75-year-olds were thought to have more problems than typical 25-year-olds across all domains of measurement: conversational skills, memory, and hearing.

This research indicates that both older and younger people generally share the same perceptions of older language and communication skills. They agree that older people have more difficulty across a range of skills, even some of those who are predicted, on the basis of information-processing research, to favor older people. The finding that self-perceptions of older people are also quite negative reflects the generally low social expectations about the communication performance of older people, and these expectations are shared by young and old alike. This should not be taken lightly because it almost certainly feeds directly into constructions of self-potential, from there to effort, and ultimately to affect performance.

Beliefs, Stereotypes, and Language Performance

Investigations using the LIA demonstrate that both older and younger people expect older adults to experience more communication difficulty than young adults. Recently, Hummert and colleagues extended these earlier findings to examine the effect of particular substereotypes of older people (as discussed in chapter 3) on judgments of language and communication skills. Different stereotypes of elderly individuals suggest different stereotypes of communication characteristics, and especially, different levels of communication competence. A recent study by Hummert, Garstka, and Shaner (1995) used the LIA (Ryan, Kwong See, Meneer, & Trovato, 1992) to assess beliefs of young middle-aged and elderly participants about their own communication skills and those of four elderly targets. Traits used to characterize the targets corresponded to two positive (Golden Ager, John Wayne Conservative) and two negative (Despondent, Shrew/Curmudgeon) stereotypes (Hummert, Garstka, et al., 1994). Participants of all ages believed that the number of communication problems in hearing and memory would be lower for the two positive targets than for the two negative targets. It should be noted that this was true even though the trait descriptions of the two negative targets gave no indication of memory and hearing difficulties. In addition, perceptions of age-related increases in word recognition and storytelling skills favored the positive targets over the negative ones.

Thus, although generalized negative views of elders can be shown to be powerful stimulants of negative evaluations (Harwood & Williams, 1998), often, beliefs about the communication competence of elderly individuals can result from categorizing them as particular types of elderly persons—an issue we revisit. Having examined the nature of expectations and beliefs about language skills, this discussion turns now to look at wider social perceptions of older adult speakers. Much of the research to be reviewed was born from the language-attitudes research tradition, which explores stereotypical expectations associated with different kinds of language, particularly with accented speech. As such, this research has been crucial in providing insight into how language and communication expectations of older people are intertwined with the stereotypes and social beliefs that chapter 3 discussed in detail.

Perceptions of Older Communicators

A number of experimental studies have taken advantage of the fact that listeners can fairly accurately attribute age to a speaker from voice cues alone (Hollien, 1987; Ryan & Capadano, 1978). As described previously, older voices typically have certain qualities of pitch, tone, and breathiness, which are easily distinguishable. However, as a caveat to this, Mulac and Giles (1996) showed that, in some circumstances, the perceptual age of an older person's voice can be quite independent of both chronological age and subjective or psychological age. In other words, you can feel young, yet nonetheless sound old. Not surprisingly perhaps, the older the perceptual age of the voice the more frailty and vulnerablility are attributed to the speaker. Doubtless, future studies will assess which cues—physiognomic (Hummert, 1994), vocal, verbal, dress, and so on—lead (in what kinds of combinations) to increased or decreased expectations.

Ryan and Laurie (1990; see also Ryan & Johnston, 1987) considered the ways in which an adult speaker's age and messages with varying levels of effectiveness might interact to affect judgments of that speaker. Age interacted with message effectiveness such that an effective message resulted in more positive evaluations for the younger speaker, but not for the older speaker. Furthermore, the older speaker giving a message with a white noise background was rated as the least competent target. As the authors pointed out, this suggests that the older speaker, in comparison to the younger one, received more blame for the poor-quality recording and less credit for the effective message.

One of the main findings arising from language-attitudes studies is that prestige-accented speakers are upgraded on traits indicating competence, such as perceived intelligence and confidence, yet are often downgraded on traits indicating solidarity, such as perceived friendliness and trustworthiness. Giles and colleagues (e.g., Giles, Coupland, Henwood, Harriman, & Coupland, 1990) argued that this evaluative profile is agist (and, in fact, sexist) to the extent that usually the listener-judges, and almost always the speakers, are young adults (and also male) and that this could theoretically be crucial. It is possible that the judgmental pattern noted previously would become virtually irrelevant when considered vis-à-vis much older speakers, given pervasive negative stereotypes associated with the competence afforded to the elderly in the West.

In this vein, Stewart and Ryan (1982) asked young participants to evaluate either old or young male speakers speaking at fast, medium, and slow rates. Both age and rate affected competence ratings, with younger and faster speakers seen as more competent than older and slower ones. However, rate played a stronger role than speaker age in causal attributions about the reasons for the speaker's performance.

Possessing a standard accent and also a fast speech rate could perhaps assume even more importance in older years, as it could stave off some of the negative connotations of being elderly because it is usually associated with speakers who have high social status. Two studies (Giles et al., 1990; Giles, Henwood, Coupland, Harriman, & Coupland, 1992) showed that agism is inherent in other decoding practices. In this (and in the follow-up) study, the speaker was a male actor (age mid-30s) whose professional viability depended on his ability to change his voice to produce different authentic age- and class-related voices (guises). This was an accomplishment that he had achieved many times on national television. In the first study (Giles et al., 1990), the speaker produced a number of different versions of the same (neutral) 320-word passage, in which he was heard talking about his car, supposedly during an interview. Although the content of the passage was the same, he systematically varied several features of his speech by *speech rate* (fast vs. medium vs. slow), *accent* (standard [British] vs. nonstandard [northwest English]), and *voice quality* (elderly vs. young adult). The different combinations of these features resulted in 12 versions of the passage so that, although the speaker sounded different in each version, it was in fact the same speaker in every case. Thus, any differences in judgments of the speaker did not result from idiosyncratic qualities of different speakers, but from the systematic variations in speech rate, accent, and voice age.

Young-adult listener-judges from South Wales, United Kingdom, rated one of these 12 versions of the passage on speaker personality traits. Manipulation checks substantiated that the speaker's guises were perceived as intended, and that when sounding elderly, he was judged to be 62 years old. Predictably, the guises using standard accents were upgraded on status and downgraded on benevolence and integrity (Ryan & Giles, 1982). The older guises were considered to be more aged (i.e., evaluated along the dimensions of frail, old-fashioned) and more vulnerable (i.e., weak, insecure), with the most vulnerable voice being the slow, nonstandard, older voice. Although the use of fast speech and a standard accent by an older speaker reduced perceived vulnerability, he was nonetheless seen as asocial and egocentric. Moreover, this guise was rated as the least benevolent of the older age variants. Thus, regardless of the other cues present, the older voice was always associated with some negative characteristics.

The researchers also gathered open-ended qualitative information by asking participants to give reasons for their particular ratings of the speaker(s), as well as by asking them to explain why the speaker had made certain statements. Findings from this aspect of the research showed that the combination of old age and nonstandard speech produced responses that drew heavily on assumptions about both old age and relative disadvantage. The researchers found that listeners differentially interpreted extracts from the text, such as the speaker saying, "I didn't know what to think," depending on the speaker's age. Hence, this statement was more likely to be attributed to the speaker's being confused if elderly (and recall he was perceived as only in his early 60s) then to his wishing to withhold judgment given the complexity of issues at hand if he was young. When asked why they rated the speaker as they had, despite the fact that he said exactly the same thing in each condition, listeners described the young standard speaker as "arrogant and pompous"; the nonstandard young speaker as "trying to impress" or "using the words of others"; the standard elderly speaker as "egocentric, living in the past, and talking of trivia"; and the nonstandard elderly speaker as "stupid and losing his grip." When invited to substantiate these accounts by recourse to pinpointing textual information, respondents very often highlighted exactly the same utterances to justify their very disparate claims. These open-ended data clearly indicate that respondents actively interpreted what they heard and tailored information to fit schemas prompted by age and class, as indicated by standard and nonstandard speech variables.

Building on this foundation, a follow-up study employed the same speaker varying the same speech qualities, but with different message content (Giles, Henwood, et al., 1992). Again, the speaker was talking about his car, but this time in the context of an interview following a car crash (no personal injury involved). The speaker's competence was held in question and the responsibility for the crash was kept uncertain. In addition, respondents were given a questionnaire asking them, among other things, to list their thoughts and feelings when the speaker was talking. Other measures included textual interpretation items (e.g., items such as "Was the speaker aware of damage?"; "Was the speaker to blame?") and a passage-recognition questionnaire administered 2 days later. Results of listener-judges' interpretations of the text revealed potent age effects. Younger speakers were perceived to be more aware of the damage caused by the accident than were older speakers. Older speakers were denigrated as doddery, vague, and rambling, seen as more upset and weak, and were commented about less than younger speakers, who were seen as stronger. A couple of days later, information spoken by younger speakers was more accurately remembered than the same information spoken by older speakers.

These studies demonstrate that speech markers such as accent, rate, and age, separately and in combination, can act as sociolinguistic triggers. In other words, as soon as such markers are heard, listeners call upon relevant cognitive stereotypes or schemas and use them for interpreting and understanding what has been said. Such biasing often means that older people's communicative behaviors are negatively evaluated, are actively processed in a stereotypical manner, and are recalled less effectively than are the comparable behaviors of younger people (see also Ryan & Johnston, 1987).

FORMULATING WHAT TO SAY TO ELDERS

It stands to reason that if respondents are using schema-driven processing in interpreting the behavior of others, then they would also use such strategies when seeking information from others. In a study by Carver and de la Garza (1984), two groups of students read the same brief five-line description of an automobile accident involving either an older (84-year-old) or a younger (22-year-old) male driver-protagonist, the impetus for the stimulus messages in the studies described previously. Respondents were presented with a list of nine empirically derived questions that could be posed to the protagonist. These questions were to be rank ordered by the respondent in terms of their perceived importance in assigning responsibility for the accident. As predicted, age labels induced stereotypical information seeking. Specifically, the elderly label (referring to a person age 84) led to differential patterns of information seeking concerning the physical, mental, and sensory inadequacies of the driver; conversely, and also concordant with stereotypes, the young label (age 22) led to questions concerning speeding and alcohol consumption.

A later study conducted in Britain extended this design to include 77-, 66-, and 54-year-olds as well as the original 84- and 22-year-old targets (Franklyn-Stokes, Harriman, Giles, & Coupland, 1988). As the age of the target increased, the importance of questions about health, physical condition, quickness of reaction, and mental competence also increased linearly. In other words, such questions were thought least important for the youngest target and most important for the oldest target. The reverse pattern occurred for questions concerning alcohol consumption. These were more frequently asked of young targets and tailed off linearly as the targets' ages increased.

In a follow-up study conducted in New Zealand (Ng, Moody, & Giles, 1991), the target ages were extended to cover the life span from 16 to 91 years (in 10-year age bands). Again, health and competence information was more frequently sought from older speakers, whereas speeding and alcohol information was perceived as more relevant for younger targets. However, rather than a steady linear trend as in the previous study, the importance of health- and competence-information seeking was observed to increase most sharply at 31 and 81 years of age. As in the previous study, information seeking based on speeding and alcohol was considered less important for older targets. In this case, therefore, not only was information seeking agist, but information seeking that seemed to rely on a decremental perception of growing older was present for middle-age targets, increasing dramatically with a target in the very early 30s. Of course, the attributions of criminal behavior (in this case, drunken driving) to the young person can also be seen as agist and can be linked to stereotypical perceptions of young people as irresponsible and reckless. So, young and old people are both characterized as incompetent, but for different age stereotype-associated reasons.

Agist information seeking, therefore, affects all age categories. An early experimental examination of how young adults might address older people when requesting different kinds of assistance (Dillard, Henwood, Giles, Coupland, & Coupland, 1990) demonstrated that young (and older) adults have beliefs that allow them to formulate what to say to each other. This research tapped into the prodigious area of inquiry known as compliance gaining (see Miller, 1983) and predates Hummert's work, which has subsequently teased apart various substereotypes of older people. Working from the premise that older adults are stereotyped as less effective communicators than their younger counterparts, this study attempted to examine two potentially stereotypical views of older communication (see Brewer, Dull, & Lui, 1981). On the basis of research by Brewer et al., researchers reasoned that an older person seen as weak and feeble would be expected to use gentle and polite influence strategies, whereas a view of egocentric and abrasive older people suggests stronger, more directly assertive strategies. Dillard et al. (1990) examined these two views while manipulating the legitimacy of the request made. Young adults completed a questionnaire designed to investigate how people set about persuading someone else to do something for them. They were asked to imagine themselves as either a typical 20-year-old or a typical 70-year-old and to ask a particular favor of either a 20-year-old or a 70-year-old. In addition, participants were told that they should either feel *justified* (legitimate request) or *unjustified* (illegitimate request) in asking the favor because they had or had not granted a similar favor about a week before. Respondents were first asked to write down what they would say and then to check off from a list the strategies they thought they might use. Although the results did not succinctly confirm either stereotype, young respondents believed that older actors in general were willing to exert more pressure than were their younger counterparts. They construed that older people were more direct with young targets than with their peers, and as more forceful and aggressive in their compliance-gaining attempts. This could reflect perceptions of older persons as authority figures who may use age status alone as justification for exerting pressure to comply.

The respondents in this study were hypothesizing about strategies that might be used in a way that allowed access to young people's perceptions of older persons' strategies. Obviously, these kinds of studies need to be replicated in an interactional context from both generations' perspectives before any hard-and-fast conclusions can be drawn. Nevertheless, the fact that age had an effect on the type of strategy used in the study indicates some profitable directions for future research about intergenerational compliance-gaining and it underscores the vital role stereotypes can often play in mediating actual communication. Whatever the strategies used in compliance-gaining, they are sure to be influenced by interactants' beliefs about what may be the most effective forms of talk (see Giles, Coupland, & Wiemann, 1992).

Do younger and older people have different beliefs about the functions of talk? Giles, Coupland, and Wiemann (1992) addressed this question by asking a sample of young (average age 19 years) and older persons (average age 70 years) to complete a questionnaire aimed at assessing own-age peers as well as eliciting attributions about other-age cohorts' beliefs about talk. Results of a factor analysis of the questionnaire study suggested that older people construed talk more positively than did their younger counterparts. In addition, young people rated their peers as likely to use talk for affiliative reasons. Older people considered their peers to have more communication problems than they did individually. That young people have a negative view of older people's beliefs about talk was suggested by their perception of older persons as assertive and valuing small talk, without these factors being apparent in the young people's views of their own-age peers. There was a recreational element of talk common to older people's ratings of both themselves and their peers; in contrast, they viewed young people as skeptical about the value of talk, but in favor of chitchat. As both groups construed each other (but not their own groups), as valuing small talk and chitchat, there seems to be considerable potential for intergenerational miscommunication with young and old engaging in overaccommodative small talk together. This section examined early research that began to open up inquiry into beliefs about intergenerational communication. These studies spawned an enormous amount of subsequent research that is discussed further in the following chapters.

LANGUAGE AND COMMUNICATION CHANGES IN OLD AGE

When considering younger and older peoples' experiences of intergenerational conversations, it is important to attempt to differentiate real life and potentially problematic aspects of these situations from myth, misperception, and so forth. In other words, although the literature has sought to establish some baseline of evidence of language changes in later life, real and expected age-related changes are often confounded with agist assumptions and expectations, and the two are not easily disentangled. Disentangling these factors is difficult because they are locked together in complex feedback loops. For example, as illustrated in Fig. 4.1, language skills may be influenced by any number of interlocking factors, including chronological age, health, environment and so forth, as well as beliefs about self. In concert with Fig. 4.1, the next section turns from stereotypes and beliefs about language and communication behavior to a discussion of language in adulthood from a life-span developmental perspective. In particular, this section examines sensory, physiological, and cognitive changes that influence language and communication in late adulthood.

In the United States, it is estimated that as many as 30% of adults age 65 and older have communication problems of one sort or another (Orange & Ryan, 1995). This includes sensory and cognitive receptive problems as well as production problems.

Sensory changes that may affect communication include both hearing and eyesight. Slawinsky, Hartel, and Kline (1993) suggest that as many as 40% of noninstitutionalized North Americans over the age of 75 have some hearing loss, but much of this is relatively minor and can easily be corrected with hearing aid devices. Using data from the 1988 National Health Interview Survey (Shewan, 1990), Villaume, Brown, and Darling (1994) estimate that 38.1% of persons over 75-years old have some hearing impairment. According to Orange and Ryan, (1995), high-frequency tones are those that are most problematic for people with hearing loss, and sometimes this can be combined with tinnitus or ringing-ears.

Villaume, Brown, and Darling (1994) suggest that there are two phases of hearing loss in later life. The first, more typical of those who are young-old, allows for adaptational strategies to aid hearing such as increased attention to paralinguistic cues involved in prosody (Wingfield, Lahar, & Stine, 1989). The second phase of hearing impairment, more typical for the old-old, deprives them of this adaptation, so they typically switch to a restricted form of conversation in which speakers take turns to dominate a topic with only minimal feedback (see also Pichora-Fuller, Johnson, & Roodenburg, 1998).

Sometimes, more severe hearing loss may cause people to withdraw from conversation, especially conversation that is rapid or distorted (Stine, Wingfield, & Poon, 1989) or, for example, when interference occurs in crowded social situations, where many sounds and different voices intermingle. Of course, this can seriously affect the quality of life for older people, and especially so when such withdrawal or repeated requests for clarification and repetition may result in perceptions of the hearing-impaired person as cognitively impaired (Bayles & Krasznaik, 1987). Thus, research shows that hearing impaired people, including those who are older, employ a range of skills to compensate for sensory losses (e.g., Johnson & Pichora-Fuller, 1994; Pichora-Fuller et al., 1998). Examples of compensation strategies include talking more in order to reduce listening demand, lip reading, repetition requests, informing others about the hearing loss, pretending to understand, avoiding others, withdrawing from communication, and preventing communication. Pichora-Fuller and colleagues report a fascinating case-study analysis in which one particular older individual, who was so skilled at both topic management and pretending to understand that she managed to continue conversation with no apparent problems in spite of severe hearing loss (Pichora-Fuller et al., 1998).

Recently, Jaworski and Stephens (1998) argued that pretending to understand, avoiding others, withdrawing, and preventing communication are not necessarily maladaptive strategies as previously suggested, but are strategies that attend to face concerns and are adaptive ways of managing relationships with hearing-able interlocutors. In many instances, such strategies could be used in order to attend to self and other negative and positive face concerns, for example, to avoid embarrassment and intrusion, which repeated repetition requests could cause to self and others. In addition to the adaptation strategies we mentioned, which apply to hearing-impaired people of all ages, research by Stine et al. (1989) has suggested that older people are able to use higher order knowledge of conversation to fill in the gaps based on what might be expected in ordinary conversation, although the associated miscommunication risks must be quite high.

Turning from sensory changes to *speech production* changes in late adult-hood, voice quality changes that are associated with age make older voices instantly recognizable, even if the other person's age is not known or he or she cannot be seen or both (Ramig, 1986; Ryan & Capadano, 1978). The pitch of female voices lowers with age, whereas in males it increases; the range of older voices' pitches may decrease, the voices may sound breathy and harsh, and this may be accompanied by slight changes in hypernasality (Orange & Ryan, 1995). Thus, older speech may have some distinctive characteristics such as slower speech rate, hoarse voice, lower volume, hypernasality, slower articulation, and imprecise consonants (Ramig, 1986). As Pratt and Norris (1994) point out, there is no evidence that these changes affect listeners' comprehension of older adult speakers, although it is likely that if such qualities do indeed distinguish older voices, they may trigger a range of beliefs and stereotypes, which in turn affect evaluations of older speakers, as discussed in previous sections of this chapter.

Research has also compiled a catalogue of cognitive changes that have been associated with advancing age. Some older adults may have problems with retrieval of names (see Cohen, 1994, for a review), a problem that has been documented through both diary (Burke, Mackay, Worthley, & Wade, 1991; Cohen & Faulkner, 1986a) and experimental studies (Burke & Laver, 1990; Crook & West, 1990). It has been suggested that this may be because there are fewer and more arbitrary or abstract links for proper names than there are for a noun and an object (Cohen, 1994). Similarly, older adults seem to experience more problems than do younger ones with word re-trieval or the tip-of-the-tongue phenomenon (Bowles & Poon, 1985; Burke & Harold, 1988; Salthouse, 1988). On the other hand, research has consis-tently shown that vocabulary increases as we age, and especially so for peo-ple who are, or have been engaged in ways that encourage this—such as those involved in education (Obler, 1989; Salthouse, 1988; Schaie, 1993).

In terms of *speech comprehension,* cognitive psychologists have studied as-pects of structural (e.g., sensory registers, working memory, and long-term memory) as well as processual (e.g., attention, reasoning, rehearsal, process-ing-speed, retrieval, etc.) functions of the normal aging cognitive system (see Nussbaum, Hummert, Williams, & Harwood, 1995, for a review). Changes in such processes carry implications for the language and communication pro-cessing and production capacities of older adults. It has been suggested that declines in both working memory capacity and processing speed affect the syntactic and discourse-processing abilities of older adults, even though their semantic knowledge remains intact (Kemper, 1992; Light, 1990; Ryan, 1991). For example, Kemper, Kynette, Rash, O'Brien, and Sprott (1989) collected both oral and written language samples from young adults and from three groups of older individuals (ages 60–69, 70–79, and 80–92). Age-related changes of syntactic complexity were noted in both oral and written modalities. In particular, the number of clauses per utterance and left-branching clauses decreased across the four age groups. *Left-branching clauses* are those which precede the main predicate of an utterance. They are typically more difficult to process and produce than are right-branching clauses because to do so requires holding information in working memory. Kemper, Kynette, and Norman (1992) followed the older participants in the previous study for 3 years, collecting annual measures of working memory and syntactic complexity. Most of the participants did not experience significant changes in working memory during that time period. However, of the small minority who did, almost all also experienced significant decreases in syntactic complexity. Notably, these were individuals who were in their late 70s to early 80s in the first year, which led the researchers to speculate that this time period may be critical for language development in older adulthood.

Just as working memory has been related to older adults' productions of complex syntactic structures, it is also suggested that working memory affects the processing of these structures in the discourse of others. In a study conducted by Norman, Kemper, Kynette, Cheung, and Anagnopoulos (1991), college students and elderly adults listened to prose passages that were interrupted by pauses. During the pauses, participants were asked to recall the immediate preceding statements. Analysis showed that college students had a better recall than did older adults for syntactically complex statements, but only differed slightly from older participants in the recall of simple statements.

Thus, although researchers agree that older adults are not significantly less able to understand single words or straightforward everyday sentences (Pratt & Norris, 1994), there is considerable debate about whether they have more difficulty comprehending complex and difficult grammatical structures that are uncommon in everyday speech, such as left-branching clauses (e.g., see Kemper, Kynette, Rash, O'Brien, & Sprott, 1989). This may be partly because much of the research that appears to demonstrate that older adults have comprehension difficulties do so under experimental conditions which, researchers acknowledge, are hard to generalize. For example, such studies often use complex, difficult, and bizarre language as stimuli, examples of which are never seen in everyday speech.

Wingfield, Stine, and their associates have conducted a number of studies about the language-processing capacities of young and elderly individuals (Stine & Wingfield, 1987; Stine, Wingfield, & Poon, 1986; Wingfield,

Lahar, & Stine, 1989; Wingfield, Wayland & Stine, 1992). Generally, they have used accuracy of recall as the dependent measure of processing capability, with an emphasis on how speaker rate and use of prosody may differentially affect recall of young and elderly persons. Results show that a fast rate leads to poorer recall from both young and older adults, but that the rate of decline is greater for older adults than for young ones. (Stine et al., 1986; Stine & Wingfield, 1987; Wingfield et al., 1992). In terms of prosody, results indicate that older adults, more than young ones, rely on prosodic cues such as pause and inflection to aid their processing of oral discourse (Stine & Wingfield, 1987; Wingfield et al., 1989; Wingfield et al., 1992). These researchers interpret their results in a similar fashion to Kemper and colleagues, namely, that working memory declines in older adulthood account for the differences between young and old adults' performances on these measures.

A variety of research has investigated a phenomenon known as *off-target verbosity* (OTV) loosely defined by Gold, Arbuckle, and Andres (1994) as talk that is both abundant and lacking in focus—"a series of loosely associated verbalizations that stray more and more from the original topic" (p. 107). An illustrative example of this is given by Gold et al. as follows:

Interviewer: How often do you see your daughter?

Respondent: I've only gone down there twice, she's only been there 3 years. Its only an hour and 23 minutes by plane, but she said, "What the poop are you coming down for?" Because it was the Royal Commonwealth Conference and since they were preparing for Prince Edward and so she said "Are you coming?" And so I phoned up Air Canada and I said I wanted a ticket. So I went the next day and it was my birthday and since it was my birthday and I had 12 little roses from my garden in a water vase.... (p. 108)

Factors such as high stress, extroversion, and lower levels of social support have been related to OTV, but these correlates are found to be independent of age. It is important to note that more stress and lowered social support may be as much caused by OTV than vice versa. The exact nature of the relationship between extroversion and OTV is uncertain, but among other explanations Gold et al. (1994) speculate that such extroverts may have lost the inhibitory mechanisms that suppress irrelevant speech. The single most important set of factors contributing to OTV may be chronic ill health, particularly losses in frontal-lobe functioning (Arbuckle & Gold, 1993) that correlate with age (Gold et al., 1994). Naturally, some people are more talkative than others, but only a very small number of older adults (15% to 20%) can be classified as overly verbose, showing the extreme unfocused and tangential talk characteristic of OTV. As Orange and Ryan (1995) argue, "only a small minority of older adults are loquacious, thus debunking the myth that *all* older adults are overly talkative" (p. 125).

Despite the evidence suggestive of language and processing effects of age-related changes in older adulthood, the implication that such effects are equal to reduced communicative competence is not supported (Light, 1988; Ryan, 1991). In fact, much of the research concerned with language changes in later life is hotly contested (Ryan, 1991). Typically, research has found that older adults experience more difficulty than do younger adults in those tasks that place high demands on sensory processing and memory. Under normal everyday circumstances (e.g., as opposed to the controlled conditions of the laboratory), it is argued that none of these changes are likely to significantly affect everyday, normal, conversational interaction with healthy older adults (Orange & Ryan, 1995).

On the contrary, researchers have argued that older adults are particularly adept conversationalists. Older adults' storytelling skills, including their ability to hold interest and increase clarity, frequently receive highly positive evaluations from younger people (Kemper, Rash, Kynette, & Norman, 1990; Williams & Giles, 1996). Research by Kemper et al. (1990), comparing personal narratives produced by college students to those produced by older adults found that older adults' narratives were often judged more positively. Although some studies are largely based on young people's perceptions, and could be heavily influenced by positive stereotypes of older people as adept story tellers, linguistic analysis of the narrative structure of older peoples' accounts has supported these perceptual reports. For example, linguistic analysis in the Kemper et al. (1990) study found that older people's stories were more complex than students' accounts, a finding that was interpreted as accounting for the higher ratings. However, whereas older adult's stories were more complex in higher order structures, they were found to be less complex in terms of lower order structures, such as subordinate clauses and anaphora. Kemper and colleagues argue that there is a trade-off here, but it is not clear whether the older adults could not use lower order structures or chose not to. An alternative interpretation is that older adults accommodated their stories to their perceived listeners. Other recent research with young college students revealed that they valued older people for their storytelling skills and felt that such skills were not only instructive and entertaining, but facilitated and eased conversation between strangers who might otherwise have little to say to each other (Williams & Giles, 1996).

Similarly, Pratt and Robins (1991) found that raters judged older people's personal narratives to be more effective than those of older students (and nonsignificantly better than those of middle-aged adults). Again, linguistic analysis revealed that this finding was probably due to the fact that older narratives conform very closely to an effective narrative structure, identified by Labov and Waletzsky (1967) and termed *high-point structure.* In this way, prototypically skilled narrators (in this case, older adults) build upon a rising story line that eventually builds to a high point of interest and high story tension, followed by a resolution. Mergler, Faust, & Goldstein (1985) suggested that older adults are skillful when reading stories aloud and facilitate listeners' recall of story content more than do younger adults.

In addition, sociolinguistic studies that have shown that older people use turn taking and higher levels of conversational organization in skillful and sophisticated ways, including question–answer sequences, use of interruption, and so forth (for a review, see Pratt & Norris, 1994). Moreover, some older people seem be able to accomplish this in spite of sensory losses such as hearing deficits that conspire against them (Pichora-Fuller et al., 1998). A conversation-analytic study of peer and intergenerational get-acquainted sessions demonstrated that older people were just as conversationally skillful as young people and also used the same conversational strategies. Unlike young people, they invoked the past when in conversation with other elders, and this was interpreted as a strategy that built a shared understanding and fostered intersubjectivity (Boden & Bielby, 1983). Such research demonstrates that older people are skillfully able to draw upon their resources to facilitate interpersonal conversations between people of different backgrounds. In a similar vein, Williams and Giles' (1996) college-student data showed that these young people valued, and were communicatively satisfied with, older people who were able to accommodate to their younger interlocutors' conversational needs and life stages by talking about college and career plans.

The previous discussion of cognition and communicative competence outlines a variety of sensory and cognitive changes that have been associated with advanced aging; researchers stress that there is considerable interindividual variability in these data. As was mentioned, health factors, pathological changes (e.g., stroke-induced aphasia, Alzheimer's disease), losses of brain function, and so on are almost inevitably connected with reduced communication competence, and are more reliable predictors of language and communication difficulties than is chronological age. With chronic ill-health such as dementia, the extent of interference may result in the profound disruption of semantic memory and coherent discourse associated with advanced Alzheimer's disease (see Kemper & Lyons, 1994, for a review).

SUMMARY

The first section of this chapter continues the discussion of stereotypes of age by exploring how those stereotypes might influence perceptions of speakers and evaluations of their language and communication competence. From the research reviewed in this section we can see that people typically make assumptions about the abilities of older people. Of particular interest are the assumptions that we make about older people's language and communication skills. Also, younger people design their talk to older partners based on stereotypic assumptions about older people's conversational needs (Giles, Henwood, et al., 1992). Several studies indicated that young people seek information from older people that is consistent with agist expectations (Franklyn-Stokes, Harriman, Giles, & Coupland, 1988; Ng, Moody, & Giles, 1991). Such expectations appear to be based on beliefs about elders' failing physical and cognitive capabilities. Thus, for example, questions addressed to an older interlocutor may be designed to elicit information about bad eyesight and hearing, failing memory, and so forth. Agist information seeking has also been observed in more naturalistic settings. For example, an interactional study conducted by Coupland and colleagues (N. Coupland, Coupland, Giles, Henwood, & Wiemann, 1988) revealed that in many cases, young women (age approximately 30 years) elicited age-stereotype congruent information when in conversation with older partners (age approximately 70–80 years).

Not only are older and younger speakers perceived in stereotyped ways, but the content of their talk is often interpreted stereotypically. By drawing on rules or stereotypes to decide what topics are appropriate for intergenerational talk, people may constrain and limit possibilities for relational development, and as a consequence may reinforce those very stereotypes. It is important to realize that respondents typically go well beyond the information provided in research studies, and this reveals an extensive use of socially shared assumptions about older and younger people. Typically this enables respondents to extend negative information and infer other negative traits and consequences from it.

Finally, it is important to note that elders are drawing on a shared set of rules when they themselves downgrade older people. This is demonstrated by investigations that used the LIA survey. In Giddens' (1991) terms then, the first part of chapter 4 continued where chapter 3 left off, examining the rules that social interlocutors operate with when involved in voice decoding, evaluating, attributing, and responding to members of other age groups.

The second part of the chapter addresses issues of actual language and communication abilities and how they develop and change through the life span into older adulthood. This section focuses on some of the sociolinguistic resources that older people bring to interaction. It is argued that, although researchers have shown that older people, especially those in late old age, might face particular communicative challenges such as loss in hearing, it is hard to disentangle physiologically associated losses in communication ability from other more social factors, which might also affect performance. As Giddens (1991) suggests, it is the combination of rules and resources that work together to keep the system in play. Rules are handy for people to draw upon to explain social events and fill in the gaps sufficiently for people to explain events. As Giddens (1991) suggests, action is sometimes opaque; we do not have access to all conditions that influence our interactions. For example, we may not know that a person is deaf, but we may notice that something about the interaction is awry and we will look for ways of interpreting and understanding what is going on. Stereotypes and schemas about aging provide handy explanations that fill in the gaps for us. That is how we may arrive at the explanation that old people are out of it, and the attribution of any number of age-associated problems, which range from deafness to dementia. In many cases, while giving us a satisfactory explanation of what is going on, our attributions may, in fact, be misattributions.

Older people may be aware of the constraints in their sociolinguistic resources and take steps to compensate or repair or both—some of those attempts are skillful—such as those described previously, which call on other conversational and strategic resources (e.g., see Jaworski & Stephens, 1998; Pichora-Fuller et al., 1998). Others may misfire and can lead to further negative attributions, especially that the older person is, in communication accommodation theory terms, underaccommodative. The next two chapters bring communication accommodation theory (see chapter 1) to center stage while they continue to explore young-to-old and old-to-young language strategies along with perceptions and evaluations of intergenerational talk. Chapter 5 begins by exploring a range of attributions and perceptions of older interlocutors' communications, particularly underaccommodation, which relates well to both the rules and resource that were presented thus far.

5

Intergenerational Language Strategies: Underaccommodation

Intergenerational talk is an issue that has received very little empirical attention across the disciplines, especially noninstitutionalized talk and everyday community interactions (see N. Coupland & Coupland, 1990). Later chapters turn attention to intergenerational communication in caring and institutional contexts, and to younger and older people who have familial or well-established long-term relationships. However, this chapter focuses initially on interactions between young and old strangers or acquaintances and everyday community interactions. Following the theoretical framework of communication accommodation theory (for a detailed account, see chapter 1), the issue of elder underaccommodation is discussed; after this the discussion is expanded by reviewing recent research that explores themes of intergenerational-communication satisfaction and dissatisfaction reported by young people.

Routine, seemingly mundane interactions between younger and older people who are strangers or casual acquaintances are a daily occurrence in health care, the service industries or in casual social settings, and are by far the most frequent type of intergenerational contact outside the family. Nevertheless, they are often considered relatively unremarkable and are relatively invisible in research. Their importance is somewhat understandably downplayed in comparison to concerns for older people in caring contexts. It is worth scrutinizing these everyday interactions because they may have serious implications in a number of ways. Intergenerational understandings and misunderstandings are created and sustained through these interactions. These interactions appropriate, enact, and reinforce intergenerational stereotypes. These older and younger people are those who often consider each other to be rather typical, generalized, and nonindividualized representatives of their age groups. Thus, as the discussion of intergroup theory in chapter 1 suggests, many of these interactions have a very strong intergroup flavor—a theme that continues through this chapter. Moreover, it is through these seemingly unremarkable intergenerational interactions that older and younger people alike negotiate their everyday domestic and lifestyle needs as consumers of products and services from business people in shops and offices, as well as from professionals such as lawyers, doctors, bank managers, and so forth.

As chapter 1 described, communication accommodation theory (CAT) has predictive and explanatory power for conceptualizing intergenerational communication as well as for specifying some social psychological antecedents and consequences of such talk. CAT has been used extensively to conceptualize elderly-to-young as well as young-to-elderly language strategies (N. Coupland, Coupland, Giles, & Henwood, 1988; Hummert, 1994; Ryan et al., 1986). In their theoretically based typology of old-to-young language strategies, underaccommodation was identified by Ryan et al. (1986) as a predominant perception from young people of older adults' talk. Underaccommodation is when some style or quality of talk is underplayed relative to the needs or wishes of an interlocutor (see N. Coupland, Coupland, & Giles, 1991).

This chapter and the following chapter overview studies that fall very broadly into these two categories. This chapter begins by discussing seminal research in this respect—interactional discourse data focusing on one particular aspect of underaccommodation, dubbed *painful self-disclosure* (N. Coupland, Henwood, Coupland, & Giles, 1990; Giles, Coupland, & Wiemann, 1991). Studies by N. Coupland and colleagues explore and describe various dimensions of old underaccommodation, its realization in talk, and young people's attempts to negotiate it when interacting with older partners.

INTERACTIONAL PAINFUL SELF-DISCLOSURE

During the 1980s in Wales, Coupland and colleagues conducted a study of get to know you conversations between younger and older women. Younger (30–40-year-old) and older (70–87-year-old) female volunteers were paired and videotaped during the first 8 minutes of their interactions (for a review of this work, see N. Coupland, Coupland, & Giles, 1991). The women were strangers to each other and were told by way of instruction to get to know one another. Apart from this, participants were given no further instructions and were left alone, knowing they were being videotaped.

The elderly women were members of two adult day centers and were mostly from upper-working-class backgrounds, lived alone, and were widowed. In fact, more than 80% of day-center participants are women, a figure which is reflective of the large numbers of women in the older population in general. So, although these studies have an arguably biased focus on women, they are a result of this structural constraint and reflect the demographics of wider society. The younger women were recruited via newspaper advertisements, they were typically married and lower middle and working class.

Of the dyads taped, 20 were intergenerational (young–old), 10 were peer–young, and 10 were peer–elderly. Following a Latin-square design, the researchers had each informant participate in two interactions, one within generation and one across generations. The initial goals of the project were to determine whether the younger women overaccommodated to their elderly partners, and also to document this verbally, paralinguistically, and nonverbally. Findings revealed distinct evidence of overaccommodation occurring from the young participants (e.g., initial and profuse nodding of the head placed at a tilt by the young, many of whom were seemingly interviewing the elderly). For all intents and purposes, however, this sample seemed positively disposed toward, and experienced in, conversing with older people. Apart from these informal observations of overaccommodation, the research team's attention turned to examining quite another, relatively unexpected sociolinguistic phenomenon, which was subsequently labeled *painful self-disclosure* (PSD; see J. Coupland, Coupland, Giles, & Wiemann, 1988).

A quantitative analysis of PSD revealed that the elderly women in this study spent approximately 17% of the time disclosing personally painful information (e.g., accidents, illness and medical problems, bereavement, social deprivation, etc.) whereas the younger women spent less than 2% of the time doing so. Of the 20 intergenerational dyads, 16 manifested instances of older PSD with only one young person reciprocating. In the 10 peer–elderly dyads, there were 9 instances of reciprocation, whereas in the 10 peer–young dyads, there were only 4 instances of the phenomenon. Even more interesting than the figures documenting the quantity of PSD, which have tended to be the primary focus of previous research (Holtgraves, 1990), are the processes by which PSDs were introduced into discourse, responded to, and curtailed.

The main findings are summarized here, and for more details readers should refer to N. Coupland, Coupland, and Giles (1991). The majority of disclosures could be characterized as introduced by the older people themselves; sometimes they were contextually related, but other times they were "out of the blue." However, a substantial portion were elicited by the younger person asking questions that led to the disclosure. An initial PSD often led to others, a phenomenon the researchers referred to as *chaining*. Such patterns of disclosure are typically regarded by communication theorists as unusual and rather inappropriate for first-acquaintance interactions (Berger & Bradac, 1982). Thus, the young interactional partners could be characterized as being faced with a number of interactional dilemmas in responding to such revelations. This could lead to considerable discomfort in the young and awkwardness as every possible or available response could be seen unfavorably. For example, the young partners could switch topics and discourage further disclosure, or they could express interest and risk, encouraging more disclosure. The first strategy may seem rather rude and dismissive, whereas the second may lead to an escalation of disclosure and further interactional dilemmas. A third option is to express sympathy, but this may seem rather overaccommodative or even patronizing. Often the young partners seemed to settle for a minimal response such as "mmm," "good heavens," or "oh dear." Elderly PSDs were textually managed quite well by a few young interlocutors, at least in procedural terms, and sometimes were even solicited by them in the first place. There was a rich variety of ways in which PSDs were creatively terminated (e.g., commenting on a positive by-product of the painful event and shifting topic), either by the discloser or by the recipient.

Among other things, this pattern suggests that the older people (in this context) were not utilizing the full range of potentially available topics. Thus, the possibility arises that in some cases, self-disclosures initiated in order to share feelings and tell who you are (see Boden & Bielby, 1983) may become ritualized into prolonged negative exchanges, which may enhance and lend salience to negative feelings, possibly reinforcing and recreating them by their very enactment (see Rotenberg & Hamel, 1988). Such unnerving experiences on a day-to-day basis could possibly deter younger people from wishing to engage in future intergenerational contact (see Notarius & Herrick, 1988).

In a follow-up study (N. Coupland, Henwood, Coupland, & Giles, 1990), a complementary sample of young women listened to and commented on audiotaped extracts of PSDs from the interaction study. In group discussions, a few of the young women denied that PSD was a problem, some thought it sad and others thought it strategic (as, e.g., an attempt to gain sympathy). Most felt that it was underaccommodative—in other words, the elderly women were seen as egocentric, focusing on their own problems and underattentive to the younger women's conversational needs. For instance, one informant claimed, "They [note the intergroup pronoun] play for sympathy, they're very much ... like young children, they want to be the center of attention for as long as possible."

We must be cautious about stretching the findings regarding PSD in the Welsh community too far beyond their context (day-care centers), cohort (working class 70- to 80-year-olds), culture (Wales, United Kingdom), and life circumstances of the interactants. However, evidence of PSDs has also been found in conversations of well-educated, middle class, community-dwelling older individuals from the Midwestern United States. Shaner, Hummert, Kemper, and Vandeputte (1994) collected intergenerational and peer conversations in a similar manner to N. Coupland, Coupland, and Giles (1991). Conversations were coded for both painful and painless self-disclosures. Although elderly participants made fewer overall self-disclosures than did young people, a higher proportion of their self-disclosures were classified as PSDs. In addition, and in contrast to the N. Coupland, Coupland, and Giles data, the researchers suggest that the older participants in this study tended to introduce these PSDs into the conversations on their own initiatives, without any prompting from the other conversant via questions. In contrast, the disclosures of young participants were primarily painless, and occurred in response to direct inquiries on the parts of their partners.

Therefore, interactional underaccommodation can be discursively realized in intergenerational talk through older people's disclosures of their ill health, painful life events, and so forth. Older people, however, are often alleged to be underaccommodative to young interlocutors in other ways. For example, by drawing on other research we can conclude that older people may also be perceived as nonverbally underaccommodative. Interlocuters are perhaps less likely to be aware of nonverbal underaccommodation and would not typically comment about it. This draws attention to the difference between practical and discursive consciousness as discussed in chapter 1. Nonverbal underaccommodation may have a priming effect, such that it may lead to contagion whereby negative evaluations spread to the entire discourse, and especially to evaluations of the older person's individual characteristics, his or her ability, personality, and so forth. The following research is suggestive of this effect, although the original research was not conducted from a communication–accommodation theory perspective.

Early research by Bromley (1978) described so-called "aversive" properties of elderly institutional residents and argued that expressive changes that are associated with age contribute to communication problems. Expressive behaviors described by Bromley as problematic could be characterized as underaccommodative. These include a decline in spontaneity and response due to stiffness of posture and gesture, and a lack of sponteneity in facial expressions and eye contact. It is suggested that such factors slow down interaction so that a younger interactant might feel that communication is breaking down. A second class of problematic, and again, in our terms, underaccommodative elder behavior suggested by Bromley is older adults' reduced ability to keep pace with the rapidity of the expressive behavior of younger persons, and difficulties in repair work when either misunderstand the other. Also, slower elder reactions reduce sensitivity to social signals and reflexively produce alterations in self-concept. Finally, it is suggested that a reduction in mobility and sitting posture in turn affects the range of expressive behaviors open to an older person, which include less control over his or her position and distance in interpersonal interaction.

This list of expressive behavioral changes in later life exemplifies the notion that communication problems occur between younger and older people because older people are underaccommodative. In this case they are identified as underaccommodative in terms of speed, sponteneity, postural mobility, nonverbal sensitivity, and so on. According to Bromley, the result of these limitations is the progressive social isolation of the elderly person, and inevitable consequences for the way he or she is perceived by others, and so forth as highlighted in the discussion of the communication predicament model discussed in chapter 1 (see Ryan et al., 1986). In social exchange terms, Bromley suggests that, for younger people, the costs of interacting with older people eventually outweigh the benefits. Although these suggestions were derived from studies with institutional residents who were suffering from poor health, they imply that in everyday interactions, young people become unconsciously aware of postural stiffness, body position, and spontaneity, which may lend them to make attributions of underaccommodation. Moreover, as was argued earlier, this could possibly contaminate perceptions of other aspects of communication, such as listening and conversational skills.

How widespread is the notion that elders are underaccommodative to young peoples' conversational needs? Do young people see this as a problematic aspect of intergenerational talk? What other problems do young people experience when conversing with elders? What are the positive aspects of intergenerational talk? These were the questions behind recent studies by Williams (1992) and Williams and Giles (1996). These researchers analyzed retrospective accounts of young college students who were asked to report conversations with nonfamilial elders that were either satisfying or dissatisfying.

INTERGENERATIONAL COMMUNICATION
SATISFACTION AND DISSATISFACTION

An initial questionnaire-based pilot study of young people's perceptions of intergenerational communication satisfaction was conducted by Williams (1992). In this study, four factors were found to significantly differentiate satisfying and dissatisfying intergenerational encounters. The first was labeled *old underaccommodative negativity* and items loading highly on this factor included: "The older person talked excessively and exclusively about his or her own problems," and "I didn't know what to say in return to the older person's complaints." Note that the latter item reflects certain accommodative dilemmas which, as we discuss next, young people frequently encounter when conversing with elders. Another factor, labeled *mutuality*, was characterized by a sense that the age gap was diminished; the partners found common interests; the elder was positive, animated, zestful, admired youth, and was nonjudgmental. *Elder individuation* was defined by the older person being individualized and not stereotyped, and the young person felt able to express feelings freely. *Young individuation* was defined by the young person feeling individualized and was not treated in terms of young stereotypes. There were relationships between these factors and reported emotions in predictable directions. For satisfying conversations, mutuality was associated with higher levels of reported happiness, relaxation, and lower frustration, but it was not related to anger. In dissatisfying conversations, mutuality was associated with higher levels of anger and frustration, and with lower levels of happiness; underaccommodative negativity was associated with increased anger, frustration, and decreased relaxation, but was not related to happiness.

In addition, young people rated their satisfaction or dissatisfaction with peer and intergenerational conversations with the result that young people rated intergenerational interactions as less satisfying overall than interactions with same-aged peers. An intergroup approach to intergenerational communication (see Harwood, Giles, & Ryan, 1995) was also a focus of the study (see chapter 1 for a detailed discussion of Intergroup Theory). For this context, intergroup communication was defined in terms of Hewstone and Brown's (1986) intergroup contact theory as perceptions of respondents that age is salient and that they and the older person were typical of their respective age groups. Results showed that dissatisfying conversations were rated as more salient along these intergroup dimensions than were satisfying conversations. In addition, those young people who reported high levels of intergroup salience were compared to those who reported relatively low levels of intergroup salience. In general, high intergroup-salience groups were less inclined to perceive satisfying or dissatisfying conversations as mutual and were less inclined to agree that the older person was individuated. In general, respondents who scored high on intergroup-salience measures were inclined to be more negatively disposed to their partners. They were more inclined to disagree that satisfying conversations were mutual, and were more inclined to agree that the older person was negative and underaccommodative in dissatisfying conversations. Thus, high intergroup salience seems to lead to more negative ratings of intergenerational conversations, at least by young people (Williams, 1992). These results are consistent with intergroup theory as discussed in chapter 1 because they indicate that intergroup salience may be an important mediator of intergenerational communication.

Given these findings, further research asked these same young people to self-report on both satisfying and dissatisfying conversations with older people (Williams & Giles, 1996). Using the procedures of Hecht, Ribeau, and Alberts (1989) in their study of interethnic satisfaction, written accounts were gathered, content coded, and analyzed to extract underlying dimensions or themes of communication satisfaction and dissatisfaction. Respondents were also asked to suggest some improvement strategies, which were also content analyzed to extract a list of frequently cited conversational improvements.

The resultant themes or dimensions were then analyzed to identify those that were associated with satisfying, versus dissatisfying, conversations. As can be seen from the summary of results displayed on Table 5.1, socioemotional support and narratives were the most frequently reported characteristics of satisfying conversations.

Reports were considered supportive when either the older or the younger person demonstrated interest and attentiveness or provided both emotional or instrumental support or encouragement or both, and welcome advice and compliments. Interestingly, almost 90% of the reported support was provided by the elder. Therefore, in most cases, it was the older person who was reportedly converging or attuning to the conversational needs of the younger person, and he or she achieved the right balance, neither going too far with advice nor being overly parental. These older people were characterized as extremely skillful communicators. For example, support was not always complicit or totally accommodative; sometimes the older person was supportive by playing devil's advocate or by sensitively and skillfully presenting an alternative opinion.

A much less frequently reported aspect of socioemotional support was that provided by the young person. These young people characterized themselves

TABLE 5.1
Themes of Intergenerational Communication Satisfaction,
With Frequencies

Category	Dissatisfied (%)	Satisfied (%)
Socioemotional support	22	78
Narratives	11	76
Mutuality	3	32
Astereotyping	0	29
Old positive emotion	2	25
Perceived older accommodation	2	14
Young positive emotion	3	17
Underaccommodative older person	72	1
Communication restrictions	38	14
Old negative emotion	30	0
Reluctant young accommodation	30	2
Defensive younger person	20	2
Stereotypes of younger person	17	10
Stereotypes of older person	22	21
Young negative emotion	9	6

as accommodating to the conversational needs of their older partners. In this respect, some reports had a flavor of new agism (see chapter 3) because young people characterized their partners rather stereotypically as deserving and grateful for the young person's support. Often, support provided by the young was associated with mixed feelings, usually happiness resulting from the young person's ability to provide support, whereas sadness was associated with sincere empathy for the older person's life circumstances.

The second largest category, entitled narratives, included instances of story telling, open disclosure about one's life and circumstances, and instances of reminiscing, all of which were reportedly welcome and enjoyable. Both age groups contributed equally to this category. Interestingly, and contrary perhaps to popular notions of older peoples' reminiscences and narratives, two thirds of the older persons' narratives were about fairly recent activities rather than about long past events. Also, the reports allowed some insight into the reasons why narratives might be satisfying for young people. Narratives provided first-hand knowledge and information about important historical and recent events, they were entertaining, and they facilitated conversation. The latter may be an important conversational resource in a situation where the two partners might feel that they have little in common (i.e., a generation gap).

There were fewer younger narratives, the most common topic of which was the younger person's college and future career plans. School and career appeared to be a readily accessible topic that young people enjoyed talking about, and perhaps one they felt was particularly acceptable for intergenerational talk because it focused on goals that typically met with an elder's approval. This talk can be characterized as accommodative from one perspective, because young people clearly felt that it was appropriate, pleasurable, and fulfilled their own conversational needs. However, we should be wary of suggesting that older people themselves found it accommodative. Indeed, older people may characterize extensive accounts from young people of school and career plans as remarkably underaccommodative, perhaps even as egocentric.

Another interpretation is that this kind of talk may be a self-presentational smoke screen whereby younger people overaccommodate to some image that they think they ought to project in order to both gain elder approval and attend to face concerns. Moreover, a few young people indicated that this kind of talk is shallow and nonauthentic because this talk does not really transmit who they are. Some earlier interactional evidence also points to young authenticity as being an issue for intergenerational communication. N. Coupland, Coupland, and Giles (1991) report a qualitative case-study analysis of particularly problematic intergenerational talk between two women. One of the women was a young married researcher in her 30s and the other was a retired teacher in her 80s who had never been married. Although the older woman was described as "frail, partially sighted, and quite immobile" (p. 39), she showed no significant cognitive or linguistic decrements. The problematical aspects of this conversation were described by the young researcher as "effortful, awkward and unsatisfying" (p. 39). Ultimately, most of the conversational work was the responsibility of the young interactant and she reportedly felt a strong sense of inauthenticity in the conversation because she felt that the pressure to accommodate to her older interlocutor inhibited her ability to be herself. In the words of N. Coupland et al., the analysis of the conversation documents "a hierarchy of ideological accommodation which begins with avoiding articulating viewpoints that an interlocutor will predictably not share, through selective putting of one's own views and modifications of them, to outright falsification" (p. 46). The issue of inauthenticity and pressure to accommodate to older interlocutors is one that is raised quite frequently, as is demonstrated further, in young people's accounts of intergenerational talk.

Turning again to the themes illustrated on Table 5.1, *mutuality* was another supportive feature of satisfying conversations, but it was distinguished from socioemotional support because it referred to young people's feelings that true common ground, equality, and mutual supportiveness with their partners had been achieved. Socioemotional support, in contrast, existed when one person or the other was reported as providing support and was therefore, arguably, more one sided. In terms of accommodation theory, mutuality involved meeting in the middle rather than accommodation by one partner towards the needs of the other.

Old stereotypes refers to instances when older people were singled out as being different from other old people. This was further divided into two subcategories, the first indicated that young people had some underlying negative expectations that, in these cases, were violated. Also, in the first subcategory, young respondents invoked a stereotypical or agist image to demonstrate that their partners did not fit the stereotype. In other words, their partner was an exception to the rule and the rule was always negative. For example, one respondent commented, "The fact that he was content and that old satisfied me … every other elder I've talked to has made me fear/want to avoid getting old." It is also worth noting that many of these accounts incorporated expressions of surprise at the stereotype violation (see also Henwood, Giles, Coupland, & Coupland, 1993). Also in this category were occasions when age had no bearing on the conversation. Although age was clearly salient, negative expectations and stereotypes were not raised as an issue, and thus these accounts were more interindividual in flavor.

Often there appeared to be an underlying assumption that older people were superior by virtue of age and experience, and thus young people tended to comment when they felt that the older person had restrained himself or herself from exercising this, which was labeled *perceived older accommodation*. By restraining themselves in certain ways, respondents inferred that older people had avoided putting them in an awkward situation. Similarly, other reports mentioned certain topic areas that older people sensitively avoided. Presumably certain topics (attitudes towards sex, drugs, etc.) are thought more likely than others to threaten intergenerational understanding. Older- and younger-positive emotional expressions were coded when it was clear that the partners were enjoying the conversation.

These categories reflect an emotional dimension to accommodative talk largely portrayed in accounts of nonverbal behavior.

In contrast, *old underaccommodation* was overwhelmingly the dimension most frequently associated with dissatisfying conversations, and was mentioned by almost 75% of respondents. In essence this reflected instances when the younger person perceived that the older person was either not listening, was interrupting, was inattentive, or was unable to align with the younger person's conversational needs because of off-target attention. In the latter case, elders were often portrayed as dominating the conversation with their own agendas. In other words, this suggests several varieties of underaccommodation. This finding suggests that young people do see underaccommodation as a predominant problem when speaking with elders.

In addition to underaccommodation, these conversations were hampered by further constraints labeled *communication restrictions,* which were differentiated from underaccommodation because the constituents were largely characterized as involuntary. These concerned (real or perceived) physical or physiological deficits such as auditory and speech production problems, which were most frequently attributed to advanced age. For example, respondents reported having problems with the older person's expressive, receptive, and comprehension, skills. Typically, comments referred to the older person's "slow" or "rambling" speech, hearing problems, ability to understand, and so forth. Although these problems were most frequently attributed to the older person, some respondents reported accommodative dilemmas they faced when attempting to manage such restrictions. For example, respondents reported "not knowing how to talk to older people," "not knowing what to say," and feeling as if they "could not communicate." Some such problems reportedly arose in very difficult circumstances, as when the older partner was suffering considerable ill health, which had a strong effect on the interaction (e.g., in at least one case the partner was suffering from Alzheimer's disease). Many interactional dilemmas, however, seem to be considered rather typical of a whole range of intergenerational encounters.

Some reports contained detailed accounts of negative emotional expression by older partners. Comments regarding the older person's negative emotional expression fell into two subcategories, the first of which seemed both emotionally as well as communicatively divergent or counterattuned. In this case, the older person was characterized as angry and complaining (and this was quite often associated with intergroup accusations). Respondents who reported angry, complaining behavior from their partners tended to report feelings of anger in response.

The second subcategory, painful self-disclosure, is perhaps better characterized as emotionally and communicatively underaccommodative. In these cases, the young persons claimed that their older partners were overly disclosive of personal details of ill-health and social problems. This links well with the findings of N. Coupland, Coupland, Giles, and Henwood (1988) described previously. Often, respondents reporting elder painful self-disclosure were likely to demonstrate some sympathy with their partners, typically reporting feeling dejection, sadness, and pity.

Reluctant young accommodation was the label used to summarize a frequently reported set of circumstances in which young people reported feeling obligated, forced, or pressured to make polite conversation, often to the point of nonauthenticity, as discussed previously. In this sense, young people commonly reported putting a cap on their feelings and "biting their tongues." This restraint appeared to be motivated by a desire not to be rude, but to be respectful, showing concern for the older person's negative face. Often this appeared to be combined with young people feeling inferior or subordinate to their conversational partners. When reasons for these feelings were given, they indicated that restraint may have been partly due to age respect and partly due to other role relationships. In many reported situations the older person was in a superior role, as for example, a customer, client, or boss of the younger person.

Although this was not an explicitly reported characteristic of intergenerational talk itself, a number of reports were classified as indicating young defensiveness in response to conflict. In this case, respondents attempted to establish that the blame for dissatisfying encounters was entirely due to their older conversational partners. Thus, accounts were considered defensive when the young person positioned himself or herself as a victim of wrongful accusations and injustice. Notably, most of these accounts began with the younger person claiming that he or she did not do or say anything dissatisfying; responsibility for the misunderstanding was placed firmly on the shoulders of the older partner—a typical strategy in conflict situations (Hocker & Wilmot, 1995).

Another category was labeled *stereotypes of young* and comprised comments about older people who were perceived to be condescending, patronizing, overtly superior, overly parental and critical of youth, or a combination of these. Thus, in many cases, this category represents younger persons' subjective perceptions of elder overaccommodation towards them (see also Giles & Williams, 1994). In dissatisfying intergenerational conversations, age differences, stereotyping, and derogatory feelings about age appeared to be highly salient either in the interaction itself or in the post hoc account. In these conversational accounts, younger people attributed the source of dissatisfaction to the older person stereotyping them. This took various forms, but three in particular were frequently mentioned by these respondents. In the first instance, talk revolved around implicit or explicit comparisons between generations. By way of example, one respondent's remarks characterize this intergroup differentiation and stereotyping quite well: "She negatively stereotyped my entire generation and she went on and on about how spoiled I was and then I got a lifetime's worth of 'when I was your age ...'" (Williams, 1994, p. 76).

The second focus of this kind of talk was on the supposed *naivety of youth* and the subsequent undervaluing or discounting of young people's opinions, especially when it came to politics or current affairs. A final subcategy was when older people were perceived as patronizing or condescending to their young partners. Prevalent in these reports were the use of pet names such as dear and sweetie and treating young people as if they were children and so forth. In some cases younger people admitted playing up to this by acting younger than they really felt.

Interestingly, stereotyping older people was evident in both satisfying and dissatisfying conversations. In reports of dissatisfying conversations, stereotyping was much more explicit and agist; for example, attributions of grumpiness, complaining, and senility were commonly linked to age. In satisfying reports, stereotyping was more often implicit and was couched positively as in, *like a grandmother* or labeling older people benevolently as *cute* and *sweet*. Ryan, Hummert, and Boich (1995) discuss how such terms may be indicative of young patronization to older people, although young respondents in this study did not often spontaneously admit to behaviors that could be classified as overaccommodation (see chapter 6). We would not expect people to immediately recognize and report their overaccommodation of others for self-presentational reasons as well as because of the very strong possibility that such overaccommodations are often below conscious awareness.

When asked about the emotions associated with satisfying and dissatisfying conversations, young respondents associated satisfying conversations with positive emotions (happiness, relaxation, cognitive arousal, high self-esteem, love, and security) and associated dissatisfying conversations with negative emotions (anger, frustration, a desire to leave, and powerlessness) as would be expected. However, a more interesting aspect of these data was the finding that satisfying conversations were not universally positive. In fact, more than one third of respondents reported mixed emotions in response to satisfying intergenerational encounters. These mixes fell into two general groups. Some respondents reported feeling anxiety and trepidation at the beginning of intergenerational conversations, but as the conversation evolved they relaxed and felt more at ease. The other frequent mix was respondents who reported mixes and blends of happiness and sadness, which were associated with empathy for the older person, who was suffering stressful or painful life events (e.g., due to ill-health). This suggests that for young people, many so-called "satisfying" intergenerational encounters are tinged with negative emotions and are therefore aversive in some respects. Whether or not this is unique to intergenerational, rather than to peer conversations, is an issue that needs to be explored in future research.

A final stage of this research elicited young people's own suggestions for improving their intergenerational encounters, and findings are illustrated on Table 5.2.

Generally speaking, suggested improvements include those wherein the older person should be more accommodative to the younger both emotionally and cognitively, by being less negative, by listening, and by increasing clarity. It was suggested that improvements would follow if both partners were more engaged and attuned to each other (involved and other orientation), and if both were more emotionally accommodative in terms of sympathy and caring. Notably, respondents felt that a large number of satisfying conversations could not be improved. A positive aspect of this is that some of these conversations were exemplars of support and understanding, and

TABLE 5.2
Suggested Improvements for Intergenerational
Conversations, With Percentages

Improvement Strategy	Dissatisfying (%)	Satisfying (%)
Nothing	7.8	43.4
More involvement (both)	16.3	29.5
More time (young)	3.1	19.4
More clarity (old)	7.8	3.9
Less negativity (old)	34.1	1.6
More other orientation (both)	27.9	3.9
More assertiveness (young)	19.4	5.4
More listening (old)	14.7	2.3
Sympathy/caring (both)	11.6	2.3
Avoidance (both)	10.9	0

particularly those in which the older person was a well-known and loved mentor or grandparental figure. The negative side of the data is that many times, the conversation was as satisfying as it possibly could be under the circumstances. In other words, the gulf created by old age, or more importantly years lived, differing lifestyles, life priorities, and ill health was so great that it could not possibly be bridged. Note, too, that for dissatisfying conversations, one reported improvement was to avoid the interaction, to avoid the person, or to avoid older people in general. In a very broad and exploratory sense then, this initial study suggested a number of communication themes of satisfaction and dissatisfaction that young people identify in association with intergenerational conversations.

Following this initial study, Williams (1996) investigated underaccommodation more systematically in a controlled quasi-experimental study designed to compare judgments of younger versus older underaccommodation. Two versions of a *vignette* (a prototypical communication scenario), which featured two women striking up a conversation in a cafe, were prepared using the previous findings regarding underaccommodation. In one version the target was characterized as underaccommodative in the ways described in the previous study (i.e., inattentive, ignoring, and using off-target domination). In the second version, the target did not engage in these behaviors; instead her speech was designed to appear more neutral. In addition, the age of the target was varied so that in some versions she was said to be 25 years old and in others she was portrayed as 70 years old. The partner was always portrayed as 20 years old and her speech was unchanged in all versions of the vignettes.

Undergraduate respondents read and judged the various versions of the vignettes, and in closed-ended format judged the target and partner's personality and feelings toward each other. In a follow-up study, the same respondents participated in focus-group discussions. Focus groups were simply asked to discuss what was going on in the vignettes, what the target and partner were like, what their motives were, and so forth.

Results indicated that the underaccommodative targets were seen more negatively than neutral ones regardless of their ages. Age differences were observed for both neutral as well as underaccommodative conversations. The 70-year-old target was viewed more positively than the 25-year-old; she was thought to be less ignoring, more listening, and more empathic in neutral versions of the conversation, and was viewed as more dominant and less negative or ineffective in underaccommodative versions. When it came to evaluations of the 20-year-old partner, she was perceived as more annoyed and less empathic when addressed by an underaccommodative compared to a neutral 25-year-old, but this was not matched by similar effects when paired with a 70-year-old. This means that respondents saw the 20-year-old as more reactive to negative behavior from a 25-year-old as a 70-year-old.

Data from the focus-group discussions revealed that respondents may have perceived the 70-year-old as well-meaning, excusing her behavior as due to the mitigating circumstances of being old (i.e., loneliness or the need to be involved and the desire to mother) combined with an age-respect norm. The focus-group data revealed that participants hypothesized about several stereotypes, which were used at different times to explain various aspects of the 70-year-old's behavior. At least two stereotypes were evident—a "typical grandma" (i.e., see the Perfect Grandparent stereotype discussed in chapter 3) and a lonely, needy person (i.e., see the Despondent stereotype discussed in chapter 3). These results have implications for theoretical models of intergenerational communication, because this demonstrates not only that stereotypes may function as post hoc attributions for conversational breakdown, but also that different stereotypes may be kept in play during conversations and drawn upon as resources for talk, attributions, and so forth as circumstances appear to require.

The general notion that young people may characterize elders as rather underaccommodative has received support from other studies. A speaker-evaluation study by Ryan and Capadano (1978) revealed that young college students judged older women speakers as more "out of it" and inflexible than younger women speakers (speakers were ages 12 to 71). All of these features are consistent with the contention that young people view older people as underaccommodative. Moreover, although elder underaccommodation is generally seen by young people as dissatisfying, underaccommodation from older people may often be attenuated by stereotyped expectations and attributions, such that some older people might be forgiven for underaccommodation, while others may not be forgiven. Considering elder stereotypes, some stereotypes (e.g., Despondent and Severely Impaired) might be expected to be more underaccommodative than others (e.g., Golden Ager, Perfect Grandparent). For example, Shaner (1996) has suggested that painful self-disclosure (PSD) can be associated with negative stereotypes of elderly persons. Indeed, it is an intriguing possibility that an initial PSD introduced early in a conversation could activate a particular stereotype of the elder, which might be followed through the conversation, and in some cases might dominate it.

Besides drawing attention to further aspects of older underaccommodation, the communication-satisfaction and dissatisfaction research has been valuable for a number of reasons. It confirmed and extended previous knowledge about aspects of intergenerational talk that young people find problematic, as well as those features that young people enjoy. It has been valuable in other respects, too, because it has supplied an initial set of ecologically valid dependent measures that could be formulated into a questionnaire for use in further studies in which respondents are required to evaluate intergenerational communication. To achieve this, the original category dimensions described by Williams and Giles (1996) have been formulated into the Perceptions of Intergenerational Communication (PIC) questionnaire, which has been used both in the Eastern and Western contexts to evaluate younger and older people's perceptions of their intergenerational encounters. The cross-cultural research using the PIC questionnaire is discussed in chapter 14; for the moment, discussion focuses on the use and development of the PICs measure in a Western context.

Harwood and Williams (1998) investigated young people's expectations for conversations with two different elder stereotypes—the Despondent, and the Perfect Grandparent. In this study, the PIC measure was combined with other items intended to assess speech adjustments, such as talking louder and talking slower (overaccommodation), that young people might make in attempts to communicate more effectively with older people. Also, in response to the notion that young people might view intergenerational talk with some anxiety, some communication-apprehension items were included along with Hecht's (1978) communication-satisfaction scale, which was included in part to test the validity of the PIC. Braithwaite, Lynd-Stevenson, and Pigram's (1993) attitudes toward aging questionnaire, with three subscales (attitudes toward contact, perceptions of older adults competence, and attitudes toward older adults' sociability), was used as a measure of generalized perceptions of older people.

Results showed that *communication apprehension* ("I could not think clearly when I spoke," "I did not know what to say," "I did not act like myself, my words became confused and jumbled"); *elder attunement* ("gave welcome advice," "told interesting stories," "was supportive"); and *positive affect* were all significantly related to the communication satisfaction scale. Elder attunement was the most powerful predictor of communication satisfaction, indicating that for young people, global communication satisfaction is substantially determined by the extent to which the older person is attuned to his or her own conversational needs.

The nature of the older target played a significant role in determining three of the seven dimensions of evaluation. Participants who were presented with the Despondent stereotype described themselves as more anxious, and described the older adult as less attuned and more likely to complain as compared to those participants who were presented with the more positive steroetype—the Perfect Grandparent. However, it is important to note that despite the role of stereotypes, general attitudes toward contact with elders was a significant predictor of five of the dimensions of conversational expectations, namely, compassion or self esteem, anxiety, communication apprehension, elder attunement, and positive affect. They were also borderline predictors of young *overaccommodation* (avoiding certain words, talking louder, talking slower, and feeling obliged to be polite). Across all measures, more positive attitudes toward contact with older adults were related to more positive expectations for this specific interaction. In addition, perceived competence of older adults was negatively associated with the level of complaining to be expected in the experimental interaction, and perceptions of adult's sociability predicted the expected degree of elder attunement.

Therefore, a number of interesting findings arise from this study. First, the findings complement the previous research; elder attunement included items described in the Williams and Giles (1996) study, which were characterized as accommodative to young people. Similarly, the elder-complaining dimension reflects one aspect of Williams and Gile's dissatisfying talk that was described as underaccommodative and is related to PSD. The two factors underlying young people's perceptions of their own behavior—communication apprehension and young overaccommodation—are closely related to both previously reported communication restrictions and to reluctant young accommodation.

Therefore, not surprisingly, we can conclude that young people have more negative conversational expectations for negative elder targets; they expect them to complain more than positively characterized elders. However, expectations such as these, which varied dramatically across targets, were not necessarily those that predicted overall satisfaction. Expectations for complaining may have distinguished targets, but elder attunement to younger person's needs was the dominant predictor of general satisfaction. This could be interpreted as meaning that younger people will tolerate an elder person's complaints, providing that he or she meets the young persons' communicative needs. Under these conditions the young person will not be overly dissatisfied.

Interestingly, younger adults described very little variation in judgments of their own behaviors across the target types. As will be seen in chapter 6, despite these self-reported expectations, young people do indeed vary their speech quite dramatically in response to elder targets.

Harwood and Williams (1998) also showed that for some conversational expectations, general stereotypes of older people were stronger predictors than were the subtypes themselves. Despite the specific information provided about the targets, evaluations on a number of dimensions were determined more strongly by global attitudes. If we turn these results around, they suggest that sometimes, even if young people are given specific information about elders, (which in real-life contexts outside the lab may be an accurate reflection of their social status, abilities, and so forth), it may be overlooked in favor of general positive or negative attitudes toward age. Thus, expectations based on general attitudes to age may be pursued regardless of the individual's particular abilities. In other words, providing specific information about the individual has no effect on some evaluations and expectations about communication, and the older person may not be individuated. This is important because in certain circumstances speech modifications made to elders may be inappropriate, and this is what causes most concern to those who are advocates for elderly people.

SUMMARY

This chapter examines evidence that suggests that not only are young peoples' encounters with older people likely to be less satisfying than encounters with peers, but also, dissatisfying encounters with older people are likely to be perceived in intergroup terms with underaccommodation as the most frequently reported communication problem. Furthermore, it is very communicatively demanding for young recipients to manage underaccommodation. All the empirical evidence points to underaccommodation as a predominant and pervasive perception of older interlocutors, perhaps especially so for those who are seen in terms of negative stereotypes (e.g., despondent).

A number of researchers have speculated about the possible motivations and consequences of underaccommodative talk, particularly PSD (Coupland, Coupland, Giles, Henwood, & Wiemann, 1988; Mazloff, Shaner & Ward, 1996). In their summary of elderly-to-young miscommunication, Coupland et al. (1988) enumerate four types of elderly underaccommodation. First, *intergroup underaccommodation* may be triggered by life circumstances especially to relatively infrequent intergenerational contact. Thus, although interactional goals may be positive, focus on the other person is attenuated; for example, the elderly person may be relatively self-focused and rather low attuning to his or her younger partner. Young recipients of this may judge it as rather passive and distant. For example, in Williams' and Giles' data described previously, some older people were judged as "out of it." In other cases, the older person can be judged as overly assertive, such as when the older person is perceived as unwilling to deviate from his or her own conversational agenda (Williams & Giles, 1996).

A second form of underaccommodation is considered *self-protecting*. The older person perceives that his or her identity is threatened by actual or perceived negative interindividual comparisons, especially given that, when in conversation with young adults, older adults may wish to avoid topics that make their own lives seem less worthwhile or fulfilled. The result is that they may attempt to exert control over the interaction most probably through discourse-management strategies by keeping to so-called "safe" topics—ones that relate to their own lives, and they may avoid social comparisons in which they would look the worst. Alternatively, they may self-protect by talking little about their own lives and by taking the focus off their own situations by attending extensively to the younger person's conversational needs.

Threatened identity was also thought to lead to forms of self-handicapping, as when the older person evaluates his or her own performance negatively and tries to save face. In this case, the older person would be attentive to the partner's potential attributions, and would try to attenuate any negative attributions by apologizing and overcompensating. Relatedly, self-stereotyping (Turner, 1982, 1986) may result from an older person's self-perception as an aged communicator and they may then both take on and act out the features perceived to be typical of their social groups. Again in this case, the focus is on the self, rather than the other person, with the consequence that the older person is judged as stereotypically elderly and underaccommodative.

Finally, intergroup divergence is thought to lead from a threat to identity. The goals are to promote intergroup distinctiveness, and to signal disapproval and dissatisfaction. Attention may be focused on the other person's productive performance (e.g., youth slang) or on emphasizing generational differences and making intergenerational comparisons. The result is divergence, and this has dubious gains for older people because such strategies can be characterized as typical of grumpy and irritable old people who disapprove of the young.

In Giddens' terms, although younger interactants perceive underaccommodation as communicatively constraining, it may in some respects be enabling for older people. By being underaccommodating to young people, older people may retain some sense of control over the conversation and may thereby reduce or avoid potentially negative intergenerational comparisons. As N. Coupland, Coupland, Giles, Henwood, and Wiemann (1988) suggest, painful self-disclosure, among other things, may be self-reinforcing because it elicits outwardly sympathetic, supportive, and flattering responses from young interlocutors as do certain forms of self-handicapping (Arkin & Baumgardner, 1985). Young people frequently express surprise at older people's disclosures and reassure older people that they are marvelous for their age (Coupland, Coupland, & Giles, 1991). On an interindividual level this is supportive and flattering. On an intergroup level it is comparable to telling a member of an ethnic minority (e.g., African American) that "they are okay for a black." There is an internal contradiction here, which in structuration theory terminology (see chapter 1 for a description of structuration theory), is opaque for elders who collude in denigration of their social groups, receiving with grace an individual compliment at the expense of an intergroup insult.

In any event, PSD is often a rational, poignant reflection of life circumstances and events that we all endure as we traverse the life span (see Coupland, Coupland, Giles, Henwood, & Wiemann, 1988, for further discussion); and it may be an important component of self-identity to be shared with others. In this sense, PSDs may serve to reveal important aspects of the individual's identity as a valiant survivor of a struggle with various life challenges.

From their ethnographic data with older adults in senior centers, Mazloff, Shaner, and Ward, (1996) also speculate about these as motivations for PSD. Interestingly, these researchers also note the frequency with which older people disclose such things to each other. The researchers suggest that older people gain a certain pleasure from this. In other words, PSD among peers may be a form of social comparison and competition with others who have also suffered. This indicates, that in some circumstances, people gain a certain covert prestige out of painful self-disclosure. Contradictions evident in this are that while gaining "brownie points" for themselves through these processes, older people are at the same time self-identifying with negatively perceived aspects of their social group, and are potentially reinforcing ill-health, poor coping, further underaccommodation, and withdrawal from active life. Whereas younger people repeatedly indicate that they do not enjoy being accomplices in such disclosures, they also may subtly encourage them in various ways by providing interactional reinforcement and support. This process can set up an intergroup comparative context from which young people derive support for their own social identities as healthy, vital, and active young people.

The fact that young people perceive underaccommodation as an intergenerational communication problem may have very wide-ranging consequences for young and old alike. Such difficulties and associated attributional processes can fuel the desire for minimal contact and can lead to sociocultural isolation of older people, and even to ill health, as proposed by the communication predicament model of aging (Harwood, Giles, Fox, Ryan, & Williams, 1993; Ryan, Hummert, & Boich, 1995) described in chapter 1. Also, this can result in political and public policy implications if the media raises fears to the point that younger people feel that elders, as a collective force, are politically and economically threatening, or are, in other words, underaccommodative.

Furthermore, negative intergenerational-conversational experiences of young people and associated management problems can lead, in turn, to negative constructions of their own aging, fear of old age, and avoidance of older people. In a social learning sense, both satisfying and dissatisfying intergenerational-communication experiences act as role models for what might be expected of these young people in the future as they grow older. This can lead to self-stereotyping. Reflexively, this may influence younger peoples' ability to relate to and associate with subsequent generations of young people as they, in turn, grow older. In this way, a cycle of problematic intergenerational contact may be produced and reproduced through successive generations.

It seems logical that, among a variety of reactions to perceived underaccommodation, young people may overcompensate to, and respond with, communicative overaccommodation. In many cases perhaps, under- and overaccommodation go hand in hand, carving out the topography of intergenerational conversations. This then, is the topic for the next chapter.

6

Intergenerational Language Strategies: Overaccommodation

Overaccommodation is a language and communication strategy that is considered to be rather typical of young peoples' communication with elders, and one which seems to have generated a considerable amount of research attention. *Overaccommodation* may be defined as the overplaying of a particular language or communication style relative to the needs, wishes, or desires of the listener (Coupland, Coupland & Giles, 1991; Ryan et al., 1986). *Overaccommodation* is further defined by Coupland et al. (1988) as a miscommunicative process wherein at least one participant perceives a speaker to go beyond a sociolinguistic style judged necessary for attuned talk. Often researchers use the terms overaccommodation and patronization as if they are interchangeable concepts, but there is danger in this. Recently, Williams and Giles (1998) defined *patronizing talk* as talk that is ideationally simpler, slower, and more childlike in intonation (for a review, see Ryan, Hummert, & Boich, 1995), and importantly, is attributed as patronizing by the recipient (Ytsma & Giles, 1997). This recent definition reflects the subjective attributional element inherent in the term *patronization*. For the most part, this chapter uses the term *overaccommodation* except when discussing research wherein researchers themselves used the term *patronization*.

This chapter explores several varieties of overaccommodative communication, but of particular interest is the research concerned with younger peoples' overaccommodation toward the elderly. It should be noted that overaccommodative communication is not limited to intergenerational contexts, having been noted in other contexts too, such as in talk to persons with physical disabilities (Fox & Giles, 1996), mentally handicapped adults, and foreign people (DePaulo & Coleman, 1986). In fact, as we shall see, overaccommodation occurs in a variety of contexts in which speakers modify their speech and communication to achieve certain interpersonal goals, such as increasing clarity and promoting understanding, or to emphasize differences and to increase interindividual and intergroup distance.

As was discussed previously, there are undoubtedly predominant and problematic intergenerational language strategies beyond under- and overaccommodation, many of which are yet to be documented and described. This chapter and the previous chapter focus on under- and overaccommodation because these two communication strategies have attracted the most attention from intergenerational researchers. In recent years, overaccommodation has dominated the literature and there has been an explosion of studies investigating this phenomenon. This chapter summarizes the main studies and charts a course through the major findings.

Researchers have concentrated research attention on overaccommodation in intergenerational contexts for a number of reasons. The most important reason is best expressed by the communication predicament model (CPA) discussed in chapter 1. As the model suggests, there is worrying evidence that if one treats people as if they are helpless, they tend to acquiesce to that treatment and give up control—a phenomenon known as *learned helplessness* (see Rodin & Langer, 1980), and one which can spiral to ill-health, both physical and psychological. Overaccommodative communication seems to carry with it considerable implications for the power relations of the individuals (and groups) involved (Ng & Bradac, 1993), because it disempowers the person being overaccommodated. In particular, overaccommodative communication modifications are not necessarily based on realistic needs of the individual, and are, therefore, often inaccurately targeted (as indicated by the stereotype activation model discussed in chapter 1). This means that adjustments can be made to many socially and cognitively active elders, many of who may view such acts as communicating a lack of respect that undermines self-esteem and dignity. It is also possible that when negative images associated with age are made salient to older individuals (e.g., by overaccommodating them) they will tend to self-stereotype (see Turner, Hogg, Oakes, Reicher, & Wetherall, 1987). In other words, if such adjustments happen frequently or are salient enough, it is possible that older people may begin to see themselves in terms of the communication directed at them and may begin to look, move, sound, think, talk, and account as older (Giles, Fox, Harwood, & Williams, 1994).

A TYPOLOGY OF OVERACCOMMODATION

Although a range of modified versions of the communication predicament model of aging have emerged (e.g., see Harwood & Giles, 1996), the central hypothesis remains intact, and it has been the dominating theoretical framework for much of the research concerned with overaccommodative communication to the elderly. According to this view (e.g., see Ryan et al., 1986), overaccommodation is mediated by stereotypes of either elderly incompetence or sensory decrements (Ryan et al., 1986). In their early summary of the sociopsychological contexts and sociolinguistic instantiation of young-to-elderly miscommunication, Coupland, Coupland, Giles, and Henwood (1988) list three categories of overaccommodation—sensory, dependency, and intergroup. *Sensory overaccommodation* is prompted by an assumption of physical or sensory handicap (e.g., hearing loss). In this case, the goal of the young person is to promote understanding resulting in attention to the other person's ability to interpret what is being said, followed by overcompensation for the assumed difficulty. In CAT terms, this would indicate an excessive use of interpretability strategies. *Dependency-based overaccommodation* is based on perceptions of social or institutional roles and is associated with a need to control, leading to regulative or controlling talk, which may seem overcontrolling or authoritative to a listener. In other words, this may be based on the assumption that the elder needs help with certain tasks, and leads to the elder being directed or told what they can or cannot do. In other words, it is an excessive use of control strategies. *Intergroup overaccommodation* would seem to be much more disingenuous, motivated by a need for psychological distance to mark out the boundaries between one's own group and that of the interlocutor (see chapter 1, this volume, for a discussion of intergroup theory).

Young-to-old overaccommodation has been labeled in various ways as "patronizing speech," or "patronizing communication" (Ryan et al., 1986; Ryan, Hummert, & Boich, 1995), "elderspeak" (Cohen & Faulkner, 1986b), and "baby talk" (Caporeal, 1981). It is important to distinguish between these various labels to point out that, beyond the value judgment inherent in the term *patronization,* the issue of whether or not speech is overaccommodative depends on one's point of view. Objective researchers armed with definitions, community listener–judges, perpetrators, and recipients of, overaccommodative speech may all have varying perceptions about whether or not a particular instance of communication overshoots its target, to say nothing of the associated intent, force, and consequences. With this in mind, the following section describes communication features that researchers have associated with various forms of overaccommodation, assuming that it could be recognized independently of attributions.

Features of Overaccommodative Communication

Overaccommodative communication labeled *patronizing* is perhaps a less extreme form of baby talk and is distinguished from normal adult speech by being slow, oversimplified (e.g., low in grammatical complexity), polite, and overly warm (see Hummert & Ryan, 1996). In addition, clarification strategies such as careful articulation and increased volume may be employed along with other content and paralinguistic features (Ryan et al., 1986). Compared to young and middle-aged adults, older people may more often be susceptible to overfamiliar communication, such as inappropriate forms of address (Wood & Ryan, 1991) and frequent patting or touching or both (Lancely, 1985). Ryan, Hummert, and Boich (1995) summarize psycholinguistic features associated with patronizing communication into two categories, verbal and nonverbal (see also Hummert & Ryan, 1996).

Verbal features include simplification of speech such as grammar and vocabulary, using both childish terms and minimizing words (e.g., just, little) and making pronoun modifications (especially overinclusive use of "we"). Inappropriate forms of address have also been placed under the rubric of patronization, as when first names are used overfamiliarly, and the use of endearments such as "darling." Ryan et al. (1996) also list certain forms of topic management as patronizing, namely, limited topic selection, interruptions, dismissing other generated topics, and exaggerated praise for minor accomplishments. Nonverbal correlates of patronizing speech include modifications to voice (high pitch, exaggerated intonation, etc.), gaze (e.g., reduced eye contact), proxemics, facial expressions (exaggerated smile), gestures (e.g., hands on hips), and touch (e.g., overfamilar pats).

Recently, Hummert and Ryan (1996) have distinguished between two forms of overaccommodation that they label *patronizing speech*. One form is overly nurturant, wherein the patronizer uses overly familiar terms, simple language, diminutives, and highly varied intonation. The other form is devoid of paralinguistic features that may indicate nurturance, but is characterized by imperatives, shortness, cold and uncaring tones, and disparaging remarks. This latter form is much more controlling and overly directive.

This form of communication even seems to persist when avoidance of such tactics has been vigorously and normatively prescribed, for example, in the training regimens of home-care assistants (Atkinson & Coupland,

1988). In addition, it has been shown that younger people may deflect and downplay some of the seriously expressed concerns, thoughts, and feelings of the elderly (Grainger, Atkinson, & Coupland, 1990). All of this can, of course, cause irritation, anger, and frustration if the elderly person does not welcome such communication.

As alluded to previously, the motivations of overaccommodative communication are generally assumed to be overzealous attempts to indicate nurturance and socioemotional support, although in some cases the motives may also include a need for dominance and control (Grainger, Atkinson, & Coupland, 1990) and a desire to emphasize the intergroup distance. To the extent that some extreme forms of overaccommodation convey little respect, the challenge for caretakers and the paradox at the center of the communication-predicament model (see Ryan & Cole, 1990; Ryan, Hummert, & Boich, 1995), is to manage communicatively two competing goals, namely, to convey nurturance and support while preserving dignity by remaining polite and respectful. The juxtaposition of these goals is nowhere more problematic than in caring contexts.

Overaccommodative Communication in Caring Contexts

For considerable time it has long been acknowledged that institutional care promotes dependence. The communication predicament and stereotype activation models described the ways in which negative stereotyped perceptions of older people could lead to stereotype-adjusted speech, which in turn leads to a cycle of negativity and decrement. Such a view is supported by research such as that by Rodin and Langer (1980), which clearly showed how the treatment of institutionalized older people could generate and perpetuate self-fulfilling prophesies of dependence and ill-health resulting in learned helplessness and further dependency. More recently, Baltes and colleagues (e.g., Baltes & Wahl, 1992; Baltes, Wahl, & Reichert, 1991) reported that independent behaviors of institutional residents are ignored and not reinforced, whereas dependent behavior is rewarded. Interestingly enough, these researchers sought to determine whether this phenomenon was age specific or was related to the very fact of institutionalization. They compared a children's institution to an elderly care facility and found that the reverse pattern prevailed in the children's care facility—children were reinforced for independent behaviors while dependent behaviors were ignored (Baltes & Reisenstein, 1986).

In consideration of the communicative aspects of promoting dependence, the field studies of Ashburn and Gordon (1981), Caporeal (1981), and Culbertson (Caporeal & Culbertson, 1986) were among the first to document forms of overaccommodative speech directed from young to elderly interlocutors. Caporeal and colleagues described an extreme form of overaccommodation used by caregivers when addressing institutionalized elderly people in long-term care facilities. Defined by characteristics of high pitch and of exaggerated intonation, it was labeled *secondary baby talk* (Caporeal, Lukaszewski, & Culbertson, 1983). Such talk was directed at elderly institutional residents regardless of functional ability, cognitive alertness, or indeed, preferences of individuals. Furthermore, it was estimated that almost a quarter of nurses' utterances could be identified as secondary baby talk. (Sachweh's, 1998, extended definition led her to suggest a far greater proportion of baby talk in her study of a German nursing home.) Caporeal and colleagues reported that caregivers assumed that older adults would prefer such talk, and that it enhanced clarity and aided attention and comprehension. Moreover, staff who used baby talk most were also those who harbored more negative evaluations of the resident's capabilities. In addition, content-filtered and taped excerpts from Caporeal and colleague's field studies indicated that secondary baby talk to elderly recipients was indistinguishable from primary baby talk addressed to children (Caporeal, 1981). Studies by Lanceley (1985) and Fairhurst (1981) also identified speech that has been considered patronizing such as the use of "we" when referring to an individual, nurses talking about the patient in the third person, informal address terms (e.g. inappropriate use of first names or nicknames or both), routinized talk, use of exaggerated praise, and persuasive or coercive talk.

Since these initial investigations, there has been a consistent and lively research interest in this phenomenon (e.g., see Sachweh, 1997). In spite of the concentration and research emphasis on secondary baby talk, there are other forms of institutional communication discussed in the literature, such as the absence of talk and task-oriented talk (Grainger, 1995). Grainger and others (e.g., Ryan, Bourhis, & Knops, 1991) point out that many nurses in institutional contexts are struggling with dilemmas such as how to get the task completed according to institutional and organizational regimes, and how, at the same time, to maintain their roles as caring and supportive individuals. The contradiction here is that to be caring and supportive would require time to listen, to discuss resident's anxieties, problems, even to build and promote more intimate relationships. But the pressures of the organization are built around the need for efficient time management and task completion. After all, to build relationships is costly for the institution. We should not overlook the potential emotional and psychological cost to the nurse that comes with more affective-relational involvement with residents. In fact, part of nurses' motivations in using patronizing speech may be to keep an emotional distance.

Grainger (1995) argues that to characterize institutional talk as secondary baby talk or patronizing talk "assumes the mechanistic use of a predetermined style and underplays the dynamism of interaction" (p. 427). Her research is insightful because of her attention to the contextual complexities in which overaccommodative, and in our terms, underaccommodative, talk together realize the institutional roles of nurse and elderly patient. Nurses overaccommodate to some aspects of the resident's needs but underaccommodate to others (e.g., emotional needs). Grainger argues that secondary baby talk as a reaction to the perceived dependency of the older person is part of an interactive process that can include other parenting talk such as directive and regulatory talk (see also Hummert, Shaner, Henry, & Garstka, 1995; Hummert & Ryan, 1996). In this case, the connection between the form and function of talk is emphasized, and as Grainger points out, such talk is often motivated by a need to gain compliance from the older person so that tasks can be completed, while simultaneously managing a considerable number of face threats. As a result of her own ethnographic and discourse-analytic research in a long-term care institution, Grainger is able to demonstrate how elderly residents' dependent and sick-role behavior complements nurses' talk. Although much research attention is placed on nurses' talk to patients, we must remember that both nurses and residents discursively construct the institutional-resident and nurse roles, albeit in a complex system of power that often finds the patient at the lowest level of the power hierarchy (Grainger, 1995).

Overaccommodation in Community Contexts

Although originally identified in institutional contexts, overaccommodative communication is by no means confined to such settings. However, its strength, prevalence, and the attention that research implies it should be afforded in everyday naturalistic contexts (especially in the family), are still relatively undocumented and remain elusive. There is a growing recognition that overaccommodative communication to older adults can be offensive and unwanted, but for the most part, this recognition is confined to those being trained as caregivers, organizations concerned with elders' welfare, and those intent on raising elder's political and social consciousness to elderly issues. For example, in 1994, the American Association of Retired Persons published guidelines for the minimization of patronizing communication to elders, advising that people should avoid terms like "sweetie" and "cute."

From a behavioral point of view, and as an extension of their earlier studies in institutional contexts, Baltes and Wahl (1992) compared interactions between community-living elderly people and their social partners to those between nurses and nursing-home residents. Both the nursing-home residents and the community-dwelling elderly were reinforced for dependency behaviors. Unlike the nursing-home context, independent behaviors of the community dwellers were sometimes reinforced, but more often elicited a dependency supporting response. Although Baltes and Wahl did not specifically consider overaccommodation as a dependency-supporting strategy, there is little doubt that both under- and overaccommodation are important components of such behaviors.

Recently, spontaneous overaccommodation to elders in community contexts was confirmed by Kemper (1994). She examined the use of "elderspeak" (characterized by shorter sentences, few sentence embeddings, and the use of few markers of discourse cohesion) by both caregivers (e.g., nurses) and service providers (e.g., craft instructors) when addressing older adults. More importantly, such talk was not used when younger adults were addressed in comparative contexts, and was not sensitive to the functional capability of the older adult groups (i.e., demented vs. nondemented).

In a family context, Montepare, Steinberg, and Rosenberg (1992) examined young college students' spontaneously produced speech to their grandparents and parents. Observer judges rated speech addressed to the grandparents as higher pitched, more feminine, more deferential and more unpleasant than speech directed toward parents. These characteristics are not unlike some of those described as patronizing, although the speech was not more simple than speech directed at parents. That the characteristics of this speech style are readily apparent to naive judges and are even sufficient to indicate, in some instances, the identity of the target (e.g., grandmother vs. mother), which illustrates the degree of communication modification that occurs here.

Community elders have commented on their perceptions of patronizing communication addressed to them. They were given this opportunity in a series of focus groups conducted with older adults (Hummert & Mazloff, 1993). Three typical situations in which participants claimed patronizing communication occurred most often were identified. The first, not surprisingly, was in health-care institutions, such as doctors' offices, hospitals, and caring facilities; another was in the family with adult children; and a third was in public settings in grocery stores, banks, and so on. Particularly problematic were instances when older adults might be behaviorally slower than younger ones. For example, older adults might be slower in walking, sorting out change in stores, and so forth. Communication behaviors that these older adults identified as patronizing included overparenting or overly directive speech, nonverbal indications of frustration (e.g., sighing, rolling eyes), disrespectful and impersonal speech, use of inclusive "we," and oversimplified speech. Nonlistening was an issue because participants expressed concerns about instances when either they or their concerns were ignored or discounted (see also Giles & Williams, 1994).

In a qualitative-comparative study, Ryan and Cole (1990) interviewed 20 institutionalized older women (mean age 83 years) and 20 community-dwelling active women (mean age 72 years). Their results revealed that these elderly women all expressed a preference for speech from young people to be more respectful as well as more nurturant. However, different communication desires were also evident in these data, and they varied according to the life circumstances of the respondents. The younger, community dwelling, more active women were not as satisfied with intergenerational speech as the institutional residents were. The institutional group, who had more health difficulties, actually preferred speech that was more accommodative, perceiving speech that was addressed to them as simpler, slower, and kinder than that reported by the community group. This indicates that what we might classify as overaccommodation on the basis of objectively defined features may not always be evaluated as such by older people. Some people, especially perhaps those who are old-old, less active, and more dependent, may be more tolerant of communication we would identify as overaccommodative. Whether or not this tolerance is part of a learned helplessness cycle is an important consideration that remains to be fully explored (see Baltes et al., 1991). The situation is probably not as simple as this. It may be a genuine paradox that whereas some speech and communication adjustments are required and welcome, they, at the same time, communicate dependency.

OBSERVER-JUDGES' EVALUATIONS OF OVERACCOMMODATIVE COMMUNICATION

Apart from more naturalistic institutional and community contexts, a series of experimental studies have been aimed at teasing apart some of the processes of patronizing or overaccommodating communication to the elderly. In recent years, patronizing communication has been extensively studied by asking groups of observer-judges to read and respond to vignettes, which vary speech style (patronizing, neutral), participants (e.g., nurses, receptionists, nursing-home residents, and neighbors as well as substereotypes) and contexts (institutional and community). A typical example is that of Ryan, Bourhis, and Knops (1991) who used a written vignette of a middle-aged nurse talking with an elderly nursing-home resident to elicit evaluative perceptions of the nurse and the elder resident. The resident was depicted as either cognitively alert and active or as forgetful and confused. Speech style was manipulated by the wording of the vignette to indicate a neutral or patronizing message. The latter contained condescending and simplified speech, for instance, presumption of the resident's inability to understand a television program and the expressions "be a good girl" and "poor dear." The results of this study revealed that patronizing speech was downgraded by observer-judges as significantly less respectful and nurturant than the more neutral variant. In addition, both the nurse and the resident were seen as significantly more frustrated in the patronizing condition, and such speech was not considered more appropriate for the forgetful or confused elder. Further, inferences elicited from respondents indicated that, in spite of the written presentation of the scenario, they could hear the patronizing conversation as louder, more shrill with exaggerated intonation, and as less understandable than the more neutral style.

That people associate a range of nonverbal behaviors with patronizing speech was confirmed in an investigation by Ryan, MacLean, and Orange (1994). Vignette respondents were both adult volunteers and a sample of service providers. Results indicated that patronizing versions of written vignettes were associated with negative nonverbal behaviors such as frowning, sighing, stiff posture, crossing arms, turning, and walking away from the resident. Moreover patronizing vignettes were less likely to be associated with positive nonverbal correlates such as smiling, maintaining eye contact, and gentle movements.

In a methodological expansion of this research, Edwards and Noller (1993) used a videotaped presentation of a vignette involving a female nurse and an elderly woman. Respondents were community-living elderly people, trainee nurses, and independent observers (psychology students). Edwards and Noller were particularly interested in comparing the subjective and perhaps divergent perceptions of these three different groups. Also, the videotape facilitated a more natural presentation of overaccommodation than did a written vignette, and also nonverbal features could be represented and subsequently evaluated. Three different overaccommodative-communication strategies were varied in the videotapes in such a way that they could be evaluated alone or in paired combinations. The strategies were: altered voice pitch, touch (a pat on the elderly person's shoulder), and an expression of endearment ("that's a good girl"). The interactional context was also varied: a bathroom setting with the elderly woman seated in a wheelchair and dressed for bed; the elderly woman lying in bed; and the elderly woman sitting in a lounge chair reading a magazine.

All three respondent groups agreed that the strategies were patronizing and found the pitch and endearment the most patronizing, but the groups differed on the extent to which they found the strategies patronizing. On many of the evaluative dimensions, the elderly women were more tolerant of the strategies than were the other two groups. Of particular importance was the expression of endearment, which the elderly group rated as less patronizing, less dominant, and more respectful than did the psychology or the nursing students. Again, in contrast to the two student groups, the elderly women rated the endearment strategy more positively than the touch or the pitch, whereas the students rated it more negatively. The elderly women (and psychology students) were also more positive than the nurses when it came to evaluating the endearment and the pitch and endearment strategies for warmth and support. In spite of the fact that elderly women rated the pitch and endearment strategy as patronizing, they also rated it as respectful and nondominant.

The important point here is that the older women were more tolerant to the patronizing forms than were either of the other two groups of respondents. They tended to rate them higher both in terms of the status as well as the supportiveness that the strategies conveyed even though they agreed that the strategies were patronizing.

Edwards and Noller did not ask their respondents to evaluate the behavior of the elderly person, but being the recipient of patronizing communication can lead some observers to assume that one is the sort of person who deserves or requires such modifications, and can thus affect evaluations of your competence. A study by Giles, Fox, and Smith (1993) followed the procedures of Ryan, Bourhis, and Knops (1991), using a vignette of a middle-aged nurse talking with an elderly nursing-home resident. Respondents were both young university students and community elders. As a result, Ryan et al. found uniformly more negative evaluations of a nurse when he or she used patronizing talk (such as "Be a good girl," "Poor dear") compared with when he or she used a more neutral style. For example, he or she was perceived as less respectful, less considerate, less competent, and less benevolent in the former condition. The resident herself was perceived as more frustrated and helpless in the patronizing condition. The researchers also found that elderly respondents were likely to be very sensitive to the characteristics of the individual receiving the patronization. When the nurse spoke patronizingly, older (but not younger) respondents rated the resident as less competent, more weak, and less alert. At one level, this implies that older adults incorporate contextual cues in their evaluations of particular episodes of talk, whereas younger individuals appear less inclined to do so. It also suggests that elderly persons may be more willing to denigrate their peers on dimensions of competence as a result of the particular kinds of talk directed toward them.

The results of a follow-up investigation with elderly respondents (reported in the same study) indicated that many of them claimed to have been patronized themselves and that it made them extremely irritated. Interestingly enough, evidence from this and from a further unpublished study (Ryan, Giles, Harwood, & Williams, 1993) indicates that elders consider themselves less likely to be patronized than others of their own age, particularly those who are considered more frail and less respected within the community.

It is essential to realize that, although the current literature may give the impression that intergenerational overaccommodation is a one-way street, this may not be the case. The following set of studies reveals that young people too may be subjected to overaccommodative communication. Overaccommodation to the young has attracted far less research attention than overaccommodation to older adults, not surprisingly, because the insidious implications of ill health, lack of control, and decline are not thought to be paralleled in the case of talk to the young.[1]

In spite of this, young people themselves identify overaccommodation directed at themselves as problematic, as is demonstrated by Giles and William's (1994) series of studies examining young people's reactions to patronizing talk from older to younger adults. In an initial study, undergraduates reported that they, too, were the recipients of patronizing speech, and this annoyed them. They were asked to describe how older people patronized them, and from a content analysis of these data, eight categories emerged. In a second study, undergraduates were presented with two examples of each of these categories and were asked to make similarity judgments of each combination. Analyses showed that they cognitively represented the different kinds of patronizing speech on three dimensions: nonlistening (e.g., "The elderly don't listen to what I have to say"), disapproving (e.g., "You're all party animals!"), and overparenting (e.g., "When you get older you will see this was best"). In a third study, these three different kinds of patronizing forms were

---

[1]Although it should be noted that it is entirely possible as, for example, in the case of parents who continue to treat young people like children, which can undermine their self-confidence and hold them back from independent development as full adults.

utilized for social evaluation in a vignette study alongside a nonpatronizing (control) variety. Patronizing of any of the types by either a 70-year-old person or by a 40-year-old person was seen very negatively by young adults, but a hierarchy of judgments did emerge depending on the question posed. Stereotypical disapproving talk was considered by judges to convey the most negative intent, but nonlistening was considered the most difficult to manage communicatively, and overparenting was considered to be the least offensive of the three. Different causal attributions were afforded patronizing targets when they were middle aged rather than elderly (e.g., age envy was, interestingly enough, associated far more with the 40-year-old than with the 70-year-old person).

Note that the strategies identified by young respondents as ways that older people patronized them closely mirror the kinds of strategies identified as young-to-old patronization. Overparenting parallels the overly nurturant forms of patronizing communication used with elders, whereas disapproving speech parallels the overly directive and controlling forms of patronization to the elderly. Also it is noteworthy that both older respondents (i.e., those in Hummert and Mazloff's, 1993, study), as well as younger respondents, identify certain forms of nonlistening as patronizing (although researchers might be inclined to categorize this form of dissatisfying intergenerational communication as under- rather than overaccommodative).

Having established that patronization is bidirectional, Harwood, Giles, Fox, Ryan, and Williams (1993) extended the Giles and Williams research in several ways. They examined patronizing talk from the young to the elderly and from the elderly to the young within a single study, and extended the research to examine the impact of various response strategies to patronizing talk. Previous research of this kind had portrayed the elderly target as a (behaviorally) passive recipient of patronization, and hence possibly as someone who was colluding with the patronizing behavior (e.g., see Edwards & Noller, 1993; Ryan, Meredith, & Shantz, 1994). Part of the intent of this research was to evaluate the effectiveness of more assertive response strategies with a view to eventually formulating recommendations for elders to adopt communication strategies that would ward off unwanted patronization. The setting for the vignette was a doctor's office where a conversation took place between a patient and the receptionist. The patient (either older or younger) was late for an appointment and was either patronized (nonlistening, disapproving, or overparenting) or was spoken to with nonpatronizing speech by the receptionist. In response, the patient was either accepting or assertive. The results showed that the receptionist was viewed as negatively when she patronized the elder person as she was when she patronized the young. Patronizing talk is therefore viewed negatively regardless of the recipient's age, and intergenerational communication was judged as far more satisfactory when the patronizing talk was not present.

When it came to evaluations of the responses, assertive responses from the patronized person led to more positive evaluations of her as higher status, more controlling, and less nurturing than when she provided a neutral response. However, patronizing individuals who were the recipients of this response mode were evaluated as less satisfied, and less in control, and of lower status than when they received an accepting response. Thus, Harwood et al. showed that assertive responses to patronizing speech influenced perceptions of both the patronizer and the patronizee.

Harwood and Giles (1996) designed another study to examine young observer-judge's evaluations of the thought processes that might accompany patronizing speech. Intergenerational patronizing vignettes were used to present respondents with patronizing talk by a young individual. This study also evaluated the relative weight that respondents might give to what is said when having some insight into what interactants might be thinking. To acheive this, the nature of the various target's thoughts were varied as well as were the older adult's responses. Responses echoed those of the Harwood et al. (1993) study as neutral–neutral, patronizing–neutral and patronizing–assertive. The younger individual's thoughts were characterized as caring (e.g., "She really tried hard to get here—I'll fit her into the schedule") or dominant (e.g., "Oh boy, this dumb person can't remember the time of her appointment") and the older individual's thoughts were varied as assertive (e.g., "I can't believe she just spoke to me in that manner") or passive ("Geez, it would be all my fault if the appointment was already filled"); a final condition provided no thoughts. Like the Harwood et al. (1993) study, this study was also conducted in a community context, but one which de-emphasized the medical nature of the context because it was suggested that perhaps the earlier study could have activated elderly stereotypes in connection with a caring context. Accordingly, the Harwood and Giles (1996) study was set in a bank, a context that would be more likely to point to the older adult's competence and high status.

Results echoed the previous findings in that the patronizing receptionist was viewed more negatively than the nonpatronizing receptionist, and the patronized client was thought to be less happy. The receptionists who were the recipients of assertive talk were evaluated as less competent, whereas clients who were assertive were thought to be less warm. However, unlike the earlier Harwood et al. (1993) study, evaluations of the client's competence were unaffected by the assertive response.

For the most part, results indicated respondents were more likely to give precedence to the thoughts than to the speech when both were provided. As might be expected, private thoughts are perceived as more important indicators of intent than is more public behavior such as speech. Results also indicate a possible additive effect when thoughts and speech are matched. For example, the receptionist who was patronizing and who was characterized as thinking dominant thoughts was evaluated as more patronizing than when the thoughts were not included.

Whether or not an assertive response can prompt more positive evaluations is still open to some discussion. A recent study by Ryan, Kennaley, Pratt, and Shumovich (1996) also looked at possible responses to patronization and showed that rather than accruing any socioevaluational gains, the older person who provided a directly assertive response to being the recipient of agism was rated as least competent and polite. Certainly observer-judges infer that people who respond assertively to patronization are less satisfied and that assertion may be one way of indicating this. Speculatively, it could be that assertion by those older people who dislike patronization would make them feel better, perhaps raising their own self-esteem by indicating that they were not the type of people who enjoy being patronized. Herein lies another paradox because assertion can threaten the positive face of the other interlocutor, who, after all, may mean well. Consequently, the asserter may seem ungrateful and insensitive to others. Further research along these lines would do well to distinguish between speech that may be attributed as assertive, versus that which is verbally aggressive (in which case evaluations would be less favorable), and argumentative (which seems to accrue more favorable evaluations according to interpersonal research by Infante and Rancer, 1996). As Harwood and Giles (1996) suggest, a central dilemma for older adults (or in other words, a communication predicament), is how to indicate their displeasure with speech that they attribute as patronizing without accruing negative attributions for their own behavior as over-sensitive, ungrateful, aggressive, or any combination of these.

STEREOTYPES OF OLDER PEOPLE
AND OVERACCOMMODATION

Studies have also addressed the predictions of the stereotype-activation model regarding the behavior of the perceiver in an interaction with an older adult. Hummert and Shaner (1994) presented college-age participants with photographs of two elderly women. One was described by the traits of the Severely Impaired stereotype (e.g., forgetful, slow-thinking, dependent, sick, etc.) and one by the traits of the Perfect Grandparent stereotype (e.g., healthy, loving capable, wise, etc.). Messages elicted from the participants and addressed to the Severely Impaired person were shorter, less complex, and more demeaning in emotional tone than were those to the Perfect Grandparent. A further study (Hummert, Shaner, Henry, & Garstka, 1995) elicited messages from young, middle-aged, and elderly participants in response to a less extreme negative stereotype (Despondent). Results showed that the Despondent target (depressed, sad, hopeless, afraid, neglected, and lonely), like the Severely Impaired target, was believed to require more age-based overaccommodations than the positive target, and these beliefs were reflected in the messages addressed to the targets.

A follow-up study (Hummert, Shaner, Garstka, & Henry, 1996) examined younger and older people's beliefs about the kind of messages that they might direct toward more positive elder stereotypes. This study also examined verbal messages directed at these stereotypes, who were depicted in either a community or a hospital setting. In the community setting, respondents were required to formulate a persuasive message designed to persuade the elder to attend a wedding. In the hospital context, respondents were required to persuade the elder to tell the nurses about painful symptoms. The targets fitted the description of either the Golden Ager (a positive stereotype) or the Despondent (a negative stereotype). Overall respondents were more likely to use patronizing talk with the Despondent target compared to the Golden Ager (as would be expected from previous studies) and used more patronizing messages in the hospital context. However, older adult respondents actually produced fewer patronizing messages than did younger respondents, and in fact, middle-aged people produced the most. Also, middle-aged people produced a higher number of nurturing messages than did younger people, but younger people produced a higher proportion of directive messages. What is particularly interesting about this study is that the messages varied according to the type of target and the context. The highest number of nurturing messages were directed toward the Despondent target featured in a hospital setting. However, the Golden Ager seemed to suffer most because this person received the highest percentage of overly directive and controlling messages when placed in the hospital context—messages that did not contain nurturant features. Presumably this was because participants prompted by the positive presentation thought the Golden Ager could handle more straight or stern talking, and they did not need to make so many allowances for age.

Of course, it could be argued that one of the major findings of these studies is that respondents do not make sweeping overgeneralized overaccommodations to elders. Instead they attempt to make appropriate and sensitive speech modifications to targets, based on very little information. In this sense then, modification attempts are quite valiant even when they misfire. Consider for example, the Severely Impaired target who was described as forgetful and slow thinking. Common sense would indicate that such a person was in need of considerable speech adjustments, which may not be inappropriate given the nature of the target, and are thus not necessarily patronizing. Far from showing that younger people are insensitive to their elders, these studies actually show considerable sensitivity by young people. Even though their attempts to communicate effectively are sometimes off target, they are by no means totally inappropriate. Indeed, there is evidence that respondents attempted to accommodate appropriately to the emotional state of the Despondent target too, because according to Hummert et al. (1996), respondents estimated that they would attempt to soften their voices and decrease the liveliness of their expressive styles.

Finally, we reiterate that it would be wrong to suggest that all communication that could be objectively identified as overaccommodative can be characterized in negative terms, which are patronizing and infantalizing to older people, who are perfectly capable of managing without such modifications. The fact is that some people in some circumstances require and enjoy communication adjustments that meet their individual needs. In particular, they may find age-adjusted speech helpful because it indicates sensitivity to some of their social and communicative needs. It is worth reiterating that when a problem does occur with overaccommodation, it is when the communication adjustments do not coincide with the target person's subjective needs or desires. In particular, overaccommodation refers to a situation wherein the speech or communication adjustments overshoot those needs, as for example, when some needs (e. g., nurturance) are overemphasized at the expense of others (e.g., politeness). The problem centers around the objective labeling of a variety of speech and communication as patronizing, and the essential subjective aspects of overaccommodation are in danger of being discounted.

This issue is amply illustrated by Kemper, Anagnopoulos, Lyons, and Heberlein (1994), who demonstrated that what might be classified objectively as overaccommodative speech could, in some circumstances, be adaptive, helpful, and appropriate. Their study used picture-description tasks to investigate speech accommodation by spouses to their partners with Alzheimer's disease (AD). The task required spouses to verbally describe pictures that their partners could not see until the partners could select the correct picture from a set. Among other things, the results showed that spouses reduced their speech complexity and increased references to highly salient aspects of the pictures they were describing. These speech accommodations closely approximated the simplified register labeled as "elderspeak" and included other modifications designed to simplify speech—reductions of lexical density and lexical redundancy, and reductions in sentence length and complexity. Moreover, such accommodations facilitated AD adult's performance on the task, probably because the accommodations reduced cognitive processing load and were thus tailored to the listener's needs. Kemper et al. (1994) suggest that these accommodations may have resulted from the spouses' experiences of communicating with their AD partners.

SUMMARY

Together, this chapter and the previous one examine research into two major categories of intergenerational communication, characterized in communication accommodation theory terms as underaccommodation and overaccommodation. This chapter considers types of overaccommodation and their communicative correlates, both verbal and nonverbal but urges caution in the case of objective classification of communication as overaccommodative, patronizing, and so on.

Research with nursing staff in institutional contexts has firmly established the presence of overaccommodative communication from nurses to elderly people, and has suggested that this plays a role in discouraging independence and encouraging dependence. Together, overaccommodative and underaccommodative talk are activities that draw upon rules and resources, and which structure intergenerational relationships within and outside institutional contexts. Both nurses and residents grapple with issues of personal power and self-determination in a system, which by its very nature, undermines them.

Compared to research in institutional contexts, the presence, and most importantly, the frequency, of overaccommodative talk from young to elderly is far less well established in the community, especially in nonmedical contexts. Perhaps this is because the combination of old age, caring, and task demands are particularly important catalysts of overaccommodative communication in medical and caring settings.

Experimental research using various forms of patronizing vignettes allows us to make a number of generalizations. Whether the patronized target is young or old, independent judges typically view patronizing communication as less desirable than nonpatronizing forms, even when an older target might be characterized as confused. Judges also tend to view patronizers negatively. However, a number of studies indicate that older people, especially institutionalized elderly, may be more tolerant of patronizing speech, perhaps because they are more likely attribute it to caring thoughts. Although there are implications that older people may become accustomed to such speech and may be unaware of the social, psychological, and health consequences it has for them.

Other evidence suggests that older people may be harsher judges of those who are patronized, perhaps assuming that the very presence of such communication indicates that the person requires it. When it comes to responses to patronization, there may be some evaluative gains for those who are assertive, although assertion must be carefully managed so as not to seem rude and insensitive. Finally, research suggests that attributions may play an important role, because overaccommodation that is considered to be motivated by caring (e.g., caring thoughts) might be more easily forgiven than that which is motivated by control and domination. Research has thus far failed to examine the possibility that the relationship between the patronizer and patronizee may mitigate the negative evaluative force of such communication, as it may be far more appropriate and more forgiven when it occurs between intimates.

Respondents in experimental studies have also shown sensitivities to different substereotypes. In this case, older people appear to be more sensitive and able to appropriately adjust their communication to the target than are younger people. Although interestingly enough, Hummert's research suggests that middle-aged people produce the highest proportion of patronizing messages, which may point to their lifestage, because they could be sandwiched between the young and the elderly. Alternatively, an intergroup stance might suggest that such overaccommodations are a means by which middle-aged people positively differentiate themselves from an outgroup, the elderly, who may be far too close for comfort. Finally, we have pointed out that some forms of overaccommodation are extremely helpful, especially for those older people who are frail and are suffering from various forms of disease and ill-health.

7

Generational Identity and Age Identity

Chapters 5 and 6 outline forms of intergenerational talk, concentrating on under- and overaccommodation. Such talk, in some sense, structures intergenerational relationships and plays an important role in the negotiation and construction of various identities for older and younger people. It is important to realize that, in an intergenerational dyad, both parties are working with various rules and resources—for the most part the rules are shared, but interactant's resources may not be. Of course, in reality, the boundary between what constitutes a rule versus a resource is fuzzy. In many cases, rules can be used as resources for talk, and creatively so. This appropriation is particularly evident in the building of identities and alignment with various versions of the self and the other person.

Beginning with a life-span developmental perspective, the processes of age–identity presentation and performance in a variety of intergenerational contexts are the foci of this chapter. Several different theoretical approaches to identity are considered, as are different dimensions of identity: individual, relational, and social identity (as described in chapter 1). The final sections of the chapter consider generational identity and generational groups or cohorts and their social construction vis-à-vis other generational groups. Among the issues discussed in this chapter are questions such as: How do people defend against negative portrayals of age identity? What constitutes a distinct identity for a cohort and does this affect relationships with other generations? If so, how?

INDIVIDUAL IDENTITY AND LIFE CRISES

There are a number of different theoretical approaches to the self and to identity. One way of viewing identity is to consider it as a findable entity entirely located within individuals. The hard version of this would portray two individuals in interaction as two distinct selves engaged in information exchange. The tendency to represent people in this way has been connected to a Western emphasis on individualism (Geertz, 1979) and to functionalist social theory and research (Taylor, 1994). In his discussion of identity in terms of relationships, Wilmot (1995) refers to this approach as Paradigm I wherein individuals exist as "independent units loosely connected by the relational thread" (p. 37). This view of identity is predominant in the stage theories of development discussed in chapter 1 to which we now return to discuss life-span identity development.

Life-span developmental theory as discussed in chapter 1 provides an important perspective when we come to consider issues of identity. During the last 30 or 40 years, developmental psychologists have devised explanations for the interconnections between society, the developing self, and identity. Early developmentalists suggested that to achieve a healthy adulthood, each of us must complete a set of essential and linear transitions through life crises or developmental tasks. Developmental tasks (Havinghurst, 1956, 1972) or crises (Erickson, 1959) of identity are closely associated with life-span stages discussed in chapters 1 and 2: childhood, adolescence, middle age, and old age. Each stage is thought to involve a unique and essential transition or crisis, the resolution of which allows us to pass successfully to the next stage. According to this view, throughout the developmental phases of life we need to be able to incorporate changes into self-concepts while continuously adjusting to different demands, contexts, relationships, and so on.

For example, during adolescence it is considered vital that a teenager develop an awareness of self as a unique individual apart from his or her family, especially apart from parents. Separation and dependence are key themes (Baltes & Silverberg, 1994; Sugarman, 1986). Adolescents are somewhere between late childhood and early adulthood and are developing a sense of self and an autonomy apart from parents, while at the same time they are dependent, as we all are, on social network and family support (Baltes & Silverberg, 1994). Developing a sense of psychological well-being is considered crucial during these years, along with a feeling of knowing where one's future is leading (Erikson, 1959, 1980). The development of sexual identity is also highlighted as a task of the adolescent years. For Havinghurst (1956, 1972), the main task of adolescence is the development of a personal ideology.

Early adulthood involves tasks such as selecting a mate, starting a family and home, building a career, and finding a social group (Havinghurst, 1956, 1972). Erickson casts the identity tasks of early adulthood in terms of an intimacy versus isolation dynamic (Erikson, 1980). Similarly, Levinson,

Darrow, Klein, Levinson, and McKee (1978) characterize this phase as an exploration of the possibilities of adult identities, considering lifestyle choices and so forth. So, for example, within interactions, this becomes the projection and rehearsal of possible selves (Markus & Nurius, 1986).

During middle age, the essential struggle between *generativity* (a concern for younger generations), and *stagnation* (a state of inertia in personal growth) is the primary identity task in Ericksonian terms (Erikson, 1980). Those middle-aged persons who have achieved generativity are able to assist younger generations more toward full adulthood and to help teenagers to become happy and responsible. Well-adjusted middle-aged persons are able to reach personal life satisfaction, maintain a career, accept and adjust to the psychological changes of middle age (e.g., lost youth), relate to their spouses as people, and adjust to aging parents (Havinghurst, 1956, 1972). Much has been written about the alleged midlife crisis (see Sheehy, 1976, for a popular account of this) which is, in part, a derivative of Levinson et al.'s (1978) suggestion that the main task of midlife is to come to terms with one's own mortality. On the positive side, midlife is also a time when we are more confident and take our places as fully contributing members of society. Some developmentalists see this as the achievement of full independence and individualism.

Late life, according to Havinghurst (1956, 1972), includes the identity tasks of adjusting to decreasing physical strength, retirement, reduced income, death of spouse, affiliation with one's age group, adapting to social roles in flexible ways, and establishing satisfactory living arrangements. For Erikson (1980), this stage is portrayed as involving the need to come to terms with impending death and loss of self-identity and esteem. The struggle here is between ego integrity versus despair and disgust.

According to the developmental-stage view, one of the main goals of development through adulthood is to achieve an integrated self. In successful aging, old age becomes a somewhat idealized state of *ego integrity* in which the older person accepts self and the life as lived, and comes to terms with unresolved conflicts. Thus, in stereotypical terms, the ideal state to achieve is that of wise old sage—the ultimate pinnacle of human development. It has been proposed that one important way this psychological state can be achieved is through the process of life review (Butler, 1963). The life review is a particular type of reminiscence said to occur in late life, which is essentially an evaluative summary of one's passage through life through which ego integrity is achieved. Thus, again perhaps rather stereotypically, reminiscing and storytelling by older people have been linked to this developmental task.

Although the phase and stage theories of developmental identity tasks, which were popular in the 1950s and 1960s have much to offer us, in the context of the late 1990s they may seem socioculturally rigid, inherently sexist and agist, and out of step with the demands of social life in the latter part of this century. The life-span perspective in recognition of social change and in concert with modern views of flexible lifestyles, and family types would prefer to cast identity development in terms of development through life events and transitions (Danish, Smyer, & Nowak, 1980) rather than through inevitable phases and life crises. Life events and transitions must be negotiated throughout the life-span; some events may be closely linked to chronological age (e.g., leaving the parental home), but others can befall persons at any age (e.g., death of a significant other). Life-span developmentalists would suggest that we develop our identities transactionally (Bronfenbrenner, 1979) and that we can both produce and be produced by our environment. In other words, individuals can be active in the production of their own developments (Lerner & Busch-Rossnagel, 1981).

Personal identity is one of the major foci of stage-model developmentalists for whom each stage of development represents a transitional point for identity, and development does not occur unless the transition is made. Rather than conceptualizing persons as undergoing identity changes in ordered, sequential, and critical stages, the negotiation of self-identity across life contexts is a necessary component of a life stream that may not be ordered and linear, but is perhaps punctuated, cyclical, or even spiral (e.g., see Werner & Baxter, 1994; Wilmot, 1995). Consider the life review, earmarked as a special task for old age. Rather than being exclusive to late life, the life review is an activity of people of any age, and is probably related to particular transitory life events (see Harvey, Weber, & Orbuch, 1990, for an analysis of accounts at times of relational loss) or life changes that occur periodically throughout the life span. Theories that characterize life-review reminiscing as a special developmental task unique to old age may unwittingly serve to reinforce agist notions about who engages in reminiscing and why, and may cloud the theoretical development of the role of reminiscing in a host of social practices (Coleman, 1995; Middleton & Edwards, 1990).

Regardless of chronological age, human beings have a need for connectivity between a past, a present, and a future, accounting for one's life and rehearsing versions through intraindividual processes reflexively, as well as in interaction with others, may be a means of tracing the self in relation to personal past, present, and projected future, situated within various dynamic social contexts (Mead, 1932; Shotter & Gergen, 1989). It is important, therefore, to view people as active participants constructing and reconstructing themselves, and it is worth noting that the self can be reorganized and represented differently according to the perceived audience. This is well illustrated by research that has looked at various self-presentations (public and private) of well-known writers and artists, such as Bielby and Kully's (1989) comparison of the more public autobiography of Beatrice Webb with her more private diaries, and also the various presentations of self by Georgia O'Keefe (Rosenfeld, 1993).

Thus, an alternative approach to identity places emphasis on the interactional nature of the self; rather than identity being carried to an interaction, it becomes negotiable through interaction (see Goffman, 1959; Mead, 1932). In a similar fashion, Wilmot (1995) refers to Paradigm II research that views the self as "embedded within relationships" (p. 41). This is the predominant perspective of researchers and theorists who work within interpretist, critical, and postmodern frameworks (e.g., see Shotter & Gergen, 1989).

Relational theorists such as Wilmot (1995) point out that it is often useful to consider identity in relational terms, whereby less emphasis is placed on the self as a discrete unit and more on the self in relation to others. Wilmot illustrates this with the example of long-married couples who, if they are close, can finish sentences for each other. Thus, in long term, in close relationships, or both, seemingly separate identities can become fuzzy, such that the identity of one person can only adequately be defined in the context of the other (or others). The relational perspective reminds us that the self develops over time, in and through a variety of relational contexts, and that a unique, individual self apart from others, particularly those in our social network, is often an illusion. This has implications for relational-intergenerational communication as is discussed further in chapters 8, 9, and 10.

Recently, Giddens (1991) convincingly argued that self-identity is a fundamental existential problem in modern Western societies. From his perspective, identity is not a given distinct trait, but has to be routinely created and sustained in the reflexive activities of the individual. In other words, people draw on rules and resources to create who they are in interaction, but also reflexively (e.g., when reflecting back on interactions). According to Giddens, predictable social roles (e.g., wife, mother), which were often based on the relationships between familial generations, are no longer valid in modern life (termed *high-modernity*). One of the major features of high modernity, according to Giddens, is advances in media and technology. Even the relationships between space and time have been redefined by advancements such as television and satellite broadcasting, jet travel, the Internet, and so forth. Such conditions stand in opposition to traditional society wherein social roles were more certain, known, and predictable, and stage models of identity development may have been more appropriate. In this way, conditions of modernity demand that personal identity be more fluid, uncertain, and complex than in premass-mediated life. We must, therefore, be more adaptable and flexible in order to fit into the fast ebb and flow of high-modernity; we must be able and ready to define and then redefine ourselves and our social roles as required. As a result, our identities are constantly updated in the stream of lived experience. According to Giddens, the self is a reflexive project constantly in a state of renegotiation and readjustment. In Giddens' own words, identity is "the self as reflexively understood by the person in terms of his or her biography" (p. 53).

Variable Identity Negotiated During Intergenerational Talk

The notion that identity may be highly negotiable and potentially variable across different contexts, rather than fixed and intransient, is not necessarily new (i.e., see Goffman, 1959; Mead, 1932). The traditional psychological debate between situational and personality determinants of behavior, and whether or not or how much people behave consistently across various contexts, is related to this issue. More recently, researchers interested in conversation and interaction have emphasized the importance of constructed selves and have turned attention away from debates about personality versus context, and toward individuals as more active in constructing their own identities across different contexts. The assumption of this approach is that individuals actively create, negotiate, and manage their selves through interaction with the social world. Then identity is expressed, attributed, and negotiated through communicative processes, in conversation and in interindividual interactions, as well as in the media.

Of course, as chapter 1 detailed, people work with personal and social identities. In an aging context, a person's social identity as a member of an age group, his or her generational alignments, and so forth are salient. In line with Giddens' approach to identity, Coupland, Coupland, and Nussbaum (1993) have appealed for more research attention to discursive formulations of the life span, particularly of age–self presentation and generational alignments. These writers point out that although Giddens provides us with an intuitively appealing approach to identity as a discursive activity, the details of how this is achieved in everyday social contexts is left for others to explore.

A discourse analytic study by Coupland, Coupland, and Grainger (1991) provides a compelling example of how identities can be viewed as variable repertoires. They report a case study of one particular older individual across two conversational contexts, one of which was peer elderly and one intergenerational. In the peer conversation, May, a 79-year-old woman, was paired with 82-year-old Nora. In the intergenerational conversation, May was paired with a 39-year-old woman, Jenny. Detailed, comparative-discourse analysis of the conversations revealed that in the peer elderly conversation, May appeared as rather vibrant, coping, and socially active. Her partner, Nora, in comparison, seemed far less so. However, when May was placed in conversation with the younger woman, Jenny, the conversation centered around more negative themes stereotypical of aging: immobility, institutionalization, economic hardship, illness, and so forth. In part, this more negative and vulnerable identity was triggered by Jenny's questions, which seem to elicit these themes from May, although May must, of course, have colluded with this. Presumably these variable identities are a function of the social-comparative processes at work in the two interactions. In the first, May perhaps saw herself as doing rather well comparatively, whereas in the second, she saw herself as doing less well comparatively. The discourse between herself and her partners both reflects and constructs these alternate self-perceptions (see also Coupland, Coupland, & Giles, 1991).

This finding led Giles and colleagues (e.g., Giles, Fox, Harwood, & Williams, 1994) to suggest that, given a certain set of cues, older people can be induced to act, think, and feel older than they are, a situation which was termed *instant aging* (Mulac & Giles, 1996). This suggests that interlocutors can discursively offer each other identities that they can each choose to attune to, to enact, to creatively appropriate, or to resist. An additional example of this can be drawn from Taylor (1992), who examined the associations between elder frailty and identity evident in the relationships between homeowners and their younger live-in caregivers. According to Taylor (1992, 1994), friends and caregivers, as well as the older people themselves, co-constructed frail identities for the older person. From a discourse-analytical and critical perspective, Taylor (1994) suggests that such identities were constructed "in order to account for problematic events, to orient conversationalists toward the older adult's impending death, to define—and thus to indirectly control—the older adult, and to locate the existing self in relation to the past and establish its moral meaning" (p. 195).

The presentation and enactment of variable identity is not exclusively the domain of the old. For example, young people may offer "sanitized" versions of themselves for the approval of older people during intergenerational talk. Chapter 5 described younger peoples' retrospective accounts of intergenerational conversations in which one of the most frequently mentioned satisfying aspects of these conversations was social support from older people. It could be suggested that much of this support was gained because the younger people portrayed themselves as diligent college students thinking about their future careers, while at the same time censoring accounts that might meet with disapproval (e.g., accounts that might invoke negative stereotypes of youth such as late-night drinking, rock and roll, and sex). When young people admit that authenticity is sometimes an issue for them during intergenerational talk, it is perhaps because they feel that they have pushed the censored version of self too far in their attempts to accommodate and thereby validate the version of youth that they imagine their older interlocutor prefers to hear (see also Coupland, Coupland, & Giles, 1991).

This strategic use of rules and resources is probably one of the ways through which positive stereotypical images of "nice and clean cut" young people emerge during intergenerational talk, and younger people collude by acting in terms of positive stereotypes. Little is known about the realization of youth identity through intergenerational communication. Anecdotally, exaggerated versions of youth are sometimes produced to win elder approval as, for example, the one young respondent who reported that, when talking to an older woman, she actually acted younger than she really was (Williams, 1992). It is probable that such self-presentations, while being inauthentic in some ways, are extremely validating in others. In such instances the young person gains considerable validation from his or her older partner for being a member of a socially advantaged age group, and his or her social identity is reinforced.

Youth identity emergent during intergenerational talk is yet to be extensively studied, but there is some research examining the discourse of elderly identity and the ways in which people can self-identify or categorize themselves as old.

Age Categorization

In their studies of intergenerational discourse between strangers (described in chapter 5), Coupland, Coupland, Giles, and Henwood (1988) examined a range of processes and strategies through which elderly identity can be realized during intergenerational talk. In other words, these are processes by which older people come to be identified as old through intergenerational talk. One observation was that the elderly women in the sample more frequently disclosed their chronological ages than the younger women did, and by doing so, they identified themselves in terms of the number of years lived. In fact, 75% of the older people in these conversations spontaneously divulged their ages in years (see Coupland, Coupland, & Giles, 1989), and virtually all older persons in the sample disclosed their ages in some form or other. Most young people responded to the disclosure of elderly age with an intergenerational conversational routine, for example, "Why, 87, good heavens, you don't look 87!" This was often linked to a statement such as, "I hope I look like you when I'm 87," and in almost every case with evaluative exclamations such as, "Marvelous!" In other words, the young person responded in accordance with the unacknowledged rule: to reach 87 without strikingly visible decrepitude is relatively unusual and remarkable and deserves congratulations.

Indeed, there are many ways by which older people reveal their ages without mentioning chronological years, which were also investigated by Coupland et al. (1989). One such age-identifying process was labeled *age-related category* or *role reference*. In this case, speakers located themselves or their conversational partners within specific age groups or generations. In this discourse, speakers engage in the process of self- and other-categorization as in the following example in which an older woman categorizes herself as a pensioner: "I think us pensioners are very lucky really" (Coupland, Coupland, & Giles, 1991, p. 60), and another who distances herself from an undesirable subgroup, geriatrics: "Some of the people at the day center are quite confused ... they're really geriatrics" (p. 60). For the most part, role references in these data were to valued social roles that invoke some of the positive stereotypes (discussed in chapter 3)—those of being grandmothers and great grandmothers. This kind of self- and other-categorizing talk opens the door to other intergroup processes and other forms of talk that serve to create distance between speakers.

Rather typically, in Coupland et al.'s data, chronological age was often produced as an account for ill health or frailty. This process, which is a form of self-handicapping, has been fairly frequently observed in studies of elderly discourse (see chapter 5). Coupland et al. categorized this as *age identity in relation to health, decrement, and death*. This is potentially quite problematic for older people because it is a self-stereotype, and as such can lead to certain self-fulfilling prophesies. Frequent association of ill-health, frailty, and decline with chronological age draws on the socially prevailing negative stereotypes of older people (as discussed in chapter 3, this volume), and at once reinforces them as legitimate and veridical. The following quotes from Coupland et al. exemplify this category: "What was I going to say (.) oh god now it shows my age" and " I'm I'm not very well these days too (,) I'm 70 last Octo(ber) ... so I find I can't do it so good" (p. 61). In these cases, the speakers draw on notions of age associated decreptitude, memory loss, and ill health to conduct a conversation, and by doing so they align themselves with negative social identities.

Talk that locates someone in a historical period of time with a considerable past was categorized as *temporal framing processes* and was comprised of three subcategories. First, in some cases, age was marked when people add time-past perspectives to current or recent-past states or topics. Quite simply, this was the discursive act of locating oneself in a stream of personal history. For example, one woman in Coupland et al.'s (1991) study said, "I retired in 1974 I'd been nursing for 46 years. ... Came down to Cardiff in 1952 ... and I was at the CRI (hospital) until I retired. ... my mother died when she was 45 in 1933." (p. 63).

One of the key features of the second subcategory—*self association with the past*—was the sense of disassociation of the elderly speaker with the present, and also with her younger partner, who was located in the present. This kind of talk is communicatively divergent; it emphasises that speakers belong to different social groups and serves to distance the speaker from the partner. An example of this is noted by Thimm and Kruse (1996), in which an older woman drew attention to the age and lived-history difference between herself and her partner by commenting, "well, you wouldn't know." Alternatively, Boden and Bielby's (1983) data show how this can be a highly accommodative and thus convergent device used to bring peer elderly speakers closer together by invoking the past to create topics of shared experiences; thus a decrease in distance occurs and the ingroupness of the speakers is emphasized.

The third subcategory was *recognizing historical, cultural or social change.* In these instances, older and younger speakers sometimes made age salient by their focus and comment on social and historical changes. In this way, the older person came to represent a previous historical period while the interactional partners made comparisons and commented on the differences between then and now. Topics such as the war, rationing, and pensions were prevalent in this talk. For example, one young person asked, "Your generation were speaking Welsh weren't they?" and another older woman commented, "but times are so different aren't they?" (see Coupland, Coupland, & Giles, 1991, p. 65). Again then, distance is created by pointing to the divergent experiences of generations, a theme picked up later. Remember that accounts of identity such as those discussed are embedded and formulated in a social climate that emphasizes the negativity of advancing age and of growing old—an agist climate. The next section addresses the ways in which people may orient to such a climate as it impacts the aging self.

Protecting Threatened Identities

Many older people appear to accept the agism inherent in our society, and this is inscribed into the passive responses to patronization in many vignette studies (described in chapter 6), as well as to being an implicit component of diagrammatic and theoretical attempts to model such processes (e.g., see Harwood, Giles, Ryan, Fox, & Williams, 1993; and models described in chapter 1, this volume). Of course, we must recognize that there are a variety of ways of coping with agism, all of which have far wider implications than the often-localized context of their enactment suggests. These issues and their interpretations in terms of social identity and intergroup theory are discussed in the epilogue.

As we enter adulthood we begin to encounter and traverse a number of threats to a positive view of self that are explicitly connected with chronological time counts. Hepworth (1995) has written extensively about the images of aging with which we are bombarded daily. As discussed in previous chapters, such images are predominantly negative, and as such, challenge a positive view of ourselves as we age. Consider, for example, the identity implications of a range of issues discussed in the preceding chapters. What are the identity implications for elders who live in and through social stereotypes, and who are routinely tolerated, patronized, avoided, and so forth? If old age is viewed negatively by our society, and societal agism is an epidemic (as argued by Butler, 1989), we must ask the question: Can older people maintain positive self-esteem in the face of threats to a positive image of the aging self, and if so how do they achieve this?

The maintenance of elders' individual self-esteem in climates that challenge a positive view of the aging self is an issue that has not frequently been considered in research (i.e., see Coleman, 1995). Now-classic research by Rodin, Langer, and colleagues (e.g., see Rodin & Langer, 1980) demonstrated how institutionally induced dependency can lead to negative psychological, social, and physical decline. Chiefly, it is thought that low self-esteem is related to negative perceptions enacted through age-adapted speech, which become integrated into older people's concepts of self- and age-identity (Kuypers & Bengston, 1973). Thus, the link between negative self-esteem and patronization has been theorized such that negative images, stereotyping, interactional patronization, and the like are thought to be related to low self-esteem, psychological and physical ill health, and so forth, according to current models of intergenerational communication (e.g., see Ryan et al., 1986, chapter 1).

However, as Pratt and Norris (1994) suggest, various strategies, such as attributional devices, can be used to protect the self, and this aspect, the protection of self-esteem, has rarely been considered in intergenerational-communication research. Chapter 5 discusses how elder underaccommodation may come about as a response to threatened elderly identities. The next section enlarges this discussion by proposing a variety of strategies that might protect threatened personal and social identity, and it discusses the ways that such strategies may themselves contribute to wider social discourses of agism (see Coupland & Coupland, 1993).

If overaccommodative talk poses a potential threat to older people's identities, we might gain some insight into identity-protection processes if we investigate how older people cope with patronization. In this respect, a pilot study by Ryan, Giles, Harwood, and Williams (1993) interviewed 20 healthy, active, community-dwelling, older adults in California about the forms of, and their responses to, patronizing talk directed at them. Four people in the sample claimed that they were not patronized, with comments such as, "Problems do not happen to me, I make sure I am capable," or that if they were patronized or talked down to they did not notice, commenting, "I don't pay much attention" and "I may be missing something." Interviewees did readily agree that other older people were patronized, especially those who were visibly frail (see also Giles, Fox, & Smith, 1993). Because the sample was active, healthy, and vital, perhaps they were less susceptible to this type of talk. However, the interview topic was in some senses quite face-threatening because older people were being asked to acknowledge that they were members of a stigmatized social group who are talked down to, treated as incompetent, and so forth. In fact, it is the self-presentational, face-management and identity-protection processes that are the most interesting aspects of the interviews. In this regard, eight people claimed that they had experienced patronization, and all but one of these related instances of problematic talk with their adult children. Six other people said that they were not patronized or talked down to, but continued to describe other instances of problematic talk with young people attributing it to lack of communication and to being the younger peoples' problem.

These data are not necessarily indicative of whether or not people are patronized, or even whether or not they are aware of it, but they do indicate that people may have a range of responses to the potential face threats of being asked about such talk. Possibly, some reactions to the interview questions could be related to a phenomenon known as the *denial of personal disadvantage* (defined as perceiving discrimination at the societal level but denying its occurrence at the personal level), and this is done in order to preserve personal self-esteem (Crosby, Cordova, & Jaskar, 1994). Naturally, it is tempting to see parallels between discursive denial in which one is treated in an agist fashion, and early studies of children's denial of racial-group membership, which was interpreted as indicating an awareness of membership in a stigmatized and thus undesirable group (Milner, 1975). Relatedly, a number of writers have commented about the behavioral denial of aging, such as when older people attempt to fend off age by trying to maintain or recreate youthful appearances. Surgery is one of the extremes of such strategies (Sontag, 1978). This theme, and its intergroup and social-identity implications, are elaborated in the epilogue chapter.

Related to denial strategies, rigorous and explicit distancing from negatively viewed subgroups is another method of enhancing self-esteem and protecting oneself from the face-threatening aspects of a negative social identity. In this case, an older person may categorize himself or herself as a member of a more positive subgroup as compared to other older people or to frail older people (see also Coupland, Coupland, & Giles, 1991). Coupland et al., identify this as *the discourse of self-exception.* This is achieved by discursively creating subgroups of "incompetent old people" (see also Ryan et al., 1986), with whom the speaking individual does not belong. (It should be noted that in data concerned with Generation X, to be discussed later, we find that when a negative image of youth is salient, young people readily do the same; Williams, Coupland, Folwell, & Sparks, 1997.) In accounts about intergenerational talk, young people actually endorse this strategy in a wider social discourse, which might be labeled the *discourse of other exception.* A similar process was noted in chapter 5 in which young people comment that older partners in some satisfying intergenerational encounters are those who are "unlike other old people." In this sense then, there is consensus that being like a category that can be labeled "old people" is undesirable, and the discourses of both younger and older people sustain this. It is partly due to this tendency that negative stereotypes of a social category are so resistant to change (see Hewstone, 1989a).

A third method of protecting self-esteem may be a form of self-stereotyping through which older people attempt to recategorize themselves positively in terms of widely accepted positive images of old age. An example of this may be found in the intergenerational interaction data of Coupland, Coupland, and Giles (1991) mentioned previously. Although positive and negative stereotypes of elders are in play in these conversations, it could be suggested that older people attempt to resist negative stereotypes by casting themselves in positive terms, for example, as grandparents. Hepworth (1995) provides convincing evidence as to why this might be the case. His analysis of images of aging as reflected by our cultural artifacts shows how the aging body is predominantly portrayed in art and literature as "decaying." Furthermore, there are undertones that decrepit bodies are immoral and are unsuccessfully aging, while candy-coated images of elders modeled as grandparental figures or statespersons can be seen as moral and successfully aging. He provides a compelling example from the book *Imaging American Women* (Banta, 1987) showing how the late 19th-century portrait by Sarah J. Eddy of the political activist Susan B. Anthony (entitled *Susan B. Anthony on the Occasion of Her 80th Birthday*) can be interpreted as reconstructing her image "in the tradition of the saintly grandmother rather than the feisty political activist" (p. 13).

Another positive image of self that older people might attempt to appropriate is the notion of *self as a survivor*—when the self is cast as a hero of his or her own story, which may include accounts of personal triumph or perseverance in the face of the trials and tribulations of a personal past (e.g., painful self-disclosures). In most instances, older people gain support from young people when aligning with such positive images of self (see also Coupland, Coupland, & Giles, 1991).

A fourth strategy of self-esteem defense may be related to what Hepworth (1995) refers to as the "mask" of aging, which describes the psychological separation of the self from the aging body. We would suggest that *the separation of young self and aging self* may also emerge discursively as a strategy to ward off identity threats associated with being seen to be old. Hepworth argues that older people, aware of the negativity of becoming and being old, experience an internal separation of self. Thus, it is not uncommon for older people to remark that they do not "feel" old. Despite advancing age, ill health, or other markers of the passage of time, they feel the same as they always have. This *same self*, the continuous and essential self, is actually an eternally young self, in other words, older people align themselves with a more positive image of self—their youth and youthful bodies. According to Hepworth, this leads to the fragmentation of the old and essential self, and interestingly enough, a distancing from a less desirable self.

In some instances, older people may gain self-serving advantages from self-stereotyping and self-presenting as old. We might call this *the strategic use of old self-identity.* For example, Coupland and Coupland's (1993) study of medical discourse revealed that some elderly patients appropriated agist and stereotypical images to resist health-related behavioral changes (such as giving up smoking). Although this appears to serve individuals' localized conversational (and particularly their behavioral and lifestyle) motivations, reliance on such notions is at the same time self-disenfranchising (Coupland & Coupland, 1993). Thus, observational research has documented older people not only accommodating or accepting agism, but also serving as unwitting coconspirators in its realization. Health professionals, caregivers, and others concerned with the welfare of the elderly may also attempt to refute agism by engaging discourses of antiagism (increasingly they are encouraged to do so by training regimens), but do so in the face of a minefield of threats to their own as well as elderly persons' face concerns (Coupland & Coupland, 1993). It is this minefield of contradictory concerns that Coupland and Coupland suggest often leads doctors to "acquiesce to ageist remarks or offer bland noncommittal responses" (p. 293), although some are prepared to challenge agism and to attempt to manage the conflict that it engenders. Sometimes even attempts to tackle agist talk backfire because stereotypes, even when produced in order to refute agism are reified by their production (see Henwood, Giles, Coupland, & Coupland, 1993).

We can envision even more confrontational and reactionary strategies that older people could use to defend their identities (Hepworth, 1995; Williams & Giles, 1998). One more confrontational strategy that has been studied directly is use of assertive responses when being patronized. Evaluations of these have been modeled in experimental studies as we discussed in previous chapters. Doubtless there are others. For example, one elderly informant described how she coped with what she felt to be inappropriate use of her first name by a family doctor by pointedly using his first name (see Ryan et al., 1993). This suggests that some form of matching or mirroring may be used to signal dissatisfaction. Undoubtedly there are a variety of other strategies for resisting agist talk and negative social identities that deserve more systematic investigation.

Confrontation can go further than this. Rather than being ashamed of aging or of being acquiescent, older people could appropriate agist images and use them in confrontational ways. This would be similar to strategies used by other stigmatized groups such as African Americans and gay people, encapsulated by phrases such as "Black Power," "Act up," and "Gay

Pride." Although this is a possible strategy for politically active elders, at this point in time there seems to be very little of this kind of reactionary behavior among older people. The recitation of the slogan "Growing old disgracefully" is gathering momentum (in the United Kingdom at least), and organizations like the AARP (American Association for Retired Persons) and Age Concern are actively campaigning for more public awareness of agism. A few years ago, the bumper sticker "Spending our children's inheritance" was popular with some retired people in the United States. The use of such catch phrases and slogans indicates that older people are beginning to resist social norms that dictate that those who are beyond retirement should gracefully submit to becoming benign, selfless, and dignified grandparental figures.

This chapter discusses theories about how individual and social identities may develop as a life-span process through various stages of development, and suggests that such processes may be better conceptualized in terms of various life-span turning points, rather than in stages. The ways in which people may discursively produce, reproduce, and at times, rework various aspects of their identities to take particular interactional stances vis-à-vis comparative others is described. Finally, some of the means by which people might defend against negative identities was considered. As we mentioned previously, many theorists would argue that identity is a purely social construction achieved across the life span through interaction with others, and that it cannot be measured outside a discursive context. However, other theorists would feel perfectly comfortable with the notion of personal and social identity as fixed entities that can be measured out of context. Perhaps the two extreme views can be balanced if we characterize identities as repertoires, or resources that people can call upon for various purposes, when in interaction. In this sense, identity is less fixed and more fluid and can be constantly updated as Giddens (1991) suggested, but can be measured in an objective way too, given that this measuring would be outside the constraints and enablements of particular interactional contexts.

For example, it could be suggested that some older and younger people have a fairly strong awareness of self as a group member, a strong age-associated social identity. Recent research has started to measure people's sense of age identity. For example, Garstka, Branscombe, and Hummert (1996) measured perceptions of age-group identity, self-esteem, life satisfaction, and status of young, middle-aged, and older adults. Out of the three age groupings, older adults had the strongest age-group identification compared to middle-aged and younger adults. Regardless of age, strong age-group identifiers tended to have higher self- and collective esteem, life satisfaction, and positive affect.

In another study Garstka, Branscombe, and Hummert (1997) asked young adults to generate advantages and disadvantages associated with both their age-group memberships and then comparatively with middle-aged and older adults. Young people's focus on the advantages of being young was associated with stronger young-age-group identities when they compared selves with middle-aged adults, and the reverse was found when young people focused on the disadvantages of being young. Garstka et al. argue that middle-aged people are perceived to command higher status, and therefore, when the young think about their relative advantages compared to this group, they enhance esteem and thus strengthen age-group identity. However, when thinking of their disadvantages relative to middle-aged adults they suffer a relative loss of esteem and thus comparative identity. There were no such differential associations when younger adults compared themselves with older adults, as comparatively, younger adults see themselves as advantaged.

Harwood and Williams (1998) used Garstka et al.'s age-identity scale and found that younger college students who identified highly with their age group expected to experience lower levels of apprehension, more attunement, and more compassion from anticipated conversations with older adults than those young people who indicated lower levels of age identity. Harwood and Williams (1998) suggest that by placing older adults in a relatively powerless position by claiming ability to take care of them, younger adults adopt a relatively powerful position for themselves. Thus younger (and middle-aged) individuals who feel more strongly about their comparative youngness are also more likely to help older adults. Putting this into an intergenerational caring context suggests that caregivers may gain self-esteem, not just as individuals who care, but as belonging to a comparatively "better-off" age group. There are perhaps social identity gains for caregivers who positively differentiate themselves from older adults in this way. As a result, younger (and middle-aged) people may seek to care and help even those who do not need such care. This could help explain why, as Baltes and Wahl (1996) have shown, older adults in nursing homes are often reinforced for dependent behavior and are not reinforced for independent behavior. There is no net self-esteem gain for a caregiver, who by encouraging an older adult to be independent, finds his or her caring to be redundant (see chapter 6, this volume, for more discussion of caring contexts).

Age identity as we have begun to discuss it, may be comprised of several components. For example, age identity might refer to a person's sense of self as a young person who is stereotypically healthy, vital, and fit, but age identity also encapsulates other aspects of identity, which might be labeled *generational identity*. This refers to people in terms of their particular cohorts and captures what it is to be a person who developed through a particular historical period.

GENERATIONAL IDENTIFICATION

The notion of a cohort is very important for understanding, in developmental terms, the vastly different experiences of different age collectivities living through distinct historical periods. In studies of human development, a cohort is most commonly defined by a 10-year age band, but the perceptual boundaries are more fuzzy than this (see Harwood, Giles, & Ryan, 1995; Williams, Coupland, Folwell, & Sparks, 1997). There is little doubt that common experiences can unite a cohort, particularly in relation to decisive and major historical events, such as the World Wars, the Depression, the Vietnam War, and so forth. It has been argued that such factors can and do transform an age cohort into a generation (Mannheim, 1952, 1972). However, historical events and social conditions would not be expected to affect all members of a generation in the same way, and we must be mindful that generations are made up of subgroups who may hold contrasting and conflicting values (Mannheim, 1952, 1972). For example, the generational experience of wealthy college-educated youth is almost certainly quite different from that of more disadvantaged, poorer youth who do not have college educations (Berger, 1971). Some commentators doubt that a generation would be significantly aware of themselves as a distinct and internally coherent social collectivity (Berger, 1971). For example, political analysts such as Bennett and Rademacher (1994) cite evidence from recent national election studies that suggests that the current generation of young people (in their terms, "Postboomers") do identify with their cohort, but that they do not necessarily identify most closely with young people (see Garstka et al., 1996).

Therefore, young people's identification through various modern media (e.g., certain generationally salient television shows, Internet, and virtual reality) versus their parent's ("Baby Boomers") identification with reference to the Vietnam War (in the United States), and grandparents' identity with reference to the Depression and World Wars I and II are examples of generational identities. Such common experiences may be used to reduce interpersonal distance (converge or attune) in talk between same-age group members as well as to increase distance (diverge or counterattune) between different-age group members (see Boden & Bielby, 1983; Thimm & Kruse, 1996) as was already discussed. It is important to understand that identities defined by such events may also be ascribed to a generational group from the outside, particularly the media, as much or even more than identities are self-ascribed. This, in itself, is an important social phenomenon worthy of study. Although in some senses, the media, particularly advertisers, may have invented current generations, as indicated by the labels "Generation X," "Baby Boomers," and "Greedy Geezers," for their own purposes we could expect such constructions to have various intended and unintended social consequences.

With such issues in mind, Williams, Coupland, Folwell, and Sparks (1997) initiated focus-group research that aimed to explore the ways in which young people discursively oriented themselves to a newsmedia clip about Generation X. Of interest was the way that young college students talked about their generational identity in the context of media portrayals that contained many negative characterizations of the generation (see chapter 3). In many ways, the young people in this study talked about the media as an outgroup, the Baby Boomers, who were negatively stereotyping young people in order to make positive intergroup comparisons and bolster their own social identities. The analysis showed that young people both appropriated and refuted media images in an effort to coconstruct their individual and collective identities, and that this was done vis-à-vis other generational groups such as the Baby Boomers. Generational identity was not accepted as a given, but was constantly reviewed in discussions. The discussants struggled with categorizing who belonged to Generation X, rejecting the implied homogeneity of the label. This is entirely as would be predicted by social identity theory because group members have a tendency to homogenize outgroups, but to see ingroup members as heterogeneic, emphasizing the diversity of the ingroup and defying categorization (i.e., "they are all the same but we are all different").

In this study, young people produced contradictory versions of whether they belonged to the generational category, rejecting media reports as negative stereotyping, which, they claimed, reflected the vested interests of older generations. This was a situation, which when described in these terms had an intergroup competitive flavor. In a similar fashion to that which we described in our discussion of older people's identity-protection strategies, young participants engaged discourses of self- and other-exception to counteract negative images of youth. At the same time, these young people talked freely about the attributes of their generation, a discourse that was age-identifying because it firmly located them as cohorts in a historical time period. According to these young people, salient themes for the generation were: shared concerns about the economy and job market, worry about divorce and family schism, monogamy and family values, the positive aspects of generational diversity, and the collective experience of media and technology. Interestingly enough, young participants reproduced popular media discourses as concerns for their generation.

Importantly, this research exemplifies how the introduction of social categories can trigger intergroup processes in an age-group context, as discussed in chapter 1. In spite of the finding that discussants' self-categorization about belonging to the generation was itself at issue, they readily oriented to this categorization, as social identity theory would predict. Accordingly, they differentiated themselves from relevant outgroups—both those older and those younger than they. Furthermore, as predicted by social identity theory, this differentiation led to denigrating those who would be considered outgroups; for example, older generations were humorously ridiculed and younger generations were criticized.

SUMMARY

This chapter has discussed identity as an important aspect of both life span and intergenerational communication. Theorists in the latter part of this century rejected earlier notions of identity development as fixed life stages or as phases, in favor of notions of identity as negotiated throughout the life span in a series of communication contexts: intrapersonal, interindividual, intergroup, and through the media. This chapter, perhaps more than any other, demonstrates the way that people work with rules and resources in communication with others. Discursive action draws upon the social fabric to fashion identities for the self and for others, which are used creatively as well as strategically to achieve interpersonal goals such as positive self-presentation, resisting negative categorization, or other goals beyond the immediate situation. These activities recreate and verify understandings about age in our society. It is not that agism is a prejudice imposed by one person or one group on another, although it can be, but this chapter demonstrates that agism is continually and inadvertently reproduced by older and younger persons working together.

Intergroup alignments, self- and other categorizations, and social comparisons are repertoires that can be used as social resources for conversation. People often use such resources strategically, often for local gains, without realizing the wider social consequences of such action. Short-term gains can often result in long-term losses for self as well as for one's social group. An example of this was provided in the discussion of older patients who attempt to use age as an excuse for not changing unhealthy lifestyles. When doctors draw attention to the inherent agism in this discourse, they begin to open up the fault lines along which Giddens (1984) suggests change may occur. On the other hand, doctors and others who choose not to draw attention to the contradictions are perhaps inadvertently colluding to keep the system in play.

Given that self-esteem and identity are interwoven, and that a positive self-esteem is essential for well-being, it is interesting to speculate about how older people achieve a positive view of self during intergenerational talk. Age is often salient in such talk, with old age being marked as divergent from the norm. This means that older people seem to need to account for old age in various ways, and to do so in the face of some rather negative social identities that these contexts might afford them (i.e., membership of a social group that is stigmatized in many respects).

Moving to conceptualizations of age identity in generational terms, emerging research about generational alignment and age-group identification suggests that people can and do identify with a particular age group or cohort, but that this too can be contextually variable, ambivalent, and negotiable. Interestingly enough, people seem to spontaneously orientate themselves to intergroup stances when age categorization and age identity are salient.

Although we are only beginning to appreciate the complexity of the matter, it is important to investigate and theorize about how people develop and transform their individual and social identities across the life span from young adulthood, to middle age, to elderliness. It is also important to investigate how age identities are constructed and resisted by the way others communicate both with and about people of different ages.

Developmental adaptation and positive personal and social identities are likely to be achieved through mutual participation in alternate social, intergroup, and interpersonal discourses that afford positive images to all age categories. It is not as simple as this, however. As a society we have a very narrow range of views about the possibilities for age identity. We try to shoehorn people into narrow bands of predictable behavior. These bands do include positive roles and identities for younger and older people alike, but they are restrictive roles and we need to be aware of the alternatives that modernity has brought to us all. We need to afford people more than just the positivity of being, for example, a typical grandmother. We need to afford people the choice and diversity of a range of possible identities.

PART II

INTERGENERATIONAL RELATIONSHIP COMMUNICATION

Chapters 1 through 6 progress from contact issues to stereotyping and agism, and trace how these issues are interlinked with and through language. In chapters 5 and 6, communication accommodation theory takes center stage while intergenerational-accommodation issues are discussed (particularly, over- and underaccommodation). Chapter 7 concentrates on language, communication, and age identity. Much of the research discussed in these chapters implicitly assumes that the interactants are either strangers, passing acquaintances, or are in professional, health-care relationships.

Clearly, intergenerational communication does not transpire within a relational vacuum. As was mentioned in the introductory chapter, we are very much aware that the great majority of intergenerational contact takes place within a well-developed, often very close, family relationship. The next four chapters of this book describe several intimate relationships within which a great deal of our intergenerational communication takes place. Each of these relationships, and many other familial as well as nonfamilial relationships, are long-term life-span relationships. It is helpful to keep in mind that these relationships are characterized by the multidirectional nature of their development, by simultaneous gains and losses in affect and power, by the great diversity of interindividual and intraindividual behavior exhibited within and between relationships, and by the significant environmental influences that frame each relationship.

It is important to keep in mind that, because of the theoretical and academic-discipline priorities of researchers interested in intergenerational relationships, these chapters move us away from a central focus on interactional theories such as CAT and the intergenerational-communication models (e.g., the stereotype activation model, the communication predicament model) discussed in chapters 1 through 7. This does not mean that such theories are redundant when we come to consider intergenerational relationships. On the contrary, we argue that such theoretical notions have important contributions to make to understanding intergenerational communication in relationships, especially long-term lifespan relationships. Researchers simply have not yet explored such contributions. Where appropriate, we endeavor to point out where the theoretical links may be made, although we cannot provide an exhaustive account of such connections.

Readers will no doubt find that the next four chapters operate at a different level of analysis than the previous chapters. Rather than focusing on social interaction and communication, many relational studies focus at the level of the individual self-report, the family, the community, and/or institutions as investigated by sociologists. Our approach, therefore, also contains within it a plea for more social-interactional research situated within enduring relational contexts. It is imperative for social-interactional studies that are not merely snapshot events (i.e., one conversation in one context at one particular moment in time), but are more longitudinal in nature, following individuals and groups through time and across multiple contexts. Studies such as this could reveal crucial communication patterns across time, and could prioritize intergenerational communication as constitutive of the relationship rather than vice versa.

The adult child–elderly parent relationship, the grandparent–grandchild relationship, the middle generation sandwiched (in between parents and children) relationship, and several nonfamilial relationships such as the physician–older patient relationship are discussed in some depth in Part II of this book. To fully understand intergenerational communication, one must come to an understanding of the relational contexts within which much of that communication occurs. Numerous other relationships could be added to this list, but these particular relationships represent some of the more central familial and nonfamilial relationships into which we enter throughout our lives. In addition, the relationships discussed in the next four chapters are defined by their essential intergenerational nature.

8

Adult Child–Elderly Parent Relationship

The popular media and the voices of numerous politicians agree strongly that the family is an institution almost beyond repair. According to these voices, marriages are collapsing under the weight of irresponsibility, children are being left on the streets for the state to raise, grandparents are shipped off to nursing homes to be cared for by underpaid illiterates, and middle aged adults have all but abandoned any sense of family values. Although this belief may cause great consternation in all of our minds and may serve to elect those politicians who blame others for the downfall of the family, there is ample evidence to suggest that the family as an institution is as strong as ever and continues to serve our civilization quite well.

This chapter describes the enduring relationship we as children maintain with our parents. The adult child–elderly parent relationship is a perfect starting point from which to discuss the impact of relationships on intergenerational communication. Although it is true that young children interact quite frequently with their young parents, and that the resulting interaction is intergenerational, the adult child–elderly parent relationship has the added bonus of two mature adults interacting within a relationship negotiated through many years of both joy and pain. In the limited space of the next four chapters, the importance of understanding, or at least considering, the dynamic nature of the familial and nonfamilial relationships in which interaction occurs are considered so as to gain a more complete knowledge of intergenerational communication across the life span.

First, as was stated in the initial chapters of the book, let us dispense with the myth that both generations, adult children and elderly parents, turn their backs on each other as they age. In other words, we want to be quite clear that familial relationships have not undergone some type of major nuclear meltdown. There is agreement within the social-scientific community that the parent–child relationship, along with numerous other family relationships, remains close and vibrant throughout life (Nussbaum, Hummert, Williams, & Harwood, 1995). Leigh (1985), in an extensive study of the interaction patterns of family members, reports that interaction rates within the child–parent relationship remain frequent and stable throughout the entire life span. Cicirelli (1981) and numerous other scholars report that not only do approximately 90% of older adults have living children, but that well over 80% of these dyads report a close relationship. As Nussbaum et al. (1995) wrote, "The myth of alienation between adult children and their elderly parents is simply not supported by the facts" (p. 28).

This chapter presents two theories that account for the continuation of a close, child–parent bond throughout the life span: intergenerational solidarity theory and life-span attachment theory. Neither of these theories are communication based; instead each seeks to explain the essential affective as well as caregiving function of the child–parent relationship across the life span. The literature addressing the adult child–elderly parent relationship has been dominated by investigations into caregiving, and this chapter reviews the pertinent findings. In addition, two areas of research have been very helpful in our understanding of this intergenerational relationship and the communication that transpires within the relationship. Problems such as late-life divorce by a parent, and psychological difficulties on the part of an adult child can impact the child–parent relationship. How these problems affect the relationship can be informative as to the nature of the relationship. Finally, a growing concern for social researchers is the number of adult children who are living in the same home as their elderly parents. The literature attempting to understand this more frequently occurring situation is also reviewed.

INTERGENERATIONAL SOLIDARITY THEORY

Intergenerational solidarity theory attempts to provide a sound explanation for the life long bond children and parents feel toward each other. Nakonezny (1996) reports that intergenerational solidarity has its roots in the classical sociological traditions of Durkheim, the social-psychological tradition of Homans and Heider, and the early family sociology scholarship of Angell and Hill. All of these traditions consider *solidarity* (defined by close feelings and cohesion) as central and essential to the structure of group encounters. Without solidarity, groups would not exist. The process is communicative; familial solidarity is invoked in everyday talk within families, at the dinner table, and so forth. Family members frequently construct themselves as an ingroup where the rest of the world is outgroup. In this way familial identity is invoked and cohesion is enforced.

Working with these strong theoretical traditions, contemporary family sociologists, most notably Bengtson, developed intergenerational family solidarity theory (Adams, 1968: Bengtson, Olander, & Haddad, 1976: Bengtson & Schrader, 1982; Mangen, Bengtson, & Landry, 1988; Nye & Rushing, 1969). Bengtson and Schrader (1982) expanded an earlier multidimensional taxonomy of intergenerational solidarity by Nye and Rushing (1969) to include six distinct dimensions:

Associational solidarity—the frequency and patterns of interaction in various types and activities;

Affectional solidarity—the type and degree of positive sentiment held about family members, and the degree of reciprocity of these sentiments;

Consensual solidarity—the degree of agreement on values, attitudes, and beliefs among family members;

Functional solidarity—the degree to which family members exchange services or assistance;

Normative solidarity—the perception and enactment of norms of family solidarity; and

Intergenerational family structure—the number, type, and geographic proximity of family members. (p. 116)

Nussbaum et al. (1995) suggest that the child–parent relationship remains strong across as many as 70 years because the participants are in consistent contact with one another; show high levels of affection toward each other; tend to help out when help is needed; know when to avoid expressing hostile thoughts; and reach a consensus on values, beliefs, and opinions. In other words, intergenerational solidarity functions to maintain the adult child–elderly parent relationship. Knowing when not to express hostile thoughts and reaching a consensus on values, beliefs, and opinions directly implies familial accommodation processes. In some way then, families manage to achieve an accommodative working consensus that works for them most of the time. We might also suggest that, in many cases, both adult children and elderly parents exercise a form of accommodative censorship that protects the solidarity of the relationship. Each party knows what topics not to discuss in front of the other and in this way a protective veneer of censensus is created.

Bengtson, Marti, and Roberts (1991) report that the dimensions of intergenerational solidarity just listed are independent, complex, and rather stable across time. They point to a tension between intergenerational solidarity and individuality between generations within the family. This tension becomes more salient if the aging parents are in need of high levels of support. The negotiation between the adult child, who desires autonomy and solidarity, and his or her elderly parents, who also desire autonomy and solidarity, is a difficult task. Intergenerational communication that takes place within this negotiation is key to the life-long nature of the relationship, which often gives rise to helping behavior as well as to feelings of unmet expectations or guilt. *Intergenerational solidarity* is the communication taking place between adult children and their parents. The communication defines the levels of solidarity and autonomy to be found within the relationship. This solidarity plays a positive role because it is both directly and indirectly related to caregiving. On the other hand, feelings of intergenerational solidarity within this relationship function to maintain feelings of obligation that may produce negative feelings of guilt related to not being able to care enough. Communication predicaments (as discussed in chapters 1 and 2) are inherent here, but have yet to be studied. For example, at the center of a communication predicament is a dilemmatic pull between the communicative accomplishment of two seemingly conflicting goals. In this case then, the accommodation dilemma of how to protect individual autonomy versus how much accommodation should be given to parents are inherent as communication predicaments. Adult children may well find themselves in the situation where they feel they cannot win. If they give too much to their parents they are losing their own independence, but if they protect their independence they feel guilty for not supporting their parents. Moreover, there is every reason why older parents might feel a similar st of pulls and pushes. The elder parent may be struggling to provide support to the adult child while trying to maintain independence as an individual in his or her own right. Parents and adult children might be actively seeking support and adult children and parents might feel obliged to give support. See chapter 14 for more discussion of filial obligations.

LIFE-SPAN ATTACHMENT THEORY

A second theory to explain the life-long bond of the child–parent relationship is *life-span attachment theory* (Cicirelli, 1991). Attachment was originally conceptualized to explain why young children, when separated from their parents for an extended period of time, failed to thrive (Bowlby 1969, 1980). "Attachment refers to the bond or tie that an infant forms with the mother; it is an internal state within the individual that is inferred from the propensity of the infant to seek proximity and contact with the mother" (Cicirelli, 1991, p. 26). The process of attachment is a simultaneous seeking by the child for his or her mother with the mother providing security, protection, soothing, comfort, and help. Each child is thought to have an innate predisposition to form a secure attachment to a parent or parents. For the next few years, the parents continue to offer support and nurturance to their dependent children.

Cicirelli (1991) reports that as the child grows into adolescence and adulthood the motivational system linked to attachment, which functions to provide safety and security, fades. The growing autonomy of the child produces less attachment, which is thought to all but disappear in adulthood. Thus, some believe that parent–child alienation in adolescence and adulthood can be explained by a loss in attachment feelings. Once the child reaches a state of independence, the child–parent bond is weakened, and we should not be surprised when children and parents grow apart with age.

An alternative position championed by Cicerelli (1991) is that attachment continues throughout the entirety of our lives, only in a slightly different form. There is overwhelming evidence to suggest that adult children interact with their parents and that adult children and parents turn to one another in times of need (this literature is reviewed in the next section of the chapter). Cicirelli proposes that as we age into adolescence and adulthood, attachment changes and communication takes on a significant role. Simple communicative behavior such as calling our parents on the phone, writing a letter, or even sending an e-mail can substitute for the face-to-face interaction so common between young children and their parents.

As adult children move from the home and increase the physical as well as the psychological distance from their parents, the mechanism of symbolic attachment emerges in adulthood. Cicirelli (1991) states that the adult child can evoke the symbolic representation of the parent, engage in imagined conversation, and gain a feeling of security and closeness without physical proximity. This imagined communication, together with actual communication via telephone, letter writing and email, maintains the high level of attachment felt by adult children and elderly parents once physical separation has occurred. Attachment survives into adulthood because we can adapt to the lack of physical proximity with the use of technology and by evoking memories of our parents by using imagined communication on a psychological level. The actual intergenerational communication, or the imagined intergenerational communication, once again helps to define the parent–child relationship.

One question that remains to be answered is how intergenerational solidarity or life-span attachment functions within our lives. In other words, why do we strive to maintain close child–parent relationships throughout our lives? Another question is: How do older adults and their elderly parents communicate attachment or solidarity during the final 20 years of life? The solidarity and attachment felt in these relationships are not only ends in and of themselves, but these feelings are known to be linked to caregiving as well as to care-receiving behaviors. The next section of this chapter reviews the existing literature about the caregiving function of the adult child–elderly parent relationship.

CAREGIVING IN THE
ADULT CHILD–ELDERLY PARENT RELATIONSHIP

Elderly parent relationship reserchers concentrated their investigations on the caregiving function of the relationship. Whereas it is acknowledged that the adult child–elderly parent relationship functions in many additional ways, such as transmission of generational values and beliefs or in fulfilling affective needs, the roles of both parent and child in fulfilling the caring needs of each other have dominated the scholarly literature.

Cicirelli (1991) points out that the great majority of elderly parents do receive some form of care from their adult children. As a matter of fact, informal care of elderly parents within the family far exceeds the formal care provided to older adults by nursing homes, hospices, adult day-care facilities, or social workers. It should also be noted that care continues to be provided throughout life to the adult children by their elderly parents. Seitzer and Ryff (1994) suggest that parenting is a life-course phenomenon. Older parents continue to provide support of various kinds, including advising, babysitting, and giving financial help, to their adult children until their health prevents such behavior.

Of related interest is the fact that the majority of older adults residing in the United States have at least one child living within 10 miles of their homes (Lin & Rogerson, 1995). A series of studies supports the notion that geographical proximity is the greatest predictor of intergenerational interaction between adult children and their elderly parents (Crimmins & Ingegneri, 1990; Kiveett & Atkinson, 1984).

Lin and Rogerson (1995) advanced a three-stage theory of intergenerational proximity. The first stage of spatial separation occurs when the young adult moves away from home and thus promotes intergenerational independence.

The second stage involves the middle-aged adult moving to various new homes to maximize job opportunities, while at the same time, considering a move closer to the parents to establish intergenerational contact between grandchildren and the grandparents. In the final stage of this migration, the adult children and their elderly parents move closer because of the declining health of the parents and the need of the adult children to care for the parents. The proximity of adult children and elderly parents toward the end of the parent–child relationship is important because it provides the interactive opportunity for caregiving behaviors to occur.

Scholars who have studied caregiving within the family context have not always agreed on a precise definition of caregiving. Walker, Pratt, and Eddy (1995) wrote that most researchers conceptualize *caregiving* as "occurring when one or more family members give aid or assistance to other family members beyond that required as part of normal everyday life" (p. 402). A common method of measuring caregiving is to use a checklist of instrumental activities of daily living (IADLs). Activities common to everyday household work such as cooking or cleaning are considered instrumental activities. Because these activities are related to work normally performed by wives or daughters, women often do not consider these activities as caregiving, whereas husbands and sons do report these activities as caregiving tasks.

A second common method of capturing caregiving behavior is to measure activities of daily living (ADLs). Activities such as bathing, walking, or more medically related tasks fall into this domain. Although older men have consistently failed to report needing help with instrumental activities, partly because they have never performed such tasks, they do report as much need as do older women with the medical aspects of daily living. In any case, each caregiver or care receiver may define caregiving relative to his or her gender or what appears normal to him or her. Often, caregiving behavior may be under- or overreported.

Walker, Pratt, and Eddy (1995) attempt to solve this definitional problem by conceptualizing the criterion for caregiving as "dependence on another person for any activity essential for daily living including both IADLs and ADLs" (p. 403). Caregiving, therefore, is based on the dependency of the care receiver rather than on any specific behaviors of the caregiver.

An additional sticky point within the rather massive literature about caregiving is that socioemotional care and the communication of this care are often ignored. Whereas all family relationships have a strong affective component, the socioemotional exchange across the life span often defines the quality of the relationship. This history of socioemotional care contextualizes the physical caregiving and may play a role in whether the care is perceived as a burden or a blessing.

Walker, Pratt, and Eddy (1995) consider both the negative as well as the positive outcomes of providing care to elderly parents. A common myth often perpetuated within our society is that once our parents age beyond 70 years they will need our constant help and this will in turn ruin our lives. A wear-and-tear hypothesis has been put forth that postulates an increase in caregiving burden as duration of caregiving increases (Townsend, Noelker, Deimling, & Bass, 1989). Walker, Acock, Bowman, and Li (1996) tested the assumptions of this wear-and-tear hypothesis and found that it is not the duration of caregiving that leads to caregiving burden, but the increases in the intensity of caregiving that are related to higher levels of stress. The research evidence simply does not support the myth that caregiving is an overwhelmingly negative burden. The vast majority of caregivers do not suffer from clinical depression, nor is there any established relationship between decline in care-receiver's health and caregiver stress. Walker, Pratt, and Eddy (1995) do report numerous studies suggesting that caregiving is more stressful for women than for men, is less stressful for African-American caregivers than for White-American caregivers, and is more stressful for those caring for cognitively challenged individuals than for physically impaired parents. Although it is true that adult children must change the normal routine of their lives when caring for their parents, it is also true that the majority of these adult children report managing their lives quite well. In addition, research has provided some very interesting information regarding the positive outcomes of caregiving. Once again, Walker, Pratt, and Eddy review a number of studies that indicate both African Americans and White Americans have a combination of high stress and high satisfaction, which increases as they provide more care. Daughters have reported "receiving valuable instrumental and socioemotional aid from their dependent mothers" (p. 407). One must not forget that the care offered by adult children is offered and given in a relational context. Thus, the stress and life complications associated with caregiving emerge within the parent–child bond. This relational solidarity or attachment often can redefine what appears to be a hopeless situation into a positive and fulfilling endeavor. Although it may be trite to think that performing good deeds makes us feel good, this good feeling serves us and the adult child–elderly parent relationship particularly well.

Caring for elderly parents is not an equal-opportunity context. As mentioned previously, caregiving is often measured by performing tasks such as cleaning, cooking, dressing, and bathing. These tasks are closely associated to the household tasks most generally performed by women in our society. It is no surprise that women provide the great majority of care to older adults in our culture. Stone, Cafferata, and Sangl (1987) report that after spouses, adult daughters are the most frequently called on source of caregiving for older adults. Daughters are far more likely to provide care for parents, and because women outlive men, these daughters are for the most part caring for their mothers (Himes, 1994). The interesting notion in this overwhelming demographic trend is how the women in our society continue to care for aging family members with a minimal contribution fro men and yet continue to describe their situation as fair and satisfactory (Thompson & Walker, 1989). Walker, Pratt, and Eddy (1995) report additional information that some caregiving daughters feel guilty that they are not caring enough, and that as long as their husbands neither resent nor interfere with their caregiving behaviors, the caregiving daughters report not being dissatisfied with the husband's or brother's lack of supportive behavior. Once again, a sound explanation for this seemingly unfair division of the caregiving effort can be found in the relational construction of the wife or daughter role. The comparison of equal effort in care is not son–daughter care, but is daughter–daughter care. The other adult daughters across the country are performing caregiving behaviors, so it seems quite normal that "I" as an adult daughter, should care for my parents, feel stress as well as satisfaction, and be unbothered that my spouse or my brothers refrain from helping around both houses.

In a recently published article, Ingersoll-Dayton, Starrels, and Dowler (1996) examined the interaction between the relationship status of the parent and the adult child (i.e., parent vs. parent-in-law), the caregiver's gender, the parent's gender, and how these three characteristics are associated with caregiving activities, the resources received from parents, and the cost of caregiving. More than 1,500 employed caregivers of parents and parents-in-law reported that women do provide more help to elders than do men (except for health care or health management), indicated no differences in the amount of help sons-in-law and daughters-in-law provide to their parents-in-law, report higher levels of stress for daughters, report that daughters-in-law experience less help from parents-in-law and report more stress than do sons-in-law, and report that older women receive and give more assistance than do older men. This study provides additional support that gender is an important explanatory factor with regard to caring for a parent or even a parent-in-law.

Race and ethnicity are additional influences on caregiving within the adult child–elderly parent relationship. Research comparing African-American caregivers to White caregivers indicates that African-American caregivers report more stress and yet also report more positive feelings toward their caregiving experiences (Hinrichsen & Ramirez, 1992). Walker, Pratt, and Eddy (1995) speculate that the intergenerational bonds in the African-American community may be stronger than those Whites have, and that African Americans may be able to handle stress better because they have adapted to many stressful situations throughout their lives. These factors may contribute to the well-being of African-American caregivers.

The Hispanic population is the fastest growing single segment of the U.S. population (Markides & Coreil, 1986). Mexican Americans compose the largest subgroup of the Hispanic population and the second largest ethnic minority group in the United States. Dietz (1995) investigated patterns of intergenerational assistance within the Mexican-American family in her attempt to discover if similar patterns of caregiving exist within this subgroup of the American population. Studying more than 700 older Mexican Americans, Dietz found very high levels of need with very low incomes in this study group. The intergenerational interaction between Mexican Americans appears to be quite strong. However, numerous needs of older Mexican Americans are not being met by family members. These needs are especially significant in the area of finances. The Mexican-American population is not financially secure. This fact, coupled with the strong growth in total numbers of older adults, will eventually lead to serious problems in the families' ability to care for their elderly members. Because African Americans and Mexican Americans experience family and aging in somewhat different ways than the dominant White culture in America, scholars should not be so fast to generalize the findings of the caregiving literature to everyone in society. Obviously, much more research about the caregiving process beyond the cultural boundaries of White America is needed.

As is quite clear from the past few pages, the adult child–elderly parent caregiver literature is extensive. The great majority of this research, however, has not studied the intergenerational communication that transpires within the actual caregiving context. An exception to this is a study reported by Cicirelli (1993) in which he attempted to investigate dyadic decision making in the adult child–elderly parent dyad in family caregiving situations. Cicirelli reasons that from young adulthood to older adulthood, the communication within our relationships functions quite consistently with a social construction paradigm (Coupland & Nussbaum, 1993). However, when a decline in the health of an elderly parent becomes noticeable and the normal communication between adult child and parent reaches a higher level of difficulty, the younger person's discourse to the elderly parent may change in a reciprocal fashion, even to the point of becoming patronizing, routinized, and paternalistic. Cicirelli defines paternalism as the imposition of one person's decision on another individual for the welfare of that individual. The process of caregiving may develop from a reciprocal interaction evidenced by joint decision making on the part of both adult child and elderly parent to a more paternalized decision process dominated by the younger, healthier adult child. The caregiving relationship that began with equal accommodation and without patronizing-speech acts may become one with the adult child overaccommodating the elderly parent and using patronizing speech. The communication predicament model outlined in chapter 1 can be very useful as a descriptor of this very process. The decline in health triggers a relationship change that may result in paternalistic decision making as well as in submissive acceptance of those decisions.

A group of 50 mother–daughter dyads with the daughters ranging in age from 33 to 70 and the mothers ranging in age from 62 to 97 participated in a study to test whether, as mothers increased in age, more paternalistic decision making by their daughters would occur. The findings of the study support Cicirelli's notions that, as the parents age and become less healthy, a daughter's belief in paternalistic decision making stabilizes and influences the pattern of communication within this decision-making dyad. The results of this study are important on several levels. First, on a practical level, the daughters who are making decisions for their parents without input from their parents must rely on relational history to anchor their decisions. Thus, previous interaction and quality communication with their mothers prior to a decline in health becomes more important as the daughters attempt to do what is best for their mothers. In addition, this study underscores the importance of studying the intergenerational communication transpiring within the adult child–elderly parent relationship. As caregiving dominates the relationship, changes can occur that help to redefine both the relationship and the communicative behavior within that relationship.

Thus far, few scholars have attempted to study the mother–daughter relationship across the life span from a social constructivist perspective. A study by Henwood and Coughlan (1993) combines feminist theory with discourse analysis to study how closeness and intergenerational solidarity are, in practice, constructed in the discourse of mothers and daughters themselves. Henwood and Coughlan view women's experiences, identities, and relationships as discursive products or constructions rather than fixed, natural realities. This perspective highlights the importance of studying the interaction, communication, and talk occurring between the mother and daughter to broaden our understanding of this life-long relationship. To truly understand the caregiving found within the adult daughter–elderly mother relationship, the construction of that relationship as expressed in the discourse is vital.

CORESIDENCE

An indication of the intergenerational solidarity or attachment felt between older adults and their elderly parents can be found in the literature addressing coresidence. Although it is not the norm that older children live with their elderly parents, Ward and Spitze (1992) report that about 15% of individuals over 65 years of age living in the United States coreside with adult children. Coward, Albrecht, and Shapiro (1996) review literature that indicates no gender difference in preference of residence. In other words, elderly parents are just as likely to live with their adult daughters as with their adult sons. In addition, the great majority of elderly parents who live with their adult children live with never-married or formerly married children. These data indicate that a child's spouse is not likely to be present in the home with the elderly parent. Older African Americans and older Hispanics are more likely to coreside with their adult children than are older Whites. This may represent a combination of the stronger intergenerational family bonds in these minority families and the greater economic needs of the White-American and Hispanic-American household (Ward & Spitze, 1992).

The circumstances that would cause an elderly parent or an adult child to move together are more complex and varied than one might anticipate. The common myth is that older adults become ill, demand help with their physical needs, and force themselves into the homes of their adult children. The evidence suggests that less than one half of all multigenerational households are formed because of health-related disabilities of the elderly parent. Older adults also move into the home of a adult child because of the death of a spouse. In addition, it can also be the case that adult children are moving in with their parents because of financial setbacks or divorce. Finally, some children never leave home and remain living with their parents until the death of their parents.

A number of recent studies have investigated the quality of intergenerational relationships in multigenerational households. Suitor and Pillemer (1988) investigated the hypothesis that adult children living with their elderly parents may be involved in a situation that exacerbates intergenerational conflict. Their data point to a rather harmonious existence in the adult child–elderly parent household. Very little evidence emerged from their study to indicate intergenerational conflict. The authors conclude that the conflict that does occur in the home does not seriously disrupt or disturb the parent–child relationship. This may be in part because those who decide to live together have a good relationship prior to the coresidence (for a more detailed discussion of intergenerational conflict, see chapter 12). However, it would be very interesting to document how the conflict that does emerge is managed communicatively and preserves the harmony of the relationship. Communication plays a significant process role in the management of relational stability.

Other researchers have pointed to examples of the possibility of conflict within multigenerational households. Coward, Albrecht, and Shapiro (1996) remind us that as intensity of care increases, so does the stress felt by the caregiver. As the intensity of care increases in the home, the possibility of conflict arising from the stress can increase and produce relational strain. In addition, there is evidence to suggest that coresidence can affect the perception of marital quality of both the adult child and the elderly parents. Thus, it is possible that both positive and negative relational outcomes can emerge from coresidence.

Coward et al. (1996) attempted to expand the existing literature about the quality of the adult child–elderly parent relationship of those who coreside by asking the elderly parents how their lives would be affected if they no longer lived with their children. Whereas the majority of parents indicated no change would occur in most aspects of their lives if their living situations changed, those elderly parents who did report a change in their lives felt that this change would be negative. The data indicates that elderly parents who are married felt that the change in living circumstances would have a much smaller negative impact than did elderly parents who were not married. In addition, elderly parents felt that moving away from their adult children would affect some parts of their lives more than others. "Specifically, older adults forecasted the greatest negative impact on their lives would be in the areas of overall happiness, companionship, and social life" (Coward et al., 1996, p. 344). In addition, elderly parents were quite concerned about their future financial needs if they no longer lived with their adult children. This study, in concert with the other evidence reported, points to the importance of the social and financial functions of the adult child–elderly parent relationship served by coresidence.

There are many ways in which communication researchers can contribute to an understanding of the forces that initiate and sustain coresidence.

For example, coresidence may be implicitly, as well as explicitly, negotiated in communication with adult children long before it ever happens. As communication specialists, we can speculate about a variety of ways that this may be done. Aging parents may introduce "in passing" discussions about coresidence, "granny annexes," and so forth. They may also rehearse with favored adult children reasons why they could or could not live with other adult children. Initiating topics in this hypothetical way could be a nonthreatening way of testing the waters with adult children to get an idea of their receptivity to coresidence, without having to deal with the face-threatening situation of asking directly. This may be just one of a variety of ways in which the ground for coresidence is prepared. The important point is that there are vast opportunities for communication researchers to bring their particular perspectives and skills to study family life. There is enormous scope for theoretical and applied advances that have yet to be fully grasped by our discipline.

LATE LIFE DIVORCE AND OTHER ISSUES

When problems arise in the lives of adult children and elderly parents, the way these problems are handled gives us clues as to the fundamental nature of the relationship. Divorce has been well documented as a breakdown of the marital bond, which often has severe implications for the children of divorce. The children referred to in the great majority of studies documenting problems in the child–parent relationship during and following divorce are the very young children of parents who are close to 30 years of age. "Popular reasoning seems to be that parental divorce is easier and less disruptive for offspring who are mature adults" (Cooney, Hutchinson, & Leather, 1995, p. 153).

Pett, Lang, and Gander (1992) cite statistics that the number of divorces for persons more than 60 years of age is increasing rapidly. More than 4% of the population over the age of 65 years report they are divorced. In addition, the number of children who experience the divorce of their parents is increasing. The question becomes, how does the divorce of a parent affect the adult child–elderly parent relationship?

According to Cooney et al. (1995) young adults who report recently divorced parents maintained less contact and less intimate relations with their fathers after divorce. Evidence also exists that adult children who had difficulties with their parents prior to the divorce are more likely to report problems subsequent to the divorce. In addition, financial problems of adult children are often linked to the divorce of elderly parents. With these factors in mind, Cooney et al. investigated the predictors of adult child–elderly parent relations following a parental divorce. Their results point toward the importance of the actual divorce process as most predictive of post-divorce relational difficulties. Prior to the divorce, parents should minimize any relational problems with their children. The timing of the divorce does not appear to lessen the relational consequences or to save children from the negative affects of the divorce. Adult children suffer emotionally as much as younger children when their parents divorce.

Pett, Lang, and Gander (1992) studied the impact of late-life divorce on family celebrations, traditions, important life-cycle events, and family contact. Divorce in this study was found to be more than a single tragic event. The divorce of older parents set in motion a process of continued negotiation and restructuring of family tasks and traditions. "The strong positive relationships between perceived disruptiveness of the divorce, present family closeness, and consequent changes in family rituals suggest that adult children of divorce struggle for years with the aftereffects of their parents' later-life separation and divorce" (p. 547). An additional finding of the study highlights the importance of mothers and daughters for maintaining kinship links. The divorced mothers, and in their absence the daughters of the divorced parents, were found to be more active negotiators in ensuring the continued existence of valued family rituals and traditions.

Beyond the late-life divorce of elderly parents, numerous problems can arise in an adult child's life that can affect the elderly parents and the child–parent relationship. Divorce on the part of a child, a financial crisis, or a drug- or alcohol-related problem can affect the elderly parents as well as other family members. If children experience these problems, parents may feel responsible, believe they have failed as parents, and may become depressed. This depression in turn leads to relational problems between the adult child and elderly parent.

Dunham (1995) investigated the relationship between adult-child problems, conflict with the adult child, social support from an adult child, and depression of aging parents. A sample was drawn from a longitudinal study of three-generation California families. Results revealed that the only intergenerational variable consistently related to depression in aging parents was the presence of support from an adult child. As support from a troubled adult child increased, depression also increased. Results also suggested that fathers of children with a drug or alcohol problem were significantly more depressed than other fathers. Finally, results revealed that older parents were able to manage the effects of the problems of their adult child upon their own lives by using support from other sources, such as friends.

Together, these findings indicate a rather dynamic, complex, relational bond between adult children and their elderly parents. As the direction of support changes, elderly parents may have difficulty coping with the redefinition of the relationship. Elderly parents, however, have a lifetime of other support mechanisms to manage the negative consequences of relational change. In addition, older fathers may be more vulnerable, than are older mothers, to the problems of an adult child. Future research is needed to address the possible reasons that the father, and not the mother, is under greater risk of depression resulting from such adult-child problems.

SUMMARY AND IMPLICATIONS

The literature reviewed and discussed in this chapter suggests that the adult child–elderly parent relationship is often a close relationship that serves our affective and mutual-aid needs throughout a large part of the life span. Any lingering doubts that children typically abandon their parents or that parents turn their backs on their children in our society should be put to rest. The child–parent relationship is likely to be vibrant, intimate, rewarding, and challenging early in life, throughout our middle years, and late in life as well.

Two theories have been advanced to explain why the child–parent relationship bond is maintained throughout the life span. Intergenerational solidarity theory was devised by sociologists to capture the structural solidarity inherent within the family. Much like various small groups build cohesion to maintain a group identity, families utilize their structures to reinforce life-long bonds and small-group identity as a family. Life-span attachment theory has been proposed by psychologists to extend the attachment feelings of mothers and infants throughout the life span through the symbolic attachment older children and elderly parents can feel when physical separation does not permit day-to-day contact. These two theories help us to understand why, unlike many living creatures, humans do not abandon their families, but instead remain close until separated by death.

The closeness found within this relationship reinforces, or even at times causes, the caregiving behaviors that are shared by adult children and their elderly parents. Not only are affect needs satiated within this relationship, but physical, medical, and daily living needs are met as well. Only a spouse will care as much for an elderly parent as will an adult child. In addition, elderly parents continue to care for their children as long as they are able. This mutual aid, which may be a function of the affective nature of the child–parent relationship, produces a quite unique intergenerational interaction.

The mutual aid and affect within the relationship are not universal. All genders and all cultures do not behave in the same manner throughout life toward their parents and children. The literature is quite clear that a great deal of the caregiving burden is shouldered by women. Mothers and daughters are the caretakers of this society. Different cultures also care for their families in different ways. African-American and Mexican-American households feel a stronger need to maintain intergenerational care. However, this need to care is often in conflict with the financial ability to care.

Various problems within the adult child–elderly parent relationship must also be understood as having a significant affect upon the maintenance of "normal life." The late-life divorce of an elderly parent, the divorce of an adult child, or the alcohol or drug problem of a child are tragic events that lead to major adaptive behavior by both children and parents. These problems have been shown to create stress not only for individuals, but for the relationship. The ability to overcome this stress can directly affect the closeness and the caregiving behaviors that once may have been taken for granted.

To date, only a handful of studies have taken the next step to capture the intergenerational communication that transpires within the adult child-elderly parent relationship. Scholars such as Cicirelli (1995) and Henwood and Coughlan (1995) have suggested that the actual negotiation of the relationship can be explained and described through the communicative behavior shared by children and their parents. This constant negotiation appears not only in the decision making of an adult child when attempting to care for a sick parent, but also in the mother–daughter interaction as they attempt to redefine their relationship throughout the life span.

A rich understanding of intergenerational communication is only made possible by first realizing that all communication takes place within a relational context. As the early chapters of this book make clear, the great majority of scholarship devoted to intergenerational communication has not placed the communicative behavior of interactants within a relational context. The intergenerational communication so important for the adult child–elderly parent relationship takes place in a context of many years of relational history, relational affect, relational turmoil, and relational caregiving. The closeness felt in this relationship over the entire life span has an effect upon each relational participant who is accommodating to the other. Of more interest is precisely the way in which children or their parents manage accommodative dilemmas in their relationships so as to maintain solidarity and caring.

9

The Grandparent–Grandchild Relationship

For many of us, the grandparent–grandchild relationship is the one relationship we can immediately point to as being truly intergenerational. In any classroom of a Western industrialized nation, if the students are asked to think about an intergenerational interaction within which they have recently participated, their interaction with one of their grandparents will be one of the first to come to mind. Whereas social scientists have only recently begun systematic explorations of the grandparent–grandchild relationship, this relationship has played a central role in the family system throughout recorded history. During the latter part of the 20th century, numerous economic, political, health-related, and structural-familial changes have occurred in our lives that have pushed social scientists to take a much closer look at the grandparent–grandchild relationship, and at the intergenerational communication that transpires within the relationship. It would not be an overstatement to suggest that many of our general conceptions of growing old and of what it may be like to be old are formed with reference to our relationships with our grandparents.

Gratton and Haber (1996) wrote a very concise history of American grandparenting to place the modern era of the grandparent–grandchild relationship in an accurate historical context. The mid-19th century was marked by the authority grandparents held within the family because of their vital economic and social roles. Rarely did grandparents live with their grandchildren. Relationships between the generations reflected the critical economic and social roles played by grandparents, and reinforced the notion of interdependence within the family. The industrialization of the late-20th and early-19th centuries changed the patterns of the grandparent–grandchild relationship. The power of authority once granted for experience and wisdom decreased, increases in life expectancy increased longevity of elderly family members who were likely to be chronically ill, the proportion of trigenerational households increased significantly, and perhaps most important, a view of aging as a burden was clearly visible in the scientific and popular writings of the time. "Physicians viewed old age as an illness, critics denigrated the capacities of older workers, and family experts opposed extended and complex households" (Gratton & Haber, 1996, p. 11). The Great Depression and the legislation that emerged from this era produced a third phase of American grandparenting, which was dominated by companionship and independence. The economic independence that flowed from social security and private pension plans removed some of the burden from younger generations and created an environment for grandparents to interact with grandchildren as friends or companions. Added to this, improvements in lifestyle and health care mean that older people live both longer and healthier lives. Although this historical overview is rather simplistic and certainly does not include all grandparents, it does place the grandparent–grandchild relationship within a continually changing context often that interacts with factors outside immediate family circumstances.

The modern grandparent–grandchild relationship exists in a very diverse environment. The dramatic increases in long, healthy lives, coupled with the fact that an increasing number of teens are bearing children, have produced a society in which three quarters of us can expect to become a grandparent and to remain in this role for many years (Giarrusso, Silverstein, & Bengtson, 1996), eventually becoming great-grandparents too. In addition, Bengtson, Rosenthal, and Burton (1990) pointed out that the shape of American families has changed from many young people at one level, to multiple generations with fewer numbers in each generation. Thus, intergenerational communication, rather than intragenerational communication, takes on added significance within the family context. Finally, such factors as financial security, one's ability to adapt to the grandparent or grandchild role, divorce, functioning simultaneously as a parent and a grandparent, and culture all place added variability on the dynamic nature and function of the grandparent–grandchild relationship. In other words, although we may talk about the grandparent–grandchild relationship as if it was a single relational entity, we must bear in mind that it is not necessarily so. We have some fairly strong expectations for what the grandparent–grandchild relationship should be, as indicated by Hummert's (1990) work.

As with the previous chapter concerning intergenerational communication within an adult child–elderly parent relationship, very little research has been produced that specifically targets intergenerational communication between grandparents and their grandchildren. However, much research has compiled an impressive body of evidence documenting the nature of the relationship(s) themselves. The majority of this literature concentrated on descriptions and classifications of grandparental style accounting for the effects of gender, culture, divorce and surrogate parenting on grandparenting style. This chapter reviews the major research findings in these areas and concludes with a discussion of the importance of these relational dynamics on the intergenerational communication for grandparents as well as for grandchildren.

Giarrusso, Silverstein, and Bengston (1996) lament the fact that little attention has been paid to large-scale surveys into the intergenerational relationship of adult grandchildren and their grandparents. It is not hard to imagine that, for some grandparents and their grandchildren, advancing age can lead to a more exciting and dynamic relationship. On the other hand, it is not hard to imagine that as grandchildren move to college and as grandparents become more mobile, a less intimate relationship may evolve. One fact remains clear, however, as life expectancy increases, the probability of a dynamic and changing relationship with our grandparents as we both age is very strong.

GRANDPARENTING STYLES

The styles of role enactment utilized by grandparents are related to the notion of grandparent role. Neugarten and Weinstein (1964) realized the importance of the grandparent–grandchild relationship and suggested several styles of grandparent behavior to help explain the diverse and complex nature of grandparenting roles. Before their comments, grandparenting was not viewed as a terribly interesting or complex phenomenon, with some individuals performing quite admirably whereas others were simply bad grandparents. Troll (1983) summarized the Neugarten and Weinstein styles of grandparenting as follows:

1. *Formal style*: maintaining clearly demarcated lines between parent and grandparent, with an occasional gift or minor service.
2. *Fun-seeker*: a leisure orientation, characterized by grandparental self-indulgence and mutuality of pleasure.
3. *Surrogate parent*: almost always the grandmother who substitutes for the children's mother if she is employed or otherwise unable to care for the children.
4. *Reservoir of family wisdom*: more often the grandfather and reminiscent of the traditional power role described by Apple (1956).

5. *Distant figure*: emerging from the shadows ritually and fleetingly.

Neugarten and Weinstein (1964) reported that the most popular styles for grandparents were the formal and fun-seeker styles. Younger grandparents had more diverse styles, whereas older grandparents typically utilized the formal and distant styles. Undoubtedly there are contextual, social, economic, and health correlates of these styles, which are enormous generalizations anyway.

Wood and Robertson's (1976) conceptualization of the grandparent role recognized the fact that we have fairly strong social norms for grandparents. Their categories are based on the belief that "attitudes and expectations on the role derive from two major sources: those that are determined almost exclusively by social or normative factors and meet the needs of society, and those that stem from personal forces within the individual and meet his (sic) needs" (p. 245). Four grandparenting styles were suggested by Wood and Robertson. The Apportioned style of grandparenting referred to individuals who were high in personal needs and high in social needs. The Individualized style of grandparenting consisted of individuals high in personal needs and low in social needs. Grandparents who fell into these two style categories were older, less educated, had more grandchildren, and engaged in more activities with the grandchildren than grandparents of the other styles. The Symbolic style of grandparenting referred to individuals reporting high personal needs and low social needs. The Remote style of grandparenting referred to individuals low in personal needs and low in social needs. The grandparents falling into these two styles were younger, more involved in community events, and more involved with friends than they were with their grandchildren. The Remote grandparents had little, if any, contact with their grandchildren.

Cherlin and Furstenberg (1985, 1986) also attempted to classify the grandparent–grandchild relationship into styles of grandparenting. In their 1985 article, they discuss five styles of grandparenting (detached, passive, supportive, authoritative, and influential). In their influential book, Cherlin and Furstenberg (1986) discuss three styles of grandparenting based on two dimensions of relational behavior: degree of contact and extent of influence. The Remote style included those grandparents who saw their grandchildren so infrequently that they could only maintain a ritualistic, purely symbolic relationship. The Companionate style of the grandparent–grandchild relationship was defined "as one in which the grandparent and grandchild had seen each other at least once every 2 or 3 months during the past year in which there were low levels of either exchanges of services or parentlike behavior" (p. 77). An Involved relationship style has the grandparents and grandchildren seeing each other more than once every 2 or 3 months and in which there were high levels of exchanges of services and high levels of parentlike behavior. Cherlin and Furstenberg viewed these styles as useful explanatory tools in understanding the nature of the grandparent–grandchild relationship. Ultimately, however, they found these styles to be much too static to capture the ever-changing, dynamic nature of this relationship.

Giarrusso, Silverstein, and Bengtson (1996) point out that the Cherlin and Furstenberg classification does not take into account the solidarity or connectedness of the intergenerational relationship. They suggest classifying grandparent styles or grandparent–grandchild styles along the same six dimensions of intergenerational solidarity discussed in the adult child–elderly parent chapter. Silverstein, Lawton, and Bengston (1994) used the six dimensions of intergenerational solidarity to create a typology of five categories of adult child–elderly parent relations. The five types of intergenerational relationships are: tight knit, sociable, cordial but distant, obligatory, and detached. Although these relationship types describe parent–child interactions, it is suggested that these same five relational types may also characterize grandparenting styles and the grandparent–grandchild relationship.

Of course, whereas these style and type classifications are interesting, we know that the grandparent–grandchild relationship is likely to be far more dynamic than style classifications seem to allow. Grandparents play different roles at different times and their interaction with grandchildren is likely to be fluid, reforming and changing as the individuals age and as circumstances and needs change across the life span. The grandparental role is one that is increasingly played out over a great many years. During the early years of a child's life, the relationship between grandparents and grandchildren is necessarily very different from the kind of relationship that a grandparent has with a young-adult grandchild. As discussed in chapter 3, work by Hummert and others has shown that we have strong positive expectations about grandparenting in our society, to the point of having prototypical schemas of what a Perfect Grandparent should be. This is bound to interact at some level with grandparenting itself, with the way grandparents think about and perform their roles, and with the expectations that parents and grandchildren might have for grandparents. Remember that families do not stand outside society with its norms, stereotypes, and expectations. We expect these factors to interact in interesting ways with close family relationships, but as yet these interactions have not been studied.

GENDER, CULTURE, AND DIVORCE

The grandparent–grandchild relationship can be influenced by numerous factors. The gender of the grandparent and of the grandchild is one factor that may have an affect upon the quality of the relationship. Obviously, cultural differences exist in the grandparent–grandchild relationship and these cultural differences can have a dramatic impact on the relationship. Perhaps even more significant than gender or cultural differences are relational differences brought about by the profound structural changes occurring within many families.

The perception of the exact nature, responsibilities, and functions of grandparenting may be different for grandmothers than for grandfathers. People draw upon social norms and expectations to figure out how to be a grandparent. Nye and Bernardo (1981) suggest that women in particular undergo anticipatory socialization in preparation for the role as grandmothers. Women develop a grandmother self-image prior to the birth of grandchildren. An enthusiasm bias may exist in our society for grandmothers-to-be that better prepares the grandmother for her nonvoluntary role change into grandmotherhood. This may account in some way for the higher levels of satisfaction with grandparenting reported by grandmothers than reported by grandfathers (Downs, 1988; Thomas, 1989). For women particularly, it is likely that the birth of a first grandchild spurs a number of identity changes and self-image contradictions that must be worked through. For example, as discussed in previous chapters, the role and self-identity of grandmother is seen very positively in our culture, and women often proudly list their grandchildren and their respective achievements as a way of gaining self-esteem. However, the birth of a first grandchild is also a significant symbolic marker of advancing age, which is not seen so positively in our culture, and so in this respect the transition into the grandparent role may be one that women do not relish quite so much.

What are the norms, expectations, and role transitions for men? Some researchers suggest that grandfathers play right into the hands of social expectations by behaving as distant, macho-male figures less interested in emotions (apparently leaving that to the Perfect Grandmothers) and more interested in practical matters. For example, Hagestad (1985) claims that grandfathers attempt to influence young grandchildren only in instrumental matters such as school and finances. Grandmothers, on the other hand, attempt to influence their grandchildren's interpersonal as well as instrumental activities. Thomas (1986, 1989) found that grandfathers tended to stress family extension through grandchildren and the pleasures of indulging the grandchildren. Grandmothers tended to stress feelings of biological renewal through their grandchildren.

Some social scientists have also suggested that grandfathers tend to be less involved in their roles as grandparents (Hader, 1965; Hagestad, 1985; Neugarten & Weinstein, 1964). Some have suggested that maintaining some distance from the grandchildren may be a response to the higher mortality rate of aging males. Hagestad (1985) describes this lack of involvement in terms of the instrumental versus expressive domains of interpersonal relationships. "Whereas grandmothers tend to discuss subjects of emotional or relational content with their grandchildren, grandfathers often communicate in terms of practical aspects of the issues being discussed—often to the point of having certain issues identified as subjects not to discuss with grandpa" (Downs, 1989, p. 267).

Research results are inconsistent with respect to uncovering differences in the grandparent–grandchild relationship due to the gender of the grandchild. Hagestad (1985) reports that grandfathers tend to be more involved with grandsons, whereas grandmothers are more involved with granddaughters. On the other hand. Thomas (1989) found no differences attributable to grandchild gender in closeness or satisfaction for a grandparent in a preadolescent sample.

Overall then, there is much evidence that people do draw on norms of behavior. Gendered roles in society are reflected in these characterizations of grandparenting behavior. It is important to note that research being discussed here was conducted with older people who grew up during the war years. Whether the "60s' generation" who grew up with liberal attitudes, feminism, and the like—the so-called Baby Boomers—will grandparent in quite the same way is very doubtful indeed.

The relationship between maternal and paternal sets of grandparents and their grandchildren has also been studied. Kahana and Kahana (1970) found that grandchildren tend to favor maternal grandmothers because the maternal grandmothers indulge the young grandchildren. Adult children also expressed feeling much closer to their maternal grandmothers. Hartshorne and Manaster (1982) report that high school students visited their maternal grandmothers more often than their paternal grandmothers. Matthews and Sprey (1985) note that the family system is quite complex and that interaction between grandchildren and their maternal or paternal grandparents is largely due to how well the parents get along with the grandparents. The findings that suggest grandchildren's tendencies to feel closer to, and interact more with, maternal grandparents are almost certainly a result of the women maintaining a kin-keeping function. In other words, the grandchild is more likely to interact with the maternal grandmother because the grandchild's mother is more likely to interact and be close to her own mother than her mother-in-law.

The responsibility associated with being a grandparent and gender differences associated with this responsibility were studied by Thomas (1989). Grandparents did not differ in the "extent to which they stressed the centrality of the relationship in their own lives, in the extent to which the relationship permitted reinvolvement with their past, or in the extent to which they valued sharing wisdom with the grandchild" (p. 278). Not surprisingly, given strong social norms, both grandmothers and grandfathers consider their relationships with their grandsons and granddaughters to be important and to be a major responsibility in their lives.

Just as scholars interested in the adult child–elderly parent relationship have not investigated cultural differences within the relationship to any great extent, the differential effects of culture on the grandparent–grandchild relationship has also received very little attention. However, given the fact that families of various cultures, both within the United States and outside the United States, experience family life quite differently, it is reasonable to assume that different cultures negotiate the grandchild–grandparent relationship in unique ways. It should be noted that the research we reviewed tells us very little about the negotiation of this relationship in the United States (see chapter 14 for a comparison with Eastern cultures).

Within African-American culture, Poe (1991) reports that grandmothers attain the highest status within the family structure. This authority of the grandmother can overshadow any more affective or companion role. Stack (1974) found that maternal grandmothers in African-American families often accepted responsibility for caregiving, especially when the mother was employed. Maternal grandmothers were found to play a significant security role, as well as providing much-needed consistency, in the lives of other African-American family members. When compared to White families, African-American grandparents contribute more to family cohesion and to more supportive family structures (Hays & Mindel, 1973). In addition, Thomas (1994) found that grandparenting has a more central role for African-American men than for male members of other ethnic groups. A study by Strom, Collinsworth, Strom, and Griswold (1993) underscored the differences found between African-American grandparents and White grandparents. In essence, African-American grandparents and their grandchildren viewed themselves and their functions within the family quite differently than did White grandparents and their grandchildren.

Numerous researchers have pointed to the significant role of the grandparents within the American Hispanic community (Lubben & Becerra, 1987; Markides & Mindel, 1987). Schmidt and Padilla (1983) studied the importance of speaking Spanish within the family. Results indicated that Spanish language compatibility between grandparents and grandchildren predicted the amount of cultural affinity in structuring intergenerational differences. The issue of language compatibility between generations may have been an important issue at the turn of the 20th century for many European immigrants to America. Today, it is no longer a salient issue for White Americans, but is a very important factor for intergenerational interaction for Hispanic Americans, Asian Americans, and many other immigrant communities. Schmidt and Padilla also report that Hispanic-American grandparents belonged to larger, more multigenerational families, had a higher degree of intergenerational contact, felt higher satisfaction with their contact with grandchildren, and counted more on family support.

The traditional role of grandparenting in the Native-American culture can best be described as more intense than the role of grandparenting in many other cultures. "In the traditional pattern of Indian family organization, grandparents were often more available for infant and toddler care and thus continued a relationship of mutual concern with grandchildren throughout the life span" (McGoldrick, Pearce, & Giordona, 1982, p. 72). Barusch and Steen (1996) describe the Navajo as a society that places elders at the core of their civilization. "The elder was placed at a central location in this static conception of traditional society and was seen as a wise one, as a source of important and useful information. Through the elders, the past was brought to the present and given to children to transmit to the future" (p. 49). Modern society has changed many things across all of the Native-American nations. Perhaps, more important than the tremendous financial burdens felt by many Native-American communities, is the destruction of numerous native languages. The traditional role of the grandparents within the Native-American community may not survive the encroachment of modern society.

Beyond the effects of gender and culture on the grandparent–grandchild relationship are those changes in family life brought about by one's own choices. Just as divorce profoundly changes the adult child–elderly parent relationship, divorce on the part of a parent can have significant implications for the grandparent–grandchild relationship. The majority of research that has investigated the effect of parental divorce on this relationship has concentrated on young grandchildren. Findings from the research indicated that the younger grandchild–maternal grandparent relationship becomes stronger with higher levels of contact and affective closeness, and more instrumental assistance (Cherlin & Furstenberg, 1986; Clingempeel, Colyar, Brand, & Hetherington, 1992; Matthews & Sprey, 1984). Focusing on paternal grandparents, contact between grandparents and grandchildren is more limited, and geographic distance is greater after the divorce. Cooney and Smith (1996) and Giarrusso, Silverstein, and Bengston (1996) attribute the differences in relational quality following a divorce to the custody arrangements of the divorce. Because the mother typically receives custody, maternal grandparent–grandchild relationships are intensified. In contrast, noncustodial fathers do not often interact with their children as often as the custodial mothers, which directly leads to much less contact with paternal grandchildren. This issue of the importance of the parental role in mediating interaction between numerous generations is more fully discussed in the next chapter.

Cooney and Smith (1996) were interested in the possible changes in the grandparent–grandchild relationship following a parental divorce if the children were older and not reliant on the parent for visits to interact with the grandparents. Grandchildren participating in this study were between 18 and 23 years old. Results from their investigation indicated that "recent parental divorce was not associated with levels of affective, functional, or associational solidarity between adult grandchildren and grandparents" (p. S94). The divorce of the parents did not seem to affect the grandparent–grandchild relationship in any meaningful way. The adult grandchild and the grandparent were able to initiate and maintain interaction without the mediating behavior of the parent. This finding is important because it points to the life span developmental nature of the grandparent–grandchild relationship, and to the relationship as having a life on its own, apart from the parents, for children old enough to maintain the relationship.

Divorce on the part of the adult child and the late-life divorce of the grandparent also have impacts on the grandparent–grandchild relationship. Of special note may be the dating behavior of grandparents. Although there is no substantial empirical evidence to suggest that grandparent dating is an issue for grandchildren, undergraduate students in Communication and Aging classes often report shock when they learn of their divorced or widowed grandmother dating and sleeping with men other than their grandfather. The scenario of step-grandparents and how one deals with such a relationship are open questions. Research needs to be conducted that considers all levels of divorce and the possible effects of these divorces on all the intergenerational relationships within the family.

GRANDPARENTS AS PARENTS

The typical picture of the American family rarely includes grandparents raising grandchildren. Kornhaber (1996) reports that 2.2 million children lived in households headed by grandparents during 1970. The biological mother resided in about one half of these households. By 1993, census data indicated that 3.4 million children lived with their grandparents (U.S. Bureau of the Census, 1993). African-American children were about three times more likely to reside with their grandparents than were White children. Generations United, an organization founded to promote cross-generational understanding and cooperation, estimates that the number of grandparents seeking support as they raise their grandchildren may be as high as 7 million.

Kornhaber (1996) paints a demographic portrait of the grandparents who raise grandchildren by using data from the U.S. Bureau of the Census, 1993. Sixty percent of grandparents raising grandchildren are grandmothers. Approximately one third of the grandparents caring for their grandchildren are older than age 65. If you are African American, you are twice as likely to be a grandparent raising a grandchild than if you are a White American. Of all the grandparents who raise their grandchildren, 68% are White, 29% are African American, 10% are Hispanic American, 2% are Asian American, and 10% are Native American. Twenty-seven percent of grandparent caregivers live at or below the poverty level. Within the United States, approximately 60% of grandparent caregivers live in the South, with the others spread evenly throughout the rest of the country.

Researchers have recently begun to address the many diverse consequences when a grandparent, either through choice or by default, raises a grandchild. The results to this date indicate that grandparents find themselves in a rather troubling paradox. On one hand, grandparents feel very fortunate to be able to help and to perform a very positive function within their families; on the other hand, the tremendous financial, health, legal, and personal burden of raising a second generation of children causes a variety of personal stresses and strains (Burton, 1992; Kornhaber, 1996). Dowd and Bengtson (1978) report that these stresses may be magnified within the minority community, when compared to the White community, because of the much lower financial stability of the families. Added to these stressors is the fact, that at least in the United States, support for grandparents raising their grandchildren is not a governmental priority at any level (Kornhaber, 1996). Grandparents can and often do seek and find support from within their families, but precious little support can be found outside the informal networks.

Kornhaber wrote that despite the negative emotions and often dire financial burdens associated with raising grandchildren, grandparents who are caring for grandchildren feel useful and derive satisfaction from the knowledge that they are rescuing their grandchildren. "Caretaking grandparents in the Grandparent Study said they had increased energy and interest in daily life and noticed an improvement in mood since they started raising their grandchildren" (p. 136). The great majority of grandparents who are caring for their grandchildren report their efforts toward raising their grandchildren have given their lives new meaning.

The intergenerational communication transpiring between a caregiving grandparent and the grandchild has not been investigated. The changing relationship from the grandparent role to a more parental role may have significant impact upon the psychological well-being of the grandparent as well as the communication shared within the relationship. Obviously, the negotiation of the new relationship would be an interesting avenue of research too, as would be the subsequent communication negotiating the new relational bond.

COMMUNICATING HISTORY—SHARING STORIES

The pivotal role communication plays in determining the nature of the grandparent–grandchild relationship has received very little scholarly attention. One study that attempted to capture intergenerational communication within the grandparent–grandchild relationship was conducted by Nussbaum and Bettini (1994). This research utilized the notion set forth by Kornhaber and Woodward (1981) and accentuated by Downs (1989), that both grandparents and grandchildren view their interaction as one in which experiences, events, and family history help to continue family tradition. Nussbaum and Bettini (1994) designed a study that provided an opportunity for both grandparents and grandchildren to interact on audiotape. During the Thanksgiving holiday, grandparent–grandchild dyads were asked to "tell a story that captures the meaning of life" to one another. A like number of the four possible dyad pairs (grandmother–grandson, grandmother–granddaughter, grandfather–grandson, grandfather–granddaughter) were formed within their own homes and were instructed to audiotape the shared stories. No other family members were present so that each participant would only be influenced by his or her immediate relational partner. The adult grandchildren in this investigation were college students, most were White with no major financial difficulties. The purpose of this investigation was to identify any patterns of storytelling that emerged, to help us better understand not only what content of communication emerges in such a situation, but to capture a small portion of communication that may help to define this intergenerational relationship.

The audiotapes were analyzed for the purpose of identifying any consistencies or patterns in the stories told by each participant. Nussbaum and Bettini point to several interesting patterns that did emerge from the interactions. First, the grandmothers talked at least twice as long as the grandfathers, regardless of the gender of the grandchild. The grandfathers not only talked less, but were quite reticent to talk at all. In numerous instances, the designated grandfather refused to participate when the recorder was turned on. The adult grandchildren reported that none of the grandmothers refused to participate. Why the grandfathers were reticent is not clear. Perhaps they were apprehensive about interacting "on-record" with their grandchildren in rather intimate, affective encounters. In other words, it is possible that the requirements of the study fell outside the grandfather's (but not the grandmother's) natural range of behavior with grandchildren.

A second pertinent finding from the audiotaped interactions was that a large majority of grandparents mentioned their ages in the course of their stories, or in the comments surrounding their storytelling. Much of the age-telling talk was straightforward: "I've learned a lot in my 82 years ...", while some alluded to their ages more subtly, "Back in 1972 when I was 52 ...". This age-telling within intergenerational talk was found to be a rather typical feature in conversations between young strangers and elderly individuals within an adult day-care center (Coupland, Coupland, & Giles, 1989). It is interesting to note that age-telling occurs not only between intergenerational strangers, but also, between very close family members participating in this communicative task. Age-telling serves to make the interaction age salient. In this particular context, it is probably used to emphasise the fact that the grandparents are older and therefore wiser. In this way then, grandparents attempt to invoke stereotypical images of wise elders whose stories should be treated seriously. Remember that transmitting wisdom through storytelling is a well-rehearsed and positive stereotypical image we have of elders.

The audiotaped interactions also revealed a content difference in the meaning of life stories among the grandparents. Sixty-five percent of grandfathers talked about youth experiences, especially wartime experiences, to emphasize the value of life. In addition, grandfathers were more likely than grandmothers to talk about major health problems that made them refocus the meaning of their own lives. Finally, grandfathers were more likely to tell a story or a parable that held a particular moral for the listener. One grandfather told his granddaughter of his rather "racy" youth and how he learned, from his misdeeds, to perform service activities in his retirement. Grandmothers, on the other hand, talked about how the family developed, how they met their husbands, and about their own parents and grandparents. Grandmother talk was filled with family and relationship talk. Much like Thorsheim and Roberts (1990) in their collection of life stories from elderly individuals, grandmothers in this investigation concentrated on relational themes, whereas grandfathers concentrated on accomplishments both in and outside the family. Grandmothers also contrasted life today with life 50 or so years ago. Grandfathers did not reminisce about the past in quite the same way. As was mentioned in previous sections of this chapter, we must be careful about generalizing these results to other grandparental cohorts. For example, because these grandmothers and grandfathers grew to adulthood in the 1940s and 1950s, their stories are influenced by gendered roles during that particular historic period. For example, many of these women would have seen their primary roles as homekeepers and housewives, and their stories will naturally reflect this.

The content of the stories told from grandparent to grandchild did not change due to the gender of the grandchild. Both grandfathers and grandmothers told grandsons and granddaughters similar stories concerning the meaning of life. Of particular interest to the researchers was the finding that grandchildren of both genders seemed to experience great difficulty in telling meaningful life stories to their grandparents. Several explanations for this lack of storytelling from the adult grandchild to the grandparent can be offered. It could be that the limited life experiences of these young adults have provided the grandchildren with no appropriate stories to share. Or, more likely, the procedures utilized within this investigation violated the natural relationship expectations of grandparents and grandchildren. Grandchildren probably felt that they had very little comparative wisdom to transmit to grandparents, that their stories would sound naive and corny, or that the grandparents would not be able to relate to the modern circumstances that produce modern, meaningful, life stories. In any event, the research reveals that grandchildren and grandparents had difficulty stepping outside a rather natural and expected complementary accommodative relationship wherein grandparents were the ones who were supposed to tell wise stories, and grandchildren were supposed to listen and take note.

SUMMARY AND IMPLICATIONS

The grandparent–grandchild relationship is reflective of the great diversity of family relationships that exist in our modern society. No greater mistake could perhaps be made than to simplify the nature of this relationship into one or two static behavioral categories or relational types. The research reviewed in this chapter points to the variety of grandparental behaviors manifested within the relationship across the life span, as well as the importance of such factors as gender of both grandparent and grandchild, parental divorce, financial resources, age of both grandparent and grandchild, the parental role of the grandparent, and the cultural background within which the relationship exists, as having profound impacts on the nature and course of the relationship. Intergenerational communication that transpires within the relationship and any possible effects of that intergenerational communication cannot possibly be understood without first recognizing the importance of each contextual factor outlined in this chapter.

One could argue that the adult child–elderly parent relationship discussed in the previous chapter has a more well-defined pattern of roles and appropriate relational behavior than the grandparent–grandchild relationship. The intergenerational communication of the grandparent–grandchild relationship, therefore, may be quite demonstrative of relationship-defining behavior.

In modern society, characterized by Giddens (1991) as "high modernity," the grandparent and the grandchild are likely to be inventing their relationship in a new world wherein stereotypic roles are influential, but are no longer appropriate or functional, and in which lifestyle changes have changed the essence of the relationship. We might also speculate about the resources that grandparents and grandchildren bring to their relationships and how these help shape and form the relationships. For example, grandparents are a potentially valuable family resource because they often provide a rich source of social and emotional support, financial stability, baby sitting or child minding services and so forth. Also, they are often able to work with, or even free themselves from, the constraints of the child–parent relationship (i.e., discipline, constant caregiving, tuition) and can construct a relationship to suit their unique needs and desires.

The nature of the grandparent–grandchild relationship will change as we live longer, become more or less financially stable, produce fewer children, and become a more mobile society. As this family relationship changes, scholars will need to uncover much more of the hidden emotional and instrumental functions of this particular intergenerational relationship. Communication between the generations, the talk shared by grandparents and grandchildren, and talk between grandparents and parents regarding the child, are all valuable and relatively untapped sources of information that reveal far more about the nature of this relationship than models of style do. When we consider the research about grandparenting to date, a myriad of questions swirl through our minds. The following are not exhaustive, but should provide a nexus to provoke further thought. Future research should investigate how grandchildren, parents, and grandparents create the grandparent role. Researchers should also investigate whether and how certain contexts or events such as ill health create communication predicaments for grandparents and grandchildren. How do families tackle and resolve communication predicaments that might be unique to this relationship? Rather than blandly asserting that grandparenting can be a highly positive and satisfactory experience versus one that is distant and disconnected, researchers should study the cut and thrust of this relationship. When the relationship is satisfying, how is this achieved? In addition, the effect of unreasonable positive stereotypes concerning the grandparent role on both the grandparent and grandchild need to be uncovered. How do people transition into the grandparental role? How do families work through the myriad of relational changes and potential tensions (i.e., contradictions and dilemmas) that accompany such transitions? When grandparents fall short of the stereotypic ideal, could this lead to much less satisfaction within the relationship?

One interesting constraint that families work with is the issue of grandparental interference in childrearing. Almost certainly there is strong self-presentational pressure for families to portray grandparents as noninterfering. This belies the importance of grandparental involvement, however. If we draw a distinction between interference and involvement, grandparents are by definition involved. Studies based on social interaction rather than self-reports might show how levels of interference, or to use a less value-laden term, involvement, are negotiated, managed, and even tolerated in a complex transaction of accommodative give and take. As we hope this chapter shows, grandparental involvement is often a valuable resource for the family.

When college students are asked to think about an older adult they often interact with, these students do not discuss their interactions with strangers. Rather, their first response is to discuss their relationships with their grandparent and/or other very familiar well-known elders. To understand intergenerational communication, a much greater effort on the part of scholars needs to be directed toward the communicative behavior found within the grandparent–grandchild relationship.

10

Sandwiched Communication

One clear message of this book is that multigenerational family relationships are increasingly common occurrences in modern society. The previous two chapters concentrate on older adult child–elderly parent relationships and grandparent–grandchild relationships. The intergenerational communication that transpires in these two familial relationships is often performed within a rather complex and dynamic family structure. Parents sometimes have their own parents present when they talk to their children, who in turn may have their own children present during the same interaction. In other words, the simple dyadic relationships often discussed by scholars in the empirical literature, and highlighted in the previous two chapters of this book, take place within a larger triadic or quadratic family-relationship system. Grandparents, parents, and children have a remarkable habit of interacting simultaneously or, at the very least, of modifying their communicative behavior because of the fact that others in the family are active participants in everyone else's lives. The simple dyad of parent–child or grandparent–grandchild operating in an interactive vacuum without being affected by various other intergenerational relationships occurring around them is a convenient but rather simplistic way to begin the study of such relationships—it is not reality. Families increasingly consist of several levels of intergenerational interaction affecting each other in complex and hitherto underexplored ways. For example, family members' identities across the life span are constructed in these multiple communication contexts—in a system of interlinked dyadic, triadic, and other multiple-interaction structures. The scholarly literature has produced only a minimal amount of discussion concerning multiple, intergenerational relationships, simultaneously affecting and being affected by one another. As part of this multilevel systemic structure we are as much affected by interactions that we do not have a direct part in as those that we do. For example, we are not always privy to those conversations other family members have about us in which they can construct scenarios and make decisions that affect us directly. This sandwich effect of a grandparent–parent relationship with consequences for a parent–child relationship, and vice versa, is the topic of this chapter.

As the decade of the 1990s comes to an end, the popular media, as well as political forces at work in many Western countries, appear to expect a major multigenerational conflict to erupt (for more discussion of this issue, see chapter 12, this volume, Halpren, 1994). According to these voices, older people are branded "greedy geezers" who spend all of society's money as they wear out the Baby Boomers caring for them, who in their turn, deplete the rich resources of the world chasing their I've-got-to-have-it-now lifestyles. These two generations, one self-absorbed and the other just plain selfish, have no time for the forgotten and faceless Generation X; their overspending and selfishness has left neither jobs nor money for the next generation. Ultimately, as described in chapter 12, this line of reasoning suggests that three generations of individuals seem to be on the verge of a catastrophic conflict for the limited social and economic resources available to lead comfortable lives. If this is true, we might expect some evidence of such multigenerational conflictual communication between the various levels of intergenerational interaction within families. Alternatively, it could be suggested that this intergenerational resentment is primarily directed at outgroup members, for example, elders who are neither family nor well known; family members may often be considered an exception to the rule (see also chapter 12, this volume). These mediated discourses would only emerge in families at certain triggering points; for example, family members will apply available media images to each other when they feel that it is strategic to do so (see Williams, Coupland, Folwell, & Sparks, 1997). For the most part, researchers paint a very positive picture of family interaction. This is probably because family members have learned to accommodate each other; they know what not to talk about and what to "let pass." In this way, families probably achieve an accommodative working consensus (see Pittam & Gallois, 1998), which is enough to keep relationships flowing smoothly and productively most of the time.

The simplest and perhaps most informative situation within which multiple generations interact is composed of the two relationships discussed previously (the adult child–elderly parent relationship and the grandparent–grandchild relationship) with the addition of the adolescent–parent relationship. Whereas the infant–parent relationship can also be included within any triad of intergenerational interaction, the adolescent–parent relationship is discussed in this chapter because during adolescence, young people are emerging from the shadows of the parent and negotiating a unique communicative identity. Thus, the multigenerational nature of communication includes at the very least three distinct relationships, each affecting, and being affected by, the other relationships. The particular focus of this chapter is on the middle generation of individuals who must relate to individuals both older and younger than themselves. Intergenerational communication will indeed be affected by the numerous multigenerational relationships occurring simultaneously in our lives, and the sandwiched generation may have the most difficult or possibly, the most interesting intergenerational roles to master. Because the adult child–elderly parent relationship and the grandparent–grandchild relationship have already been discussed, it is appropriate to summarize the existing literature concerning the adolescent–parent relationship prior to a complete exploration of multigenerational communication.

THE ADOLESCENT–PARENT RELATIONSHIP

Any scholar who studies the life-long development of humans can compellingly argue that the most developmentally interesting time of our lives occurs during our adolescence. While all of us move through adolescence into adulthood and feel the massive physical, psychological, and social changes that are often beyond our control or reason, we must somehow cope with these changes and the demands they impose on our lives. Although it may seem to adolescents that these changes are occurring only to them within an individual vacuum, these massive individual changes certainly affect, and are affected by, the family who surround the adolescent. Noller (1995) emphasizes the importance of the family in this critical period of our development by stating, "Families that provide close, supportive environments for adolescents, while at the same time encouraging autonomy and independence, seem to produce adolescents who can best cope with the transition to adulthood" (p. 77). This statement, which seems like common sense to most of us, belies the difficulties that dog the accomplishment of this task. One major key to the adolescent environment is the adolescent–parent relationship. This intergenerational relationship exists at the very heart of our individual development into adulthood. Stated quite simply, to understand the dynamic changes in adolescence, one must come to understand the intergenerational relationship and the communication that transpires while both parent and adolescent reinvent their relationship as old interaction patterns give way to new ones.

Noller (1995) identified five functions of communication in families with adolescents: "(a) enabling the renegotiation of roles, rules, and relationships, (b) providing an appropriate climate for identity exploration, (c) enhancing rather than diminishing self-esteem, (d) providing appropriate modeling and teaching of problem solving, and (e) enabling adolescents to make the important decisions that affect their lives" (pp. 77–78). Each of these five functions of communication adds to our knowledge of this relationship. However, the first function of communication mentioned by Noller, enabling the renegotiation of roles, rules, and relationships within the adolescent–parent relationship, is most central to an understanding of the dynamic nature of this particular relationship, and to the multigenerational relationships within which the adolescent–parent relationship is embedded.

Just as the nature of the adult child–elderly parent relationship changes and is constantly renegotiated, the adolescent–parent relationship is in a heightened state of intense change. For the most part, adolescents strive for greater autonomy and independence in their lives, often more than parents feel comfortable with, and so an accommodative struggle ensues. Typically then, adolescents initiate bids for freedom and parents must reframe, accept, or reject such bids actively or passively. The parents may wish to respect or to temper adolescent needs and demands or may attempt to maintain control. Exactly how this is achieved communicatively is not yet known. We have little doubt that this process is at times conflictual, miscommunicative, and may be under constant repair. In any event, the rebirth of the adolescent–parent relationship can have a profound impact upon the family. This relational transition or turning point is quite normal, although it is at times quite intense, dramatic, and painful for both parties. However, only in very rare instances does this turning point reach a point of true crisis in which the relationship is damaged beyond repair. Adolescent–parent conflict is quite predictable and is ultimately positive and helpful if it serves to spur and move the relationship forward. Without some tension and conflict, change in the relationship might be impossible and both adolescent and parent would surely suffer.

Noller (1995) points to several factors that manage the intensity of conflict during the renegotiation of the adolescent–parent relationship. First, adolescents and parents view the family quite differently. Adolescents perceive their families to be more negative, less open, less cohesive, and less adaptable than their parents do. Second, the extent to which parents resist adolescent moves toward independence can intensify conflict. "Adolescents are likely to want more change, and at a faster rate, than their parents can comfortably handle" (p. 80). Third, peer pressure may play a role in the conflict between adolescents and parents. Adolescents begin to seek advice from peers as they move into middle school or junior high school. The need to manage peer relationships can often create impossible situations for both the adolescent and the parent. Fourth, adolescents must come to grips with the fact that their parents are not always correct and can make mistakes. The opposite is also true. Parents must come to grips with the fact that adolescents are not always wrong, and actually can make mature, reasonable decisions. Finally, the core values of each generation may provide fuel for more intense conflicts. The adolescent generation may place more emphasis on shared societal responsibility for the poor, the aged, or the environment, and may blame their parents for numerous problems, such as the sorry state of the schools and the lack of employment opportunities. Parents may feel that their adolescent children are lazy and spoiled. These perceived value differences can intensify conflict (for a more complete discussion of intergenerational conflict, see chapter 12, this volume).

The second and third functions of communication in the adolescent–parent relationship center on the adolescent discovering his or her place in the world and maintaining positive self-esteem. The quality of the adolescent–parent relationship appears to play an important role in these psychological states for the adolescent. In families in which parents provide solid emotional support, manage conflict in an appropriate manner, and are not overly controlling toward their adolescent children, positive outcomes, with adolescents coming to terms with their own identities and developing positive self-concepts, are more likely to appear (Noller, 1995).

The fourth function of communication within the adolescent–parent relationship is to provide appropriate modeling of interpersonal behavior. The adolescent–parent relationship provides valuable experience for both participants about how to behave appropriately in numerous other relationships. This, of course, is most important for other intergenerational relationships both within and outside the family. Barnes and Olson (1985) report that families can benefit from a democratic style of adolescent–parent communication. These families report being closer and more loving, and obtaining a higher level of satisfaction with their family life. The democratic style of family interaction and stressing of positive negotiation is likely to produce adolescents who can function as effective, independent adults.

Results from numerous empirical investigations indicate that male and female adolescents may be socialized into different ways of communicating within the adolescent–parent relationship (see Noller, 1995). Older adolescents report interacting more with mothers than with fathers. "In addition, female adolescents reported more self-disclosure to mothers than did male adolescents across such areas as interests, sex roles, relationships, sexual information, and sexual problems, and they reported more self-disclosure to fathers in the areas of future plans, rules of society, and general problems" (Noller, 1995, p. 98). Noller concludes that parents provide models of communication that fit sex-role stereotypes and that adolescents follow these same sex-role stereotypes in their interactions with their parents.

The final communication function of the adolescent–parent relationship concerns decision making in the lives of adolescents. As adolescents age, they attempt to gain more control over their lives by making more and more of the decisions that affect their lives. Parents, on the other hand, have difficulty handing over the decision-making process to their adolescent children. Decisions of extreme importance are faced by adolescents and parents each day. Drug use, sexual exploration, future educational goals, and many other issues can lead to serious conflict between adolescents and their parents. If parents or adolescents feel uncomfortable with a discussion concerning these important life issues, both adolescent and parent may make poor decisions. Noller (1995) points out that adolescents who have a poor relationship with their parents tend to interact more with peers about these serious issues and to ignore the advice of parents. This in turn often leads to more serious problems including a spiraling of relational problems.

What seems most interesting for communication researchers is how families can acheive these five goals while attempting to manage a number of contradictions and communicate through a myriad of accommodative dilemmas. Parents may feel conflicting needs to hold on to and to let go of adolescents, who also feel conflicts of dependency and autonomy as they develop resources outside the family of origin. In fact, communicative underaccommodation, nonaccommodation, and even divergence away from parents may be normal parts of an adolescent bid for freedom. The adolescents put communicative distance between themselves and their parents in order to achieve personal and social distance. At the same time, parents may be ambivalent about "letting go" of their children. For example, at times they may try to hold on to their youngsters. In communication terms this would be indicated by various accommodative behaviors such as overaccommodating as discussed in earlier chapters (e.g., see chapter 3, this volume). There may be times when the adolescent and the parent feel and act as members of different social groups, hence the intergroup end of the interindividual–intergroup dialectic may be engaged. This can exacerbate tension and conflict in spite of parents' good intentions and best efforts to do what the experts suggest they should do to aid healthy development through adolescence.

By late adolescence this early transition has typically been worked through. Thornton, Orbuch, and Axinn (1995) studied the transition from late adolescence to young adulthood within the parent–child relationship. Several interesting findings emerge from this study. First, Thornton et al. report that their sample of late adolescents indicates the existence of positive and supportive relationships with their parents. Only a very small minority of parent–child relationships were characterized in negative ways. Late adolescents who are moving into young adulthood report more positive relationships with their mothers than with their fathers. In addition, adolescents who report positive relationships with their parents are more likely to maintain positive relationships into young adulthood. If the relationships are not so positive, evidence exists that many parent–child relationships become more positive as the child ages into young adulthood.

Thornton et al. also indicate strong support for the notion that parent–child relationships are evaluated differently by parents and children. Perhaps more important, is the suggestion that neither parent nor child recognizes the fact that this one relationship has two perceived realities. These different perceptions of the nature of the relationship can lead to miscommunication and trouble when parent and child attempt to handle any uncomfortable situation.

Although much more empirical research has concentrated on the various factors involved with adolescence as a life stage, the short discussion of the adolescent–parent relationship included in this chapter certainly underscores the importance of communication within this family relationship. The adolescent–parent relationship is challenging to both participants. It is a critical time both the adolescent and the middle-aged adult, when many changes are occurring and many relational challenges must be met. Beyond simply dealing with this particular intergenerational relationship, both adolescent and parent must maintain additional intergenerational relationships within the family. The remainder of this chapter attempts to capture the multigenerational nature of relationships faced by family members. Of particular interest are those middle-aged adults who are sandwiched between adolescent children and elderly parents.

THE SANDWICH GENERATION

Middle-aged adults are faced with multiple challenges in their increasingly complex lives. Social scientists have speculated that factors such as the increased longevity of older individuals, the changing role of women in our society, and the timing of childbirth have placed this generation of adults in a rather troublesome situation (Brody, 1981; Treas, 1979). Middle-aged adults may find themselves "sandwiched" between caregiving for their elderly parents and parenting their adolescent children. The popular media has magnified the possible stress and pressure placed on this middle generation and has created a dilemma as to who the middle generation is most responsible for—their parents or their children. Social scientists have only recently begun to investigate this sandwich generation and their multigenerational responsibilities. The two previous chapters, as well as the first part of this chapter, present the literature about what we currently know of the nature of the older adult–elderly parent relationship and the adolescent–parent relationship. The major functions within these relationships—emotional support, socialization, financial support, caregiving of all sorts, and so on—were discussed and found to be mutually satisfying. In other words, for the most part, research suggests that the relationships work well enough. Parents generally do socialize their children to become productive members of society, who in turn support their parents as they age and if they should become dependent. However, the discussion to this point assumes that the parent is not simultaneously caring for both adolescent children and older adults. As a matter of fact, most empirical investigations ignore the fact that middle-aged adults may find themselves in this very position. Therefore, any possible consequences of multigenerational responsibility have been rather absent from the scientific literature. The question becomes whether this middle generation can perform these multigenerational tasks without major psychological and physical distress to themselves and to the various intergenerational relationships in this increasingly complex world.

Rosenthal, Matthews, and Marshall (1989) and Spitze and Logan (1990) investigated the number of middle-generation women caught between parenting responsibilities and caregiving for an elderly parent. They find that very few middle-aged women are caught between responsibilities of work, children, and caring for elderly relatives. Himes (1994) utilized sophisticated demographic techniques to further explore the possibility of women finding themselves in this situation across the life span. Results indicate that it is quite rare for middle-aged women to be both parent to adolescents or younger children and to be a primary caregiver to an elderly parent. However, the probability of one day becoming a caregiver for an elderly parent is quite high. As elderly individuals remain healthy well into their 70s, the possibility that middle-aged women will both care for children or adolescents and their elderly parents grows increasingly smaller. The time spent caring for both generations also may be limited, given the fact that adolescents grow to leave home, and that ill elderly people eventually die. However, this is by no means an indication that middle-aged women will not face such a multigenerational dilemma. At any rate, the probability that at some point in the life span caregiving will dominate the lives of middle-aged women is quite high.

A few studies have investigated the possibility of adverse effects on middle-generation adults who find themselves caring for parents as they parent their own children. Horowitz (1985) found that adult daughters of elderly parents reported declines in psychological well-being due to the time constraints of their family responsibilities of caring for both children and parents. Stoller (1983) investigated the amount of care middle-aged women with children at home provided for their elderly parents. Results indicate that middle-aged women did not provide less care to their parents, suggesting that these middle-aged women tried to pack more caregiving activity into smaller amounts of possible time, thus promoting significant stress in their lives. These women were trying to be super providers. Noelker and Wallace (1985) report evidence suggesting that married middle-generation parents experience numerous personal and physical problems related to caring for their coresiding elderly parents, which unmarried, childfree, middle-generation adults do not suffer.

Loomis and Booth (1995) tested the notion that multigenerational caregiving does adversely affect the lives of this sandwich generation. Only a small amount of empirical evidence exists suggesting that middle-aged adults who simultaneously care for children and parents do experience multiple problems. Some researchers suggest that multiple caregiving roles may actually be beneficial because these duties provide a sense of fulfillment and increased self-esteem. A study was conducted to test whether the adoption of multigenerational caregiving responsibilities adversely affects caregivers' well-being. Utilizing a national sample of middle-aged individuals with an average age of 48, who were simultaneously caring for at least one child less than 17 years of age and one parent or parent-in-law, multigenerational caregiving responsibilities were correlated with marital happiness, marital interaction, marital conflict, marital instability, psychological distress, financial strain, satisfaction with leisure time, and division of labor. Results indicate that, as middle-aged adults take on the added burden of multigenerational caregiving, little or no effect on caregivers' well-being is recorded, even after considering factors such as caregiver gender and weekly hours of outside employment. Loomis and Booth conclude that middle-aged adults who have children at home and assume the added responsibility of caring for a parent or parent-in-law experience no significant changes in their well-being. "Moreover, we suggest that the multigenerational responsibilities of children and elderly parents do not develop into an especially difficult situation for most middle-generation adults and that troubles of the sandwich generation may be a myth" (p. 147).

Three plausible explanations are proposed to explain this lack of any decline in well-being by middle-aged caregivers with multigenerational caregiving responsibilities (Loomis & Booth, 1995). First, the children as well as the parents have an existing relationship prior to the additional caregiving for the parents. The existing relationship provides each participant with much-needed information about how to cope with the new, renegotiated relationships and any sacrifices needed to be made concerning their own lives. In addition, the relational history of all three generations permits each participant to anticipate many of the demands of the relationship prior to reaching a crisis point. Second, there may be a selection effect so that those individuals who can most handle the added caregiving burden are the ones who take on the additional multigenerational responsibilities. The research evidence does suggest that middle-aged caregivers already have strong relationships with their spouses, children, and parents prior to the added parental caregiving. These strong relationships can be the foundation to actually help the middle-aged adult perform as a spouse, parent, and caregiver to a mother or father. Third, the middle-aged adults may have a value system that reinforces the positive aspects of caregiving. These individuals appear to have an unlimited ability to successfully parent their children as they care for their ailing parents.

Levitt, Guacci, and Weber (1992) investigated multigenerational support, relationship quality, and well-being in a bicultural sample of young adult women (mean age of 21 years), their mothers (mean age of 46 years), and their maternal grandmothers (mean age of 73 years). Thirty English-speaking and 23 Spanish-speaking triads participated in this investigation. Results from this study provide evidence that women in the middle generation gave significantly more support than they received.

Both the older mothers and the younger daughters report receiving more support from the middle-aged women than they gave to the women in the middle generation. This evidence supports the contention that the middle generation may be squeezed between two needy generations.

Additional findings from this study point to generational as well as cultural differences in perceptions of relationship quality. "Relations with daughters were viewed more positively by older than by middle-generation women, and there was a significant discrepancy in perception between older-generation mothers and daughters regarding quality of their relationship" (Levitt et al., 1992, p. 477). The younger mother–daughter dyads perceived a similar level of relational quality and support exchanges. These results may indicate a closer and more interdependent relationship between the younger mother–daughter dyad. These results suggest that a larger generational difference may exist in the older mother–daughter relationship than in the younger mother–daughter relationship.

Cultural differences emerged within the data that reflect a general empirical trend for intergenerational tensions in acculturating groups (Szapocznik, Scopetta, Kurtines, & Aranalde, 1978). The Spanish-speaking respondents in the older and middle generations reported less positive relations with the younger generations than did the English-speaking respondents.

Research discussing the possible consequences of multigenerational interactions within the family context is quite sparse. From the empirical evidence just discussed, several major conclusions can be reached. First, at any one point in time, the great majority of individuals living in Western society do interact within multigenerational family relationships. It is very common for adolescent children to coexist with their parents, grandparents, and even great grandparents. The four generations may not always live under the same roof, but these four generations do interact and influence one another. Second, at any one time, it is rare for a middle-aged adult to simultaneously care for an elderly parent and raise adolescent children. This sandwich generation of middle-aged adults caring for two generations of family members is quite small. Third, those middle-aged adults who find themselves within a sandwich of caregiving may or may not report extreme stress as a result of their caring responsibilities. Research supports psychological distress on the part of the sandwich generation due to caregiving responsibilities. On the other hand, research supports positive affects of this sandwiched caregiving that enhances one's sense of self-worth. We simply do not know at this point the exact nature of the consequences inherent within multigenerational caregiving. Finally, the way different generations of family members view their relationships with one another may be quite disparate. For example, adolescents' perceptions of the parent–child relationship are different from those of their middle-aged parents. In addition, these same middle-aged parents' perceptions of their relationships with

their elderly parents are quite different from their elderly parents' perceptions. The multigenerational, perceived relational differences are very intriguing because they are at the core of a constant shift and change of
relational identities within the family. The role that communication plays
within this multigenerational context of relational change is the content of
the next section of this chapter.

MULTIGENERATIONAL COMMUNICATION

As mentioned at the beginning of this chapter, middle-aged adults who are
raising adolescent children while they continue a very active relationship
with their own parents inhabit a fascinating communicative niche. Communication, of course, is always located in the context of a developing relationship. The question becomes, how does communication function within
such a complex, multigenerational, relational, family environment?

As yet, social scientists who study intergenerational communication
have not addressed this real-world issue. Unfortunately, we know very little
about how communication transpires or the possible functions or effects of
communication within these multigenerational families. We can, however,
speculate as to form and importance of such communication by extending
what we do know about intergenerational communication, both within and
outside the family, to the more complex communicative situation of multi-
ple-intergenerational relationships. For example, we could investigate if,
when, how, and why intergroup and stereotyped communication emerges
between intergenerational family members.

Research has suggested that at the core of the multigenerational family
relationship is the perception of an honest, deep-felt closeness. Whether
or not this closeness is defined as solidarity or attachment, the empirical
evidence is clear that multiple generations of family members report feeling close throughout their lives. It is normative for adolescents, their parents, grandparents, and great grandparents to report frequent interaction
with one another, and for this interaction to transpire within close relationships. It is also normative for these close relationships to be in a constant state of flux and change. The feelings of closeness may remain quite
high as each individual attempts to redefine control and power within the
relationship. At the very minimum, then, we are faced with a series of
multigenerational family relationships that remain stable along affective
relational dimensions, but that often change quite dramatically in terms
of relational power distributions. We can assume that the communication

within these relationships creates and reflects feelings of intimacy, and is therefore attuned and accommodative. On the other hand, a constant repositioning of power differentials as family members negotiate their independence or dependence would be indicated by incidents and periods of under-, over-, or nonaccommodative communication or some combination of these.

In any case, it is the middle-aged generation of adults who are likely to be brokering a power dimension in opposite directions with the younger and older generation, and may be embroiled in, and feel responsible for, several communication predicaments at the same time. Triadic communication predicaments seem to be important unexplored phenomena. For example, adolescents may be attempting to negotiate more autonomy and power over their lives, while the older generation may be positioned as losing power and as more submissive to the middle-aged adult, especially if health care or other difficulties that threaten independence are at issue. Of course, the great majority of older adults wish to remain independent as long as possible. All this points to the fact that the dependence versus independence issue is likely to be one nexus of intense familial maneuvering, and three generations may be simultaneously negotiating various positions along this continuum. In this way, middle-aged adults can be sandwiched between two dramatic relational repositionings. This sandwich effect is much more than the caregiving phenomenon discussed earlier in this chapter; it is a relational communication phenomenon.

The closeness felt within each intergenerational family relationship must be nurtured. Much communicative work is necessary to maintain the high levels of closeness often taken for granted by these relational participants. For example, according to parents' self-reports, they do not respond to the intergenerational conflict caused by their adolescent childrens' demands for more freedom or to their parents' wishes for more interactive time by ending or limiting the affection in the relationship. Interactive data would illuminate this further and may show how closeness is somehow maintained as the relational power is distributed, conflict deflected, solutions proposed, and so forth. In other words, how do we manage such a complex communicative task without destroying the relationship? If the relationship has taken a severe turn for the worse, how do we rebuild it? Perhaps it is the history of closeness across the life span, as well as access to other familial resources (e.g., practical support), that enable the relationship to survive serious intergenerational conflict that would predictably tear apart nonfamilial relationships.

SUMMARY

For the middle-aged adults who have been a major focus of this chapter, relationships with their children and their parents are long-term, intense, and highly affective. Most investigators choose to study these relationships as if they are purely dyadic. Indeed, we have chosen this dyadic path to present the most up-to-date empirical literature concerning intergenerational family relationships and the intergenerational communication shared within these relationships. We do this because it is the simplest and most direct format for discussion. However, these relationships are neither purely dyadic nor purely two generational. At the very least, it should now be obvious that the great majority of us interact in a familial, multigenerational world with up to five generations of family relationships coexisting.

Recognizing the importance of this leads to questions such as: While the adolescent negotiates autonomy with his or her parents, what role does the grandparent relationship play in this renegotiation of control? Research has shown that the grandparent–grandchild relationship is not only a significant familial relationship, but that it can be a highly diverse relationship. In some instances, we can foresee great participation by grandparents in the renegotiation for adolescent autonomy from the parents. The adolescent child may form a coalition with his or her grandparents to gain an upper hand in the autonomy challenge. In other instances, the grandparents may sit back, watch, and share a chuckle. The grandparents in this case remain separate from the negotiation or serve as a back-up to either parent or child, hoping that their grandparent–grandchild relationship will not be affected by the outcome of the parent–child renegotiation.

Empirical research has also been clear that grandchildren can become involved in caring for, or at least helping their parents care for, their grandparents. The grandparents have lost some level of independence and must renegotiate this with their children. Often, the grandchildren can be a great help to this renegotiation by offering to share caregiving responsibilities. This, in essence, changes the nature of the grandchild–grandparent relationship as well as the nature of the parent–child relationship. The communicative dynamics of these multiple-relational redefinitions across generations should be a focus for future research.

The life-span nature of all familial, multigenerational relationships is often overlooked. We must keep in mind that all participants in these relationships are aging. Although this may appear to be a simple concept to discuss at this time, social scientists have virtually ignored the changes that occur to the parent–child relationship, the grandparent–grandchild relationship, or any other relationship while that relationship moves through time. The middle-aged adult who is sandwiched between adolescent children and older parents will remain sandwiched in an evolving set of relationships for some number of years. Research should follow these multiple generations through time and observe the actual relationship turning points and the communicative behavior utilized to manage simultaneous relational changes. One could compare numerous families as they develop across the life span, and could monitor similarities and patterns that may be predictive of relationship turning points.

The overwhelming majority of multigenerational, familial relationships seem to manage the enormous changes occurring throughout life quite well. However, there are times of severe relational crisis that occur in relatively well-managed relationships that have the potential to destroy the relationship. In addition, numerous families do not function well, and multigenerational relationships within these families never seem to generate any level of happiness—family members seem to be locked into patterns of mutually unsatisfying communication but somehow they stay together in a dysfunctional trajectory. The stress that middle-aged adults feel as they simultaneously care for their elderly parents and manage their adolescent children will manifest itself in the communicative behavior of the family. This intergenerational communication is not a symptom or manifestation of family crisis—it is the crisis—and can be the cause and cure of familial dysfunction too.

A major demographic trend that affects families and has been ignored by social scientists who study communication are the increasing number of families involved in divorces or remarriages. Research has indicated that grandparents can be helpful during the divorce of their children, for both those who are being divorced and for the grandchildren, but we know very little how this help manifests itself in the communication between all the various relational participants. The United States is also a society with a deep tradition of excess litigation. The legal rights of multiple generations concerning their continued interaction is currently a hot legal topic. Just what are the legal, communicative rights of grandparents with their grandchildren once a remarriage has occurred? The complexity of multigenerational relationships within the family is only made more complex by a disruption in the relational bonds of any family member.

At this time, research has not uncovered the communicative keys to successful multigenerational relationships within the family. Indeed, these keys may not exist. However, the major difficulties with intergenerational communication found within some families are not disruptive for the great majority of families. The process by which individual family members can communicate their individual and relational needs that lead to highly satisfying relationships across both generations and the life span should not be a mystery. Future research into the communicative behavior of these multigenerational families will be immensely productive. It is imperative that communication scholars get involved in the study of multigenerational interactions; demographic and sociological studies simply have not answered many of the important questions.

The previous two chapters and this chapter attempt to place intergenerational communication within the family context. A great deal of empirical research has produced a substantial body of literature that outlines the important functionality of familial, intergenerational relationships. The research is quite clear. The parent–child bond is generally close and caring throughout life. The grandparent–grandchild relationship is close, diverse, and dynamic for both relational participants throughout life. These familial, intergenerational relationships are constantly changing through frequent interaction across the entirety of the life span. The middle generation of older adults can find themselves in a unique communicative position sandwiched between the generations. It is also clear, however, that researchers have only just begun to observe and understand the important role intergenerational communication plays in competent family functioning.

The next chapter concentrates on some important, potentially long-term and relatively intimate intergenerational relationships outside the family. Although intergenerational friendships do exist, we focus our discussion on intergenerational relationships that are common yet are more professional. Intergenerational communication within the physician–patient relationship and the teacher–student relationship, for instance, has been studied and shown to be important in accomplishing vital individual as well as societal goals. The next chapter brings together the literature about several important nonfamilial, intergenerational relationships, and the intergenerational communication transpiring within those relationships.

11

Intergenerational Relationships Beyond the Family

As previous chapters reveal, intergenerational communication is not limited to family interactions. A number of the most influential and significant relationships we form and maintain in our lives occur within professional, intergenerational interactions. This chapter discusses two professional contexts within which intergenerational relationships are quite common, health care and education. Chapters 2 through 7 explained some of the major dimensions and contexts of nonfamilial intergenerational relationships. For instance, intergenerational relationships form through organized religion, service organizations, mail delivery, various friendships, sporting activities, and so on. However, the contexts of health care and education may not only be among the most significant contexts within which intergenerational relationships are formed; they may have also produced some of the most interesting and relevant research to enhance our overall goals of discussing and understanding intergenerational communication across the life span. The chapter concludes with a brief discussion of interesting and recent research concerned with intergenerational friendships.

As discussed in the previous three chapters, intergenerational relationships formed within the family are generally both positive and productive. Although the intergenerational communication that defines these familial relationships may at times seem to be quite destructive and marginalizing, for the most part, intergenerational communication within families is caring and life enhancing. Unfortunately, the same is not always true for intergenerational communication outside of the family. The vast majority of the research and theory dedicated to intergenerational communication (reviewed in the first part of the book) has concentrated on nonfamilial interactions and has consistently shown that intergenerational communication can be problematic. Negative stereotyping based on prejudice and bias appears to be rampant in nonfamilial intergenerational communication. These preexisting stereotypes on the part of both the young and the old in any encounter may have significant implications for intergenerational relationships, and could obviously influence the outcomes of relational transactions.

The communication that transpires within health care interactions and educational interactions has the potential to produce significant, life-maintaining, and enhancing outcomes. Any problematic feature of the interaction due to the inherent difficulties of intergenerational communication can prove to be significant in the lives of the interactants, and needs to be addressed.

HEALTH CARE

The quality of the formal health care provided to each individual living in Western societies is certainly one of the greatest accomplishments of the 20th century. The biomedical model that has influenced, and now dominates, the great majority of health-care professions has produced a monumental amount of medical knowledge that affects each one of us every day. It is not an understatement to recognize the fact that medical science has added years to the life span of those individuals living within countries where that science has emerged. This being said, this same biomedical model and the health-care community in general, which is dominated by this model, has also produced a context of science and care that promotes extreme intergenerational miscommunication. The many medical advances that each of us celebrate at the societal level can be totally obfuscated by communicative problems at the relational level.

Health care is in a dramatic state of change. In the United States, the transformation from a fee-for-service system to a managed-care system is having, and will continue to have, significant impact upon the way health care is provided and managed for years to come. The financial instability of health care necessitates not only a change in the way society defines and deals with health care, but also changes the way each health care provider interacts with each patient. These changes may produce a much "friendlier" health-care context for older adults, or the various changes may produce an even more intergenerationally difficult context.

The health care that is of interest in this chapter occurs at the relational level. A health-care provider interacts with an older patient and both individuals attempt to solve a health problem. The health-care provider and the patient bring with them into the encounter many personal characteristics and, at the same time, are influenced by the physical context within which the interaction occurs. The extent to which their intergenerational differences affect the interaction and the outcomes of the interaction is of great concern to many health-communication scholars and should be of great concern to both patients and providers.

Several key intergenerational contexts within health care are discussed. Although one could write quite extensively about middle-aged nurses, physical therapists, dentists, and so on, interacting with infants or adolescents, we primarily focus on the older adult patient–middle-aged physician interaction as our prime example of an intergenerational health-care relationship whose communication has been shown to be troublesome. Although space limits a thorough discussion of this one particular interaction, this particular intergenerational event is informative and can serve as the foundation on which to build a case outlining the importance of productive and competent intergenerational communication.

A second focus in the health-care context is on those elderly individuals who live within long-term care facilities (see also chapter 6, this volume). These facilities are designed to manage the physical well-being of their residents. At the same time, these facilities provide an excellent arena for the practice and study of intergenerational communication. Finally, the emerging context of adult day care will be discussed. Much like the long-term care facility, and often associated with it, adult day care is a relatively new health care phenomenon. It is designed to provide a place of recreation and activity for older adults who are physically able to take advantage of the context, and at the same time, may not be able to independently navigate the outside community. Once again, adult day care provides an excellent opportunity for intergenerational contact.

The Older Patient–Physician Relationship

The importance of focusing on the older patient–physician relationship as an example of problematic intergenerational communication within health care is reinforced not only by the large number of studies recently dedicated to this topic (see Beisecker & Thompson, 1995; Haug & Ory, 1987; "Research Issues," 1996, for excellent reviews of this literature), but is also evidenced by the frequency of visits, and therefore interactions, between older individuals and physicians. The U.S. Senate Special Committee on Aging (1991) reported that people over age 65 average eight visits to a physician per year as compared to an average of five visits by the general population.

"Older people spend a significant portion of their time interacting with physicians, and these interactions have important consequences for the quality of life of elderly patients" (Beisecker & Thompson, 1995, p. 397). Because physicians retire when they are close to age 65, much like the rest of us, it is not unreasonable to assume that these older individuals enter into an intergenerational interaction with a physician who may be as many as 50 years younger than they are the majority of times that health care is needed.

The following event observed by one of us illustrates the potential problem that may exist when an older individual visits a younger physician. This event occurred during a journal club meeting at a major medical school in the midwestern United States. Physicians who are in their residency training in family practice are required to present a journal article to a small group of medical researchers as part of their 1-month rotation in geriatrics. On two separate occasions, journal articles were presented by residents that provided evidence linking exercise and diet on the part of older adults to positive health outcomes. The two residents were surprised by these findings when presenting these results. The residents believed that diet and exercise were important for younger individuals, but until the reading of these particular articles, never considered exercise or diet to produce positive outcomes for older adults. These residents are highly trained, sophisticated health care providers. What appears to be information that any 5th grader who watches television might know, that exercise and diet are important for our entire life span, somehow escaped the training of these health professionals. This anecdotal occurrence provides some insight into the total lack of knowledge on the part of some heath-care providers concerning the aging process, partly due to minimal geriatric training (remember that most family physicians practicing in the United States have not received formal training in geriatrics or gerontology beyond some minimal time spent while on rotation). The possible intergenerational miscommunication in the older patient–physician interaction only begins with a lack of information about aging on the part of physicians. It continues with widespread reliance on assumptions about old age and the aging body, and insensitive communication of objective medical information. For example, in one anecdote of which we know, a healthy woman in her early 70s with a minor health complain was horrified to be told by her physician, "Well, the human body wasn't designed to last this long, you should not really be alive right now." The communication difficulties of the medical interaction are further complicated by the fact that older patients themselves rely on (often inaccurate) assumptions about health and old age.

Beisecker and Thompson (1995) made special note of the fact that, in many ways, older patients are quite similar to younger patients in medical encounters. We should not assume that just because an individual is older that he or she is somehow significantly different from all others who seek medical advice. This being true, research has provided a number of characteristics of older individuals and therefore patients that may impact the interaction with a younger physician. Whereas the majority of older adults are healthy and quite independent, when an older person visits the physician a real or perceived physiological problem has probably initiated the encounter. Adelman, Greene, and Charon (1991) point to numerous physiological factors in the lives of older adults that complicate the patient–physician interaction. Factors such as sensory deficits, cognitive impairment, functional limitations, and multiple, simultaneous medical problems, many of which are chronic and thus cannot be cured tend to complicate the medical encounter (see chapter 4, this volume). Add to this stereotypes, inaccurate assumptions, and expectations about aging, and we have quite a problem.

Haug and Ory (1987) emphasize the obvious fact that older patients have a long medical interactive history that may or may not be positive. Older adults have simply been to the doctors more often during many different circumstances than younger patients have. This history may produce a great respect for health care, or it may produce a skepticism about health care that surfaces during the interaction.

Chapter 4 described a large body of research beginning to emerge within the field of communication that highlights the differences between the interactive behaviors of younger and older adults (Hummert, Wiemann, & Nussbaum, 1995; Nussbaum & Coupland, 1995). Specifically, older individuals may have more difficulty processing and producing complex syntactic structures (Kemper, Kynette, Rash, O'Brien, & Sprott, 1989), may report more problems with receptive and expressive skills (Ryan, Kwong See, Meneer, & Trovato, 1992b), often are or can be perceived as overly verbose (Gold, Arbuckle, & Andres, 1994), may exhibit different patterns of self-disclosure and age-telling (Coupland, Coupland, & Giles 1991), and may utilize different strategies during interpersonal conflict (Bergstrom & Nussbaum, 1996). Within the medical encounter, Beisecker and Thompson (1995) report evidence suggesting that "younger patients have been found to ask questions more frequently and with more precision, talk about their problems more, give information in more detail, and be more assertive" (p. 399). In general, it can be stated that as we age, our communicative behavior may change and have some impact upon the patient–physician interaction.

Physicians also bring to the interaction a number of possible interactive barriers (Haug, 1996). It is reasonable to state that physicians are highly educated, well paid members of a rather segregated portion of our society. Physicians, at least in the United States and United Kingdom, are not very similar to their patients on many sociological factors. In addition, the communication behavior of physicians when interacting with older patients has been reported to be quite different from their behavior with younger patients. Physicians are more condescending, abrupt, and indifferent (Adelman et al., 1991), spend less time, and appear to utilize their "power" more, while in medical interactions with older patients (Haug & Ory, 1987). In addition, the work of Greene and Adelman has shown quite consistently that physicians are very reluctant to interact about psychosocial content with their older patients. The evidence that agism on the part of physicians is endemic, problematic, and can lead to negative outcomes for the patient has been moderated by several recent investigations. For example, Coupland and Coupland's (1993) observational data show that physician's attempts at antiagist discourse are sometimes undermined by a plethora of face threats as well as elder patients' own agist expectations. This points to some significant communication predicaments for doctors who attempt to counteract agism in social contexts that challenge their every attempt to do so. Other evidence from older patients suggests that they are satisfied with their medical care and their interactions with physicians (Breemhaar, Visser, & Kleijnen, 1990; Hall, Roter, & Katz, 1988). The overwhelming majority of studies conclude that communication between older patients and physicians can be troublesome.

An additional factor that may cause problems for both older patients and physicians, and one of the major points made in this book, is the effect of negative attitudes toward the aging process. Hummert, Nussbaum, and Wiemann (1994) state that beliefs and cognitions about the communicative competence of people of differing ages can influence individuals' linguistic and paralinguistic choices in conversations. Coupland and Coupland (1989), Ryan, Giles, Bartolucci, and Henwood (1986), and many others have provided evidence that attitudes and beliefs held by younger participants during intergenerational interactions can lead to instances of inappropriate communication or miscommunication. McCormick, Inui, and Roter (1996) state very specifically that "physicians may bring negative attitudes and suboptimal skills to encounters with elderly patients" (p. 121). These agist attitudes and negative beliefs about the aging process can very easily lead to intergenerational miscommunications as well as to bad medical decisions and outcomes.

An additional component of the older adult–physician interaction that is rather unique among health-care encounters is the presence of a companion. Elderly individuals, as well as younger children, are most likely to be accompanied to the physician by a companion, who in most instances is a family member. The presence of the companion will affect the patient–physician interaction and can create a multigenerational communicative encounter (e.g., the patient, the patient's daughter, and the young physician). Beisecker (1989) identified three roles played by the companion: (a) watchdog, verifying information for both patient and physician; (b) significant other, providing feedback regarding the appropriateness of various behaviors within the medical interaction to both older patient and physician; and (c) surrogate patient, answering questions for the patient. Research by Glasser, Prohaska, and Roska (1992) and Morgan and Zhao (1993) points to various communicative changes within the interaction, such as the companion asking the physician for more information about the particular illness and more about the prognosis. The inclusion of a companion within the older patient–physician encounter adds to the complexity and further challenges the competencies of each interactant.

Institutionalization.   Beyond the intergenerational communication that transpires within a rather comfortable physician's office, Western society has produced a rather segregated institution in whch we can care for our older citizens who no longer are able to care for themselves. Nursing homes, which within the United States are to a large extent the creation of the federal government, are not only a unique communicative environment, but, for the most part, force intergenerational communication on the residents as well as on the staff (Nussbaum, 1983a, 1983b, 1985, 1990, 1991). Van Nostrand (1981) described the typical nursing home resident as "a person who is female, widowed, white, age 81, who has a disease of the circulatory system as a primary diagnosis, and who depends on assistance to bathe, dress, use the bathroom and get about" (p. 403). More recently, the nursing home industry within the United States has responded to the everchanging medical and financial environment of health care by turning facilities into rehabilitation centers. Nursing homes today are more likely to include older residents who will, with rehabilitation, become independent and leave after a rather short stay. Nevertheless, nursing homes are medical facilities built and organized to provide care for older individuals who cannot be cared for at home or in hospitals (see also chapter 6, this volume).

Those who do the caring within nursing homes range from highly paid and educated physicians to volunteers. At risk of overgeneralizing, it has been our experience that physicians rarely enter the nursing home, that nurses (both RNs and LPNs) are typically administrators, and that nurse aides interact most frequently with the older residents. Nurse aides are the least educated, most poorly paid, and youngest (therefore, most inexperienced) of the professional staff. The majority of intergenerational communication that transpires within the nursing home is between the older residents and these nurse aides.

In order to understand the intergenerational communication that takes place in nursing homes, one can never underestimate the influence that the institution has on the lives of the residents and the nursing home staff. Despite evidence that positive relationships between residents and staff increases longevity, improves resident quality of life, decreases physical pain, and provides residents with more verbal praise and attention (Miller & Lelieuvre, 1982; Noelker & Harel, 1978), nursing homes are structured to minimize all communication, but especially to minimize resident–staff interaction (Nussbaum, Bergstrom, & Sparks, 1996), and to maximize staff control. Nursing home staff reinforce dependency behaviors while simultaneously extinguishing independence (Baltes, Neumann, & Zank, 1994; Baltes, Wahl, & Reichert, 1991). The nursing-home staff control the residents' daily activities and keep their interaction with the residents as efficient and professional as possible (Nussbaum, 1990). To run an efficient, money-making institution, it is better to have a highly structured, controlled environment than to permit too much freedom on the part of the residents or staff.

Nussbaum (1990) investigated the possibility of a close relationship occurring between elderly residents of a nursing home and the nursing staff. A first theme to emerge from interviews with the elderly residents was that a close relationship with a member of the nursing staff, while not actually occurring, was not considered abnormal. A second theme that emerged from the conversations with the elderly residents was the notion that a close relationship with a member of the nursing staff could fulfill the affiliation needs that exist and are not being met within the lives of the residents. A third theme centered on the fact that the nursing staff are in control of the nature of the resident–staff relationship. The residents did not feel that it was their place to initiate a closer, nonprofessional relationship with the nursing staff. However, if an individual on staff made relational overtures, residents could see no reason why friendly behaviors could not be returned. These interviews provided a small amount of evidence that closer intergenerational communication between elderly residents and the nursing staff of a nursing home was at least possible.

In another study, 20 registered nurses and 20 nurse aides were asked to report the content of conversations between themselves and the residents of their nursing homes (Nussbaum, Robinson, & Grew, 1985). The most common topics for conversation reported by the nursing staff included: the patient's family, problems of old age, hobbies of old age, death, and the patient's health. Topics of conversation about which the nursing staff reported very little conversation included: community events, world and national events, 'family of the staff, personal problems, plans after work, 'their job, and their own health. The results of this study do not reveal close, relational talk occurring between nursing home staff and elderly residents. In fact, the authors of this study suggest that the talk appears to be very controlled and unidirectional. For instance, disclosure about the resident's family is not reciprocated by disclosure about the staff member's family. Talk concerning the personal lives of the staff is often defined as nonprofessional and to be avoided.

Additional data were collected to compare the reported conversational content of those members of the nursing home staff who did report at least one close relationship with a resident. Both nurses and nurse aides discuss more intimate topics with those residents to whom they feel close. For instance, more talk about religion, community events, their own family, and personal problems emerged from closer resident–staff relationships. Although this type of talk is discouraged within the nursing home, it does emerge with little negative result.

Nussbaum (1991) interviewed an additional 17 residents over the age of 65 and 20 nurse aides to further explore the interactive structure of relationships in a moderate-sized nursing home in Oklahoma. Results from these interviews suggest a strong difference in the interactive goals of the two intergenerational participants. Simply put, the task dimension of the interaction far exceeded any relational dimension on the part of the nurse aides. On the other hand, the relational dimension was just as important as the task dimension of interaction for the elderly residents. Beyond the normal intergenerational problems associated with communication, the nursing home environment produced a significant difference in interactive and relational goals for both residents and nursing staff. Even though the research is quite clear that more intergenerational psychosocial talk as part of a closer relationship between nursing-home residents and the nursing staff is positive for both interactants, the medical atmosphere and the structural limitations imposed within nursing homes create an environment that may impede competent intergenerational communication.

Adult Day Care.   A growing segment of the elderly population is not ill enough to become nursing home residents and is not healthy enough to live independently. These individuals are often cared for within families, and need a place to go during the day for activity and entertainment. Beyond help for the older adults, it is also very important to help the caregivers have time for their own employment or enjoy time away from the caregiving chores. Although the United States, with no national long-term care policy, remains very far behind other Western societies, more than 3,000 adult day-care centers are currently operating in the United States. Adult day care is often a community-based center designed to provide supervised activities for those older adults who are mobile and who will not prove to be disruptive. The adult day-care centers often provide breakfast and lunch as well as activities such as exercise, dance, music and some field trips (Hertzer, 1996). Many of these adult day-care centers are associated with nursing homes.

Adult day care presents several opportunities for intergenerational communication. Staff within adult day-care centers are often younger than the older participants. In addition, these centers often invite younger groups, such as the Girl Scouts or local high school and college groups, to entertain the older center participants. Perhaps the most innovative intergenerational exchanges occur when the adult day-care center expands to include a child day care center.

Stremmel, Travis, Kelly-Harrison, and Hensley (1994) report that intergenerational day care is becoming much more popular across the United States. "Intergenerational day care is meant to be an organizational structure in which adult day care and child care are offered in the same facility, and where participants engage in joint as well as age-segregated activities" (p. 513). Based on attitudinal research, which suggests meaningful intergenerational contact has a positive effect on prejudicial biases and attitudes toward the other generation (Caspi, 1984; Dooley & Frankel, 1990; Seefeldt, 1987), it is thought that these facilities and programs can increase older adults' sense of well-being, self-worth, general attitudes toward life, as well as helping them to feel part of the lives of the children with whom they come in contact.

Travis, Stremmel, and Kelly-Harrison (1995) investigated the frequencies and types of intergenerational exchanges found in adult day-care and child-care centers. The authors ranked seven intergenerational activities from most to least beneficial and appropriate. Free conversation time was ranked at the top of the list, followed by singing, telling or reading stories, cooking, arts and crafts, games, and field trips. Intergenerational activities that include "routine, 'family style,' activity appear to be among the most appropriate and beneficial activities for young children and dependent older adults to express themselves and 'share' their experiences with each other" (p. 48). Although it is not a universally accepted principle that such intergenerational exchanges within adult- and child-care centers are beneficial for all of the interactants, it is at least theoretically plausible that such intergenerational exchanges, if supervised properly within the centers, can have a powerful effect on the lives of the children as well as on the older adults. These intergenerational exchanges must be well organized so as not to create impossible communicative situations that could do more harm than good.

Intergenerational Communication Within Health Care.   The major focus of this book is to constantly and consistently point to the importance of intergenerational communication in our daily lives. The research that has been cited throughout the book points to some major difficulties that may occur within interactions between individuals from different generations. We cannot overestimate the importance of intergenerational miscommunication within the health-care environment. Unlike most family relationships that develop over long periods of time with constant interaction, health-care relationships are becoming very short interactions with no long-term investment. The intergenerational research reviewed in this chapter shows that the older patient–physician interaction can be filled with miscommunication. In addition, the institutionalization of older individuals within nursing homes can marginalize elderly residents and create an environment of interactive starvation. Finally, as adult day-care centers spring up across the country, it will be important to monitor their performance. If these centers become a human warehouse, further segregating the generations, whether they will form closer ties to child day-care centers and become part of the larger community remains to be seen. Whether this is a positive development needs also to be evaluated.

The theoretical perspectives and the research reviewed in the first several chapters of this book can be very informative about the nature of intergenerational communication within health care. As discussed in chapter 1, the communicative predicament of aging and the stereotype activation models suggest that contextual cues often associated with old age may activate negative stereotypes. These stereotypes may lead to the patronizing speech patterns often found within the health-care setting (Caporael, 1981; Caporael & Culbertson, 1986). Nussbaum, Hummert, Williams, and Harwood (1995) suggest that overaccommodation and underaccommodation, found within intergenerational communication due to stereotyping, may have significant consequences for both older patients and the younger health-care workers. The changes in language that accompany stereotyping can very easily lead to miscommunication and an inability to solve the medical problem (see chapter 6, this volume, for a detailed discussion of over- and underaccommodation in health-care interactions).

Of additional importance within the health care profession are the societal consequences of misinformed notions of the aging process. We have built thousands of nursing homes with highly structured environments to care for individuals who are very ill. These same facilities, however, can totally isolate and marginalize those who are placed in the institution to be physically cared for. Society is sending signals that make intergenerational communication more rather than less problematic. The research is rather consistent that the health-care industry can improve the competency levels of intergenerational communication. At the same time, those individuals who are in need of medical care must do their parts to improve their communicative behavior when interacting with a provider from a different generation.

EDUCATION

Since social reformers and policy makers first attempted to promote public education, individuals in Western societies have, for the most part, been convinced that formal education should be available to all segments of a population. It has always been true that older generations taught the skills and values of a society to its younger members. Formal education was limited to the very wealthy, the aristocracy, or to religious groups until the ideal of public education became well established. This public education is the personification of an older generation educating a younger generation. When we think about the formal education of our society, we think about adults teaching children. This intergenerational contract has served society very well for more than 300 years. It would not be an overstatement to suggest that, beyond the context of the family, the context of education has produced the most valuable intergenerational contact and the most productive intergenerational communication.

Intergenerational contact within education has traditionally been one way. As stated previously, adults teach children to provide society with a literate and skilled workforce. Besides a host of other social factors, as long as working people had one job or one career for the entirety of their lives, and no new skills were required to adapt to the environment physically or mentally, the model of younger individuals being educated by older individuals for employment worked very well. The world, of course, has changed. For example, people often have two or even three careers throughout their working lives. This leads to a need for adult education, even if only to help people reskill. Views of the role of education in society are also being challenged by modernity. Education is no longer seen as merely providing workers for business and industry; it is seen as a component of personal development across the life span. Also, as the numbers enrolling for adult-education evening classes attest, education is regarded as a leisure pursuit. Education is increasingly becoming part of peoples' life projects (Giddens, 1991). For all these reasons, the concept of life-long learning has emerged. Thus, the hope and concern of gerontologists is for a wider recognition of the need for all of us to be involved in education throughout our lives. In the context of this book, education is no longer a one-way process from adult to youth, but can become an expanded intergenerational process from a younger generation to an older generation. It is valuable to consider this new intergenerational contract within the education establishment and the challenges of life-long learning for intergenerational communication.

One myth of aging that responsible gerontologists have attempted to discredit is the notion that as we age not only our intelligence but also our motivation to learn declines. Something akin to "you cannot teach old dogs new tricks" is a product of the biomedical model of thinking made quite popular during the past few decades (Glendenning, 1995) and discussed in the previous section of this chapter. Hundreds of research reports led by Schaie (1990) and others have provided evidence that many types of intelligence do not decline with age and, moreover, that motivation to learn remains quite high as well. In addition, as we age we may even become wiser (Seppa, 1996) and more adept at handling complicated issues such as moral dilemmas.

The stereotype that adults past the age of 30 years should not participate as learners in our education system marginalizes any older student and certainly creates a difficult atmosphere for both the teacher and the older student. Older adults who want to become learners within the traditional educational system must contend with learning strategies designed for younger learners and learning opportunities that do not meet their needs. Stated quite simply, the way we "do" education is concerned with preparing children for work, and therefore the entire design of the educational system is age biased toward younger learners being taught by older, more experienced teachers (Moody, 1987–1988).

The most successful late-life learning program is Elderhostel, founded in 1975 as a short-term residential college program for people over the age of 65. Elderhostel is now providing noncredit educational experiences to older adults across the world. Although the success of Elderhostel speaks to the destructive nature of the myth that older individuals are not interested in learning, the age-segregated nature of the program may add to the marginalization of the elderly population, and does little to promote intergenerational contact and communication (see chapter 2, this volume).

Intergenerational Communication in Education

Two very important questions face the education establishment. First, is education, and therefore learning, a life-long phenomenon? Second, can education help to bridge the gap between generations? The answer to the first question appears rather easy if one considers all the literature that supports a life-span view of learning. Of course, the financing of education is strongly tied to politics and it is by no means the case that life-long learning is a priority in any community. People wedded to the notion that education is primarily provided to train workers for employment would undoubtedly argue that money and resources should not be wasted on educating those who do not have enough years ahead of them to pay their debts back by being productive workers. The tradition of formal learning ending after high school for the majority of individuals will not be expanded easily because it is so deeply enforced and supported by social rules and resources. The contradictions in the system, as described at the beginning of this section, are only recently being exposed. Once the perception that education, as we traditionally conceived it, no longer provides what we need for society, the system will change. At the present time, we are left to press home a solid conceptual point that learning is a life-long process; therefore education can be a life-long process. Unfortunately, in many cases education and even learning are still not considered in this light.

The second question, asking what role education plays in the connection made between generations, is central to the point of this book. Moody (1987–1988) states quite clearly that "education should not be viewed exclusively as an instrumental activity tied to productivity in a monetized marketplace. Education is an arena where young people and old can meet, where the gap between generations can, in part, be 'bridged'" (p. 7). As was suggested in early chapters of the book, the reality may not be as simple or as positive as we would hope. Unlike the health-care setting described earlier wherein intergenerational communication needs to be competent to serve a functional purpose outside of the interaction (good health), intergenerational communication within the educational setting can serve the communication itself.

Elderhostel is a program designed for self-enlightenment, self-enrichment, and the pursuit of individual goals and pleasure. With very few exceptions, traditional higher education, as well as secondary education, has turned away from creating well-rounded, classically educated individuals to producing potential employees ready for the job market. In a very real sense, formal education in Western societies has become vocational and technical training. This mind-set cannot grasp the potential for education to provide an opportunity for such ideals as bridging the generations. Programs such as Elderhostel, while providing an opportunity for older adults to continue their education, exacerbate the goal of intergenerational contact because they are segregational. They do not, therefore, promote or produce intergenerational communication beyond that with the professor. While providing for the development needs of older individuals, Elderhostel reinforces norms and suppositions that individuals of different ages should be segregated, and thereby it is in danger of reinforcing agism.

The potential within higher education to promote intergenerational communication rests with the expansion of the traditional classroom to include students beyond those in their teens and 20s. The changing economy, the fact that fewer young adults will be available to attend college, along with the fact that each individual will pursue many different jobs, if not careers, during his or her lifetime is forcing educational administrators to expand their vision of a traditional student. The opportunity for students to learn within an intergenerational classroom will increase for the foreseeable future. The success of these classrooms will be dependent on successful intergenerational communication. Both students and teachers must cope and adapt to a classroom full of stereotypes and myths of aging. The pitfalls of intergenerational communication described in the initial chapters of this book will be part of any classroom with students of various ages. Neither instructional communication scholars nor interpersonal communication scholars have provided empirical evidence to inform us whether or not the intergenerational-communication difficulties found within interaction will adversely affect classroom learning.

The intergenerational classroom will, at the very least, provide the forum for individuals from various cohorts to interact and to observe one another. The mere fact that individuals with diverse life experiences are entering a learning environment for an extended period of time can itself be enlightening. However, the classroom can often be an intergroup experience wherein mature students become a relatively excluded and stigmatized minority among the wider student population. The mere fact that people sit in the same room together does not in itself promote intergroup communication and understanding. The challenges for the intergenerational classroom are quite daunting, and the experience of multiple generations interacting will be a rich arena for research by communication scholars.

INTERGENERATIONAL CONTACT PROGRAMS

Recognizing the inherent problems with minimal community contact, programs of organized contact have been devised to promote intergenerational understanding. Negative perceptions of old age, combined with evidence that there is minimal intergenerational contact outside the family, have spurred the growth and development of formal intergenerational contact programs designed to counteract such forces.

Young and Elderly Contact Interventions

The hypothesis that contact improves relationships between groups has a certain face-value appeal; after all, if we can increase different groups' knowledge of each other we can foster understanding and so improve relationships. Because of these inherent assumptions, intergroup contact (mostly as it relates to ethnic groups) has been the focus of a substantial amount of research and theory during the last few decades (see Hewstone & Brown, 1986; Pettigrew, 1986). Unfortunately, findings consistently failed to live up to early expectations that contact per se would improve attitudes, perceptions, and ultimately intergroup relationships (e.g., see Allport, 1954). Working from a social-cognitive, intergroup perspective, Hewstone and Brown (1986) suggest that, in order to change outgroup stereotypes, contact "should have the dual aim of emphasizing typicality and creating a less monolithic, more differentiated view of the outgroup" (p. 29). Therefore, this perspective suggests, that in order for intergenerational encounters to disconfirm agist stereotypes, both young and old interactants should perceive each other as typical representatives of their respective social groups, and the evaluative outcomes should be positive (e.g., satisfying).

Until recently, intergroup contact theories have neither explicitly considered intergroup communication, nor have they been concerned with intergenerational issues (Fox & Giles, 1993). As Fox and Giles point out, it is crucial that such theories acknowledge the pivotal role of language and social interaction in producing, reproducing, and even changing social structures, including negative stereotyping. Contact research has rarely been conducted within a communication framework, but communication is, at least implicitly, at the heart of Hewstone and Brown's (1986) suggestion that in order to promote positive intergroup relations, in their words: "the aim of intergroup encounters is a positive outcome, whether perceived in terms of successful cooperation, superordinate goals, or an enjoyable meeting" (p. 31).

Efforts to change attitudes toward aging and the elderly include (usually short-term) programs of intergenerational contact (Allen, Allen, & Weekley, 1986; Chapman & Neal, 1990). Recently, Fox and Giles (1993) undertook a critical review of such programs from the perspective of intergroup theory. Among other things, they point to the operationalization of contact as problematic for making comparisons across programs. In other words, promoters define contact and the reasons for it in very different ways. Also, studies designed to evaluate contact programs use very different dependent measures and have very different rationales of practice. For example, some target relational development whereas others are primarily concerned with attitude change (Fox & Giles, 1993).

In their review of studies dating from the 1950s to the 1990s, which was designed to evaluate the effects of intergenerational contact, Fox and Giles classify research concerned with intergenerational contact into various types of formal and informal contact with and without educational programs designed to increase awareness about aging.

Fox and Giles argue that intergenerational contact programs have failed in certain key areas and that these failures make hard and fast conclusions about the efficacy of such programs (e.g., in generating positive and long lasting attitude changes) difficult to draw. They claim that contact research suffers from a lack of guiding theory, that attitude measures cannot predict future behavior, that research is notoriously short term when longitudinal assessment is required. Many studies are limited by their lack of contextual and ecological validity, which limits their generalizability. Studies often focus only on outcomes for younger age generations and not on the outcomes for older people; they concentrate on cognitive attitudinal outcomes and fail to measure behavioral outcomes. However, Fox and Giles argue that although almost 69% of the studies they reviewed claimed some positive gains as an outcome of intergenerational contact; for the most part, results are very mixed and patchy, showing positive gains when representative elderly people are healthy and vital, but negative effects for those who are disabled, sick, and infirm.

Rather than writing off intergenerational contact programs as ineffective for attitude change maybe we should ask what such programs can offer to those who take part. For example, are there possible gains in terms of the development of specific friendships between older and younger people and their effects on both (see Rawlins, 1995)?

Of course, in intergenerational educational contexts, negative societal representations, individual ignorance, and uncertainty could be challenged with objective as well as with subjective information. Schemes such as "adopt-a-grandparent" might benefit from systematic multidisciplinary evaluations, to assess their potential for both good and harm. Despite the increasingly accepted assumption that mere contact per se is not enough, largely nontheoretical, short-term schemes with an overemphasis on attitude (rather than on communication) change continue, and are construed as positive. On the contrary, research examining the nature of community contact with the elderly indicates that contact between the elderly and younger groups is limited, and is frequently dissatisfying for the young (Williams, 1992).

INTERGENERATIONAL FRIENDSHIPS

A very exciting new area of research emerging within the communication discipline revolves around the interaction taking place between intergenerational friends (Holladay & Kerns, 1997). Typically, social scientists who explore friendship across the life span ignore intergenerational friendships or report that these friendships are rather strange (Reisman, 1981, 1984). After all, friendships are formed because of attitudinal similarity, support, geographical proximity, age similarity, and so on (see Nussbaum, 1994; Rawlins, 1992, 1995, for reviews of the older adult friendship literature). However, it is becoming increasingly clear that intergenerational friendships do form and may provide the relational partners with valuable, life-affirming interactions.

Bettini and Norton (1991) investigated intergenerational friendships in a sample of young and older adults. They found that 85% of the older adults with an average age of 84, and 33% of the younger adults with an average age of 20 responded that they do indeed interact within an intergenerational friendship. Of particular interest is the fact that more older adults report intergenerational friendships than do younger adults. This indicates not only the likelihood that, as we age our range of possible friends may expand, but also highlights the notion, as previously discussed in this book, that our society can segregate the young from the old and make it difficult for young adults to interact across generations.

Older adults reported that they formed intergenerational friendships through their interactions with their own children, grandchildren, or church. They reported that these friendships were of a different nature than their friendships with individuals of their own age. The differing degree of equality in the intergenerational friendship was cited as one fundamental difference between this friendship and the age-peer friendship.

Younger adults reported that they formed intergenerational friendships through interactions with their parents. The young adults did not consider their friendships with individuals within their parents' generation to be fundamentally different from their age-peer friendships. The fundamental activities of friendship, talking, seeking advice, and spending time together were similar in both friendship relationships.

Holladay and Kerns (1997) extended this research by conducting interviews with adults of all ages concerning their intergenerational friendship experiences. Participants were asked to consider one intergenerational friend from whom they differed in age by at least 10 years. During the face-to-face interviews, participants were asked how they met their intergenerational friend, what they talk about, what they do together, if they noticed a generation gap, how others react to their friendship, and how the friendship has changed over time.

The initial interview question asked in what context the intergenerational friendship was formed. The most frequent response was the workplace. Over one half of the interviewees mentioned how important the workplace is for interacting and forming friendships with individuals of differing ages. The second most frequently reported location for forming intergenerational friendships was a school setting. As mentioned previously in this chapter, the extent to which we segregate education and make it difficult for older individuals to return to school, the more we eliminate a possible context for intergenerational interaction. Additional contexts for intergenerational friendship formation include church and recreational activities.

A second question asked of the subjects in this study concerned what the participants of the intergenerational friendship talked about. More than 60% of the participants reported discussing their families and/or their relationships with a boyfriend or girlfriend. Forty percent reported talking about work-related activities. Other topics of intergenerational friendship talk included sports talk, recreational activities, and travel. From answers to this particular question one can conclude that talk within intergenerational friendships is very similar to talk in age-peer friendships.

A third question concentrated on the kinds of things that the intergenerational friends do when they are together. The overwhelming majority of responses centered on recreational activities, such as participating in sporting events, working out, traveling, and going to bars. Close to one third of participants within this study mentioned eating together and numerous individuals listed "just talking" as a primary activity shared with their intergenerational friends. Holladay and Kerns (1997) note that these activities seem to be mutually enjoyable and very "normal."

A fourth question attempted to explore the role of intergenerational friendships. It had been suggested in the literature that an intergenerational friendship may be less an "equal" friendship and more a mentoring relationship. The majority of respondents in this study considered their intergenerational friendship to be a true friendship. Several individuals did comment that the intergenerational friendship was similar to a mother–daughter relationship or mentoring relationship. However, the majority of respondents considered the intergenerational friendship to be similar in nature to their peer relationships.

A very important question for this study was how intergenerational friendship differed from age-peer friendships. Participants were equally divided as to whether there was a difference in their intergenerational friendships. "Interestingly, a difference identified by several participants was that they experienced a greater sense of 'validation' or 'acceptance' from their intergenerational friends than their age peers" (p. 21). Several respondents also indicated a difference in friendships because of life-stage worries of older individuals. The authors of the study conclude that the differences in intergenerational friendships that do exist lead them to value, rather than to denigrate, the friend.

An additional question sought responses to how others react to the intergenerational friendship. Fifteen percent of respondents reported that they received negative reactions from others. Others appear to question why one needs an age-discrepant friend or that they felt awkward around such an older person. The answers to this question touch on much of the theme of this book. We often have expectations about how one should behave across the life span, and these expectations and attitudes direct our communicative behavior. If we expect friends to be of a similar age and then witness an intergenerational friendship, we are in a communication situation that often is uncomfortable.

The next question asked whether respondents experienced a generation gap in their intergenerational friendships. Once again, about 50% of respondents did see a generation gap. Those who reported a generation gap noted differing tastes and popular events (music, historical occurrences like the Vietnam War, etc.), values, relationship experience, maturity level, and work experience. Interestingly, several respondents emphasized the point that differences in the generation gap did not hinder their friendship.

The final question asked how the friendship had changed over the years. The majority of respondents reported growing emotionally closer over time. Thirty percent reported interacting less frequently over time due to retirement, school attendance, or general relocation; 14% reported that the intergenerational relationship had become more equal over time.

The results of this investigation pose many more questions about intergenerational friendships than are answered. Intergenerational friendships appear to be viable and to serve an important function in our lives. We do know from the two studies discussed previously that intergenerational friendships will form and may not be totally unique from age-peer friendships in a variety of contexts. We do not know precisely how these friendships function within our lives, or what communicative skills are necessary to maintain these friendships across long spans of time. In addition, we do not know whether intergenerational friendships change the way we as individuals view the aging process.

SUMMARY

This chapter has links that spread across the entire book. Chapter 2 looks at intergenerational contact, and in many ways this chapter picks up those themes again, but focuses on a small number of intergenerational-contact situations wherein relationships are potentially able to form. The intergenerational contexts and relationships examined here are health care (the older patient and physician relationship, nursing care in institutions, and adult day care), education, and intergenerational friendships.

These contexts also create and reinforce the rules and resources for intergenerational interaction discussed throughout the book. In health care, for example, physicians and patients bring such rules and resources with them to the interaction. Physicians draw on stereotypes and assumptions about age to dispense advice and practical care, older patients draw on assumptions about age in order to ask questions, to interpret advice, and so forth. Agism does not rest solely with the doctor and is not the responsibility of the doctor alone; some socially aware physicians struggle valiantly to counteract agist expectations in a social climate that discounts and denies almost every attempt to do so. In addition, the doctor–patient interaction (like many other interactions) is a multiple intergroup context as, for example, the doctor may be a young, well-educated, middle-class male who is attempting to treat an elderly, poorly educated, working-class female. The bottom line is that both doctors and patients must negotiate a number of accommodative dilemmas as they dispense and receive medical treatment.

Post modernity has brought with it new social pressures. As Giddens points out, we can no longer depend on traditional social structures to guide us through the life span. We can no longer educate adolescents as factory fodder for an industrial society—as people who will operate machines, dig out coal, or make steel for 30 or 40 years until retirement are anachronistic throwbacks to the early industrial revolution. Instead, we are dealing with modern, computerized, highly technological societies, the world of finance and commerce and so forth—and our economy is global. These are societies wherein many people can expect to change their careers three or even four times throughout their life spans and this will almost certainly necessitate a reskilling at each juncture. This means that education will increasingly become an intergenerational context in which young middle-aged and older students will be obliged to interact if only in superficial ways. Undoubtedly, if this multiple-age context is seen as an intergroup situation, it will introduce a new and unique set of stereotypes and intergenerational-communication predicaments; as such it is a context that is already worthy of investigation. Programs designed to promote contact and change attitudes need to be carefully crafted, and their success needs to be monitored and evaluated along multiple dimensions with an awareness of the intergroup potential inherent in intergenerational communication. Finally, this chapter looked at recent research specifically designed to investigate intergenerational friendships. These associations are interesting because they may be characteristically different, in some crucial respects, from peer friendships. Also of interest is that intergenerational friendships are frequently explicitly and implicitly discouraged because they tend to violate social pressures to act your age, and they challenge the assumption that people will prefer to be with someone their own age. All too often, perhaps, we regard intergenerational friendships suspiciously as indiating that one or both of the friends are "weird."

Intergenerational communication that defines and transpires within nonfamily, professional relationships has been shown to be far less positive than intergenerational communication within family relationships. The health-care industry is rife with agism and stereotypic behavior that can do great harm to the lives of both young and old. The education establishment has not embraced intergenerational learning. The segregation of learning environments remains the norm across many Western societies. Yet, the promise for effective intergenerational communication within health care, and the possibility of multiple generations learning from one another should not be allowed to wither. We feel that the intergenerational communication within familial, professional, relationships and friendships can be studied, understood, and improved. The task for social scientists is to devote the time and energy studying intergenerational communication, both within families and outside the family, to provide solid information on which to base future, competent, intergenerational encounters.

PART III

MACROSOCIETAL PERSPECTIVES

Readers will observe that the book moves back and forth between what might be called microissues and macroissues. In some senses, this is a false division between levels of analysis at the microlevel of interaction versus the macrolevel of the community and media. We have struggled with this division ourselves because macroissues are inevitably created and reformed during interaction. Chapter 12 makes the link moving from interindividual conflict to community and mediated conflict. Then, chapters 13 and 14 consider macroissues at the level of the community and culture.

12

Intergenerational Conflict

We all experience conflict as a natural, important, integral and (contrary to popular opinion) often constructive part of our daily lives and relationships. Within the communication discipline, there is an extensive literature that documents at least a decade of interpersonal-conflict research (for reviews, see Hocker & Wilmot, 1995; Krauss & Krauss, 1990).

According to Hocker and Wilmot (1995), conflict occurs "when people are interdependent, have a perception that something is in short supply (e.g., money, esteem, power, space, computers), see the other as interfering with what they want, and see their goals as mutually incompatible" (Wilmot, 1995, p. 94). In communication studies, most interpersonal-conflict research has been concerned with conflict in relationships, especially in romantic and marital relationships (Hocker & Wilmot, 1995).

This chapter begins with a general overview of interpersonal-conflict research, which provides a baseline against which to examine intergenerational conflict. In the space provided here, it is not possible to provide an exhaustive review of interpersonal-conflict research. For this, interested readers should refer to Hocker and Wilmot (1995). The main goal of this chapter is to introduce intergenerational conflict in interindividual, familial, and institutional settings, and to integrate the possible role of intergenerational stereotyping and intergroup perceptions in mediating conflict. The chapter concludes with a discussion of mediated intergenerational conflict and its implications for the welfare of both older and younger people in society at large.

INTERPERSONAL CONFLICT IN OVERVIEW

Researchers tend to agree that the way conflict is managed is crucial for the development or the termination of relationships (Wilmot, 1995). For this reason, a number of theoretical approaches to communication and conflict are sketched in terms of strategies or tactics of conflict. According to Sillars and colleagues (e.g., Sillars, Coletti, Parry, & Rogers, 1982), conflict strategies also vary in terms of the level of engagement and the amount of affect. In general, a variety of research has identified three major categories or types of conflict strategy: competition, cooperation, and avoidance (Sillars et al., 1982), or nonconfrontation, solution orientation, and control (Putnam & Wilson, 1982).

The *competitive* or *controlling style* is characterized by high engagement and low positive affect. This style is associated with tactics such as personal criticism, rejection of another, hostile imperatives, jokes or questions, denial of personal responsibility, and presumptive remarks attributing thoughts and feelings to others that they may not own or acknowledge.

A *cooperative* or *solution-oriented style* is characterized by high engagement and positive affect toward the other and/or the relationship. This style is said to demonstrate a desire for mutual resolution. Here we find descriptive, nonevaluative remarks about the conflict, disclosive nonevaluative statements, solicitation of nonevaluative disclosure, qualification of the nature or extent of the conflict, nonhostile solicitation of criticism of self, supportive remarks, concessions, and acceptance of responsibility (Sillars et al., 1982). *Nonconfrontation* or *avoidance* is characterized by implicit or direct denial of conflict, evasive remarks, topic shifts and/or avoidance, noncommittal statements or questions unrelated to the conflict, and abstract and/or irreverent remarks like friendly joking (Sillars, 1986). *Avoidance* is considered to be a low engagement and low positive-affect style.

Rusbult (1987) distinguishes between two dimensions of responses to conflict as active or passive and constructive or destructive. Along these dimensions he distinguishes between strategies that he labels *voice* (expressing conflict), *loyalty* (related to cooperation), *exit* and *neglect* (avoidant). Voice is active and constructive, loyalty is passive and constructive, neglect is passive and destructive and exit is active and destructive.

Preferences for, and selection of, one style above another have been the subject of a great deal of research (e.g., see Beryman-Fink & Bruner, 1987; Kilman & Thomas, 1977). Among other things, attributions have emerged as important predictors of conflict tactics (Sillars, 1980a). According to attribution theory (Hewstone, 1989b), we attribute the causes of events either to external (situational) or to internal (dispositional) factors. People are thought to (unconsciously and/or consciously) select conflict strategies based on attributions about the partner's intent to cooperate, the locus of responsibility, and the stability and/or globality of the conflict. For example, Sillars found that college roommates who believed that the other person was the cause of a conflict were more likely to use distributive or avoidant strategies, whereas integrative strategies were positively related to the perception of personal responsibility for the cause of conflict. It follows that biases in the attribution process or in misattribution affect modes of conflict resolution. One particular attributional bias concerns intergroup processes. Ingroup members are more likely to attribute negative outgroup behavior internally to outgroup member's traits and personality characteristics, whereas positive events are attributed externally to the situation. Intergroup research has shown that when negative ingroup behavior is at issue, ingroup individuals attribute it to the situation, whereas positive behavior is attributed internally to ingroup traits and characteristics (e.g., see Hewstone, Gale, & Purkhardt, 1990). This theme is elaborated further in the next section.

Naturally, conflict researchers have related conflict management to certain outcome variables. Research findings across a variety of relationships and settings indicate that cooperative or integrative tactics produce the most communication satisfaction (Canary & Cupach, 1988), and also produce feelings of trust and commitment (Canary & Spitzberg, 1990; Sillars, Pike, Jones, & Redmond, 1983). A very general view is that escalation, distributive, or confrontational strategies, controlling strategies, and avoidance are not rated as satisfying (e.g., see Newton & Burgoon, 1990). The most favored is cooperation (Metts & Cupach, 1990; Sillars, 1980b). However, there are cultural differences in conflict-style preferences: Members of individualistic cultures (which stress individual needs above group needs) prefer high-engagement strategies such as cooperation and competition over avoidance, but members of collectivisitic cultures (which stress group needs above individual needs) generally prefer low engagement, such as avoidance, over high engagement (Ting-Toomey, 1994). There is also some emerging evidence of developmental or age differences in conflict preferences and selection of conflict tactics. Naturally, this is of particular interest here, because it would predictably impact intergenerational conflict communication in significant ways.

Life-Span Approaches to Conflict

There is a small but growing literature that takes a life-span-developmental approach (see chapter 1, this volume) to interpersonal conflict, which emphasizes that the ability to handle conflict develops as a life-span skill. Some of this research addresses age differences in younger and older peoples' conflict styles or tactics. Recently, Sillars and Zietlow's (1993) behavioral observation study investigated married couples' (23 to 83 years of age) conflict behaviors. They found that young couples were more inclined toward explicit conflict negotiation, being more engaging and direct when discussing marital conflict. In contrast to this, midlife couples exhibited higher percentages of denial, equivocation, topic management, and noncommittal styles, combined with lower frequencies of confrontation. Retired couples, for the most part, had the highest percentage of noncommittal behavior. Sillars and Zeitlow (1993) suggest that younger couples were more inclined to actively engage and acknowledge conflict and that they employed different forms of engagement. Midlife couples were somewhere between the passivity of the majority of retired couples and the intensity of the young. There is also some evidence that older couples may be more inclined than young couples to choose their battles because they were more willing to engage salient topics. Interestingly enough, Sillars and Zeitlow also found that a small number of older couples appeared to be locked into cyclical combative-conflict sequences, which they suggest may be due to unresolved conflicts throughout their relational life histories.

Although this study suggests developmental trends in conflict behavior, the exact nature of such trends is not entirely clear. An early study by Sillars (1980a) suggested that young people (in this case, college students) tend towards passive-indirect strategies, which involve an aggressive concern for their own needs and self-interest, but exhibit a passive-unconcerned attitude towards the needs of conflict partners (Hocker & Wilmot, 1995). A questionnaire study by Bergstrom and Nussbaum (1996) suggested that younger adults favor controlling styles, whereas older adults favor cooperative conflict styles. When *depth* (conflicts rated as long-standing with highly incompatible solutions, high blame, and little chance of resolution) of conflict increased, both older and younger adults reported decreased satisfaction, but younger adults' preferences for avoidance increased whereas older adults preferred cooperative, solution-oriented tactics regardless of the depth of conflict. In support of this, Bergstrom (1997) looked at reported conflict strategies of young, middle-aged and older adults when in conflict with their mothers. He was able to show a consistent linear increase in preference for solution-oriented styles of conflict, and a corresponding decrease in preferences for controlling styles as age increased.

In agreement with suggestions that conflict may develop as a life-span skill (Sillars & Weisberg, 1987), Bergstrom (1997), and Bergstrom and Nussbaum (1996) argue that the skill to negotiate conflict in an engaging way, but by using solution-oriented, cooperative tactics, may be learned throughout the life span. Accordingly, younger people's relatively more limited life experiences may be connected to their preferences for competitive engagement tactics, their tendency to opt for withdrawal or avoidance or both when conflicts become more difficult to manage (Bergstrom & Nussbaum, 1996), and their tendency not to distinguish salient from nonsalient issues (Sillars & Zeitlow, 1993). On the other hand, older people's preferences for cooperative tactics, which may ultimately be more successful and appropriate, may be a result of their fuller life experiences (we can interpret Sillars and Zeitlow's results described previously in a similar fashion). There are also a number of other explanations. It is possible that older respondents are more practiced at presenting themselves in socially desirable ways for the researchers or the results just presented may indicate a cohort effect in that confrontational styles are more socially acceptable now than they were a couple of decades ago.

We must also consider the possibility that different findings may be related to different methods (questionnaire vs. observation), relational differences (marital partners vs. relative strangers) and so forth. Relatedly, Hocker and Wilmot (1995) noted the tendency for objective questionnaire studies of conflict to be more susceptible to response bias because respondents, eager to cast themselves in a positive light, opt for positively perceived conflict strategies such as cooperation. However, behavioral measures such as those of the Sillars and Zeitlow study may tend to pick up different trends such as a tendency toward symmetrical reciprocity. Sillars and Zeitlow (1993) describe a strong tendency for the individuals in their study to reflect back, or to reciprocate, their partners' immediate preceding remarks. This is a phenomenon known as the *reciprocity norm* and should not be underestimated as a powerful influence in conflict interactions. It is not as easily observed in questionnaire studies. Indeed, conflict theorists have noted that such patterns can lead to degenerative spirals wherein negative conflict is reciprocated quid pro quo in an escalating sequence, and this is especially prominent in relationships that are perceived by partners as dissatisfying (Fincham, Bradbury, & Scott, 1990; Wilmot, 1995). In communication accommmodation theory terms this could be characterized as matching or mirroring styles.

As we just indicated, most research about interpersonal conflict has concerned married and romantic partners. Yet there is ample evidence to suggest that there may be some very important differences between this conflict and conflict between people of vastly different ages, as well as conflict that involves people who are relative strangers, in contrast to conflict between close friends or romantic partners. In the context of intergenerational communication, these differences could be due to developmental or cohort differences or to differential effects of age stereotyping and intergroup perceptions. Stereotyping and intergroup processes may make intergenerational conflict more entrenched and harder to overcome than conflict that is more interindividual in nature (Cooper & Fazio, 1986).

Before embarking on a discussion of intergenerational conflict within families, between nonintimates, and mediated conflict, it may be worth reviewing some important and useful definitial distinctions provided by Schlesinger and Kronebusch (1994). They distinguish between different levels of intergenerational conflict. First, they distinguish a *stressor*, when another person's needs are perceived to be a burden. According to Schlesinger and Kronebusch, stressors are intergenerational when they involve different generations of the same family. Second, Schlesinger and Kronebusch discuss intergenerational tensions, which are defined as any stressor, or burden, that an individual judges to be unfair. In terms of equity theory or exchange theory, a tension occurs when the costs of the intergenerational relationship outweigh the benefits, and this imbalance is thought to be inequitable. Third, a *friction* refers to a tension whose cause is attributed to the conscious actions of some other person or group. In other words, the other person or persons are responsible and accountable for the inequity. Schlesinger and Kronebusch argue that stressors, tensions, and friction can build upon one another to have an additive effect on intergenerational conflict.

Familial Conflict

Earlier chapters of this volume discussed various aspects of family and relational communication. For example, chapter 8 considered relationships between adult children and their parents, and chapter 10 discussed sandwiched communication between family members of different ages with an adult positioned at the center of an intergenerational sandwich between older and younger family members. An important part of these earlier chapters was discussion about caregiving for older family members. Certainly, the stresses of caregiving for familial elders are well documented and can evolve into tension and friction if the caregiver feels used, unnecessarily burdened, and powerless to change the situation (Gelles, 1983). Nonfamilial relationships in which an unequal balance of exchange exists are considered to be in danger of dissolution (see Wilmot, 1995). In a family caregiving context, however, dissolution or changes in the balance of helping may not be feasible (Gelles, 1983). Thus, conflict may evolve from unbalanced caregiving exchanges, particularly those in which individuals feel powerless to change (Chappel, 1980; Suitor & Pillemer, 1988). Examples of intergenerational-familial stressors include provision of child care, college-education funding, providing emotional and/or financial support for adult children, caring for elderly parents, and so forth (Schlesinger & Kronebusch, 1994). In other words, stress can arise from perceptions that family resources are not equitably distributed or exchanged.

Intergenerational conflicts between adolescents and parents (e.g., Montemayor, 1983) as well as between adult children and aging parents (Myers, 1988) often seem to center around issues of control, autonomy, and responsibility (see also Baltes & Silverberg, 1994). In a communication context, for example, this would entail parents using control messages to gain their adolescent child's compliance—a negotiation that can be something of a conflictual struggle (Vangelisti, 1992). Comstock and Buller (1991) note that, in line with a reciprocity norm, the parent's initial conflict strategy sets the tone for conflict with adolescents.

In summary, intergenerational conflicts may evolve around the management or mismanagement of a number of relational-dialectical tensions—between autonomy–connection or independence–interdependence, openness–closedness or expressiveness–protectiveness, and predictability–novelty (for a review of dialectics, see Werner & Baxter, 1994). Of particular importance seems to be the life-span negotiation of the autonomy–connection dialectic. For example, referring to adult children who return to reside in the parental home, Ward and Spitze (1992) suggest that conflict may arise when there is disparity between expected life-course transitions (i.e., those by which adult children gain independence from parents) and the perceived reality that adult children have failed to achieve such transitions (e.g., marriage, financial independence, etc.) and are thus still dependent on their parents.

In a similar fashion, such dialectics can be traced through other sources of intergenerational conflict within families. Researchers note that conflicts between middle-aged people and their parents center around issues of health, unresolved childhood problems, childrearing issues, managing affairs, living arrangements, and lifestyle differences (Smith, 1989). Lewis and Lewis (1985) argue that although middle-aged people may have achieved a high degree of independence from their parents, they may still need to be "parented." At the same time, according to this view, older parents are getting more dependent and less able to parent, and this too may result in conflict. Along similar lines Myers (1988) suggested that familial stresses also occur as both older people and middle-aged children may find their roles and relationships in new and relatively uncharted territory because life patterns and the nature of relationships and identity have changed dramatically over the past few decades. Such changes may cause a great deal of uncertainty about parents' and adult children's relative roles.

Some research has attempted to estimate the prevalence of intergenerational conflict within families. Suitor and Pillemer (1988, 1991) investigated intergenerational conflict between cohabiting adult children and their parents, and found rather low levels of conflict among this group, which declined even more as the length of time of cohabitation increased. This was corroborated by Aquilino and Supple (1991), who reported high parental satisfaction and positive parent–adult child interactions. However, other research has indicated that parent and adult–child coresidence can result in conflict (e.g., Schnaiberg & Goldenberg, 1989); for example, Umberson (1993) suggested that coresident parents reported feeling tension in their relationships with their adult children, and were less satisfied with the parental role. We must bear in mind that adult children who coreside with their parents are likely to be those who had positive relationships with them in the first place, and are thus less likely to experience tension in a coresidence-relational context.

It is important to stress that often conflict between adult children and their parents may result as much from the adult children's perception that parents are getting more dependent as it can from actual dependence. Often perhaps, conflict may occur when older adults urge their parents to slow down (e.g., to retire, to stop driving, etc.). Essentially, the view that conflict can occur as parents become more dependent need not result from any objective reality, but rather from popular expectations about the roles and abilities of older people. This can be the site of a conflictual struggle between adults and their parents. However, as suggested in chapters 8 and 10, researchers seem to have concentrated their efforts on debunking supposed myths that family relationships are an endangered species, are typically discordant, or are a source of deep dissatisfaction. Researchers have concentrated efforts on investigating the prevalence or frequency of intergenerational conflict, with the result that the nature of familial-intergenerational conflict and especially how individuals communicatively negotiate conflicts over the life span is largely unknown.

Very little research has examined the negotiation of intergenerational conflicts outside intimate relational contexts. A start in this direction has been initiated by Small, Montoro, and Kemper (1996), who investigated intergenerational conflict between nursing home staff and residents. As these authors suggest, very little is known about how such conflicts are resolved (if they are at all). Their small-scale study looked at the extent to which staff showed a preference for cooperative versus controlling styles of conflict resolution, comparing a Special Care Unit (SCU) versus a Skilled Nursing Unit (SNU). They also looked to see if staff's self-reported style preferences matched their actual uses of conflict resolution styles in interaction with residents. Results showed that the staff showed a self-reported preference for the solution-oriented styles of conflict, as would be expected. Although there was a match between self-reported conflict styles and actual styles, there was also considerable individual variation. However, more interesting perhaps is the finding that SCU staff showed a greater preference than did nonSCU staff for nonconfrontational indirect strategies. This finding perhaps reflects the nursing staff's sensitivity to the vulnerability and low power of residents in SCU units. Clearly, there is a need for much more research because mismanaged or unmanaged conflict in institutional (as well as other) contexts can affect vulnerable individual's lives in very significant ways. On a theoretical level, many of the processes (e.g., stereotyping, overaccommodation, underaccommodation) discussed previously are implicated here.

Intergenerational Conflict and Age Stereotypes

It is possible that stereotypes, expected role relationships, and so forth play into intergenerational conflict within as well as outside family contexts. This is especially the case if stereotypes are appropriated as resources in conflict exchanges, attributions for conflict, and so on. It is conflict between relative strangers, acquaintances, neighbors, and even coworkers that may be most susceptible to the intervening and mediating influence of stereotyping, intergroup processes, and so forth.

Stereotypes of old and young are part of the expectation and attribution process, and as such may well exacerbate positive processes and outcomes, conflict resolution, satisfaction, and the like. For example, extreme negative stereotypes of young people (e.g., as a nuisance, destructive, irresponsible) can predispose older people to make attributions that are internal, stable, and global as characterized by well-known clichés such as "the youth of today" and "I don't know what the world's coming to." The same applies to extreme negative stereotypes of elders (e.g., as interfering, dominating), encapsulated in the cliché of the "disagreeable old geezer." Such perceptions may influence the choice of conflict tactic, making solution orientation less likely, but making avoidance or competition or both more likely.

Thus, older people in conflict with a negatively stereotyped younger person may choose either to avoid conflict (not get involved), or may opt for competitive strategies (call the police). Images of the stereotyped intergenerational confrontation, wherein the older person takes avoidance measures, such as hurrying away as a youth makes obscene gestures or swears, are readily available as rather prototypical scenarios of a conflict between old and young strangers. These are regularly used by the media. Overall, when a younger and an older person are engaged in a conflict, stereotypes may be used to make attributions as well as to influence relational outcomes. For example, an older person who experiences conflict with a younger person may attribute the conflict to stereotypical aspects of youth naiveté, irresponsibility, and so forth, and may avoid getting into such disputes with the young person in the future.

Considering stereotypes of older people, different negative and positive stereotypes would predictably stimulate different conflict attributions, strategies, and so forth. Several researchers have noted the potential applicability of stereotyping and communication accommodation theory (see chapter 1, this volume) to conflict strategies (Berens, 1996; Bergstrom & Williams, 1996; Williams & Bergstrom, 1995). Considering an amalgamation of CAT and conflict styles realizes some interesting predictions based on various aspects of conflict reciprocity. Presumably, convergence would involve matching the style of the conflict partner, whereas nonconflictual convergence is often attributed positively. Convergence or matching competitive or avoidant conflict styles would predictably be perceived as unsatisfactory. In a conflict situation, nonaccommodation to cooperative strategies, divergence, and convergence toward competitive or avoidant strategies are likely to cause dissatisfaction. Conversely, convergence to partner's cooperative styles and divergence from a partner's competitive or avoidant style would predictably be related to increases in satisfaction.

Thus, successful conflict management (in Western cultures) would more often be expected if a partner diverged away from avoidant and confrontational styles and toward cooperation. It has to be said, however, that cooperation may not always the best strategy. For example, if a partner is hostile and violent (at the extreme of competitive), temporary (and perhaps longer term) avoidance might be wise (see also Cloven & Roloff, 1993). Thus, accommodation theory might predict that the most successful communicators would probably be those who are able to exercise flexibility in managing conflicts by appropriately using avoidance, cooperation, and competition to enhance relational and other outcomes. In other words, those who can effectively choose their battles are the most successful communicators.

Another important distinction can be made between conflict that is inter-individual and conflict that is intergroup in nature (see chapter 1, this volume, for a detailed discussion of intergroup theory). Intergenerational situations can be seen as intergroup when age-group membership is salient, and stereotyping is more likely, as are the associated assumptions and age-based communication adaptations. Moreover, in such cases, the causes of conflict as well as any outcome dissatisfactions are more likely to be attributed internally to the outgroup, and thus to feed back into and give support to stereotyping processes. Internal attributions are likely to involve attributions about personality or enduring behavioral characteristics rather than more transitory situational explanations. Because of this, groups may be less likely to see potential for conflict resolution.

As already mentioned, *stability* (the consistency of the conflict over time) and *globality* (the number of issues involved) also seem to be related to conflict strategies. Increasingly stable and global conflict perceptions are related to more negative behaviors (Bradbury & Finchham, 1990). Thus, if the context is age salient and the old and/or younger person identifies strongly with his or her age group, stereotypes are likely to play an important role in the conflict (note that stereotypes tend to be internal, stable, and global attributions) and attributions will predictably be group serving (Hewstone, 1989a). An intergroup theory of attribution suggests that negative behaviors of the outgroup would be attributed internally, whereas self- or ingroup negative behaviors are attributed externally. This suggests that when negative stereotyping and intergroup factors are salient in intergenerational conflict, conflict-avoidance and/or distributive strategies are more likely, and participants are less likely to seek solutions. The potential for spiraling negative effects on intergenerational contact—increasing avoidance and decreasing high-quality communication, as well as the consequences, particularly for older people, should be obvious.

Recent research by Bergstrom and Williams (1996) compared older and younger people's attributions, conflict expectations, and responses to a hypothetical conflict in an organizational context. They provided a conflict scenario and asked younger and older participants to imagine that they were in conflict with a coworker who was described as either 63 or 23 years of age. Participants were required to respond to the coworker, who was described as engaging in one of the three main conflict strategies described previously: cooperative, avoidant, or distributive.

Investigating spontaneously produced personality descriptions of the hypothetical coworker, Bergstrom and Williams found that both younger and older participants more frequently described the older coworker positively than negatively. On the other hand, a younger coworker in exactly the same scenario was more often described negatively than positively. Thus, when able to spontaneously produce trait descriptions, both age groups more frequently produced positive characterizations of the older woman (age 63) and negative characterizations of the younger woman (age 23). Although we cannot be sure why participants characterized the young target negatively, their characterizations of the older target could be related to the notion that older people are upgraded on dimensions of sociality (Braithwaite, Lynd-Stevenson, & Pigram, 1993). Particularly noteworthy in this regard is that this older person was characterized as young–old (i.e., age 63) and interestingly enough a number of character descriptions mentioned terms such as "motherly" and "grandmother."

Interestingly enough, when judging the likelihood of various conflict tactics, regardless of age of target, younger and older participants thought that engagement tactics of competition and cooperation would be more likely than avoidance tactics. To a certain extent, expectations for the partner's conflict strategy were in line with the invoked images of her personality. For example, both younger and older participants were more likely to expect the younger target coworker to compete instead of to avoid. While young participant's expectations were in line with the positive stereotype of the older coworker—they expected her to cooperate more than to avoid—older participants showed no differences in expectations of the older coworker. Perhaps this indicates that younger people were more inclined than older people to appropriate stereotypes of older people's wisdom (Baltes, 1993) and sociality (Braithwaite, Lynd-Stevenson, & Pigram, 1993) when evaluating expectations of the older coworker.

When it came to rating satisfaction, both older and younger people indicated that they would be more satisfied with cooperation than with avoidance or competition, which were equally dissatisfying. Young participants, however, again favored the older coworker by tending to be more satisfied with her, overall. In some ways, the older participants seemed to favor the younger target coworker over the older target coworker. For example, the older coworker did not accrue any comparative gain by cooperating, whereas the younger coworker did. In addition, older participants were more likely to judge the older, as compared to the younger, coworker as responsible for the problem in the first place, whereas younger participants did not differentiate.

If participants were making allowances for age in this study, it appears that older participants made allowances for the young person, and younger participants made allowances for the older person. In fact, both groups could draw on stereotypes to do so, in the one case these included age-associated inexperience and in the other, sociality.

In a final and telling stage of the study, participants were asked to write down their responses to the coworker's conflict strategy. Regardless of differing personality attributions, expectations, and satisfaction, the most powerful predictor of the responses for both age groups was a simple matching or reciprocation of the coworker's prior conflict strategy. One way of explaining this would be to point to the relatively ecologically impoverished experimental conditions necessary to conduct such a study in which respondents role played and wrote responses to a hypothetical partner. However, the results are supported by, and do corroborate, those found by Sillers and Zietlow (1993) discussed previously in circumstances that have very strong ecological validity. Also, the norm of reciprocity has been noted in other research contexts such as those of self-disclosure.

This study raises more questions than it answers. It does seem to indicate expectations of elder cooperation and prosocial conflict strategies in association with positive stereotypes (at least for younger participants), although this did not follow through to influence the response strategy. More interesting are speculations that could be made regarding elder stereotypes, as described in chapter 3. For example, how would a despondent, a severely impaired, or golden ager target be perceived and responded to in conflict situations? Most likely, expectations for perfect grandparent and golden ager would be associated with sociality and cooperative tactics. Interesting gender and substereotype combinations are also possible. For example, would the John Wayne conservative stereotype be seen as more authoritarian and thus more confrontational? Also, what would be the associated expectations and responses to young stereotypes? Importantly, we might ask questions about the relative strength of the reciprocity norm in influencing conflict processes. These questions and others must be left to future research. For the present, the discussion continues by moving from the interpersonal and intergroup levels of analysis to consider mediated and community level intergenerational conflict.

Mediated Intergenerational Conflict

It is when we bring the media into the frame that the intergroup- and social-identity theory perspectives outlined in chapter 1 are able to provide an explanation. In recent years, there has been considerable and growing media discourse of intergenerational conflict, sometimes characterized as *age-wars*. The groups at war are old people versus young people. The media frequently carry articles and news reports that draw explicit social comparisons between the old and the young and the labels such as Boomer versus Buster help to delineate the perceptual boundaries between the two groups.

A number of writers have suggested that the media portray younger and older people as engaged in conflict for scarce resources (Binney & Estes, 1988; Pollack, 1988; Walker, 1990), and there are fears that such characterizations are precursors to a justification of cuts in social security and Medicare entitlements for older people (Walker, 1990). The rhetoric recycles various social and demographic statistics, such as those about the increasing numbers of aging persons in the population putting pressure on the U.S. federal budget, combined with perceived political power of the aged (Coombes & Holladay, 1995). Popular press and television media report that the economy is going to be unable to support the swelling numbers of elderly as the Baby Boomers age into retirement. The burden, according to press reports, will fall squarely on the shoulders of the current 20-year-olds, the Busters. According to this view, young people are facing economic and social instability (hence the label Busters).

The "twentysomethings" of the 1990s are characterized as economically and socially worse off than their parents were at a comparable age, and they will continue to be worse off, shouldering the burden of an aged and dependent population. In other words, they are experiencing relative deprivation and this may be a cause of some grievance. The two groups, then, are in competition.

Comparisons which portray "twentysomethings" as relatively disadvantaged are fairly frequently framed in terms of current or impending intergenerational conflict in the so-called serious news media as well as in current popular literature. In 1994, Nelson and Cowan (1994) coauthored the book *Revolution X: A Survival Guide for Our Generation,* in which they warn of a clash between generations brought on by the alleged greed of Baby Boomers, shrinking social security, and the budget deficit. These authors characterize the Boomers and the Busters as heading toward conflict. Their response was to found the organization: Lead ... or Leave and to encourage young people to become politically active, outlining what they should do to rescue their future from a Washington dominated by Boomers.

There are several flash points of potential intergenerational conflict in media discourse. One is the potential for conflict between the current generation of 20-year-olds and those of their parent's age, popularly named the Busters and the Boomers, respectively. As was described in chapter 3, alongside the reports of the burden of the elderly, we find that all too frequently, news media reports are couched in terms of imminent intergenerational conflict between Boomers and Busters. The media can become a forum for trading intergroup insults (described in chapter 3). Some news media reports carry parental and disapproving headlines about young people, and in a mediated retaliation younger journalists and writers line up to add their voices to the fracas. For example, *Newsweek* columnist Jeff Giles (a self-declared Buster) writes, "most of the bad PR comes from boomers, who seem engaged in what Douglas Coupland (1991) defined as 'Clique maintenance.' To wit 'the need of one generation to see the generation following it as deficient so as to bolster its own collective ego'"(1994, p. 63). This is not an uncommon view, which is expressed by self-styled spokespersons for the Buster generation. Referring to divorce and working parents, young media spokespersons charge that Boomers are responsible for the latch key kids, referring to the economy, they ate the lunch leaving their kids only crumbs. Older and younger writers and journalists have their social identities tweaked, and enter into a full-blown mediated-intergroup conflict wherein the outgroup is labeled, stereotyped, denigrated, and blamed for the problem. In fact, the quotation from Giles is exactly as predicted by both intergroup and social-identity theory. In other words, once groups are established, group members seem to have an inherent need to bolster their own group relative to the outgroup, so that when social comparisons are made, the ingroup looks better than the outgroup. In fact, almost all of the media rhetoric surrounding this issue can be explained in terms of intergroup theory.

In terms of the definition of conflict, media discourse fulfills all the criteria outlined by Hocker and Wilmot (1995). We have generations who are essentially interdependent; the media is generating or fostering a perception that resources, money, welfare benefits, and so forth are, or are going to be, in short supply, and it is either going to be older people or younger people who will suffer cutbacks. Thus, a cluster of scarce resources may affect younger peoples' education and job prospects, among a host of other considerations. Economic observers point out that today's young people were born in a time of immense economic prosperity, which turned into economic recession (hence the labels "Boom" and "Bust"). Employment prospects for new graduates are declining (Van Sant, 1993), they will pay more in, and get less out of, social security (Malkin, 1994) and will experience a reduced standard of living (Howe & Strauss, 1993). The aura of negative social conditions spreads wider than the economy and family life is characterized as under siege for these youngsters. Especially cited as indicators are divorce rates and the changing structure of the family. For example, the United States had the world's highest divorce rates in the 1970s (40% of marriages ended in divorce), and women had entered the workforce in increasing numbers with the result that many youngsters grew up in families with stepparents and stepsiblings, with both parents in full time employment.

There is by no means consensus about this catalogue of social suffering. Samuelson (1993) points out that prosperity is still gradually increasing and living standards are dramatically higher than half a century ago. Other commentators suggest that demographically smaller generations typically fare better in the economy than demographically larger ones because they are in competition with less people for resources (Easterlin, cited in Quinn, 1994). An article in Newsweek pointed to at least seven ways in which Busters will be better off both socially and financially than their predecessors (Quinn, 1994). Also, the focus of energy and interest of advertisers in the Busters demonstrates their belief in the potential spending power of this generation. In addition, Coombes and Holladay (1995) effectively and convincingly debunk media-propagated images of older people as Greedy Geezers. So, in reality, it is unlikely that the young will be cheated by their elders.

Attempts to set the record straight and to debunk media myths are laudable but regardless of the facts, it will be important to assess how people receive and integrate mediated information and how they may use it in subsequent interactions. As was argued, media reports concerning this generational schism have a very strong intergroup flavor—groups are identified and labeled (i.e., Busters or Generation X vs. Boomers) and trait attributions are made forming handy stereotypes (e.g., Generation X members are lazy, whining slackers), and group members are talked about as if they were one homogeneous mass. Journalists and spokespersons seem to have their own social identities and in-group loyalties uppermost when they write rebuttals and derisory comments about the outgroup. This is where headlines such as "Grow up crybabies you are America's luckiest generation" (directed at "Twentysomethings") come from. Just as intergroup theory would predict, once group stereotypes are developed, they are generalized to all outgroup members. Ingroup members attempt to demonstrate that they are superior along important evaluative dimensions. Hence, we find that the negatively labeled Generation X fights back with accusations aimed at Boomers. This is the scenario played out in the media and the popular press, and is one that is vulnerable to all the intergroup attributions and processes that were outlined in detail in chapter 1. There is potential for considerable intergenerational tension if this media discourse enters the public psyche and becomes available as a resource in a host of other social discourses from macrolevel-political policy decision-making, all the way to interindividual discontents.

Is there any evidence of intergenerational tension as a result of these social discourses, or are people sophisticated consumers of media images and able to discount extremist positions? Certainly some researchers are concerned about the trickle-down effect of intergenerational conflict (e.g., Rosenbaum & Button, 1993). On the basis of their research, Schlesinger and Kronebusch (1994) estimate that the potential for intergenerational conflict is, in fact, relatively modest, limited to about 10% of the population. However, they suggest that tensions are more widespread, although they claim that most who feel tensions are unlikely to act on them, and that some tensions are diffused by ties of cross-generational empathy, especially within families. They conclude from their survey that the scope and intensity of intergenerational stressors could increase, depending on factors such as changes in direction of government spending as well as perceptions of fairness of the changes—and the media play an important role in shaping perceptions.

As Schlesinger and Kronebusch (1994) point out, there are a number of competing and contradictory images of the elderly as a group (see also Hummert, 1990); there is also conceptual confusion. Are we talking about tension, conflict, or even age wars? Data from the 1990 AARP Intergenerational Linkages Survey suggest that intergenerational tensions are most likely to be created when there is a disparity between how age groups are seen to be treated and how it is believed they should be treated. Their data indicate that the potential for intergenerational conflict exists most strongly among a small percentage (5%–10%) of Americans. They found that a much larger group (15%–20%) felt some intergenerational tensions. For example, some people believe that certain age groups get more than their fair share of government benefits. A still larger group (30%–65%) perceives unfair intergenerational burdens, depending on the type of burden. About 30% reported burden at the level of government, while up to 65% felt some familial-intergenerational burden.

Finally, Schlesinger and Kronebusch (1994) looked at the potential future growth of tensions. According to their survey, tensions are not most prevalent among those who are politically or economically disenfranchised. They show that younger (18–44-year-old) Americans as a whole do appear to be less optimistic about their future opportunities, and are more likely to feel burdened by familial obligations such as child care, than are elder Americans. The authors feel that there is some danger in such tensions growing and being translated into political debate, policy action, and so forth. However, they point out that one of the most striking results is that the elderly are not a homogeneous group and do not speak with one voice. Individuals hold very different views which makes intragenerational tensions equally possible also.

In summary, they argue that intergenerational conflict is less likely to express itself as competition among organized interest groups and is more likely to reside in individual perceptions and norms, analogous to racial tension and conflict. A prediction that, in the light of the stereotype-activation model, we should be concerned about because it would translate into prejudicial-communication behavior activated by certain stereotypes of elders. In this vein, Schlesinger and Kronebusch (1994) argue that such individualized tensions may involve differences in norms, which have the potential to exacerbate intergenerational discord. In other words, these researchers doubt the likelihood of age wars, but do express concerns about individuals who perceive sociopolitical conflicts and suggest that this might translate into a certain amount of interactional agism.

Certainly, as we indicated, subjective perceptions of elders' command of public economic and social resources matters as much as, or even more than, objective reality. Ingroup perceptions that an outgroup is homogeneous and is therefore perceived to speak with one voice on social policy as well as other issues matter also. This subjective perception of a group's standing (relative to other groups) in society is known as *vitality* (Giles & Johnson, 1987; Sachdev & Bourhis, 1993). Vitality can be subdivided into the subjective or cognitive comparison of groups relative to each other in terms of their institutional support (e.g., in the media, education), demographics (e.g., numbers, distribution), and status (sociohistorical, economic). For the most part, vitality has been an important dimension for understanding an ethnic group's social standing relative to others but it also has utility for measuring the relative social strength of nonethnic groups (e.g., gender: see Kramarae, 1981). The concept of vitality for understanding the perceived relative strength of different age groups (see Harwood, Giles, Pierson, Clement, & Fox, 1994) may be an important way of understanding how young, middle-aged, and older adults perceive their respective groups. At the present time, research suggests that people perceive the middle aged to have the strongest vitality among the young, the middle aged and the old. However, interestingly enough, young people believe that the elderly have more vitality than do the young. It will be important to continue to track this relative perceived vitality because changes in perception could well match an increase in intergenerational tensions.

SUMMARY

This chapter begins by outlining concepts and findings from interpersonal-conflict research. This is used as a springboard to launch a discussion about the various levels and contexts of intergenerational conflict. Possible cohort or developmental differences or both, which correspond to changing conflict styles across the life span were considered. Research suggests that as people age they also may become more mellow in their approach to avoiding conflict in nonimportant battles, but gently and cooperatively engaging those that are more important. In Giddens' terms, then, *conflict* is action that draws upon various rules and resources. The rules, norms, schema stereotypes, and the like for intergenerational interactions also would be expected to influence conflict. It was suggested that stereotypes and intergroup attributions can influence conflict strategies. People do indeed have different expectations and attributions about conflict strategies depending on the their ages relative to the age of their conflict partner.

In addition, this chapter refers to resources that people may call on in intergenerational-conflict situations. Such resources may be social—their own understandings of how to do conflict effectively, and this chapter discussed both the possibility that people develop conflict styles through the life span, and the possibility that social norms for how to best conduct and resolve conflict have changed over the last few decades. Of course, in intergenerational conflict situations, authoritative resources are also going to be important—older people are typically granted a certain amount of respect by younger people, and are often seen as authority figures in both workplace and family situations. We can also examine the allocative resources that may play a central role in conflict situations. Allocative resources in families may be located in the allocation of material benefits, while at the level of the community, this chapter discusses how allocative resources in the form of social welfare, medicare, and so on can be at the very heart of intergenerational conflict. In this regard, the chapter attempts to demonstrate how the media has creatively generated generational stereotypes and fueled a mediated-intergenerational conflict, which centers around competition for social, authoritative, and allocative resources.

The final part of the chapter discussed intergenerational conflict in the context of media images, and of perceptions of intergenerational status and vitality. Although media images of Greedy Geezers, Generation X, and the like tend to be overblown, there is some concern that such images may feed into some individual's perceptions of unfairness in the distribution of resources amongst the generations. This, coupled with disparate perceptions of age groups' vitality, may have the potential to fuel misunderstandings and intergenerational tensions in the future.

13

Societal, Political, Public Policy Issues, and Intergenerational Communication

Beyond each individual's attitudes toward aging, the language used in intergenerational interaction, and the intergenerational relationship factors that frame intergenerational communication, consistency and change in macrosocietal issues impact on the communication that transpires between generations. We, as individuals, often have no choice but to interact with one another in a world with existing parameters or barriers constructed by the institutional rules and regimes with which we work. Economic, political, and other institutional factors may seem beyond our individual or relational control. For example, the decisions made by politicians to differentiate one age group from another, a housing community that discriminates on the basis of age, a mandatory retirement age, segregating younger and older workers from each other, or a state that must choose between spending public money on education for the young or long-term care for the elderly. As discussed in chapter 1, social institutions provide a series of constraints and enablements with which people actively work to create and sustain social structure.

The fact that we can, to a certain extent, have certain social conditions imposed upon us does not mean that we are passively subjected to macrosocial conditions. People working with rules and resources shape and reshape social institutions. This means that there is a transactional relationship between people and the institutional order. Institutions can only influence from above when people take up the rules and resources offered by institutions and work with them. For example, legislators may initiate antiage-discrimination legislation, but this does not mean that agism will be eliminated or that employers will not discriminate against older workers. The notion of people drawing on and working with the social order and with this activity reinforcing the status quo, is a focus for much of the book. This should be kept in mind as macroforces are discussed in this chapter.

This chapter concentrates on a variety of macrosocietal factors such as political agendas, public policy, and mass-media effects that impact our intergenerational interactions in various ways. Political activity based on age, the politics of intergenerational equity, the luxury of a comfortable retirement, the age-based political interest groups that lobby for special programs, and the effects of a mass media that portray both young and old in a stereotypic manner are discussed at some length. Each of these factors can play an important role in influencing intergenerational communication in a top–down fashion, but are also important parts of the intergenerational equation because we appropriate them to communicate intergenerational relationships too.

AGING AND POLITICS

As discussed in the previous chapter, a myth that has been created and nurtured by politicians and the media during the past 10 years is that of growing conflict between generations fueled by very different political agendas. According to this viewpoint, the young see their futures being squandered by excess spending on very expensive programs designed exclusively for the older population. Huge interest groups and lobbyists flood the capitals of each industrialized nation, pressuring politicians and influencing the media, to concentrate solely on their agenda of cushy retirement and free health care. The government only cares about older adults, and therefore cannot spend any time, energy, or money on issues of concern for the young, such as education, child care, or the environment. This popular view dichotomizes political agendas and attitudes and predicts a coming intergenerational catastrophe. The intergroup nature and potential for intergenerational conflict is discussed in more depth in chapters 7, 12, and in the epilogue. The present discussion will concentrate on questions that frame any discussion of incompatibility of different generations' interests at the societal or individual level:

1. Do older adults themselves as individuals or as a group have a political agenda?
2. How does the agenda manifest itself in actual voting behavior or political activity?

3. Do aged interest groups exist that push this agenda?
4. Do the politicians favor the older age agenda over all other agendas?

Perhaps the one undeniable fact concerning politics is that everyone has an agenda. It is not unreasonable to state with some certainty that older adults, at least those living in the United States, do have a political agenda. This agenda is perhaps best outlined by Coombs and Holladay (1995) who studied the publications of numerous major interest groups for the aged (people over 65) and found that the following issues are central to their agendas: government subsidizing for long-term care, raising the supplemental income for social security and protecting cost of living adjustments, and providing national health care with universal access for all children. Other than the final item in this list, it appears that older adults, as reflected in the data from interest groups for the aged, have an agenda that may be quite different from other aged-based agendas. The motives are open to interpretation, too. For example, rather than being evaluated as altruistic, the notion that older Americans support universal health care for all ages may be reframed as indicative of the "laziness" of the older generation, who no longer want to spend time caring for infants and younger people in general. Regardless of the way it is framed by different interest groups, it does appear that a political agenda exists for older adults.

A second way to capture political agenda for the aged, or any differences between generations in political agendas, is to study the political orientations and political attitudes of older adults. Older adults do have political attitudes. "In fact, interest in politics seems to increase with age in the United States, peaking in late middle age or beyond, and dropping very little, if at all, after age 70" (Binstock & Day, 1996, p. 363). Older people report, on average, the highest interest in both political campaigns and public affairs of any age group. Binstock and Day attribute this high interest in all things political by older adults to an increase in activity in community events by older adults, to retirement, to a higher level of formal education, to a higher standard of living, and to a larger stake in government assistance. In combination with this high interest level by older adults in politics, however, is a feeling held by older adults that they will not be able to influence the political process. Jennings and Markus (1988) and Miller, Gurin, and Gurin (1980) report that a sense of powerlessness in one's ability to effect political policy increases with age. It appears that as we get older, our interest in political issues grows, but at the same time we become more cynical about the effect we can have on politics.

An additional myth that does not reflect the political attitudes of older adults is the notion that as we age we become much more conservative. It is believed, in other words, that older adults would agree much more with the beliefs and values of conservative candidates and conservative interest groups. In the United States at the end of the last century, the Republican party and those candidates supported by the Republican party were much more likely to call themselves conservative and to give voice to the conservative agenda. Binstock and Day (1996) report that most of the evidence about self-described conservatism and liberalism in the United States refutes this myth. Generational differences in conservatism and liberalism are due primarily to such factors as one's financial condition or one's cohort socialization, rather than to advancing age (Inglehart, 1977). It does appear, however, that party loyalty is age related. In the United States at this time, older Americans are more likely to call themselves Democrats than are younger Americans. Binstock and Day and others attribute this to older adults coming of age during the Depression and a great loyalty to the New Deal Democratic agenda of Franklin Roosevelt. The shift in recent state and national elections in the United States toward more conservative agendas may be a reflection of growing up during the 1950s and early 1960s.

It may seem surprising that a great deal of research evidence (see Binstock & Day, 1996, for a more detailed discussion) supports a general lack of intergenerational differences in age-related governmental policies. "Support for spending increases in Social Security, Medicare, and old-age benefits in general appears to be very high among adults of all ages, with older people no more likely than younger people to favor expanded benefit levels" (p. 365). Rather than age being a major predictor of support for age-related benefits and possible increased spending, factors such as political partisanship and economic standing appear to divide the electorate. Older adults do not think or vote as a solid block of opinion; in these terms they are as heterogeneous as any other social group. To portray older adults as a homogeneous group of opinion can be an intergroup move related to stereotyping. Such positions can be used in public (and private) discourses to promote certain interests and agendas. In fact, older adults are quite divided in their support of age-based agendas, and like all age groups, can support or reject political agendas on numerous factors other than age.

Excellent indicators of possible intergenerational discord due to societal factors are the voting patterns of the diverse generations. There is a general feeling, encouraged by the popular media, that voting patterns are influenced by age. Binstock (1997) suggests that "journalists who cover elections, prospectively and retrospectively, ubiquitously assert and imply that older people vote differently from other age groups because of their self-interests regarding old-age policy issues such as Medicare" (p. 15). In addition, this self-interest paradigm is often used as the best argument for fanning the flames of intergenerational conflict because older individuals are characterized as voting in a solid block to sustain the old-age welfare state that eliminates any possible government assistance to younger individuals or support to their agendas.

One fact does remain quite clear. Older adults do vote at higher rates than younger individuals. Binstock and Day (1996) cite numerous sources who agree that "controlling for socioeconomic and demographic characteristics, particularly education level, have shown for many years that voter turnout is highest among the elderly, declining only slightly after the age of 70 or 80 years in the United States" (p. 367). The myth associated with the high voter turnout of the elderly is that the elderly vote as a block for the programs and candidates who pander to their special needs. However, older people are as diverse in their voting patterns as every other age group. "Older voters have shown little inclination to base their votes on aging policy issues and perceptions of how the candidates stand on supporting the elderly" (p. 368).

The 1996 presidential election in the United States presents a remarkable piece of evidence indicating that older Americans were not much different in their voting patterns than individuals between 30 and 44 and 45 and 59 years of age ("Portrait of the Electorate," 1996). It should be remembered that at the time of this election Bob Dole was a man well past his 65th birthday, whereas Bill Clinton was in his late 40s. Despite efforts on the part of both campaigns not to allow age to become an issue, a dramatic age difference between the two candidates was quite obvious. Individuals between 18 and 29 years of age voted by a 53% to 34% margin for Bill Clinton, whereas the oldest age group, those over 60 years, voted for Bill Clinton at a 48% rate and for Bob Dole at a 44% rate. This difference is the greatest of all the age groups, but certainly does not reflect a huge voting shift between generations. Perhaps the most interesting difference in voting patterns across the previous two presidential elections in the United States is the reluctance of individuals over the age of 60 to vote for independent candidates. In contrast to older voters, the youngest age group has been the most likely to support an independent candidate, in this case, Ross Perot. Binstock (1997) attributes this reluctance to vote for independent candidates to their political parties and to the wisdom gained in their voting experience that their vote for an independent candidate may be valueless.

There is some evidence to suggest that older voters were more likely to oppose school-bond issues, but not other tax issues (Button, 1992). However, it was not clear that this voting difference was entirely related to the self-interests of the older voters. Voting for school-bond issues does tend to increase the value of homes in the school district, but in spite of this, older people who own homes still tended not to support the bond issues.

If one were to look around the world and pay special attention to the top elected leaders of each democratic country, one would notice that a disproportionate share of high political offices are held by older adults. This fact is somewhat disturbed by the recent election of Bill Clinton in the United States and Tony Blair in Great Britain. However, Guttman (1988) asserts that older individuals attain high leadership posts more often than younger individuals because of an accumulation of resources and the political experience that comes with advancing age. Also, older politicians are better able to fit the stereotype of elder statespersons who may be perceived to have more wisdom and experience. An interesting question that has not received research attention is whether the election of much-older political leaders can be influenced in any way by stereotypes and age-related expectations. It appears that at certain times in history, most recently when a young Bill Clinton defeated a once popular, but much older, George Bush, the populace threw out the older generation to give a younger generation its turn to govern. This may be spurred on by media propaganda such as "time for a change," "the government's ideas are old and tired," it is time for "refreshing and radical ideas," and so forth. While this theory of generational revolution may sound quite "sexy," there is little evidence to suggest that voters were tired of George Bush or John Major because of their age or their particular policies regarding their own age group. More likely, discourses of youth and vitality versus age and experience may be drawn on to further other political interests in one direction or another. It is reasonable to speculate that Bill Cinton's youthfulness when compared to George Bush's staleness may, at some level, be related to our perceptions of vitality and change.

Coombs and Holladay (1995) clearly articulate the notion that political power is often found within interest groups that lobby politicians. Although the power of these interest groups may often be overestimated by the media, it is undeniable that certain interest groups play a major role in policymaking in the United States. An indication that intergenerational differences exist in a society is the extent to which interest groups have been formed to lobby for policies favorable to one generation over policies advantageous to another generation.

Old-age interest groups have expanded in an unprecedented manner within the United States in the past 20 to 30 years. We now have more old-age interest groups, with more members, with higher visibility, performing more political activities than in the 220-year history of the country. Binstock and Day (1996) account for the proliferation and stability of these interest groups by pointing to the expansion of government into aging policy. Simply having an interest group, or a thousand interest groups, working for your particular cause does not guarantee access to politicians or positive action by those politicians. The question becomes whether the old-age interest groups have clout. Once again, a myth exists in the United States that interest groups dedicated to the advancement of favorable policies to the older population are, by definition, detrimental to all other age groups and have a great deal of political power, directly influencing policy decisions.

"The truth is that U.S. aged interest groups are powerful grass-roots lobbyists because they have large numbers, high social status, and are well organized" (Coombs & Holladay, 1995, p. 326). Interest groups such as the American Association of Retired Persons, the National Council on Senior Citizens, the National Council on Aging, the Alzheimer's Association, the Older Women's League, and the Gerontological Society of America are well financed, and often their members are called before Congress or are appointed to presidential commissions to address policy issues. In addition, old-age interest groups often find their causes to be very popular, while facing weak competition. Even when facing the most powerful interest groups, such as the American Medical Association or the National Rifle Association, the old-age interest groups can hold their own.

There is no doubt that old-age interest groups have multiple channels for access to political decisions and can focus the attention of politicians, the media, and the voters on issues of concern to their members. However, the power to influence the actual adoption of favorable policy for U.S. aged-interest groups is only average (Coombs & Holladay, 1995). The fragmentation of policy implementation in the government prevents the aged-interest groups from exercising much influence. "The fiction is that aged interest groups write and pass their own policies" (p. 327).

The discussion concerning aging and politics points to the differences between myths held to be true in our society and the research evidence. Although it is true that different generations may support different political agendas, it is not true that these agendas are in conflict. It is true that older voters show up at the polls and vote in higher numbers than younger voters, but it is not true that younger and older voters vote in significantly different ways. Although it is true that aged-interest groups have been formed and have an agenda supportive of their older memberships, it is not true that this same agenda is unpopular with other age groups or that this agenda is detrimental to the lives of younger people. It is true that old-age interest groups have high levels of access in political-policy discussions, but it is not true that these same interest groups write the actual policies and can guarantee implementation. All of the objective evidence, however, may have very little meaning if members of different generations believe that the generations are in fact quite different and actively attempt to undermine one another. A great deal of anxiety and potential conflict can emerge from the perception of one generation dominating or hoarding the goods of society. This is a very important point because these perceptions can feed into intergenerational communication at all levels: mass media, community interaction, and interpersonal interaction.

Retirement

It may seem rather obvious to those reading this book that human workers are not always able to take vacations or to retire. As a matter of fact, retirement is a creation of the 19th century. Prior to industrialization and several rather forward-thinking European rulers and industrialists, workers began their labor at a very young age and retired as they were buried. Concepts such as retirement, pensions, sick days, and vacations were nonexistent for most workers until well into the 20th century. Retirement, now an accepted phase of the life span, is a rather new phenomenon in human history. It is also an event that typically occurs when a worker is approaching old age. Kohli and Rein (1991) assert that modern states have become responsible for the income maintenance of substantial sections of older adults as well as the organization of the rules governing access to retirement.

Bernard and Phillipson (1995) divide the most recent history of retirement into two distinct halves. From about the 1960s on, retirement for both working men and women has become a normal feature of the life course. Retirement is synonymous with old age, and the defined features of retirement are controlled and heavily influenced by governmental policies. "The most recent retirement trends, starting toward the end of the 1970s, are marked by a number of critical changes, those focusing on the new pattern of early exit and early retirement from the labor force" (p. 287). Four factors are noted as playing a key role in the recent retirement trends. First, there is a marked decline in semi- and unskilled jobs in industrialized societies. Second, there has been an increase of women laborers in the work force. Third, early retirement due to ill health has increased. Finally, there is a growing number of older workers who freely choose early retirement because they value not working and they have the financial wherewithall to support a comfortable retirement. The traditional notion of a worker retiring after 40 years of service to one company and receiving a combination of public and private funds so that he or she can enter the twilight years in relative comfort may only have been true for a few short years following World War II. Older workers in today's industrialized countries find their paths to retirement to be much more flexible and less predictable. "Indeed, the very definition of retirement has become increasingly ambiguous as older workers and retirees have combined intermittent part-time employment, retirement benefits, and income from savings to support them in their later years" (Quadagno & Hardy, 1996, p. 325). Research by Atchley (1971, 1976, 1982, 1993) and others has stressed the positive correlates of retirement for workers in the 1970s and 1980s. However, with the changing economy and the many older workers who face a forced-early retirement, recent research has focused on the negative aspects of retirement (Bernard & Phillipson, 1995). Stress and tension from role loss and feelings of being cast aside by society are not uncommon for individuals who are forced to accept retirement before they ask to leave their jobs.

Although retirement is certainly a complex economic, social, and psychological issue that faces not only individuals but entire societies, we are most interested in how retirement functions to frame intergenerational communication. There are several different consequences for intergenerational communication that appear to be influenced by public and private sanctioned retirement. First, because retirement is not a random process, but instead is highly correlated with old age, older workers are being separated from younger workers. Intergenerational interaction, or at least the possibility of intergenerational interaction at the workplace is forcibly reduced. An indirect effect of this exodus of older workers, at least in the United States, is movement to retirement communities in warmer climates: Arizona, Florida, Texas, and North Carolina. Some older workers elect to leave their traditional communities in colder climates and move away to segregated retirement communities (e.g., Sun City, Arizona), adding to the lack of intergenerational contact (see chapter 2, this volume).

Second, younger workers see and often long for the retirement exodus. Why do only older workers receive such a great benefit? In addition, younger workers may feel as if they are paying for this laziness and recreation on the part of older workers with part of their pay checks, perhaps a form of age envy. Not only do bad feelings exist because of paying for the retirement of older workers, but younger workers may have a feeling that when their time comes to retire, these older nonworkers will have spent all the available money. The 1996 presidential campaign in the United States was fueled by speculation that social security will soon be nonexistent. This governmental program that all working Americans pay into to support the lives of individuals over the age of 62 may not be available to those of us who are in our 20s or 30s. There is a possibility that these feelings produce intergenerational tensions.

Third, older, retired workers now enjoy increased standards of health and longevity and may want to continue to work in the exact jobs from which they were forced to retire. While some workers look forward to retirement, others prefer to work. One reason corporations mandate retirement is that the younger replacement workers can be paid less salary and are (agistly) construed as more productive. There is the possibility of resentment toward those younger workers by the retired. Once again, even the perception of forcing older workers to retire to give jobs to younger workers may lead to intergenerational conflict. In the United Kingdom there has been an upsurge of resentment because companies blatantly discriminate against older workers. The Labor government is under pressure to introduce antiage discrimination legislation to put a stop to these agist practices. As in the United States, though, agist practices in employment will probably continue, but covertly.

A pragmatic, interactive consequence of retirement is the increased amount of time retired individuals now possess to spend with their families. Grandparents no longer have to go to work each and every day and thus can interact on a more frequent basis with their children and grandchildren. Previous chapters in this book reviewed both the positive and negative consequences of intergenerational family communication. It is not easy to predict whether a retirement within a family will benefit intergenerational family interaction. However, retirement, at the very least, provides the time for intergenerational family interaction to transpire, and the possibility for that communication to be competent and productive.

Social Security and Medicare

The two public-policy programs in the United States that represent an intergenerational transfer of money to help older individuals are social security and Medicare. The United Kingdom has an institutionalized social health and welfare system. Germany's Chancellor Otto von Bismark proposed a national old-age pension program for the elderly in 1881, mainly to prevent a revolt by workers (Schulz, 1996). Liberal democracies in the

United Kingdom, Belgium, France, the Netherlands, and Switzerland responded to electoral pressures in the early 20th century by instituting their own reforms to help older individuals. Much later, the United States responded to the Great Depression with its own national old-age pension plan. These early public benefits for the aged "were social assistance (by another name) 'for the elderly'—who were for the most part indigent, unable to support themselves, and increasingly unable to get adequate support from children" (Schulz, 1996, p. 412).

In the United States, the Social Security Act of 1935 established the federal Old-Age Insurance program as a governmental system of unemployment insurance. In succeeding years, survivors' and dependents' benefits were added, with disability insurance, to help disabled workers. Medicare was instituted by the federal government in 1965, establishing a comprehensive health-insurance program for the elderly. Total annual expenditures for these two programs have increased from close to $1 billion in 1950 to more than $400 billion in 1996.

The growth in these programs and similar programs throughout the world has been attributed to a shift away from social assistance to social security (Schulz, 1996). The shift away from minimal assistance to a maintenance of living standards from pre- to post-retirement for all older individuals generated large and still growing transfers of money through the federal and state governments. In essence, the working young have maintained an intergenerational contract with older individuals to, at some level, both maintain their standards of living and pay for their health care. This willingness of multiple generations giving to older generations may represent the best example of nonfamilial intergenerational solidarity in the history of the civilized world. However, it is most important to note that discourse of different age groups can characterize this social security in much different ways. For example, it is not uncommon to hear younger adults asserting that "we are paying for them" while older adults assert "we have earned our checks."

During the 1990s, it has become quite popular to use both social security and Medicare as the prime examples of how government is much too intrusive into the lives of ordinary (young) citizens, and soon will bankrupt not only the government and the nation unless draconian cuts in the programs are made immediately. Two retired United States senators, the recently deceased Democrat Paul Tsongas and Republican Warren Rudman, formed The Concord Coalition in the early 1990s to maintain a public debate concerning the large federal-budget deficits and the effect these deficits have on economic growth. By far, the greatest concerns of this coalition are the extent to which federal expenditures on the elderly threaten the survival of the federal government, and the financial security of all the citizens.

Perhaps the best example of the tension between The Concord Coalition and supporters of social security and Medicare (at least academic supporters) came at a panel discussion held during the 1996 Washington, DC, meeting of The Gerontological Society of America. The panel was composed of one member of the Coalition and three prominent gerontologists, including Vern Bengtson. The Coalition member pointed out the economic impact of the demographic catastrophe about to occur. Essentially, she argued that Baby Boomers are getting older and will soon demand their entitlements, and that these would essentially come at the expense of younger individuals. There are so many Baby Boomers that the young will soon be unable and unwilling to pay for the social security and health care of these older individuals. The gerontologists not only questioned the economic assumptions of the coalition, but chastised the coalition representative for adding her voice to the social construction of intergenerational conflict. It was the feeling of all three academic gerontologists that older adults are not "greedy geezers" and, in fact, have earned their social security not only financially, but in terms of their investment in the good of the nation through the war years, and so forth.

The economics of this debate are not as important to the content of this chapter as is the fact that the focus of the debate is a possible intergenerational conflict at a collective level. For the first time since a federal government attempted to redistribute the wealth of its citizens to help older adults, a public debate is raging as to how much help is enough, and whether this help should be organized and mandated by governments. Should one generation be taxed to maintain the lifestyles and health of another generation? There is little formal research that investigates whether this public debate has trickled down to a debate at the interpersonal level. However, recently we followed with interest a debate waged in the letters pages of a local U.K. newspaper. The letter writers were either older people (over 65) or younger people (under 65). Essentially, the younger people were complaining about retired elders who took their time shopping when the stores were busy, while younger people fumed behind them in the line. As the debate waged, the letter writers took various positions. One writer suggested that elders should be considerate to the young, who were supporting them financially. She argued that elders would not have any money to spend if younger people were not financially supporting their pensions. Older writers retaliated by pointing out that they had paid for their own pensions, and added fuel to the debate by suggesting that younger people were a generation who had forgotten their manners; they were rude and should respect elders. We suggest that these letters indicate a potential for underlying tensions to be expressed as intergroup communication. It demonstrates that discourses, which are already available in the public domain, are taken up and used by people to further their own interests. The letters also illustrate how popular stereotypes can be called on and used rhetorically.

We know that the public debate divides the major political parties in most industrialized countries, and that it is covered quite often in the news. The media urges us to be interested in this debate and to be concerned that one generation may be taking advantage of other generations. As our anecdotes indicate, we need to discover whether these societal messages are framing conversations at the more intimate interpersonal levels too.

Mass Media

As was mentioned, a public debate concerning the transfer of wealth from younger generations to older generations is occurring at a societal level. It is generally accepted that the agenda-setting function of the mass media influences this debate, and that we work with this as active viewers constructing and deconstructing our own realities. It is reasonable to state that the mass media profoundly affects all of our lives. One possible way the mass media affect our lives that is of interest to the content of this book (see chapter 2, this volume) concerns how the generations differentially consume the media and how different generations are portrayed in the media. If individuals of different ages consume and are portrayed differently, there is a very good possibility that different generations are translating their differing experiences with the media into perceptions and behavior that affect intergenerational communication. Perhaps, for example, people are using the media to support and confirm their own age biases.

Throughout the 1960s and early 1970s, the popular mass media often reported on the so-called "generation gap." In the early 1990s numerous media outlets such as MTV and *Newsweek* magazine had switched to reports on the Generation X phenomenon. The sound bite changed, but the message remained the same. In both cases the media were telling us that generations are different and that the younger generation resented the older generation for trying to send them off to war, or for using up all the resources of the earth without providing opportunity for future generations. The older generations did not understand the younger generations, and felt very disappointed by how the younger generations were conducting their lives. In these two cases, the media were presenting, in a direct way, a conflict between generations. A not-so-obvious conflict between generations may be the result of differential media consumption and portrayal of the media by the different generations (see chapter 12 for a detailed discussion of the intergroup nature of this mediated intergenerational communication).

An excellent review of the media usage and media portrayal of individuals across the life span can be found in an article written by Robinson and Skill (1995). A portion of this research was presented in chapter 2 of this book. We present the main points and conclusions reached by these authors once again to highlight the importance of the mass media in framing intergenerational communication. (For an in-depth review of the pertinent literature, see Robinson and Skill, 1995.)

A number of facts have become clear after several decades of mass-media research. First, television viewing increases across the life span to the point that older adults watch more television than any other segment of the population, including children. This increase in television watching for older adults is not due to age, but to an increase in leisure time. When one is no longer employed or raising children, one has more opportunity to watch television. Second, older adults watch more community-access programming, local news, and television programs that contain elderly characters than do younger adults. Third, many differences in viewing patterns are not so much correlated with age, as they are correlated with income and gender differences. For instance, affluent males, regardless of their age, tend to view different programming than do nonaffluent females.

Unlike television viewing, radio usage generally declines with advancing age. These differences in listening to the radio may not be directly related to age, but to spending less time listening to the radio at work or in the car. When older adults listen to the radio, they tend to listen to quite different programming than do younger adults. The elderly prefer listening to country music, talk radio, adult contemporary music, news, and nostalgia programming, such as old radio plays. The younger adults who have been studied prefer music on FM radio. Older adults prefer the AM stations.

The reading of books and magazines remains a popular activity throughout life, with a sharp decline starting around 65 years of age if eyesight begins to fail. The reading habits of older adults are also different from the reading habits of younger adults. *Reader's Digest*, *TV Guide*, and *Better Homes and Gardens* are the most popular magazines read by adults over the age of 65. *Reader's Digest*, *People*, and *Sports Illustrated* are the most popular magazines read by 18 to 34-year-old readers. It should be clear, by the short discussion concerning media usage, that different age groups consume not only different amounts of certain media, but that the media being consumed by these individuals are also different. We should keep in mind that different factors of life associated with aging, such as work status, income, leisure, and health-related factors such as eyesight, have an impact on what we watch, listen to, or read.

A second major factor reflecting the influence that mass media have on our intergenerational communication revolves around the portrayal of different-aged characters on television. A simple assumption for most of us is that television closely mirrors the real world. Characters portrayed on dramas and comedies should have some resemblance to their real-world counterparts. In other words, the number of older adults portrayed on television should roughly correspond to the proportions of older adults in the general population. Robinson and Skill (1995) conclude from their research review of articles published prior to 1990 that "there are not many elderly characters on television, males outnumber females three to one, and most elderly characters have minor roles" (p. 377). To update the literature, Robinson and Skill performed a content analysis of prime-time television during the 1990 season, to measure any changes in the proportion of elderly characters due to such factors as an increased awareness of the changing demography or to marketing associated with the population redistribution. Results from this most recent content analysis reveal very little change in the portrayal of elderly characters on television. Older adults continue to be underrepresented, with elderly male roles far outnumbering elderly female roles. In addition, as discussed in chapter 2, older adults on television continue to be unidimensional, and are placed in supporting situations. Robinson and Skill conclude their study by stating that "there is clearly a great deal of room for improvement in the way the elderly are depicted on television" (p. 385).

Intergroup Vitality

The notion of intergroup vitality refers to one social group's subjective perception of another group's relative social standing (i.e., their access to social resources, political power, and so forth) respective of their relative objective vitality (see also chapter 12, this volume). At numerous points this chapter draws distinctions between the real- and perceived-social standing of older people. For example, older people are perceived to be a politically self-interested coherent group, but the objective evidence shows that they are not. *Subjective group vitality* is a cognitive construct indicative of perceptions of groups' standing vis-à-vis others within a given society (Giles & Johnson, 1987; Sachdev & Bourhis, 1993). Subjective vitality is important because it can directly affect intergroup perceptions and intergroup communication, regardless of any objective state of affairs. The subjective perception that older people might have more vitality than younger people has the potential to fuel intergenerational tensions. Dimensions of vitality include the perceived status (e.g., sociohistoric, economic, demographic strength (or numbers), and institutional support (e.g., political, media education) of a group. Perceptions that the elderly as a group have a strong vitality could, therefore, rest on the perceived power of being economically secure, having access to Medicare and social security. Also perceptions could rest on the perceived power that increasing numbers of elderly in the population bring in terms of their ability to influence policy by applying pressure and so forth. The group that has the strongest vitality, in these terms, will achieve the highest social success; they will have access to a larger share of the social resources. Put this way, it is no wonder, then, that there is so much controversy about social security and Medicare, and so much attention to grass-roots pressure and lobbying among the various age-concerned pressure groups.

Another aspect of institutional support refers to the media—older people are at present underrepresented and negatively portrayed in the media and so by this token have less vitality than young. As numbers of older people in the population increase, we could anticipate that older peoples' interests and concerns will increasingly be reflected in a media and advertising industry geared to looking after the majority and economically rewarding interests. Education is another area that promises to become shared between the young and the old. It is in this climate of relative perceived vitality that younger generations may begin to think that they lose out compared to older people, and it is this feeling of relative deprivation that has the potential to add tension to the intergenerational equation as Schlesinger and Kronebusch (1994) argued and outlined in chapter 12.

SUMMARY

This chapter examines some of the macrocommunity features that feed, at various points, into intergenerational communication at several institutional levels. Intergenerational communication in politics, in the community, in the media, and so forth are part and parcel of interindividual communication among members of different age groups. It is argued in this chapter and chapter 12 that political, legal, and social-welfare agendas are important considerations when discussing intergenerational communication. In terms of intergroup discourses, such agendas allow younger and older people to draw on a number of assumptions that may fuel intergenerational miscommunication and even avoidance of intergenerational contact.

The macrosocietal features just reviewed only begin to touch the surface of community and instutional features that may affect intergenerational communication. We did not mention the segregated housing projects built in the 1960s and 1970s for low-income elderly, or the numerous segregated retirement communities for the wealthy elderly, or the numerous vacation destinations for older adults that are "kid free," or the eating establishments that cater to either a very young clientele or an older clientele, or the numerous educational facilities that have no facilities for older learners. Each of the communication and aging models mentioned in this book, along with most other models or theoretical descriptions of interpersonal communication, mention the possible effects of outside, environmental factors on a dyadic interaction. However, few researchers who study interpersonal communication bother to account for these effects. Within intergenerational communication, these societal factors are integral in the communication process, and thus should not be so easily ignored. One of the assumptions behind such policies, which is at the same time communicated by such policies, is that intragenerational communication is more desireable and natural than intergenerational communication. In other words: Stick with your own age group.

A second message that appears to be constructed at the societal level is that each generation is fighting for limited social resources and that only one can win. These resources may just be used up entirely by one age group, even though all of us need the resources. The political agenda of the elderly to save all budget cuts in social security will cause no money to be spent on immunizations for the young. The continued increases in social security taxes will soon prevent any spending on necessities for the young worker. The younger voters will never support an increase in Medicare coverage or a continuation of social security, and thus must be considered a political enemy. Although researchers continually assert that there simply is no evidence that the political agendas of older citizens or younger citizens create any poverty or hardships for other generations, the perception that this may be true—the perception that one social group has more vitality—can drastically affect intergenerational relations and can ultimately also affect intergenerational communication.

The environment of cities, neighborhoods, mass transit, crime, political agendas, governmental policies, and the media portrayal and reporting of all these factors can create a communication climate difficult for younger and older individuals to master. Prior to any communication shared by the generations, each individual must first battle the real or perceived barriers to a successful communicative encounter. We wish to point out that on many levels—cognitive, language practices, relational, and societal—intergenerational communication can be rather difficult and complex. The key to understanding the entire picture of intergenerational communication is to realize that treating institutional and macrofactors as if they are forces that act outside intergenerational interactions, to shape people's behavior within them, is a false division. People appropriate and creatively use macrofactors in their interactions, whether those interactions are directly intergenerational or consist of talk about other generations. It is this active use of what we have called *macrosocial factors* that gives life to intergenerational relationships.

14

Cultural Perspectives on Intergenerational Communication

This chapter examines cultural perspectives on intergenerational communication. At the time of writing, and in spite of the recent surge of research interest in communication and aging, there is very little research that specifically examines intergenerational communication across different cultures. Most of the existing research about communication and aging is almost entirely Western. However, interest in life-span issues and intergenerational communication across different cultures is growing, and there is increasing potential for future research across a variety of cultural contexts. This chapter discusses intergenerational communication in Eastern contexts. Beginning with a brief overview of the philosophical roots of Eastern cultures, recent research concerned with aging and communication and intergenerational relationships is reviewed. Much of the research that is closely examined here is the result of a recent international project designed to investigate communication and aging across the Pacific Rim (e.g., see Gallois et al., 1996; Harwood et al., 1996). The results of this project and of other research outlined here are beginning to reveal some intriguing and unexpected differences between Eastern and Western approaches to age and communication. For the most part, this chapter focuses on comparisons between various Eastern and Western contexts, and on perceptions and attitudes based on survey data.

The state of knowledge about the different approaches to aging in the East and the West has, for a long time, been largely based on hearsay and lay wisdom and has had no solid basis in research or theory. Recently, however, there have been a number of empirical research studies designed to investigate aging and intergenerational relationships in Eastern nations, studies that form the basis for this chapter. There is increasing interest in interpersonal relationships across different cultures (see Gudykunst, Ting-Toomey, & Nishida, 1996) as well as research that looks at intergenerational and relational communication within various cultures (e.g., see Ng, 1998). These developments hold great promise for future research and theoretical innovations.

It would be a mistake to leap into a discussion of intergenerational communication in Eastern cultural contexts without stressing the fact that cultural assumptions that we make in Western contexts may not be valid in the East. As many writers point out, understanding the philosophical roots of culture is crucial to understanding the why and how of cultural differences.

PHILOSOPHICAL ROOTS
OF INTERCULTURAL DIFFERENCE

The field of intercultural communication has been one of the main growth areas of communication study in recent years, especially as it relates to Eastern versus Western cultures, with the effect that we do know that Eastern and Western cultures differ in some crucial and interesting ways (e.g., see Gudykunst & Ting-Toomey, 1988). The work of scholars such as Hofstede (1980) and Hall (1976) was crucial in pinpointing some fundamental underlying cultural differences. In very general terms, intercultural scholars describe Eastern cultures as relatively more *collectivistic* or ingroup oriented, whereas Western cultures may tend to be relatively more *individualistic* or individually oriented (Hofstede, 1980). According to the work of Hall (1976), Eastern cultures are thought to be *high context* (e.g., relying on the context to disambiguate communication) whereas Western cultures are relatively *low context* cultures (e.g., favoring verbally explicit communication).

Having established such generalizations, we must be wary of using them to make sweeping distinctions. Herein lies the danger of feeding into popular stereotypes such that any sign of difference is glibly attributed to culture, and individuals are labeled as collectivistic or individualistic. Triandis, Leung, Vallareal, and Clack (1985) and others (e.g., Markus & Kitayama, 1991) argue that all cultures include individuals who may have relative individualistic (idiocentric) or collectivistic (allocentric) orientations. Some researchers and theorists would take this further to suggest that such labels are themselves overgeneralizations, because individuals can behave in ways that can be seen as either idiocentric or allocentric depending on the interaction context.

The East has varying, and sometimes contradictory, philosophical influences and in fact, the internal contradictions, for example, between Taoism and Confucianism are often downplayed by communication theorists. In China, early historical teachings of Taoism viewed persons and the environment in constant relational flux and harmony. In this view, the person is part of the environment and should accord with natural forces to maintain harmony. Not only do such beliefs echo through Chinese and many other Eastern cultures today, they have even been imported into the West in certain aspects of New Age beliefs and have been popularized in the media. Arranging one's furniture according to ancient beliefs about harmony and energy flow (Feng Shui), and the practice of Tai Chi are examples of direct descendants of ancient Taoist teachings that seek harmony between person and environment.

Other teachings and influences interacted with early Taoism. In China for example, Buddhism came across the border from India and together these two philosophies contributed to the very obtuse philosophical writings that we typically associate with inscrutability. The reason for the perception of inscrutability is probably due to the fact that both Taoists and Buddhists had a basic mistrust of verbal communication, believing that words could be used disingenuously to disguise intent, and that spiritual, universal truth could not be transmitted by inadequate verbal codes (see also Chang, 1997). Therefore, although it is common practice to link many Eastern communication behaviors to shared traditions of Confucianism, we must be mindful that Confucianism, too, interacted, and at times clashed, with other philosophical traditions.

In spite of these varying traditions, the single most frequently cited philosophical influence on Eastern communication patterns is Confucianism, which spread throughout the East to influence many Asian cultures in a variety of ways (Chang, 1997; Kiefer, 1992; Kim, 1994; Kim & Yamaguchi, 1994). For example, five codes of Confucian ethics are inscribed into the Confucian Analects (e.g., The Great Learning) which children were instructed and socialized to accept as the moral basis of society. The five codes all relate to harmony and personal righteousness through respect for, and attendance to, ordered social relationships, affection and righteousness between parent and child, a power distinction between husband and wife, and sincerity between friends. These codes highlight the order between young and old, interdependence between people, and the importance of attending to status and role in a social hierarchy. Herein, social orderliness is implicitly and explicitly tied to environmental orderliness. Hence, the self as a socially and environmentally interdependent being emerges (Markus & Kitayama, 1991).

In Eastern contexts social harmony is thought to evolve from the maintenance of ordered and hierarchical relationships. Such relationships are often based on age hierarchies (e.g., father–son), familial and social roles, and long-term life span outcomes are important. In fact, obligation to parents and familial elders can extend even beyond the grave, as inscribed in the ancient tradition of ancestor worship (Lee, Parish, & Willis, 1994). Perhaps then, it is not surprising that we expect elderly people in such cultures to be better viewed and more sympathetically treated than in the West.

The philosophical orientation of the West, by contrast, is said to rest on Liberalism. Here, the primary unit of social life is the individual, whose rights and autonomy are paramount (Kim, 1994; Kim & Yamaguchi, 1994). Thus, individuals operate as units quite separate from their social or environmental backgrounds; they act rationally, pursue their own rights, and search for personal fulfillment independent from their ingroups (Gudykunst & Matsumoto, 1996; Markus & Kitayama, 1991). In the West, stigmatization of the elderly is attributed to the pressures of Liberalism, including industrialization, short-term relationships, independence, and activity orientation (e.g., Bennett & Eckman, 1973). These are all dimensions that can be characterized as devaluing the role of older people. Older people are considered historical remnants in a world of modern industrial and technological sophistication, they are relationally demanding—requiring time and long-term relational commitments, which increase with increased age, and they are relatively more dependent and less active than younger people. Now, contrast this view more closely with Eastern approaches to communication and the elderly. We are all familiar with popular cultural stereotypes of venerated old Asian sages and of Easterners who respect and protect the elderly in caring extended families. The next few pages begin to assess whether or not such images are reflected by empirical findings.

Eastern Perspectives on Communication and Aging

Some research paints a very positive picture of Eastern views of old age, akin to our lay impressions. For example, Sher (1984), as a result of field work in Shenyang, presents a very positive image of older people within Chinese society. She claims that traditional respect and honor of the elderly has remained in the face of substantial recent changes in Chinese society. Wong (1979) suggests that the life experience and knowledge of the elderly is valued in Chinese culture because it provides a link between past and present generations, and provides a continuous link with ancestors, history, and cultural traditions. Other writers make links between Eastern attitudes to age and traditional values of harmony, suggesting that aging is seen as a positive personal experience because it reflects harmony with a natural process, and thus reflects harmony with the environment. Finally, it has been proposed that East and West differ because Eastern cultures view older people as more productive than do their Western counterparts. Nagasawa (1980) characterizes older people's productivity in providing intergenerational bonding within families. Some of this research is more impressionistic than empirical, however, and does not set out to test a priori hypothetical expectations.

Others present empirical data to suggest that stereotypically positive views of the elderly in the East may be little more than popular myths (Koyano, 1989; Levy & Tsuhako, 1994; Tien-Hyatt, 1987). Such an alternative view is proposed by Ikels and colleagues (Ikels et al., 1992) who suggest that, like their Western counterparts, Easterners may have rather negative stereotypes of the elderly. These stereotypes include attributions of physical decline, material insecurity, and poor intergenerational relations (e.g., long-winded and nagging). In addition, these authors suggest that a common Eastern approach to the elderly is one whereby older people should be treated well, but their views need not be taken seriously. In other words, elders may be treated with a veneer of respect and tolerance, but can be covertly dismissed as irrelevant.

Considering what may happen when Easterners immigrate into Western cultures, a number of researchers document a decline in traditional values and subsequent problems for elderly immigrants (Chang, Chang, & Yung, 1984; J. Chen, 1980). Wu (1975) indicates that a lack of endorsement of the filial-piety norm among young generations of Chinese Americans, as well as language barriers in the new culture, can lead to stress and an inability to access needed services among Chinese-American elders. In the Korean context, it has been suggested that a multigenerational household structure can significantly reduce such stress and trauma (Kiefer et al., 1985).

It is, therefore, also possible that impressions of venerated elders are a throwback to traditional values. It has been suggested that, as Eastern cultures become more industrialized and urbanized, and more economically successful and driven (the so-called "economic Dragons"), the elderly may be the unwitting victims of this success. This is especially so for those cultures who have experienced massive economic and technological boom in the last few decades. In these cultures, older people are characterized as being left behind in the rush for modernization. For example, Ikels (1975) suggests that such a pattern may be particularly evident in Hong Kong. She explains negative attitudes to the elderly in terms of extensive Westernization and rejection of traditional values, especially among young-Hong Kong–Chinese people. Tien-Hyatt (1987) discusses similar patterns in Taiwan where Taiwanese–Chinese elderly have less positive self-perceptions of aging than either Anglo–Americans or Chinese–Americans. She suggests that the elderly may have trouble adjusting to recent rapid economic and technological changes occurring in Taiwanese culture. In Hong Kong, Chow (1983) outlines how changes in family structure resulting in the predominance of the nuclear family increase the need for government and community care of older people, and there has been some comment about such changes in the press. In Japan too, the number of older people living on their own or in nursing homes has increased in recent years, leading to comments and concern about the breakdown of the traditional extended-family structure.

Filial Piety and Intergenerational Relationships

For many cultures around the world, there is an expectation that family members will provide social and practical support to each other throughout the life span, varying according to need. As discussed in previous chapters, grandparents may provide services such as childcare to their adult children, and as parents grow older, adult children may assume the responsibility of caring for their aging parents. A duty to care for and respect the elderly, particularly family members, is a concept known as *filial piety*. It is commonly assumed that the strength of the filial obligation varies according to culture. Traditionally it has been thought that filial piety is particularly strong in Eastern cultures and less so in the West (Kiefer, 1992; Palmore, 1975). Here, it is important to point out that it is a mistake to assume that Western nations do not have a tradition of filial piety. Earlier chapters explained how the intergenerational bond (intergenerational solidarity, analogous to filial piety), social and practical support, and helping in families is maintained in the West through a diversity of means. However, as is argued in the next section, the exact nature of intergenerational solidarity may be quite different in the East as compared to the West.

The Eastern traditional ethic of filial piety has been strongly linked to collectivism and has purportedly guided relations between the generations for more than 2,000 years. Filial piety, the Confucian doctrine of *Hsiao Ching*, teaches that elderly people should be respected, and that it is the children's responsibility to care for parents and grandparents in their old age

(J. Chen, 1980; P. N. Chen, 1979). This applies particularly within the family, but is not necessarily limited to family members, because as Yuan (1990, p. 32) claimed in China, "any acts of disrespect or abuse toward the aged are restricted by law and open to moral condemnation." At one point, the Hong Kong government (1965) declared that it was the family's moral responsibility to care for the aged or infirm. Likewise in Korea, Park and Kim (1992, p. 399) claim that "growing old represents signs of grace, respect and piety, and age is the first consideration when Koreans communicate with each other." There is a considerable body of research suggesting that elderly individuals command a powerful and respected role in Eastern cultural contexts (see, e.g., Ho, 1994; Levy & Langer, 1994; Martin, 1988; Sung, 1995; Yum, 1988). The ethic of filial piety itself has been well documented across the Asian Pacific Rim, for example, in Korea (Kim, Kim, & Hurh, 1991), China (Turkowski, 1975), Japan (Tobin, 1987), Taiwan (Lee, Parish, & Willis, 1994), and Hong Kong (Ikels, 1975). Do people in the East endorse stronger norms of filial piety compared to people in the West? In other words, are young people in Eastern cultures more likely to respect, support, help, and care for older family members than are young people in Western cultures? Does endorsement of such values translate into very different perceptions of aging and intergenerational communication in Eastern as compared to Western contexts? These are the main questions that will be addressed in the remainder of the chapter.

Intergenerational Exchange, Support, and Obligation

A comparative survey of young students' attitudes to filial piety across four Western (Australia, New Zealand, the United States, and Canada) and four East- and Southeast-Asian (Japan, Korea, Hong Kong, the Philippines) nations was conducted by Gallois and colleagues (Gallois et al., 1996). Results showed that judgments of filial piety varied according to whether the person being considered was family or nonfamily, and varied according to the age of the person being considered. Judgments of filial piety could be grouped into these dimensions: practical support (e.g., financial assistance) versus communication (e.g., listen patiently), and respect versus contact and support. Respondents indicated that they thought young people should give practical support to their elderly parents, that parents expect continued contact with their children, and that older adults in general expect respect. Compared to Western students, Asian students responses pointed to a larger generation gap between what young people intended to provide versus what was expected of them. Asian students indicated that they intended to provide practical support, but they perceived their parents and other older adults as expecting continued contact and respect. In addition, Asian students felt more obligated to provide practical support than did Western students, while Western students emphasized continued communication and contact with older adults. Asians, more so than Westerners, were aware of filial piety pressures toward general nonfamily, as well as family, elders, but they indicated that they did not willingly practice such filial behaviors.

In general then, Asian students reported that their intentions to care for and communicatively support older people were actually lower than they thought was expected of them, whereas Westerners felt they would provide more support of all types than was expected of them. In other words, Asian young people expect to fall short, an expectation, which if realized, could lead to intergenerational tensions and even conflict.

Studies in Korea by Youn and Song (Song & Youn, 1989; Youn & Song, 1991) add an interesting angle to these findings because they focused on expectations and perceptions of older people. These researchers suggest that Westernization and urbanization have led to the breakdown of the Korean traditional extended-family structure wherein the eldest son resided with his aging parents. They suggest that aging Koreans are discontented with these changes because their roles and duties have changed from being protectors and governors of their offspring, to being protected and governed by their offspring (Song & Youn, 1989). In addition, according to Song and Youn (1989), younger family members do not attempt to understand their parent's resulting psychological distress. Youn and Song (1991) surveyed a large sample (623) of elderly Koreans (ages 55–84 years) about their perceptions of conflicts in their relationships with their adult children. Findings indicated that increasing age was associated with perceptions of increasing conflicts as indicated by unpleasantness in communicating, and by perceptions of more disrespect and more alienation from children. Older Koreans expected to have better relationships with their children as they grew older, but this was not always realized. Parents who were bereaved and noncohabiting also perceived more conflicts, which again, could be a function of increased expectations that were not realized.

It seems then, that expectations that older people should be cared for, respected and honored by younger family members in Eastern cultures is very high, perhaps too high and unrealistic for modern urban communities. Certainly young people may be aware of this, because they do not feel that they can meet such expectations. Particularly perhaps, young people feel that they cannot meet the emotional or psychological expectations of elders whereas they can at least contribute with practical and financial support. It seems that this may well cause considerable strain on intergenerational relationships, especially within the family. Young people fail to meet elder's expectations, and the reviewed research indicates that both elderly and young people may increasingly perceive a gap between their own expectations and the reality, a gap that may increase as parents grow older.

Having seen the cracks in the rosy stereotypes of honored and venerated Asian elderly people so long touted in Western popular media, the next section considers research that investigated stereotypes in a comparative context. From there, the discussion turns to examine perceptions of intergenerational communication. As the discussion of filial piety foreshadowed, a continued empirical exploration of intergenerational relationships in the East reveals that in this contrastive context, Western attitudes toward the elderly begin to look quite favorable on some dimensions.

PERCEPTIONS OF INTERGENERATIONAL COMMUNICATION IN EASTERN AND WESTERN NATIONS

Traits and stereotypes, particularly those that younger people have of older people, have been important features for discussion throughout this book. Chapter 3 details a number of substereotypes of elderly people, which has typically found in the United States (e.g., Perfect Grandparent, Despondent, Golden Ager, Severely Impaired, and so on) and subsequent chapters described studies that looked at the ways in which such stereotypes influence intergenerational communication. Naturally then, when considering intergenerational communication in Eastern contexts, comparative questions about stereotypes can be asked. For example, what elder stereotypes exist in the East, or for that matter, what is the nature of youth stereotypes in Eastern cultures, and do they differ from those found in the West? How would such stereotypes impact intergenerational communication in the East? Assuming that such questions, which are drawn from a Western cultural context, are valid for Eastern and other cultural contexts, the answers will have to wait because at present there is little available empirical evidence. However, emergent research begins to address some of these issues and draws comparisons between Eastern and Western cultural contexts.

An initial study conducted by Giles, Harwood, Pierson, Clément, and Fox, (in press) found that adult's stereotypes toward the elderly were actually more positive in California than in Hong Kong. Also, further comparative data showed that Californian students perceive older people to possess more vitality in terms of status and institutional support than do their Hong Kong counterparts (Harwood, Giles, Pierson, Clément, & Fox, 1994). In addition, Hong Kong students afford more vitality to young people than do Californian students.

Harwood and colleagues (Harwood et al., 1996) further investigated the traits that younger adults associate with younger (20–30-year-olds), middle-aged (45–55-year-olds) and older (65–85-year-olds) adults, comparing Australia, Hong Kong, Korea, New Zealand, the Philippines, and the United States. Factor analysis of a series of nine traits (Attractive, Active, Healthy, Strong, Liberal, Wise, Kind, Generous, and Flexible) revealed two primary dimensions entitled Personal Vitality and Benevolence. Across all nations there was a decline in ratings of Personal Vitality and an increase in Benevolence with increased target age, so that, for example, older adults were rated as the least personally vital, but the most benevolent, a pattern that fits well with previous Western research. Variations of this theme were also evident as, for example, young respondents in the Philippines and New Zealand did not differentiate between middle-aged and older adults. The most striking finding was that there was very little evidence of a positive view of elders' increasing benevolence in the Eastern cultures—Hong Kong and Korea. In fact, the most negative evaluations of aging emerged from Hong Kong, the only location wherein respondents perceived no positive gains for increased age. Obviously, this research is a first important step in the investigation of traits and stereotypes of older and younger people in cultural contexts other than the West.

There are many questions to be answered by future research. For example, could we find, in other cultural contexts, old-age substereotypes similar to those identified by Hummert (1990)? If not, what subtypes might exist and how do they relate to the unique and particular cultural and social contexts in which they are formed and perpetuated?

What do these findings mean for intergenerational relationships in Hong Kong? As shall be demonstrated further, the data indicate that Hong Kong may emerge as a special case with respect to such issues, and we cannot discuss intergenerational relationships without considering wider implications of the cultural contexts, not just in terms of cultural philosophy, but also in terms of modernization, expansion, influences from outside, the economy, and so forth. In the case of Hong Kong, Harwood et al. (1996) argue that Hong Kong has enjoyed a special economic and prosperous status in the world (e.g., entreport trade, international commerce, and finance) so that through non-Confucian influences (especially during the British administration) a free and open society emerged. Thus, in Hong Kong, older adults, especially those who can be associated with mainland China, tradition and so forth may have been left behind by modernization and are perceived to be leading traditional and out-of-date lives. Young people may be keen to disassociate from older people and a life stage, which for them, has no redeeming qualities. Moreover, in Hong Kong, urbanization and industrialization have occurred without the propagandizing pressure of traditional Confucian values such as might be found in some other Eastern cultures such as Singapore, Taiwan, and Korea. In this context, older adults remain something of a vestige of the previous society, and the generation gap may be much more salient. In spite of these social pressures, according to Ng (1998), young people in Hong Kong strongly endorse notions of filial piety (see also Ota et al., 1996).

Recent research extended the investigation of perceptions of intergenerational communication to compare Eastern and Western nations around the Pacific Rim. Using the PICS questionnaire described in chapter 5, Williams and colleagues (Williams et al., 1997) investigated dimensions of intergenerational communication across nine nations, which included Hong Kong, Japan, Korea, China, the Philippines, New Zealand, Australia, the United States, and Canada. Findings indicated that across all nations, the data fell into four initial dimensions. Three dimensions were directly interpretable in communication accommodation theory terms (see chapter 1, this volume). The first was labeled *Elder Nonaccommodation* (when older people were perceived as inattentive to young peoples' communication needs and they also negatively stereotyped young people). Second, *Accommodation* was when older people were perceived as supportive, attentive and generally encouraging to young people. Third, age status was recognized by a dimension labeled *Respect/Obligation* wherein young people need to accommodate to older people in terms of their intergroup status. The fourth dimension was *Age-Irrelevant Positivity,* which described a situation in which young people reported that conversations with older people were emotionally positive, satisfying, and in which age did not matter. The data were compared in a cross-cultural analysis that divided the sample into East (China, Hong Kong, Korea, Japan, and the Philippines) versus West (the United States, Australia, New Zealand, Canada) differences and then looked at differences among the Eastern nations and among the Western nations in the study. Compared to the West, Eastern nations appeared to be less positive in their perceptions of intergenerational communication on some dimensions. The Eastern nations differed from the Western nations in that they were less likely to agree that elders were accommodative to them (i.e., supportive, attentive, etc.) and were more likely to disagree that conversations with elders were emotionally positive, satisfying, and that age did matter. These are the general differences, but a closer look at comparisons between particular nations reveals more detailed differences.

Hong Kong and China were similar in many ways because they could be characterized as the least positive about their conversations with elders. Compared to the other nations, Hong Kong respondents tended to disagree that elders were accommodative to them and tended to agree that elders were nonaccommodative. This was combined with the lowest levels of respect or obligation. The People's Republic of China showed a similar pattern, apart from more positive ratings of elder nonaccommodation.[1] Korea and Japan could also be clustered together in many ways. Like Hong Kong and Chinese respondents, these respondents were relatively less positive in their ratings, but unlike Hong Kong and China, this was combined with higher pressure to be respectful and obliging to elders. The findings also support the contention that, in Korea at least, age is always an important consideration in any interaction (Park & Kim, 1992).

The Philippines, Australia, and New Zealand also showed somewhat similar profiles. In particular, the Philippines stood apart from the other Eastern nations as being much more similar to the Western pattern of judgments. Thus, the evaluative profile of these three nations could be situated as somewhere between the relatively less positive far East and the relative more positive West. Australians, New Zealanders, and Filipinos were more positive than were people from the far East with medium levels of respect and obligation. They felt more obligated to be polite and respectful than did the Hong Kong and Chinese respondents, but less pressured perhaps, than the Koreans and Japanese. Age did not matter as much as for Korea and Japan. Finally, Canada and the United States could usefully be grouped together, being the most positive among this set. This general relative positivity for Canada and the United States was combined with moderate levels of Respect/Obligation. Perhaps, the higher profile of antiagism in these Western nations, along with social welfare programs for the elderly, and open discussion of the needs of an aging population help explain these results. Also there is less distance between the generations, they are more on an equal footing, and although it leads to a lowered respect norm for Western elders, the alternative seems to involve high respect, which com-

---

[1]At first glance, this finding may seem somewhat anomalous, even contradictory. However, this pattern of findings runs through several studies and suggests that older people may be perceived to be both communicatively accommodative and nonaccommodative albeit on different evaluative dimensions which might actually coincide with the stereotyped dimensions of high benevolence but low competence.

bined with hierarchical relationships, creates more intergenerational power-distance (see Hofstede, 1980). This leads to increases in communicative distance, increased intergroup (intergenerational) distinctions, and so forth.

A final finding of this research was that there was more variability among the evaluations of the Eastern nations than there was among the Western nations. This underlines the potential problematicity of grouping Eastern cultures together and labeling them as collectivistic.

DISTINGUISHING BETWEEN FAMILY AND NONFAMILY ELDERS

So far, the discussion considered young people's perceptions of intergenerational communication with nonfamily elders. As previous chapters suggested, nonfamily elders, especially strangers, may be differentiated from elder family members or from those elders who are known well and are loved. Strangers and acquaintances are much less likely to be individuated and are more likely be treated in terms of generalized stereotypes of the elderly—in intergroup terms (see chapter 1, this volume). Certainly, young people in Western cultures appear to enjoy satisfying and fulfilling relationships with grandparents and other family elders (e.g., see chapters 8 and 9, this volume).

Family members can be categorized as ingroup members whereas those outside the family can generally be considered outgroups. There is some evidence that people in Eastern cultures also might discriminate in interesting ways between ingroups and outgroups—family elders and strangers. For example, Ting-Toomey (1994) suggests that Asians may use different conflict strategies with ingroup people and family members versus outgroups or those outside the family, adopting an avoidance style when in conflict with ingroups such as family members, and a more confrontational style when in conflict with outgroup members. The reason for this can be linked to philosophical traditions and filial piety, as for example, one might be more reluctant to be confrontational and openly conflictual with those with whom one is tied in a long-term respect hierarchy across the life span.

Taking the possible differentiation between family and nonfamily members into consideration, Noels et al. (1997) extended research of perceptions of intergenerational communication to compare perceptions of communication with family and nonfamily elders as well as with peers. This study was conducted with young adults from five nations: the United States, Canada, New Zealand, Korea, and the Philippines. Researchers used the PICS questionnaire. Extending inferences from the patterns of data discussed in the Williams, Giles, et al. (1997) study, it could be suggested that Korea is the only Eastern-patterning nation in this data set. Furthermore, the United States and Canada should predictably show similar profiles, as should New Zealand and the Philippines.

Looking first at comparisons between nonfamily elders and same-age peers, the findings indicate that, for all the nations in the study, nonfamily elders were generally viewed as more *Nonaccommodative* (i.e., elders were closed-minded, out-of-touch, made angry complaints, complained about their health and lives, and negatively stereotyped young people) and less *Accommodative* (elders were supportive, told interesting stories, gave useful advice, complimented the young people, were attentive, did not act superior, and did not pry) than same-age peers. In other words, interactions with nonfamily elders were evaluated more negatively than those with same-age peers, and respondents enjoyed conversations with same-age peers much more than those with nonfamily elders. Moreover, results indicate that young people in these nations may behave in a more obsequious manner toward nonfamily elders, feeling more obliged to be polite and biting their tongues than they do with same-age peers. These findings should not be surprising in the light of the extensive discussions of agism, stereotyping, and negative perceptions of older people that were featured in the early chapters of this book.

However, not all elders are perceived in the same way. Indeed, the second comparison to highlight is the one made between familial and nonfamilial elders. As one might suspect on the basis of previous chapters, familial elders were perceived as more accommodating and less nonaccommodating than nonfamilial elders in all the nations studied. Interactions with family elders were perceived as emotionally more positive than those with nonfamily elders in all countries except New Zealand and the Philippines, where the two were not differentiated. The only exception to this pattern was Koreans' ratings of polite, bite tongue, and defensive, where family elders did not gain relative to nonfamily elders. This suggests that far more than the other nations, Koreans are communicatively guarded, even with elders they know well.

This shows that older people who are not family are negatively differentiated from both peers and older family. In this respect, relationships with family elders are bathed in a positive light. The third comparison of interest here is that between family elders and same-age peers—do family elders still come out relatively favorably? In some instances young family members might prefer to turn to elderly family members for support and encouragement instead of peers, and this is what findings indicated. Family elderly were rated as more accommodative than same-age peers in Canada, and the United States; New Zealand and the Philippines showed much the same trend. For Korea, however, family elderly did not do better on this dimension than did peers. At the same time, across all nations, family elderly were judged as more nonaccommodative than peers. Also, across all nations, family elderly scored higher than peers on dimensions of politeness obligation, bite tongue, and defensive. This indicates that all the nations under study share certain respect norms for family elders over and above peers. Korea and the Philippines rated peers as more emotionally positive than family elderly, whereas Canada, New Zealand, and the United States rated family as more emotionally positive than peers. For satisfaction, Koreans showed a large satisfaction difference, rating peers as more satisfying. Canada rated peers and family elderly as the same in terms of satisfaction, while the United States rated family elderly as more satisfying.

These results emphasize that a distinction must be made between those elders who are family and those who are not. Being a family member can be seen as a mitigating circumstance that allows family elders to be taken out of the outgroup category older people, and this carries across all nations. As we indicated in earlier chapters, in the West at least, young people may have particularly high social and emotional bonds with grandparents and other family elders, and it should not be surprising that these people would be perceived as more attentive, supportive, complimentary, and interesting often even than peers. The positivity relative to peers does not carry across all dimensions of judgment, however. While family elders were judged as more accommodative than peers and elderly strangers, they were at the same time evaluated as more nonaccommodative than peers. This indicates that respondents, while acknowledging that family elders are emotionally supportive and nurturing, also regarded family elders as being comparatively closeminded, out-of-touch, complaining and stereotyping young people, and that young people may feel obligated to remain polite and respectful to older family members too.

Returning more explicitly to cultural comparisons, the findings also show that, on many dimensions, Korea shows a different pattern than the other nations. Generally, we can reiterate findings that suggest that Koreans view elderly people less favorably than do many Western nations, including the Philippines. For example, compared to the United States, Koreans' best conversational experiences were with same-age peers, and there was a substantial gap between evaluations of same-age peers and elderly people (both nonfamily and family). Koreans, far more than any of the other nations, differentiate same-age peers from the two groups of elders (nonfamily and family). This suggests that the underlying ingroup–outgroup distinction for Koreans is between elderly and young and was not necessarily between family and nonfamily, as might have been have predicted. This contrasts sharply with the United States, wherein the best conversational experiences were with family elderly and same-age peers, followed by nonfamily elderly. So, there are clearer gains for family elderly here, which are not shown in the Korean data. This is supportive of the overall view that Americans have special intimate relationships with family elders, relationships that are more open, less distant, draw less boundaried generational distinctions, and with more equality between the age groups. In general, perhaps young Westerners may have a more equality-based and less intergroup style with family elders.

A study conducted in New Zealand by Ng, Liu, Wetherall, & Loong (1997) used the Williams and Giles dimensions (see also PICS) to ask young New Zealanders of European and Chinese extraction about their communication experiences with family and nonfamily elders as compared to peers. Young people estimated that they had the most contact with peers and the least with nonfamily elderly, and females estimated that they had more contact with family elderly than did males.

Overall results echo those discussed previously: Nonfamily elderly were evaluated as the most nonaccommodative followed by family elderly, but the difference between the two groups of elderly was not significant. Of the three groups, peers were judged as the least nonaccommodative. Unlike the study reported previously, there were gender differences. Females judged peers as equally accommodative to family elderly, whereas males judged their peers as less accommodative than family elderly. Females thought that their peers were more accommodative than nonfamily elderly, but males judged nonfamily elderly and peers as equally accommodative. In fact, overall, females thought they got more accommodation, more frequent contact, and more nonaccommodation from peers than males did.

Again, as would be expected, nonfamily elderly were associated with the least positive and most negative feelings, followed by family elderly, but peers were associated with the most positive and least negative feelings. Intimacy, too, was rated in similar fashion, except that family elderly were rated as intimate as peers, and family elderly were rated as most likely to be interacted with in privacy.

There were very few cultural differences. Chinese New Zealanders had more negative feelings about communication than did European New Zealanders, and reported less frequency of contact with the elderly than did Europeans. On the other hand, Chinese thought elderly had more vitality than did the Europeans, and rated elderly European men more positively than did Europeans. In interviews, Chinese respondents stressed their adherence to norms of politeness and respect for older people.

This study confirms the emergent findings that family elderly are viewed more positively than nonfamily elderly, but, for the most part, in this study peers were viewed most favorably. It is also essential to note that in the Ng et al. study, as in others, ratings of elderly people are on the positive, not the negative, end of the scale.

These are the only direct comparisons of young peoples' evaluations of communication with family elders, peers, and nonfamily elders of which we know. The studies do indicate some provocative directions for future research into familial-intergenerational communication that might begin to elucidate the dynamics of family intergenerational communication. Rather than generalizing that family communication is positive overall, future research might investigate the accommodative pushes and pulls of family life and how family members manage these sufficiently to achieve harmony and satisfaction.

So far the research focused on young people's evaluations of intergenerational communication, but older peoples' perceptions and evaluations are just as important. There is very little research that elicits elders' perceptions, but an initial move in this direction was undertaken by Cai, Giles, and Noels (1997). In their study, a group of Chinese older-adult respondents aged from 48 to 86 years were asked to evaluate conversations with young family members, young nonfamily members, and older adults. Also, this study explored the possibility that aspects of the intergenerational communication climate might be linked to self-assessed indices of mental health. Recall that the connection between intergenerational communication—specifically young-to-old communication and negative psychological and health consequences—is one of the underlying assumptions of the communication predicament model discussed in chapter 1.

ELDERS' PERCEPTIONS
OF INTERGENERATIONAL
COMMUNICATION

Cai et al. (1997) used the PICS questionnaire (described previously and in chapter 5, this volume), which was modified and extended to include emotions. The results indicated that, like the younger people in other nations,

Chinese adults (between 46 and 86 years old) distinguished between accommodative and nonaccommodative communication behaviors. Respondents also distinguished between positive and negative interactional emotions, and between perceptions of their own accommodative and obligated communication versus perceptions of their own behavior as restrained and avoidant toward other people.

Looking first at general evaluations of older people, in this study as in others, evaluations indicated that older people were simultaneously perceived as more nonaccommodative and more accommodative than younger family members. This particular finding could be due to the very wide age range of participants used, such that some respondents (e.g., the older age range) adults were evaluating peers (an ingroup) whereas others (in the younger age range) were evaluating older people who may have been perceived as an outgroup. Additionally, it was already suggested that accommodation and nonaccommodation may not be mirror images of each other. It is entirely possible that older people are viewed as both accommodative (supportive, attentive, respectful, polite, etc.) and nonaccommodative (closed-minded, complaining, controlling, etc.). This finding may be reflective of the multiple stereotypes and ambivalent feelings we typically have towards elders.

Looking at the results for family young people suggests that some communication behaviors of young family members were perceived more positively than those of old and young nonfamily members. These adults indicated that they were rather more comfortable with young family members than with nonfamily adults (older or young) because they did not have to search for conversational topics or feel self-conscious about how they should express themselves. They also felt less guarded, less anxious, and more emotionally positive.

These Chinese adults' evaluations of conversations with older adults were compared to their evaluations of conversations with young adults (family and nonfamily). The findings indicate that older adults were perceived to be more accommodative than nonfamily young adults, but as more nonaccommodative (i.e., closed-minded, complaining, controlling, etc.) than young adults (family or nonfamily). In addition, these older adult respondents reportedly felt more obliged to be polite and respectful, and felt the need to adapt their communication (to speak more slowly and louder, and to adapt topics and vocabulary) to older adults more than they did with younger people. They also indicated that they tended to experience more negative emotions with older adults than with young people, particularly with young family members. This means that Chinese adults appear to evaluate their conversational experiences with older people (some of whom may be peers) in much the same way as do young Westerners. Older adults are perceived as accommodative on some dimensions (e.g., emotional support) but nonaccommodative on others (e.g., complaining), and people observe a respect norm with older adults. It appears, as well, that these older people feel the need to make speech and communication adjustments, which in some instances may well be viewed as overaccommodative, in order to interact with older people, just as would be expected in the West.

A cross-generational analysis compared young-Chinese adults' evaluations of intergenerational communication with older Chinese adults' evaluations of intergenerational communication. Overall, results revealed a discrepancy in the evaluative profiles such that the older adult group was more positive about communication with the young, than the young people were about their communication with older people, in this cultural context.

As was mentioned, this study also addresses whether or not these dimensions of intergenerational and peer communication have any implications for health. Results showed that there were relationships between evaluations of interactions and certain self-evaluated aspects of psychological health in the form of depression and self-esteem. Positive feelings about interactions with young family members were related to greater self-esteem, and nonaccommodation from young family members was related to greater depression. However, interactions with young nonfamily people did not seem to contribute to self-rated psychological distress. Interestingly enough, high self-esteem was related to avoidance of older people, to more negative emotions, and to more nonaccommodation.

Interpreting this in intergroup terms, it is tempting to suggest that these respondents wished to differentiate themselves from elders by endorsing stereotypes of intergenerational communication, as demonstrated by the positive correlations of certain dimensions, with older adults' self esteem. In other words, if older people can differentiate other older people as nonaccommodative, complaining, unsatisfying to interact with, and people whom they would rather avoid, then they can take themselves outside the undesired ingroup category and differentiate themselves from the negative connotations of belonging to that category. When put in these terms, this begins to look like a quantitative manifestation of the discourse of self-exception discussed in chapter 7.

These findings raise the possibility that these Chinese older adults experience problems when communicating with elders. The results also have important implications for theoretical models, such as the communication predicament model, because it may well be that psychological health is not affected by problematic interactions with nonfamily members, strangers, or loose-network ties. This research reinforces findings from extensive research on social support—that good health rests on communicative relationships with closer network ties such as family members and peers (e.g., see Albrecht, Burleson, & Goldsmith, 1994).

SUMMARY AND THEORETICAL IMPLICATIONS

This chapter discusses intergenerational communication in Eastern cultural contexts. The philosophical differences between Eastern and Western cultures can be viewed in very general terms as rules that influence interaction across a wide range of social relationships. This chapter explores the means by which such differences influence language and communication processes, particularly attitudes toward age and intergenerational communication. Research evidence indicates that young people in Eastern cultures do indeed feel strong obligations in terms of filial duties, respect, and politeness toward older adults. Although Hong Kong especially, and China to a lesser extent, do not seem to endorse strong respect norms in terms of feeling obliged to be polite and to "bite their tongue" when conversing with elders, there may be more filial pressure, and a stronger awareness of age difference, in Eastern as compared to Western cultures. Ng (1998) has noted that even as recently as 1960, it was common practice for people in Hong Kong to exchange ages as well as names when introduced.

However, evidence also suggests that young people in the East may be less positive than their Western counterparts when it comes to certain dimensions of intergenerational communication—they tend to characterize older people as less accommodative and more nonaccommodative. Perhaps this means that older people in these cultures, being aware of strong respect norms, are less inclined to accommodate the young, and this may be emphasized as a way of demanding respect in situations wherein older people may be aware that they are losing their previously enjoyed group status as respected elders. In any event, the findings do point to harder intergenerational boundaries and distinctions based on age hierarchies, which are conditions ripe for intergroup differentiation, stereotyping, negative evaluations, and so forth.

When thinking about intergenerational communication in terms of culture, it is important to take account of the social and economic conditions prevailing in that culture. Intergenerational communication takes place in a context that is influenced by the norms or rules for interaction—some of those were explored here. In addition we must examine historical precedent (such as traditions of filial piety) and the way they might interact with modern conditions to throw up contradictions that may bring about social change. This chapter suggested that rapid modernization and economic boom in some Asian cultures has placed a strain on intergenerational relationships. For example, in Hong Kong there is some evidence that many elders can be characterized as belonging to an underclass of uneducated, poor people with outdated ideas and value systems (Cheng, 1993). Such older people commanded certain resources (social, allocative, and authoritative) in agrarian economies, which gained them respect and a place in a neatly arranged social hierarchy, resources that they do not command in modern economies.

Turning to look at this profile for older family members indicates that, indeed, family members do seem to command a special relational status and are characterized more positively even than peers are on some dimensions. This finding has implications for Western research about familial intergenerational relationships and it reinforces, with some important qualifications, the general relative positivity of familial-intergenerational relationships. However, the tendency even for family elders to be rated as rather nonaccommodative is also evident.

Data from Chinese adults is intriguing because it suggests that essentially older adults (aged 46–86) agreed with the overall accommodative or nonaccommodative profile of older peoples' communication, and there was some indication that these adults may make age-associated communication adaptations (of the sort discussed in chapter 6, this volume) to elderly people, too. Of course, this research is just a drop in the ocean of needs to be accomplished in the future. For example, this is the only study that takes a fairly direct look at the possible connections between intergenerational communication and health. The Chinese study discussed here points to the importance of the quality of communication with young family members for self-esteem and psychological well-being.

Comparative studies of Western versus Eastern nations have only just scratched the surface of cross-cultural research into intergenerational relationships. Many other cultural contexts have yet to be explored within Europe as well as in the East (e.g., see Cohen, 1987; Zandpour & Sadri, 1996). Even within the West there are cultural differences that are worthy of exploration vis-à-vis communication and aging. For example, there are probably differences between Britain and the United States, because anecdotally, older people in the United States are less accepting of the reduced status that might accompany old age, and are perhaps less inclined to accept, and more eager to reject, images of themselves as decrepit and declining towards death.

Whether or not varying profiles of intergenerational communication at different locations around the globe will be found must for the moment remain as speculation, until further empirical evidence emerges. As demonstrated with nations in the Pacific Rim, the cultural stereotype of intergenerational relationships may bear little resemblance to emergent profiles based on data.

Epilogue

One of the primary goals of this book is to bring together a variety of theories and research about intergenerational communication in various relational and community contets to present a fresh look at this area of research inquiry. This epilogue summarizes the main themes of the book and in doing so revisits some of the main theoretical perspectives in a final attempt to bring the theories and research together. This is done to elucidate various aspects of intergenerational communication and to point to some avenues for further research. This epilogue goes one step further as well, conceptualizing older adults as a social group, it picks up several of the tenets of structuration and intergroup theory to explore the means by which social changes in the status of old age in Western society might occur.

LIFE-SPAN DEVELOPMENT AND INTERGENERATIONAL RELATIONSHIPS

The life-span perspective was presented in chapter 1 to provide an orientation to our unique view of intergenerational communication. The life-span perspective posits that the potential for development extends throughout the entire life span, that development is multidirectional, that development is a gain–loss dynamic, that understanding and discovering the range and limits of intraindividual plasticity and interindividual diversity are key research agendas for social scientists, and that individuals and environments both influence, and are influenced by, each other as we age. We view communication as both the mechanism that enables our social development throughout the life span, and as the vehicle through which we define, construct, and understand our development in a world dominated by social interactions. At the core of individual life-span development are numerous relationships within which we engage as we adapt to the life-long aging process. A significant portion of these relationships, which serve both affect and instrumental needs throughout our lives, are intergenerational.

284

The child–parent dyad is a complex, life-span relationship that proves to be an excellent example of a dynamic intergenerational bond (chapter 8). Research that has attempted to uncover and understand the child–parent relationship consistently finds that parents and their children remain close and provide mutual support throughout their lives. Intergenerational-solidarity theory and life-span attachment theory were advanced to explain this strong life-span bond. Although the frequency of communicative contact, the quality of closeness, and the direction of support all change across the life span, the great majority of children and parents manage to negotiate and renegotiate their relationships through most of life's challenges. Older children and their elderly parents are now facing the new challenge of prolonged caregiving with the possible complication of Alzheimer's disease, or some other form of dementia. The children find themselves caring for the parents who once cared for them. The ability of many adult children to care so competently for their parents is a wonderful testament to the strength of this life-long intergenerational relationship. However, massive, often brutal, relational complications can emerge and must be more fully understood.

The grandparent–grandchild relationship recently captured the attention of social scientists interested in intergenerational relationships (chapter 9). The ever-increasing length of our life spans has ensured that this particular familial relationship will have time to mature and serve affective and instrumental functions never dreamed of in families only 30 years ago. Grandparents are in the unique position to not only care for their grandchildren when they are very young, but to serve also as vaults of family wisdom to teenagers and even to help care for great grandchildren. Grandchildren, on the other hand, can help grandparents remain active in family or community matters and can eventually help in the caring process. There are no scientifically grounded sets of interpersonal rules about how to perform as a competent grandparent or grandchild. This is especially true for those individuals fortunate enough to spend 40 or 50 years in this relationship. The fact that the parents are also involved in the communicative dynamics of a grandparent–grandchild relationship only make this particular intergenerational relationship more interesting to comprehend.

There is much talk and discussion in numerous media outlets concerning the generation of adults who find themselves sandwiched between caring for adolescents at home and an older parent at home (chapter 10). Although the number of individuals who find themselves within sandwiched relationships is relatively small, the probability of this occurring to any one of us during some point in our life spans is significant. For the most part, the adults who are simultaneously caring for children and parents do an excellent job and maintain a healthy level of successful coping. However, when the children or the parent are in dire need of intensive care, or if the caring behavior becomes prolonged, the caregiving burden can seriously affect the caregiver's psychological wellness. The ability that caregiving individuals possess to maintain numerous healthy relationships, and to provide care in numerous directions simultaneously, is truly remarkable.

Numerous other nonfamilial relationships beyond the stranger or acquaintance status are maintained and flourish throughout the life span (chapter 11). Some of the more fascinating relationships that emerge are the bonds we form with teachers, students, health-care professionals, coworkers, and neighbors. Several of these long-term relationships are intergenerational by their very nature. These relationships, however, are often formed and maintained within structurally agist institutions. Both education and health care have struggled with the role of older adults, as students or patients, within their systems. Often older adults are relegated to nonlearner status or to unhealthy, frail status. The intergenerational relationships that form between younger teachers and nontraditional older students, and between young health-care workers and their older patients, may need to surmount significant communicative barriers within their intergenerational interactions.

The life-span perspective can inform us as to how to organize the existing literature about the intergenerational relationships discussed in this book, and where to direct future research efforts. These intergenerational relationships and the communication that maintains and defines these relationships occurs throughout the life span of the individuals who form these long-term bonds. The parent–child relationship, the grandparent–grandchild relationship, and various other familial and nonfamilial relationships not only last for significant periods of our lives, but also change as the participants reconstruct the relational nature of those bonds numerous times. The key to grasping these changes may be found in the communication within the relationship. These intergenerational relationships, and the communication that maintains and defines these relationships, often develops in multiple directions. Life-span intergenerational relationships develop closer levels of intimacy as the power dynamic changes within the relationship. The individuals within the intergenerational relationship, as well as the various relationships themselves, have much diversity across the population. Not all parent–child relationships develop in the same predictable ways. Not all communicative behaviors serve the same predictable

functions within each intergenerational relationship. Perhaps most important, the context, both sociocultural and historical, greatly influences the
very nature of the intergenerational context. At times it matters how many
years separate the interactants. At other times, gender or education level,
or how hot the day is, or relational history, or the various roles individuals
must play, or any combination of factors affect the communication that
transpires within that particular relationship. Our task as students of
intergenerational communication is to consider each of these factors, so
that a systematic study of intergenerational communication may soeday
lead to a much richer understanding of how we are able to maintain and to
redefine the very nature of our intergenerational relationships to best serve
our individual needs as we develop throughout the life span.

Communicating Age Across the Life Span

Communication across the life span with intimates, in the family as well as
with peers and others in the community, moves people through the life
span. Life-span communication is as much a location or telling of the self in
our own talk as it is reflected in the way others talk to us and the way we
work with such talk to create and sustain life-span identities (see chapter 7,
this volume). In terms of life-span identity, people have many more choices
for how to be across the various phases or turning points of life than they did
at the turn of the century. Among other things, this may result in fundamental changes in the way we, as a society, conceptualize middle and old
age. Intergenerational and life-span communication researchers should
continue to theorize and investigate such issues across the entirety of the
life span (for a detailed critique of communication and aging research, see
Williams & Coupland, 1998). The discussion of life-span communication
research in this book was limited largely because there are so few communi-
cation-research studies investigating the life span other than those about
old age. There is enormous scope for communication researchers to make a
meaningful contribution to life-span research by extending their investigations to adolescence, young adulthood, middle age, and so forth.

One of the goals of this book was to bring together theory and research
concerned with family and community intergenerational communication.
Families grow, and family members develop and change as they pass from
childhood to adolescence and into adulthood and beyond. Most families
have contact with each other across the entire life span, which typically
spreads across many years. We therefore develop across the life span in
multigenerational groupings within the family, (see chapter 10, this vol-

ume) as well as outside it, with varying degrees of interindividual contact. It would be a mistake to suggest that intergenerational relationships outside the family tend to be intergroup in nature, while suggesting that intergenerational relationships within families tend to be interindividual in nature. In reality, the situation is much more complex than this. It is probably more accurate to see the interindividual–intergroup split as a dialectic that is continuously in play across all our interactions. Intergroup processes (categorization, stereotyping, social comparison, outgroup denigration) are available as part of our communicative repertoires, and we can draw on them when we are motivated to do so—when an intergroup stance serves our communicative needs, or when an intergroup explanation best fits the immediate context and so forth.

We can track patterns of accommodation across the life span to show how individuals approach and communicatively negotiate turning points. For example, adolescents who communicatively distance themselves from their parents and grandparents may become communicatively closer when they enter young adulthood, get married, and buy a first home. As our individual needs change, we draw on family resources in different ways. Our parents may be baby-sitters for our very young children; years later this may be reciprocated in the form of social and instrumental support provided by those children, now young adults, to the aged grandparents.

In very crucial ways, people, within as well as beyond the family, communicate the life span; it is communication, including patterns of accommodation in families across the life span, that maps and shapes life-span development and change. In spite of the fact that a number of research studies outside the family have utilized intergroup and accommodation theory to frame and explain intergenerational communication in very useful ways, communication scholars have only just begun to address these issues in relational contexts. For example, initial research comparing perceptions of communication with family versus nonfamily elders was discussed in chapter 14. In terms of accommodation theory, research seems to indicate that family elders may be seen by young people more positively than are nonfamily elders, but that family elders are seen as both accommodative (supportive, complimenting, and so forth) as well as nonaccommodative (nonlistening, out of touch, etc.). The dynamic interplay of these dimensions in families has yet to be fully investigated. Indeed elder's own views of communication with family and nonfamily young people also need further investigation (see chapter 14, this volume). In general, despite the best efforts of researchers, there is still an enormous underrepresentation of older adults as participants in research.

Many of us can relate to the discussion of familial life-span communication if we think about the changing patterns of our own comunication with members of our families across our life spans. For example, earlier chapters (e.g., chapter 3, this volume) mentioned that young people feel that elders stereotype and talk down to them along various dimensions, do not listen, are disapproving, and overparent. In many ways, such evaluations are reached when young people are treated as children—their behavior is corrected (*disapproving*), their opinions are not worth regarding (*nonlistening*), and they need to be taken care of (*overparenting*). It is not surprising that young college students might point to such dimensions as annoying if we consider the possibility that many of these people are in the midst of renegotiating such issues with their parents and other older family members. Leaving home and going to college is a significant turning point for most young adults. For many it is the first time that they have relative independence from the family. Young people on the crest of this turning point may well perceive older family members as frequently overaccommodating to them, and may seek to increase communicative distance (e.g., nonaccomodation or even *communicatively diverge*) in various ways to indicate their dissatisfaction (see Yeh, Williams, & Maruyama, 1998) and to spur a change in the parent–child communication. For example, we are all familiar with popular images that portray this dynamic: the doting mother fusses over her offspring, giving far more help than is wanted or needed, while her son or daughter draws away in embarrassment. Most of us can personally relate to the sitcom image of the parents dropping off their teenager at a nightclub and demanding a goodbye kiss in front of all the teenager's friends!

Structurating Age in Society

The discussion of structuration theory outlined in chapter 1 suggested that this theory might provide a wholistic and unifying perspective under which to gather a host of research theories and findings. Admittedly, our use of structuration theory is ex post facto, rather than a priori, inductive rather than deductive. We feel that it is a useful rubric and may provide a grounding for more research. In what follows, we can only provide illustrations of how structuration theory can be used to elucidate various aspects of intergenerational relationships, and this is in no way intended to be an exhaustive account. The discussion here spans different levels of analysis, interindividual, the family, the community, and culture. It is important to realize that structuration theory argues that there is no discontinuity across these levels. The family, the community, and the society exist because individuals create and sustain them through their interactions.

The foregoing chapters demonstrated numerous ways in which we actively reconstruct systems of intergenerational relations in our society, and how this is achieved through intergenerational interaction (as well as by avoiding interaction). For example, chapter 3 reviewed research that relates very well to Giddens' (1984) rules—reviewing the assumptions we make about others based on commonly held stereotypes and how these activities create and perpetuate various kinds of agism in our society.

The stereotype activation model illustrates how stereotypes act as rules that influence action in the form of age-adapted versus normal adult speech. The communication predicament model shows how such rules can become self-fulfilling prophesies for people caught in such predicaments. Thus, communication predicaments reproduce the system. Remember that Giddens uses the term *rules* to indicate habitual practices—we have considered them as similar to action schema or norms operating in various social contexts. Rules often constitute knowledge that is shared by persons in given situations, and when it comes to agism and stereotypes of older and younger people, the rules are shared by all interactants. This means that stereotypes may not be simply imposed by one group and accepted or resisted by another. Stereotypes are, in fact, rather more complex joint understandings and constructions in which, for example, older people share the same rules as do younger people, and use them in action too. For example, older people may acquiese to stereotypes in a passive fashion (as portrayed in the communication predicament model) or may use them to garner positive outcomes for the self (as discussed in chapter 7 and illustrated in chapter 13, this volume), or they may attempt to bring the rules up for negotiation by resisting them in various ways, as indicated in assertion to patronization (chapter 6 and chapter 7, this volume). This resistance in intergroup encounters is the foundation of affirmative action, which groups (e.g., race & gender) have urged and used in the past to bring about change in the system and are discussed in a following section.

We can, therefore, see the operation of rules when interlocutors draw on socially shared images of younger and older people to guide interaction. There are several illustrations of how these rules can be used creatively. For example, they flux and change and take innovative directions in social discourses, as demonstrated in media reports of Baby Boomers, Greedy Geezers, and Generation X. To the extent that media images serve speakers' purposes, they then become resources for talk in intergenerational, as well as in intragenerational, discussions about age relations in society. Previous chapters have illustrated how such discourses can become translated into competitive and even conflictual communication between members of different age groups in community and in interindividual discourse (see, e.g., chapters 12 and 13, this volume).

Other rules that are drawn on during intergenerational interaction include intuitive understandings about language abilities in adulthood, norms about being respectful to older people, and so forth. We can also examine intergenerational talk in different contexts to look at the way morality and power (see Giddens, 1984) are distributed among age groups. For example, overaccommodative and underaccommodative communication can reflect and/or establish a power balance between interactants, as exemplified by the discussion of overaccommodation in chapter 6. Such acts are loaded with contradictions, one of which is at the heart of the communication predicament model—how to dominate and control while maintaining respectful and nurturant behavior. Interestingly enough, as structuration theory would suggest, the respect norm for interacting with elderly people draws on a sense of morality and order—in the West as well as in the East—and also reflects patterns of power and authority, especially so in Eastern cultures where there is more power-distance (Hofstede, 1980) between age groups than there is in the West. Self-report studies show that young people are aware of social norms regarding older people's social authority, and that they should command respect—young people work with those norms.

Resources refer to the ability of social actors to command authority over the social and material conditions of others. In this respect, structuration theory identifies three important resources—social, authoritative, and allocative resources. Such resources within intergenerational contexts are too numerous to detail here, but some illustrations will suffice. Chapter 2 argued that the sheer ability to move into different intergenerational contexts and to interact with people of different ages can be considered as a social resource. In fact, chapter 2 attempts to take a brief look at the time (*historical precedents*) and space (*social domain*) constraints on intergenerational relationships. In intergenerational-contact terms, chapter 2 suggested that outside the family, such resources are scarce and are not often sought out because they are heavily constrained, not only by sheer opportunity for contact, but they are heavily influenced by implicit rules for who should be socialized with and what other generations are like as social or interactional partners (chapter 3, this volume). Chapter 4 discussed individual's lingusitic resources and showed that older adults often communicate very well in spite of some of the developmental constraints of late old age. In other chapters, social idenitity and intergroup alignments can be seen as a resources. For example, the studies of Generation X described in chapter 7 demonstrated how young people are able to draw on social identity and intergroup positioning to make sense of media portrayals of youth. Even though these young people did not readily see themselves as a coherent social group, the study demonstrated how they were able to use such understandings creatively, when it was relevent to do so.

It is important to note that there is not a succinct dividing line between rules and resources because rules can be used as resources for everyday social interaction. Chapters 5 and 6 focused on accommodation theory to review the way that the rules and resources feed into communication as action in interpersonal contexts, in this case, patterns of over- and underaccommodation in intergenerational encounters. When using questionnaires and self report measures, researchers draw largely on respondent's discursive consciousness to investigate intergenerational communication. Part of the reason that young people may not self-report that they overaccommodate older people (or indeed, that older people self-report that they underaccommodate the young) is because these activities are part of practical consciousness and are therefore not necessarily available to conscious scrutiny. In discussing identity in chapter 7 and conflict in chapter 12, we provide illustrations of the ways that people draw upon social rules and resources creatively in discursive activity to construct and coconstruct identities for themselves, for other individuals, and for groups. Much of this research entailed researchers drawing on participant's practical consciousness, tracing implicit rules and resources being used in communicative action.

Thinking in terms of the kinds of social, allocative, and authoritative resources, which social groups command, leads naturally to thinking in terms of both social identity and intergroup theory. Chapters 12 and 13 stressed that perceptions of other social groups' resources are often more important indices of intergroup tension than are objective assessments because this can affect the way that individuals behave as group members. This extends all the way from perceptions of older people's language skills and abilities to perceptions of elders' political power and command over economic and social welfare resources. At a wider social level then, government agencies and departments command allocative resources such as medicare, social welfare, and so forth. If members of different age groups feel they must compete for such resources, it is no wonder that concerns about intergenerational conflict are raised. Incidentally, in this case, there may well be a certain amount of payoff for older individuals, both individually and collectively, in collaborating with deficit views of aging.

MOVING FROM SOCIAL STABILITY
TO SOCIAL CHANGE

Society is not static. Increasingly, older people–grandparents, for example—are people who have second careers, travel widely, play football, fly gliders, and take over the parental care of their grandchildren. These are not the traditional stereotypes we have about the roles that older people should fulfill. As we go forward into the new millennium, older people are going to be doing these things long before we are able to change our expectations of what they should be doing. If old age begins with retirement (around age 65), we have a potentially huge and heterogenous group of individuals playing different roles in society (a chronological definition of old age is itself a contentious issue). From this perspective, it is perhaps more likely to be great grandparents—those in late old age—who may, for a while at least, conform most closely to our stereotypes of decremental old age. This is because it is in late old age that people begin to suffer hearing and eyesight losses and other physical challenges that may be characterized as underaccommodative and that are typically associated with more negative stereotypes. This is not to say that everybody will be this way, just that the weight of probability makes it more likely than at younger old ages.

Contradictions and Social Change

We may be seeing a change. Note that structuration theory suggests that social change occurs when contradictions in a system become exposed and supply fault lines which become a nexus for conflict[1] (see Poole, Seibold, & McPhee, 1985, cited in chapter 1 for an outline of conditions that cause contradictions). The first factor that may spur this change on would be the increase in the numbers of elderly people as we approach the millennium, and this is predicted to grow. The contradictions inherent in how to allocate economic resources to these people are already being regularly rehearsed on our television screens. The elderly people of the near future will be the age cohort born between 1946 and 1964—the so-called Baby Boomers.

The Baby Boomer generation grew up in a distinct social, economic, and political climate (Reich, 1970). They are frequently characterized as the free-loving hippie generation who dodged the draft, protested against the war in Vietnam, and attended Woodstock, and they have enjoyed economic

---

[1]It should be noted that conflict as used in this context does not necessarily mean overt and hostile combat as in social uprising (although in some cases it could) but can (and is more likely in this case) to refer to a situation where two or more opposing values can no longer be reconciled, which can lead to tension.

prosperity in their middle years. Some commentators point out that this is not a quiet and acquiescent generation; they are accustomed to raising their voices in social protest and they might be expected to bring about immense social and political change (Delli Carpini, 1986; Jones, 1980; Wheeler, 1984). This is a possibility because, as a very large cohort, this generation of people wield a lot of power and may cohere around political and social concerns of the elderly. They are not a minority group and may not accept minority group status, which means that they may help put agism more centrally on our social agenda.

It has been suggested that agism is the third great "ism" of our time. Until recently, agism has been an underrecognized social issue. According to Giddens (1984), there are three limiting conditions that govern the emergence of conflict: the *opacity of action* (i.e., actors' lack of knowledge, similar to the notion of false consciousness); a *dispersion of contradictions* (i.e., many contradictions prevent focus on any one), and *direct repression* (i.e., preventing dissent by various means). In the case of agism it is unlikely that direct repression would apply, but we can look for other conditions that help keep the system in play. For example, there have been many instances throughout this book in which we illustrated what might be called the opacity of action. In this regard we have provided numerous instances of people taking agist stances in interindividual discursive activity as well as publicly in mediated discourse, and being almost completely unaware that they are being agist (e.g., see chapter 13, this volume).

We can also look for dispersions of contradictions which can, for example, be recognized in the varying positive and negative stereotypes, and in many forms of agism (discussed in chapter 3, this volume), some of which are benevolent in their intent. This means that we cannot point the finger at one stereotype or one type of agism as negative and as the problem to be addressed. Another dispersal of contradictions occurred because of the lack of coherence of older people as a social group—their lack of organization for political action. These people are members of multiple social groups and their membership in other groups and associated social identities may be more important to them. Furthermore, they may not have a particularly strong awareness of themselves as older, and in fact may personally resist and avoid such a classification precisely because it is undesirable.

SOCIAL IDENTITY AND SOCIAL CHANGE

Chapter 7 discussed a variety of ways that individuals managed threatening and negative age identities at the individual level. Dealing with, and attempting to eradicate, age discriminations can occur, of course, at other levels too, for example, at a group or community level. Undoubtedly, social change is a very slow and nonlinear process, which can be observed at all levels of analysis and instigated through a number of different agents, such as the media, interpersonal contact, pressure groups (e.g., the American Association of Retired People [AARP]), political policy, and so forth. Moreover, it should also be noted that change in one part of a social system may have far-reaching, often unintended, consequences in another (Giddens, 1984).

The identification, naming and salience of an issue must be one of the first steps toward social change because this brings it into the public awareness (DeVine & Monteith, 1993). Intergroup and social identity theorists (e.g., Tajfel & Turner, 1986) outlined a number of routes for social change for ethnic and other groups. If we can draw comparisons among age, ethnic, and other category-based processes (see Harwood et al., 1995), this theoretical perspective may prove useful in analyzing the changing status of age in society as well as the ways in which this status is communicated.

Tajfel and Turner's (1986) routes for change provide a central role to a group's awareness of cognitive alternatives to the status quo as prerequisites to change strategies. For group members to begin to change their social status, at least three questions might be considered. First, are individuals aware of their group's negative identity or low status vis-à-vis other groups? Second, do they envision alternatives to their current identity status? Finally, to determine whether or not a group strategy is likely, we must ask whether and how strongly individuals self-identify as group members. In other words, for individuals to engage in group-based strategies for social change, they must be aware of, and attach value to, a social identity.

In recent years, books and articles propounding an awareness that older people constitute a denigrated or oppressed group have begun to emerge (e.g., Bytheway, 1995). This awareness is most prevalent among academics and professionals concerned with aging (see, e.g., Coupland & Coupland, 1990), however. There seems to be far less awareness among the lay public (evident in the proliferation of unchecked agist jokes, birthday cards, etc.), although it has to be acknowledged that grass-roots pressure groups such as the AARP are trying to raise group-based awareness, much as feminists did for women during the 1950s and 1960s.

An individual strategy for social change is mobility wherein group members may try to pass out of a denigrated group and into a more positively viewed group. For example, Western advertising media very commonly market age defying and age correcting products, which in effect promise social mobility or the passing of women from being old back to being young. In other words, such products portrayed as fighting back the ravages of time can be equated with fighting signs that one belongs to an undesired and stigmatized outgroup and attempts to promote mobility. Aging in Western media is not promoted as a process in which one can mature gracefully and positively. Rather, valued attributes of particular older people are heralded as rarities or even exceptions (perhaps thereby to be discounted; see Hewstone, 1989a); witness headlines of the ilk, "Still provocative at ...," "Still creative at ...," "Life is still fun at ...," and "Still attractive at ...." Some ads also draw explicit attention to the itemized physiognomic features—and hence criteria—for what is to be considered physical aging (and demise).

It is when individuals identify with a denigrated group and attempt to change the status of it that they may engage in group-based strategies for change. Intergroup theorists suggest that a social group will attempt to bring about a change with respect to its position vis-à-vis other more favored groups when it perceives the status quo as illegitimate but stable (Tajfel & Turner, 1986). In this case, *social creativity* may be the preferred strategy whereby the image of the group is redefined in more positive ways, painful ingroup and outgroup comparisons are avoided, attributed group values are changed in a more positive direction and/or new dimensions are used to make ingroup/outgroup comparisons.

As with the case of racism and sexism, negatively valenced perceptions of a group may be reinterpreted and represented positively by charismatic spokespersons (e.g., Martin Luther King, Germaine Greer). Notably recently feminists such as Greer (1991), Friedan (1993), and Sontag (1978) have taken up the cause of agism, especially with reference to aging women—we have yet to hear slogans such as "Gray is beautiful" or "Gray Pride" from older folk themselves (apart, that is, from within very common advertising which is explicitly and shamelessly aimed at the presumed large, prosperous, elderly market). Very recently we have noted, in the United Kingdom context at least, the growing popularity of the slogan "Growing old disgracefully." This is a creative twist on an old adage, which in itself heralds resistance to accepted norms of how we should age. Another form of social creativity was promoted by Greer who argued that the so-called sexual invisibility of older women is not negative, but is, in fact, liberating, although we doubt the popular acceptance of this.

In a similar fashion, we can recognize some of the themes of ingroup redefinition, avoidance of painful comparisons, and so forth in the following quotation from Friedan (1993). In this excerpt, she urges older people to stop the quest for youth (i.e., the individual strategy of social mobility) and embark on a new venture, effectively to redefine (more positively) who they are as a group:

The problem is not how we can stay young forever, personally ... the problem is, first of all, how to break through the cocoon of our illusory youth and risk a new stage of life, where there are no prescribed role models to follow, no guideposts, no rigid rules of visible rewards, to step out into the true existential unknown of these new years of life now open to us, and *to find our own terms for living it* [italics added]. (p. 33)

In parallel, a recent birthday card stated on the outside: "D'you know how the well adjusted age?" and inside: "Neither do I!" Such sentiments capture a sense of a vacuum here for older people. Negative images are so ubiquitous, and positive ones are so confining. What is old age, what are its positive attributes beyond agist ones, how can old-age attributes be redefined more positively without mimicking youth, what does well-adjusted old age look like? How can we creatively reinterpret images of aging without denying the very real (health and life quality) challenges that some older people face?

According to intergroup theory, if group members perceive the status quo as illegitimate and unstable, they may begin to confront perceived injustices by engaging in processes of social competition, but the risk of outgroup or dominant group retaliation here is high. Social competition is a more confrontational strategy in which groups actively resist their subordinate status and may either campaign for social justice or compete for resources. We witnessed some of these processes with racism and feminism while pressure groups campaigned for social justice and won legislative victories for racial and sexual equality. Some of Palmore's (1990) calls for action against agism can be characterized in terms of social competition. Among his many suggestions are: resisting agist language and jokes, writing letters of complaint to advertisers and so forth, boycotting agist consumer products, and using the power of the ballot. In spite of the fact that both the Gray Panthers and the AARP have tried to campaign on behalf of both younger and older people, their activity has often been reinterpreted as self-interest at the expense of younger generations. For example, electronic and print media commonly express fears that the swelling ranks of the elderly will burden younger generations by sending social security and Medicare costs spiraling out of control. In this light, elders' efforts to protect Medicare and other services for the aged are interpreted as selfish—in media sound-bite terms they are greedy geezers (Coombs & Holladay, 1995). Not only does this further feed negative stereotypes, but it sets the stage for intergenerational conflict by putting age groups in competition for economic and social resources. We already discussed this issue extensively in

other chapters and noted pockets of backlash from pressure groups advo-
cating youth interests (e.g., Nelson & Cowan, 1994). In this respect, the
media and researchers have spoken of intergenerational conflict over resources, especially health care and social security. Of course conflict is the
ultimate intergroup-competition strategy.

What happens in the next few decades remains to be seen—whether or
not agism and stereotyping of elders gets put on our collective social agenda,
whether or not older people find a collective voice, whether or not that
voice is heard, whether or not we begin to fundamentally change our views
about the status of old age in society. One thing we urge is that whatever
happens, life-span communication researchers should continue to take a
critical, theoretical, and practical interest in intergenerational communication within interindividual, intergroup, relational, and mediated contexts.
They should continue to expand their areas of investigation to make significant contributions to both the study of intergenerational communication at
all ages across the life span, and to all social contexts in both the community
and in the family.

References

Abrams, M. (1978). *Beyond three-score and ten: A first report on a surveyed the elderly.* Micham, Surrey, England: Age Concern.

Adams, B. N. (1968). *Kinship in an urban setting.* Chicago: Markham.

Adelman, R. D., Greene, M. G., & Charon, R. (1991). Issues in physician–elderly patient interaction. *Ageing and Society, 2,* 127–148.

Albrecht, T. L., Adelman, M. B., & Associates (Eds.). (1987). *Communicating social support.* Newbury Park, CA: Sage.

Albrecht, T. L., Burleson, B. R., & Goldsmith, D. (1994). Supportive communication. In M. L. Knapp & G. R. Miller (Eds.), *Handbook of interpersonal communication* (2nd ed., pp. 419–449). Thousand Oaks, CA: Sage.

Allen, S., Allen, J., & Weekley, J. (1986). The impact of a practicum on aging and reminiscence on gifted students' attitudes toward the elderly. *Roeper Review, 9,* 90–94.

Allport, G. W. (1954). *The nature of prejudice.* Reading, MA: Addison-Wesley.

American Association of Retired Persons. (1994). *Truth about aging: Guidelines for accurate communications.* Washington, DC: Author.

Andersen, P. A. (1993). Cognitive schemata in personal relationships. In S. Duck (Ed.), *Individuals in relationships* (Vol. 1, pp. 1–29). Newbury Park, CA: Sage.

Apple, D. (1956). The social structure of grandparenthood. *American Anthropologist. 58,* 656–663.

Aquilino, W., & Supple, K. (1991). Parent–child relations and parent's satisfaction with living arrangements when adult children live at home. *Journal of Marriage and the Family, 53,* 13–27.

Arbuckle, T., & Gold, D. P. (1993). Aging, inhibition and verbosity. *Journal of Gerontology: Psychological Sciences, 48,* 225–232.

Aries, P. (1962). *Centuries of childhood: A social history of family life.* New York: Vintage.

Arkin, R. M., & Baumgardner, A. H. (1985). Self-handicapping. In J. H. Harvey & G. Weary (Eds.), *Attribution: Basic issues and applications* (pp. 169–202). Dubuque, IA: W. C. Brown.

Ashburn, G., & Gordon, A. (1981). Features of a simplified register in speech to elderly conversationalists. *International Journal of Psycholinguistics, 8,* 7–31.

Atchley, R. C. (1971). Retirement and leisure participation: Continuity or crisis? *Gerontologist, 1,* 13–17.

Atchley, R. C. (1976). *The sociology of retirement.* Cambridge, MA: Schenkman.

Atchley, R. C. (1982). Retirement as a social institution. *Annual Review of Sociology, 8,* 263–287.

Atchley, R. C. (1993). Critical perspectives on retirement. In T. Cole, A. Achenbaum, P. Jakobi, & R. Kastenbaum (Eds.), *Voices and visions of aging* (pp. 3–20). New York: Springer.

299

Atkinson, K. & Coupland, N. (1988). Accommodation as ideology. *Language and Communication, 8,* 321–328.

Bakan, D. (1971). Adolescence in America: From idea to social fact. *Daedalus, 100,* 979–995.

Baltes, M. M., Neumann, E. M. & Zank, S. (1994). Maintenance and rehabilitation of independence in old age: An intervention program for staff. *Psychology and Aging, 9.* 179–188.

Baltes, M. M., & Reisenzein, R. (1986). The social world in long-term care institutions: Psychosocial control towards dependency? In M. Baltes & P. Baltes (Eds.), *The psychology of control and aging* (pp. 315–343). Hillsdale, NJ: Lawrence Erlbaum Associates.

Baltes, M. M., & Silverberg, S. B. (1994). The dynamics between dependency and autonomy. In D. L. Featherman, R. M. Lerner & M. Perlmutter (Eds.), *Life-span development and behavior* (Vol. 12, pp. 41–90). Hillsdale, NJ: Lawrence Erlbaum Associates.

Baltes, M. M., & Wahl, H. W. (1992). The dependency–support script in institutions: Generalization to community settings. *Psychology and Aging, 7,* 409–418.

Baltes, M. M., & Wahl, H. W. (1996). Patterns of communication in old age: The dependency–support and independence–ignore script. *Health Communication, 8,* 217–231.

Baltes, M. M., Wahl, H. W., & Reichert, M. (1991). Successful aging in institutions? *Annual Review of Gerontology and Geriatrics, 11,* 311–337.

Baltes, P. B. (1993). The aging mind: Potential and limits. *The Gerontologist, 33,* 580–594.

Baltes, P. B., Reese, H. W., & Lipsitt, L. P. (1980). Life-span developmental psychology. *Annual Review of Psychology, 31,* 65–110.

Baltes, P. B., Smith, J. & Staudinger, U. M. (1992). Wisdom and successful aging. In T. B. Sonderegger (Ed.), *Nebraska symposium on motivation: Psychology and aging* (pp. 123–167). Lincoln: University of Nebraska Press.

Banks, S. P., & Riley, P. (1993). Structuration theory as an ontology for communication research. In S. A. Deetz (Ed.). *Communication Yearbook* (Vol. 16, pp. 167–196). Newbury Park, CA: Sage.

Banta, M. (1987). *Imaging American women: Idea and ideals in cultural history.* New York: Columbia University Press.

Barbato, C. A., & Feezel, J. D. (1987). The language of aging in different age groups. *The Gerontologist, 27,* 527–531.

Barnes, H. L. & Olson, D. H. (1985). Parent adolescent communication and the circumplex model. *Child Development. 56,* 437–447.

Barusch, A. S., & Steen, P. (1996). Keepers of community in a changing world. *Generations, 20,* 49–52.

Bayles, K. A., & Kraszniak, A. W. (1987). *Communication and cognition in normal aging and dementia.* Boston: Little, Brown.

Beisecker, A. E. (1989). The influence of a companion on the doctor–elderly patient interaction. *Health Communication, 1,* 55–70.

Beisecker, A. E. & Thompson, T. L. (1995). The elderly patient–physician interaction. In J. F. Nussbaum & J. Coupland (Eds.), *The handbook of communication and aging research* (pp. 397– 416). Mahwah, NJ: Lawrence Erlbaum Associates.

Bell, J. (1992). In search of a discourse on aging: The elderly on television. *The Gerontologist, 32,* 305–311.

Bengston, V. L., Harootyan, R. A., & Contributors. (1994). *Intergenerational linkages: Hidden connections in American society.* New York: Springer.

Bengston, V. L., Marti, G., & Roberts, H. E. L. (1991). Age-group relationships: Generational equity and inequity. In K. Pillemer & K. McCartney (Eds.), *Parent–child relations throughout life* (pp. 253–278). Hillsdale, NJ: Lawrence Erlbaum Associates.

Bengston, V. L., Olander, E. B., & Haddad, A. A. (1976). The generation gap and aging family members: Toward a conceptual model. In J. E. Gubrium (Ed.), *Time, roles, and the self in old age* (pp. 237–263). New York: Human Science Press.

Bengston, V. L., Rosenthal, C., & Burton, L. M. (1990). Families and aging: Diversity and heterogeneity. In R. H. Binstock & L. K. George (Eds.), *Handbook of aging and the social sciences* (3rd ed., pp. 263–287). New York: Academic Press.

Bengston, V. L., Schaie, K. W., & Burton, L. M. (1994). *Adult intergenerational relations: Effects of societal change.* New York: Springer.

Bengtson, V. L., & Schrader, S. S. (1982). Parent–child relations. In D. Mangen & W. Peterson (Eds.), *Research instruments in social gerontology* (pp. 115–128). Minneapolis: University of Minnesota Press.

Bennett, R., & Eckman, J. (1973). Attitudes toward aging: A critical examination of recent literature and implications for future research. In C. Eisdorfer & M. P. Lawton (Eds.), *The psychology of adult development and aging* (pp. 575–595). Washington, DC: American Psychological Association.

Bennett, S. E., & Rademacher, E. (1994, May). *The politics of "Generation X": America's post Boomer birth cohort comes of age.* Paper presented at the Annual Meeting of the American Association for Public Opinion Research, Danvers, MA.

Berens, E. (1996, May). *A cognitive, cultural model of intergenerational conflict.* Paper presented at the Third International Conference on Communication, Aging and Health, Kansas City, MO.

Berger, B. (1971). *Looking for America.* Englewood Cliffs, NJ: Prentice-Hall.

Berger, C., & Bradac, J. J. (1982). *Language and social knowledge: Uncertainty in interpersonal relations.* London: Edward Arnold.

Bergstrom, M. J. (1997, May). *Cooperative conflict behaviors of adults: A test of three life-span stages.* Paper presented at the Annual Meeting of the International Communication Association, Montreal, Canada.

Bergstrom, M. J., & Nussbaum, J. F. (1996). Cohort differences in interpersonal conflict: Implications for older patient–younger care provider interaction. *Health Communication, 8,* 233–248.

Bergstrom, M. J., & Williams, A. (1996, May). *Older people's perceptions of intergenerational conflict: Some evaluations and response strategies.* Poster presented at International Communication Association Conference, Chicago.

Berman, L., & Sobkowksa-Ashcroft, I. (1986). The old in language and literature. *Language & Communication, 6,* 139–145.

Bernard, M., & Philipson, C. (1995). Retirement and leisure. In J. F. Nussbaum & J. Coupland (Eds.), *Handbook of communication and aging research* (pp. 285–311). Mahwah, NJ: Lawrence Erlbaum Associates.

Berry, D., & McArthur, L. Z. (1985). Some components and consequences of a babyface. *Journal of Personality and Social Psychology, 48,* 312–323.

Berry, D., & McArthur, L. Z. (1988). What's in a face? Facial maturity and the attribution of legal responsibility. *Personality and Social Psychology Bulletin, 14,* 23–33.

Berryman-Fink, C., & Bruner, C. C. (1987). The effects of sex of source and target on interpersonal conflict management styles. *Southern Speech Communication Journal, 33,* 38–48.

Bettini, L. M., & Norton, M. L. (1991). The pragmatics of intergenerational friendships. *Communication Reports, 4,* 64–72.

Bielby, D. D., & Kully, H. S. (1989). Social construction of the past: Autobiography and the theory of G. H. Mead. *Current Perspectives on Aging and the Life Cycle, 3,* 1–24.

Binney, E. A., & Estes, C. L. (1988). The retreat of the state and its transfer of responsibility: The intergenerational war. *International Journal of Health Services, 18*(1), 83–96.

Binstock, R. H. (1997). The 1996 election: Older voters and implications for policies on aging. *Gerontologist, 37,* 15–19.

Binstock, R. H., & Day, C. L. (1996). Aging and politics. In R. H. Binstock & L. K. George (Eds.), *Handbook of aging and the social sciences* (pp. 362–387). San Diego: Academic Press.

Bishop, J. M., & Krause, D. R. (1984). Depictions of aging and old age on Saturday morning television. *The Gerontologist, 24,* 91–94.

Bleise, N. (1982). Media in the rocking chair: Media uses and functions among the elderly. In G. Gumpert & R. Cathcart (Eds.), *Intermedia: Interpersonal communication in a media world* (pp. 624–634). New York: Oxford University Press.

Boden, D., & Bielby, D. D. (1983). The past as resource: A conversational analysis of elderly talk. *Human Development, 26,* 308–319.

Bond, J., & Coleman, P. (1990). Aging into the twenty-first century. In J. Bond & P. Coleman (Eds.), *Aging in society: An introduction to social gerontology* (pp. 276–290). London: Sage.

Bowlby, J. (1969). *Attachment and loss: Vol. 1. Attachment.* New York: Basic Books.

Bowlby, J. (1973). *Attachment and loss: Vol. 2. Separation, anxiety and anger.* New York: Basic Books.

Bowlby, J. (1980). *Attachment and loss: Vol. 3. Loss, sadness and depression.* New York: Basic Books.

Bowles, N. L., & Poon, L. W. (1985). Aging and retrieval of words in semantic memory. *Journal of Gerontology, 40,* 71–77.

Bradbury, T. N., & Fincham, F. D. (1990). Attributions in marriage: Review and critique. *Psychological Bulletin, 107,* 3–33.

Braithwaite, V. A. (1986). Old age stereotypes: Reconciling contradictions. *Journal of Gerontology, 41,* 353–360.

Braithwaite, V., Lynd-Stevenson, R., & Pigram, D. (1993). An empirical study of ageism: From polemics to scientific utility. *Australian Psychologist, 28,* 9–15.

Branco, K. L., & Williamson, J. B. (1982). Stereotypes and the life cycle. In A. G. Miller (Ed.), *In the eye of the beholder: Contemporary issues in stereotyping* (pp. 364–410). New York: Praeger.

Breemhaar. B., Visser, A., & Kleijnen, J. (1990). Perceptions and behavior among elderly hospital patients: Description and explanation of age differences in satisfaction, knowledge, emotions, and behaviour. *Social Science and Medicine, 31,* 1377–1384.

Brewer, M. B., Dull, V., & Lui, L. (1981). Perceptions of the elderly: Stereotypes as prototypes. *Journal of Personality and Social Psychology, 41,* 656–670.

Brody, E. M. (1981). Women in the middle and family help to older people. *The Gerontologist, 21,* 471–451.

Bromley, D. B. (1978). Approaches to the study of personality changes in adult life and old age. In A. D. Isaacs & F. Post (Eds.), *Studies in geriatric psychiatry* (pp. 17–40). Chichester, England: Wiley.

Bronfenbrenner, U. (1979). *The ecology of human development.* Cambridge, MA: Harvard University Press.

Brown, B. B., Mory, M. S., & Kinney, D. (1994). Casting adolescent crowds in a relational perspective: Caricature, channel, and context. In R. Montemayor, G. R. Adams, & T. P. Gullotta (Eds.), *Personal relationships during adolescence* (pp. 123–167). Newbury Park, CA: Sage.

Burke, D. M., & Harrold, R. M. (1988). Automatic and effortful semantic processes in old age: Experimental and naturalistic approaches. In L. L. Light & D. M. Burke (Eds.), *Language, memory, and aging* (pp. 100–116). Cambridge, England: Cambridge University Press.

Burke, D. M., & Laver, G. D. (1990). Aging and word retrieval: Selective age deficits in language. In E. A. Lovelace (Ed.), *Aging and cognition: Mental processes, self-awareness, and interventions* (pp. 281–300). New York: Elsevier.

Burke, D. M., Mackay, D. G., Worthley, J. S., & Wade, E. (1991). On the tip of the tongue: What causes word finding failures in young and older adults? *Journal of Memory and Language, 30,* 542–579.

Burleson, B. R. (1987). Cognitive complexity. In J. C. McCroskey & J. A. Daly (Eds.), *Personality and interpersonal communication* (pp. 305–349). Newbury Park, CA: Sage.

Burton, L. M. (1992). Black grandparents rearing children of drug-addicted parents: Stressors, outcomes, and social service needs. *The Gerontologist, 32,* 744–751.

Butler, R. N. (1963). The life review: An interpretation of reminiscence in the aged. *Psychiatry, 26,* 65–76.

Butler, R. N. (1987). "Ageism." *The encyclopedia of aging.* New York: Springer.

Butler, R. N. (1989). Dispelling agism: The cross-cutting intervention. In M. W. Riley & J. W. Riley (Eds.), *The quality of aging: Strategies for interventions. The Annals of the American Academy of Political and Social Science, Special Issue: 503,* 138–148.

Button, J. W. (1992). A sign of generational conflict: The impact of Florida's aging voters on local school and tax referenda. *Social Science Quarterly, 73,* 786–797.

Bytheway, B. (1995). *Agism.* Buckingham, England: Open University Press.

Bytheway, B., & Johnson, J. (1990). On defining ageism. *Critical Social Policy, 27,* 27–39.

Cai, D., Giles, H., & Noels, K. (1997, May). *Intergenerational communication in the people's republic of China: Perceptions of communication climate in older and younger adults and their link to mental health.* Paper presented to the 6th International Conference on Language and Social Psychology, Ottawa, Canada.

Cameron, P. (1970). The generation gap: Beliefs about sexuality and self-reported sexuality. *Developmental Psychology, 3,* 272–280.

Canary, D. J., & Cupach, W. R. (1988). Relational and episodic characteristics associated with conflict tactics. *Journal of Social and Personal Relationships, 5,* 305–322.

Canary, D. J., & Spitzberg, B. H. (1990). Attribution biases and associations between conflict strategies and competence outcomes. *Communication Monographs, 57,* 139–151.

Caporael, L. R. (1981). The paralanguage of caregiving: Baby talk to the institutionalized aged. *Journal of Personality and Social Psychology, 40,* 876–884.

Caporael, L. R., & Culbertson, G. H. (1986). Verbal response modes of baby talk and other speech at institutions for the aged. *Language and Communication, 6,* 99–112.

Caporeal, L. R., Lucaszewski, M. P., & Culbertson, G. H. (1983). Secondary babytalk: Judgements by institutional elderly and their caregivers. *Journal of Personality and Social Psychology, 15,* 746–754.

Carver, C. S., & de la Garza, N. H. (1984). Schema-guided information search in stereotyping of the elderly. *Journal of Applied Social Psychology, 14,* 69–81.

Caspi, A. (1984). Contact hypothesis and inter-age attitudes: A field study of cross-age contact. *Social Psychology Quarterly, 47,* 74–80.

Chang, B. L., Chang, A. F., & Yung, A. S. (1984). Attitudes toward aging in the United States and Taiwan. *Journal of Comparative Family Studies, 15,* 109–130.

Chang, H. C. (1997). Language and words: Communication and the Analects of Confucius. *Journal of Language and Social Psychology, 16,* 107–131.

Chapman, N. J., & Neal, M. B. (1990). The effects of intergenerational experiences on adolescents and older adults. *The Gerontologist, 30,* 825–833.

Chappell, N. (1980). Aging and social care. In R. Binstock & L. George (Eds.), *Handbook of aging and the social sciences* (pp. 438–454). San Diego: Academic Press.

Chen, J. (1980). *The Chinese of America.* San Francisco: Harper & Row.

Chen, P. N. (1979). A study of Chinese-American elderly residing in hotel rooms. *Social Casework, 60,* 89–95.

Cheng, S.-T. (1993). The social context of Hong Kong's booming elderly home industry. *American Journal of Community Psychology, 18,* 449–467.

Cherlin, A., & Furstenberg, F. F. (1985). Styles and strategies of grandparenting. In V. L. Bengtson & J. F. Robertson (Eds.), *Grandparenthood* (pp. 97–116). Beverly Hills, CA: Sage.

Cherlin, A., & Furstenberg, F. F. (1986). *The new American grandparent: A place in the family, a life apart.* New York: Basic Books.

Chow, N. W.-S. (1983). The Chinese family and support of the elderly in Hong Kong. *The Gerontologist, 23,* 584–588.

Chudacoff, H. P. (1989). *How old are you? Age consciousness in American culture.* Princeton, NJ: Princeton University Press.

Cicirelli, V. G. (1981). *Helping elderly parents: The role of adult children.* Boston: Auburn House.

Cicirelli, V. G. (1991). Attachment theory in old age: Protection of the attached figure. In K. Pillemer & K. McCartney (Eds), *Parent–child relations throughout life* (pp. 2–42). Hillsdale, NJ: Lawrence Erlbaum Associates.

Cicirelli, V. G. (1993). Intergenerational communication in the mother–daughter dyad regarding caregiving decisions. In N. Coupland & J. F. Nussbaum (Eds.), *Discourse and lifespan identity* (pp. 215–236). Newbury Park, CA: Sage.

Cicirelli, V. G. (1995). Intergenerational communication in mother–daughter dyad regarding caregiving decisions. In N. Coupland & J. F. Nussbaum (Eds.), *Discourse and lifespan identity* (pp. 215–236). Newbury Park, CA: Sage.

Clingempeel, W. G., Colyar, J. J., Brand, F., & Hetherington, F. M. (1992). Children's relationships with maternal grandparents: A longitudinal study of family structure and pubertal status effects. *Child Development, 63,* 1404–1422.

Cloven, D. H., & Roloff, M. E. (1993). The chilling effect of aggressive potential on the expression of complaints in intimate relationships. *Communication Monographs, 60,* 199–219.

Cohen, G. (1994). Age-related problems in the use of proper names in communication. In M. L. Hummert, J. M. Wiemann, & J. F. Nussbaum (Eds.), *Interpersonal communication in older adulthood: Interdisciplinary theory and research* (pp. 40–57). Thousand Oaks, CA: Sage.

Cohen, G., & Faulkner, D. (1986a). Memory for proper names: Age differences in retrieval. *British Journal of Psychology, 81,* 335–349.

Cohen, G., & Faulkner, D. (1986b). Does 'elderspeak' work? The effect of intonation and stress on comprehension and recall of spoken discourse in old age. *Language and Communication, 6,* 91–98.

Cohen, R. (1987). Problems of intercultural communication in Egyptian-American diplomatic relations. *International Journal of Intercultural Relations, 11,* 29–47.

Coleman, J. S. (1974). Background/history of age grouping in America. In J. S. Coleman (Ed.), *Transition to adulthood* (pp. 9–31). Chicago: University of Chicago Press.

Coleman, P. (1995). Facing the challenges of aging. In J. F. Nussbaum & J. Coupland (Eds.), *Handbook of communication and aging research* (pp. 39–79). Mahwah, NJ: Lawrence Erlbaum Associates.

Comstock, J., & Buller, D. B. (1991). Conflict strategies adolescents use with their parents: Testing the cognitive communicator characteristics model. *Journal of Language and Social Psychology, 10,* 47–59.

Coombs, W. T., & Holladay, S. J. (1995). The emerging political power of the elderly. In J. F. Nussbaum & J. Coupland (Eds.), *Handbook of communication and aging research* (pp. 317–343). Mahwah, NJ: Lawrence Erlbaum Associates.

Cooney, T. M., Hutchinson, M. K., & Leather, D. M. (1995). Surviving the breakup? Predictors of parent–adult child relations after parental divorce. *Family Relations, 44*, 53–61.

Cooney, T. M., & Smith, L. A. (1996). Young adults' relations with grandparents following recent parental divorce. *The Journals of Gerontology: Social Sciences, 51b*, S91–S95.

Cooper, J., & Fazio, R. H. (1986). The formation and persistence of attitudes that support intergroup conflict. In S. Worchel & W. Austin (Eds.), *Psychology of intergroup relations* (pp. 183–189). Chicago: Nelson-Hall.

Coupland, D. (1991). *Generation X: Tales for an accelerated culture.* New York: St. Martin's Press.

Coupland, J., Coupland, N., Giles, H., & Wiemann, J. M. (1988). My life in your hands: Processes of self-disclosure in intergenerational talk. In N. Coupland (Ed.), *Styles of discourse.* London: Croom Helm.

Coupland, J., Coupland, N., & Grainger, K. (1991). Intergenerational discourse: Contextual versions of ageing and elderliness. *Ageing and Society, 11*, 189–208.

Coupland, J., Robinson, J., & Coupland, N. (1994). Frame negotiation in doctor–elderly patient consultations. *Discourse and Society, 5*, 89–124.

Coupland, N. (1997). Language, ageing and ageism: A project for applied linguistics? *International Journal of Applied Linguistics, 7*, 26–48.

Coupland, N., & Coupland, J. (1989). Language and later life: The diachrony and decrement predicament. In H. Giles & W. P. Robinson (Eds.), *Handbook of language and social psychology* (pp. 451–468). New York: Wiley.

Coupland, N., & Coupland, J. (1990). Language and later life. In H. Giles & W. P. Robinson (Eds.), *Handbook of language and social psychology* (pp. 451–468). New York: Wiley.

Coupland, N., & Coupland, J. (1993). Discourses of ageism and anti-ageism. *Journal of Aging Studies, 7*, 279–301.

Coupland, N., Coupland, J., & Giles, H. (1989). *Telling age in later life: Identity and face implications.* Text, 9, 129–151.

Coupland, N., Coupland, J., & Giles, H. (1991). *Language, society and the elderly: Discourse, identity and ageing.* Oxford, England: Basil Blackwell.

Coupland, N., Coupland, J., Giles, H., & Henwood, K. (1988). Accommodating the elderly: Invoking and extending a theory. *Language in Society, 17*, 1–41.

Coupland, N., Coupland, J., Giles, H., Henwood, K., & Wiemann, J. (1988). Elderly self-disclosure: Interactional and intergroup issues. *Language and Communication, 8*, 109–133.

Coupland, N., Coupland, J., & Nussbaum, J. (1993). Epilogue: Future prospects in lifespan sociolinguistics. In N. Coupland & J. F. Nussbaum (Eds.), *Discourse and lifespan identity.* Newbury Park, CA: Sage.

Coupland, N., Giles, H., & Wiemann, J. M. (1991). *Miscommunication and problematic talk.* Newbury Park, CA: Sage.

Coupland, N., Henwood, K., Coupland, J., & Giles, H. (1990). Accommodating troubles-talk: The management of elderly self-disclosure. In F. McGregor & R. S. White (Eds.), *Reception and response: Hearer creativity and the analysis of spoken and written texts.* London: Routledge & Kegan Paul.

Coupland, N., & Nussbaum, J. F. (1993). *Discourse and life span identity.* Newbury Park, CA: Sage.

Covey, H. C. C. (1988). Historical terminology used to represent older people. *The Gerontologist, 28*, 291–297.

Coward, R. T., Albrecht, S. L., & Shapiro, A. (1996). The perceptions of elderly parents about the possibility of discontinuing their coresidence with adult children. *Research on Aging, 18*, 325–348.

Cowgill, D., & Holmes, L. (1972). *Aging and modernization.* New York: Appleton-Century-Crofts.

Cowgill, D. O. (1984). The disengagement of an aging activist: The making and unmaking of a gerontologist. In S. F. Spicker & S. R. Ingman (Eds.), *Vitalizing long-term care* (pp. 221–228). New York: Springer.

Crimmins, F., & Ingegneri, D. G. (1990). Interaction and living arrangements of older parents and their children. *Research on Aging, 12,* 3–35.

Crockett, W. H., & Hummert, M. L. (1987). Perceptions of aging and the elderly. In K. W. Schaie (Ed.), *The annual review of gerontology and geriatrics* (Vol. 7, pp. 217–241). New York: Springer.

Crook, T. H., & West, R. L., (1990). Name-recall performance across the adult life span. *British Journal of Psychology, 81,* 335–349.

Crosby, F., Cordova, D., & Jaskar, K. (1994). On the failure to see oneself as disadvantaged: Cognitive and emotional components. In M. A. Hogg & D. Abrams (Eds.), *Group motivation: Social psychological perspectives.* London: Harvester-Wheatsheaf.

Danish, S. J., Smyer, M. A., & Nowak, C. (1980). Developmental intervention: Enhancing life-event processes. In P. B. Baltes & O. G. Brim (Eds.), *Life-span development and behavior* (Vol. 3, pp. 131–186). New York: Academic Press.

Davis, R. H., & Kubey, R. W. (1982). Growing old on television and with television. In D. Pearl, L. Bouthilet, & J. Lazar (Eds.), *Television and behavior* (Vol. 1, pp. 201–208). Rockville, MD: National Institute of Mental Health.

Delli Carpini, M. X. (1986). *Stability and change in American politics: The coming of age of the generation of the '60s.* New York: New York University Press.

DePaulo, B. M., & Coleman, L. M. (1986). Talking to children, foreigners, and retarded adults. *Journal of Personality and Social Psychology, 51,* 97–100.

DeVine, P. G., & Monteith, M. J. (1993). The role of discrepancy–associated affect in prejudice reduction. In D. M. Mackie & D. L. Hamilton (Eds.), *Affect, cognition, and stereotyping: Interactive processes in group perception* (pp. 317–344). San Diego: Academic Press.

DeWit, D. J., & Frankel, B. G. (1988). Geographical distance and intergenerational contact: A critical assessment and review of the literature. *Journal of Aging Studies, 2,* 25–43.

Dietz, T. L. (1995). Patterns of intergenerational assistance within the Mexican American family: Is the family taking care of the older generation's needs? *Journal of Social Issues, 16,* 344–356.

Dillard., J., Henwood, K., Giles, H., Coupland, N., & Coupland J. (1990). Compliance-gaining young and old: Beliefs about influence in different age groups. *Communication Reports, 3,* 84–91.

Dooley, S., & Frankel, B. G. (1990). Improving attitudes toward elderly people: Evaluation of an intervention program for adolescents. *Canadian Journal of Aging, 9,* 400–409.

Dowd, J. J., & Bengston, V. L. (1978). Aging in minority populations: An examination of the double jeopardy hypothesis. *The Journal of Gerontology, 33,* 427–436.

Downs, V. C. (1988). *The grandparent–grandchild relationship: Communication and continuity between generations.* Unpublished doctoral dissertation, University of Oklahoma, Norman.

Downs, V. C. (1989). The grandparent–grandchild relationship. In J. F. Nussbaum (Ed.), *Lifespan communication: Normative processes* (pp. 257–281). Hillsdale, NJ: Lawrence Erlbaum Associates.

Dunham, C. C. (1995). A link between generations: Intergenerational relations and depression in aging parents. *Journal of Family Issues, 16,* 450–465.

Edwards, H., & Noller, P. (1993). Perceptions of overaccommodation used by nurses in communication with the elderly. *Journal of Language and Social Psychology, 12,* 207–223.

Emry, O. B. (1986). Linguistic decrement in normal aging. *Language and Communication, 6,* 47–64.

Erikson, E. H. (1959). Identity and the life cycle. *Psychological Issues, 1,* 1–171.

Erikson, E. H. (1980). *Identity and the life cycle: A reissue.* New York: Norton.

Estes, C. L., & Binney, E. A. (1979). The biomedication of aging: Dangers and dilemmas. *The Gerontologist, 29,* 587–596.

Fairhurst, E. (1981). *A sociological study of the rehabilitiation of the elderly in an urban hospital.* Unpublished doctoral dissertation, University of Leeds, Leeds, England.

Farkas, J. I., & Hogan, D. P. (1995). The demography of changing intergenerational relationships. In V. L. Bengston, K. Warner Schaie, & L. M. Burton (Eds.), *Adult intergenerational relations* (pp. 1–18). New York: Springer.

Featherstone, M., & Hepworth, M. (1990). Images of aging. In J. Bond, P. Coleman, & S. Peace (Eds.), *Aging in society* (pp. 304–332). London: Sage.

Featherstone, M., & Hepworth, M. (1994). Images of ageing. In J. Bond, P. Coleman, & S. Peace (Eds.), *Ageing in society: An introduction to social gerontology* (2nd ed., pp. 304–332). London: Sage.

Fincham, F. D., Bradbury, T. N., & Scott, C. K. (1990). Cognition in marriage: Retrospect and prospect. In F. D. Fincham & T. N. Bradbury (Eds.), *Cognition in marriage: Basic issues and applications* (pp. 118–129). New York: Guilford.

Fiske, S., & Neuberg, S. (1990). A continuum of impression formation, from category based to individuating processes: Influences of information on attention and interpretation. In M. P. Zanna (Ed.), *Advances in experimental social psychology* (Vol. 23, pp. 1–74). Orlando, FL: Academic Press.

Fiske, S. T., & Taylor, S. E. (1991). *Social cognition.* New York: McGraw-Hill.

Fox, S., & Giles, H. (1993). Accommodating intergenerational contact: A critique and theoretical model. *Journal of Aging Studies, 7,* 423–451.

Fox, S., & Giles, H. (1996). Interability communication: Evaluating patronizing encounters. *Journal of Language and Social Psychology, 15,* 265–290.

Franklyn-Stokes, A., Harriman, J., Giles, H., & Coupland, N. (1988). Information seeking across the lifespan. *Journal of Social Psychology, 128,* 419–421.

Friedan, B. (1993). *The fountain of age.* London: Jonathan Cape.

Gallois, C., Franklyn-Stokes, A., Giles, H., & Coupland, N. (1988). Communication accommodation theory and intercultural encounters: Intergroup and interpersonal considerations. In Y. Y. Kim & W. B. Gudykunst (Eds.), *Theories in intercultural communication.* Newbury Park, CA: Sage.

Gallois, C., Giles, H., Jones, E., Cargile, A. C., & Ota, H. (1995). Accommodating intercultural encounters: Elaborations and extensions. In R. L. Wiseman (Ed.), *Intercultural communication theory* (pp. 115–147). Thousand Oaks, CA: Sage.

Gallois, C., Giles, H., Ota, H., Pierson, H. D., Ng, S. H., Lim, T.-S., Maher, J., Somera, L., Ryan, E. B., & Harwood, J. (1996, August). *Intergenerational communication across the Pacific Rim: The impact of filial piety.* Paper presented at the International Association of Cross-Cultural Psychology, Montreal, Canada.

Garstka, T. A., Branscombe, N. R., & Hummert, M. L. (1996, June). *Age group identity, self-esteem, and the benefits of being young.* Paper presented at the annual meeting of the American Psychological Society, San Francisco.

Garstka, T. A., Branscombe, N. R., & Hummert, M. L. (1997, June). *Age group identification across the lifespan.* Paper presented at the annual meeting of the American Psychological Society, Washington, DC.

Geertz, C. (1979). From the native's point of view: On the nature of anthropological understanding. In P. Rabinow & W. M. Sullivan (Eds.), *Interpretive social science,* (pp. 225–241). Berkeley: University of California Press.

Gelles, R. (1983). An exchange/social control theory. In D. Finkelhor (Ed.), *The dark side of families: Current family violence research* (pp. 151–165). Beverly Hills, CA: Sage.

Gerbner, G., Gross, L., Signorielli, N., & Morgan, M. (1980). Aging with television: Images on television drama and conceptions of social reality. *Journal of Communication, 30,* 37–48.

Gerstein, L.H., & Tesser, A. (1987). Antecedents and responses association with loneliness. *Journal of Social and Personal Relationships, 4,* 329–363.

Giarrusso, R., Silverstein, M., & Bengtson, V. L. (1996). Family complexity and the grandparent role. *Generations, 20,* 17–23.

Giddens, A. (1976). *New rules of sociological method.* New York: Basic Books.

Giddens, A. (1984). *The constitution of society: Outline of a theory of structuration.* Cambridge, England: Polity Press.

Giddens, A. (1990). Structuration theory and social analysis. In J. Clark, C. Modgil, & S. Modgil (Eds.), *Anthony Giddens: Consensus and controversy* (pp. 297–316). London: Falmer.

Giddens, A. (1991). *Modernity and self-identity: Self and society in the late modern age.* Cambridge, England: Cambridge University Press.

Giles, H., & Coupland, N. (1991). *Language: Contexts and consequences.* Milton Keynes, UK: Open University Press.

Giles, H., Coupland, N., & Coupland, J. (1991). Accommodation theory: Communication, contexts and consequence. In H. Giles, N. Coupland, & J. Coupland (Eds.), *Contexts of accommodation: Developments in applied sociolinguistics* (pp. 1–68). Cambridge, England: Cambridge University Press.

Giles, H., Coupland, N., Henwood, K., Harriman, J., & Coupland, J. (1990) The social meaning of RP: An intergenerational perspective. In S. Ramsaran (Ed.), *Studies in the pronunciation of English: A commemorative volume in honor in A. C. Gimson* (pp. 191-210). London: Routledge & Kegan Paul.

Giles, H., Coupland, N., & Wiemann, J. M. (1992). "Talk is cheap" but "My word is my bond:" Beliefs about talk. In K. Bolton & H. Kwok (Eds.), *Sociolinguistics today: International perspectives* (pp. 218–243). London: Routledge & Kegan Paul.

Giles, H., Fox, S., Harwood, J., & Williams, A. (1994). Talking age and aging talk: Communicating through the life span. In M. L. Hummert, J. F. Nussbaum, & J. Wiemann (Eds.), *Interpersonal communication in older adulthood* (pp. 130–161). Thousand Oaks, CA: Sage.

Giles, H., Fox, S., & Smith, E. (1993). Patronizing the elderly: intergenerational evaluations. *Research on Language and Social Interaction, 26,* 129–149.

Giles, H., Harwood, J., Pierson, H. Clément, R., & Fox, S. (in press). Stereotypes of the elderly and evaluations of patronizing speech: A cross cultural foray. In R. K. Agnihotri & A. L. Khanna (Eds.), *Research in applied linguistics: IV. The social psychology of language.* New Delhi, India: Sage.

Giles, H., Henwood, K., Coupland, N., Harriman, J., & Coupland, J. (1992). Language attitudes and cognitive mediation. *Human Communication Research, 18,* 500–527.

Giles, H., & Johnson, P. (1987). Ethnolinguistic identity theory: A social psychological approach to language maintenance. *International Journal of the Sociology of Language, 68,* 69–99.

Giles, H., & Williams, A. (1994). Patronizing the young: Forms and evaluations. *International Journal of Aging and Human Development, 39,* 33–53.

Giles, J. (1994, June 6). The myth of Generation X: Seven great lies about twentysomethings. *Newsweek,* 63–72.

Glasser, M., Prohaska, T., & Roska, J. (1992). The role of family in medical care-seeking decisions of older adults. *Family and Community Medicine, 15,* 59–70.

Glendenning, F. (1995). Education for older adults: Lifelong learning, empowerment, and social change. In J. F. Nussbaum & J. Coupland (Eds.), *Handbook of communication and aging research* (pp. 467–490). Mahwah, NJ: Lawrence Erlbaum Associates.

Goffman, E. (1959). *The presentation of self in everyday life.* Garden City, NY: Doubleday.

Gold, D. P., Arbuckle, T. Y., & Andres, D. (1994). Verbosity in older adults. In M. L. Hummert, J. M. Wiemann, & J. F. Nussbaum (Eds.), *Interpersonal communication and aging* (pp. 107–129). Thousand Oaks, CA: Sage.

Golde, P., & Kogan, N. (1959). A sentence completion procedure for assessing attitudes toward old people. *Journal of Gerontology, 14,* 355.

Gould, R. L. (1978). *Transformations: Growth and change in adult life.* New York: Simon & Schuster.

Grainger, K. (1995). Communication and the institutionalized elderly. In J. F. Nussbaum & J. Coupland (Eds.), *Handbook of communication and aging research* (pp. 417–436). Mahwah, NJ: Lawrence Erlbaum Associates.

Grainger, K., Atkinson, K., & Coupland, N. (1990). Responding to the elderly: Troubles talk in the caring context. In H. Giles, N. Coupland, & J. Wiemann (Eds.), *Communication, health, and ageing* (Proceedings of Fulbright International Colloquium 1988, pp. 192–212). Manchester, England: Manchester University Press.

Gratton, B., & Haber, C. (1996). Three phases in the history of American grandparents: Authority, burden, companion. *Generations, 20,* 7–12.

Greer, G. (1991). *The change: Women, aging, and the menopause.* London: Hamish Hamilton.

Gudykunst, W. B., & Matsumoto, Y. (1996). Cross-cultural variability of communication in personal relationships. In W. B. Gudykunst, S. Ting-Toomey, & T. Nishida (Eds.), *Communication in personal relationships across cultures* (pp. 19–56). Thousand Oaks, CA: Sage.

Gudykunst, W. B., & Ting-Toomey, S. (1988). *Culture and interpersonal communication.* Newbury Park, CA: Sage.

Gudykunst, W. B., Ting-Toomey, S., & Nishida, T. (Eds.). (1996). *Communication in personal relationships across cultures.* Newbury Park, CA: Sage.

Guttman, D. (1988). Age and leadership: Crosscultural observations. In A. Mcintyre (Ed.), *Aging and political leadership.* Albany: State University of New York Press.

Hader, M. (1965). The importance of grandparents in family life. *Family Process, 4,* 228–240.

Hagestad, G. O. (1985). Continuity and connectedness. In V. L. Bengston & J. F. Robertson (Eds.), *Grandparenthood* (pp. 31–48). Beverly Hills, CA: Sage.

Hagestad, G. O. (1987). Able elderly in the family context: Changes, chances, and challenges. *The Gerontologist, 27,* 417–422.

Hall, E. T. (1976). *Beyond culture.* Garden City, NY: Doubleday.

Hall, G. S. (1904). *Adolescence: Its psychology and its relations to physiology, sociology, sex, crime, religion and education.* New York: Appleton.

Hall, J. A., Roter, D. L., & Katz, N. R. (1988). Meta-analysis of correlates of provider behavior in medical encounters. *Medical Care, 26,* 657–675.

Halpren, J. (1994). The sandwich generation: Conflicts between adult children and their aging parents. In D. Cahn (Ed.), *Communication conflict in personal relationships* (pp. 143–160). Hillsdale, NJ: Lawrence Erlbaum Associates.

Hamilton, D. L., & Trolier, T. K. (1986). Stereotypes and stereotyping: An overview of the cognitive approach. In J. F. Dovidio & S. L. Gaertner (Eds.), *Prejudice, discrimination and racism* (pp. 127–163). Orlando, FL: Academic Press.

Hareven, T. (1982). The life course and aging in historical perspective. In T. Hareven & K. Adams (Eds.), *Aging and lifecourse transitions: An interdisciplinary perspective* (pp. 1–26). New York: Guilford.

Harris, L. (1981). *Aging in the eighties: America in transition.* Washington, DC: The National Council on Aging.

Hartshorne, T. S., & Manaster. G. J. (1982). The relationship with grandparents: Contact, importance and role conception. *The International Journal of Aging and Human Development, 15,* 233–255.

Harvey, J. H., Weber, A. L., & Orbuch, T. L. (1990). *Interpersonal accounts: A social psychological perspective.* Oxford, England: Basil Blackwell.

Harwood, J. (1992). *"Don't make me laugh": Representations of age in a humorous context.* Unpublished masters thesis, University of California, Santa Barbara.

Harwood, J. (1997). Viewing age: Lifespan identity and television viewing choices. *Journal of Broadcasting and Electronic Media, 41*, 203–213.

Harwood, J., & Giles, H. (1992). "Don't make me laugh": Age representations in a humorous context. *Discourse and Society, 3*, 403–436.

Harwood, J., & Giles, H. (1996). The role of response strategy and attributed thoughts in mediating evaluations of intergenerational patronizing talk. *Journal of Language and Social Psychology*, 395–421.

Harwood, J., Giles, H., Fox, S., Ryan, E. B., & Williams, A. (1993). Patronizing young and elderly adults: Response strategies in a community setting. *Journal of Applied Communication Research, 21*, 211–226.

Harwood, J., Giles, H., Ota, H., Pierson, H., Gallois, C., Ng, S. H., Lim T.-S., & Somera, L. (1996). College students' trait ratings of three age groups around the Pacific Rim. *Journal of Cross-Cultural Gerontology,11*, 307–317.

Harwood, J., Giles, H., Pierson, H. D., Clément, R., & Fox, S. (1994). Vitality perceptions of age categories in California and Hong Kong. *Journal of Multilingual and Multicultural Development, 15*, 311–318.

Harwood, J., Giles, H., & Ryan, E. B. (1995). Aging, communication, and intergroup theory: Social identity and intergenerational communication. In J. F. Nussbaum & J. Coupland (Eds.), *Handbook of communication and aging research* (pp. 133–159). Mahwah, NJ: Lawrence Erlbaum Associates.

Harwood, J., Giles, H., Ryan, E. B., Fox, S., & Williams, A. (1993). Patronizing young and elderly adults: Response strategies in a community setting. *Journal of Applied Communication Research, 21*, 211–226.

Harwood, J., & Williams, A. (1998). Young people's communication and affective expectations of interactions with different elderly substereotypes. *International Journal of Aging and Human Development, 47*, 11–33.

Haug, M. R. (1996). Elements in physician/patient interactions in late life. *Research on Aging, 18*, 32–51.

Haug, M. R., & Ory, M. G. (1987). Issues in elderly patient–provider interactions. *Research on Aging, 9*, 3–44.

Havinghurst, R. J. (1956). Research on the developmental task concept. *School Review, 64*, 215–223.

Havinghurst, R. J. (1972). *Developmental tasks and education.* New York: McKay.

Hays, W. C., & Mindel, C. H. (1973). Extended kinship relations in Black and White families. *Journal of Marriage and the Family, 35*, 51–56.

Heaven, P. C. L. (1994). *Contemporary adolescence: A social psychological approach.* Melbourne, Australia: McMillan.

Hecht, M. L. (1978). The conceptualization and measurement of interpersonal communication satisfaction. *Human Communication Research, 4*, 253–264.

Hecht, M. L., Ribeau, S., & Alberts, J. K. (1989). An Afro-American perspective on interethnic communication. *Communication Monographs, 56*, 385–410.

Henwood, K., & Coughlan, G. (1993). The construction of "closeness" in mother–daughter relationships across the lifespan. In N. Coupland & J. F. Nussbaum (Eds.), *Discourse and lifespan identity* (pp. 191–215). Newbury Park, CA: Sage.

Henwood, K., Giles, H., Coupland, J., & Coupland, N. (1993). Stereotyping and affect in discourse: Interpreting the meaning of elderly, painful self-disclosure. In D. M. Mackie

& D. L. Hamilton (Eds.), *Affect, cognition, and stereotyping: Interactive processes in group perception* (pp. 269–296). San Diego: Academic Press.

Hepworth, M. (1995). Images of old age. In J. F. Nussbaum & J. Coupland (Eds.), *Handbook of communication and aging research* (pp. 5–37). Mahwah, NJ: Lawrence Erlbaum Associates.

Hertzer, B. (1996, February 17). Farewell to the nursing home: A host of alternatives help the aging live independently. *Business Week,* 100–101.

Hewstone, M. (1989a). *Causal attribution: From cognitive processes to collective beliefs.* Oxford, England: Blackwell.

Hewstone, M. (1989b). Changing stereotypes with disconfirming information. In D. Bartal, C. F. Graumann, A. W. Kruglanski, & W. Stroebe (Eds.), *Stereotypes and prejudice: Changing conceptions* (pp. 207–223). New York: Springer-Verlag.

Hewstone, M., & Brown, R. (Eds.). (1986). *Contact and conflict in intergroup encounters.* Oxford, England: Blackwell.

Hewstone, M., Gale, L., & Purkhardt, N. (1990). Intergroup attributions for success and failure: Group-serving bias and group-serving causal schemata. *Cahiers-de-Psychologie-Cognitive, 10,* 23–44.

Himes, C. L. (1994). Parental caregiving by adult women: A demographic perspective. *Research on Aging, 16,* 191–211.

Hinrichsen, G. A., & Ramirez, M. (1992). Black and white dementia caregivers: A comparison of their adaptation, adjustment, and service utilization. *The Gerontologist, 32,* 375–381.

Ho, D. Yau-Fai. (1994). Filial piety, authoritarian moralism, and cognitive conservatism in Chinese societies. *Genetic, Social and General Psychology Monographs, 120,* 347–365.

Hocker, J. L., & Wilmot, W. W. (1995). *Interpersonal conflict* (4th ed.). Dubuque, IA: W. C. Brown.

Hofstede, G. (1980). *Culture's consequences.* Beverly Hills, CA: Sage.

Hogg, M. A., & Abrams, D. (1988). *Social identifications.* New York: Routledge.

Holladay, S. J. & Kerns, K. (1997, November). *It's a generation thing: Exploring intergenerational friendships.* Paper presented at the annual meeting of the National Communication Association, Chicago.

Hollien, H. (1987). "Old voices": What do we really know about them? *Journal of Voice, 1,* 2–17.

Holtgraves, T. (1990). The language of self-disclosure. In H. Giles & W. P. Robinson (Eds.), *Handbook of language and social psychology* (pp. 191–208). New York: Wiley.

Hong Kong Government. (1965). *Aims and policy for social welfare in Hong Kong.* Hong Kong: Government printer.

Horowitz, A. (1985). Sons and daughters as caregivers to older parents: Differences in role performance and consequences. *The Gerontologist, 25,* 612–617.

Howe, N., & Strauss, B. (1993). *13th generation: Abort, retry, ignore, fail?* New York: Vintage.

Hummert, M. L. (1990). Multiple stereotypes of the elderly and young adults: A comparison of structure and evaluations. *Psychology and Aging, 5,* 182–193.

Hummert, M. L. (1994). Stereotypes of the elderly and patronizing speech. In M. L. Hummert, J. M. Wiemann, & J. F. Nussbaum (Eds.), *Interpersonal communication in older adulthood* (pp. 162–184). Thousand Oaks, CA: Sage.

Hummert, M. L., Garstka, T. A., & Shaner, J. L. (1995). Beliefs about language performance: Adults' perceptions about self and elderly targets. *Journal of Language and Social Psychology, 14,* 235–259.

Hummert, M. L., Garstka, T. A., Shaner, J. L., & Strahm, S. (1994). Stereotypes of the elderly held by young, middle-aged, and elderly adults. *Journal of Gerontology: Psychological Sciences, 49,* 240–249.

Hummert, M. L., & Mazloff, D. (1993). *Elderly adult's views of patronizing speech: A focus group study.* Unpublished manuscript, University of Kansas at Lawrence.

Hummert, M. L., Nussbaum, J. F., & Wiemann, J. M. (1994). Interpersonal communication and older adulthood: An introduction. In M. L. Hummert, J. M. Wiemann, & J. F. Nussbaum (Eds.), *Interpersonal communication in older adulthood* (pp. 1–14). Thousand Oaks, CA: Sage.

Hummert, M. L., & Ryan, E. B. (1996). Toward understanding variations in patronizing talk addressed to older adults: Psycholiguistic features of care and control. *International Journal of Psycholinguistics, 12,* 149–169.

Hummert, M. L., & Shaner, J. L. (1994). Patronizing speech to the elderly as a function of stereotyping. *Communication Studies, 45,* 145–158.

Hummert, M. L., Shaner, J. L., Garstka, T. A., & Henry, C. (1996, November). *"Arthur, Arthur, Arthur—Are you nuts ?": Types of patronizing messages to older adults.* Paper presented at the annual meeting of the Speech Communication Association, San Diego.

Hummert, M. L., Shaner, J. L., Henry, C., & Garstka T. A. (1995). *Patronizing speech to the elderly: Relationship to subject age and stereotypes.* Manuscript in preparation.

Hummert, M. L., Wiemann, J. M., & Nussbaum, J. F. (Eds.). (1995). *Interpersonal communication in older adulthood.* Thousand Oaks, CA: Sage.

Huston, A., Donnerstein, E., Fairchild, H., Feshbach, N., Katz, P., Murray, J., Rubinstein, E., & Zuckerman, D. (1992). *Big world, small screen: The role of television in American society.* Lincoln: University of Nebraska Press.

Ikels, C. (1975). Old age in Hong Kong. *The Gerontologist, 15,* 230–235.

Ikels, C., Keith, J., Dickerson-Putman, J., Draper, P., Fry, C., Glascock, A., & Harpending, H. (1992). Perceptions of the adult life course: A cross-cultural analysis. *Aging in Society, 12,* 49–84.

Infante, D. A., & Rancer, A. S. (1996). Argumentativeness and verbal aggressiveness: A review of recent theory and research. In B. R. Burleson (Ed.), *Communication yearbook 19* (pp. 319–351). Thousand Oaks, CA: Sage.

Ingelhart, R. (1977). *The silent revolution: Changing values and political styles among western publics.* Princeton, NJ. : Princeton University Press.

Ingersoll-Dayton, B., Starrels, M. E., & Dowler, D. (1996). Caregiving for parents and parents-in-law: Is gender important? *The Gerontologist, 36,* 483–491.

Itzin, C. (1986). Ageism awareness training: A model for group work. In C. Phillipson, M. Bernard, & P. Strang (Eds.), *Dependency and interdependency in old age: Theoretical perspectives and policy alternatives* (pp. 114–126). London: Croom Helm.

Jaworski, A., & Stephens, D. (1998). Self-reports on silence as a face-saving strategy by people with hearing impairment. *International Journal of Applied Linguistics, 8,* 61–80.

Jennings, M. K., & Markus, G. B. (1988). Political involvement in the later years: A longitudinal survey. *American Journal of Political Science, 32,* 302–316.

Johnson, C., & Pichora-Fuller, M. (1994). How communication goals may alter handicap. *Journal of Speech and Language Pathology Association, 18,* 235–242.

Johnson, J., & Bytheway, B. (1993). Ageism: concept and definition. In J. Johnson & R. Slater (Eds.), *Aging and later life* (pp. 200–206). London: Sage.

Jones, L. Y. (1980). *Great expectations: America and the baby boom generations.* New York: Ballantine.

Kahana, F., & Kahana, F. (1970). Grandparenthood from the perspective of the developing child. *Developmental Psychology, 3,* 98–105.

Kalish, R. (1979). The new ageism and the failure models: A polemic. *The Gerontologist, 19,* 398–402.

Karp, D. A., & Yoels, W. C. (1982). *Experiencing the life cycle: A social psychology of aging.* Springfield, IL: Thomas.

Kemper, S. (1992). Language and aging. In F. I. M. Craik & T. Salthouse (Eds.), *Handbook of aging and cognition* (pp. 213–270). Hillsdale, NJ: Lawrence Erlbaum Associates.

Kemper, S. (1994). "Elderspeak": Speech accommodation to older adults. *Aging and Cognition, 1,* 17–38.

Kemper, S., Anagnopoulos, C., Lyons, K., & Heberlein, W. (1994). Speech accommodation to dementia. *Journal of Gerontology: Psychological Sciences, 49,* 223–229.

Kemper, S., Kynette, D., & Norman, S. (1992). Age differences in spoken language. In R. West & J. Sinnot (Eds.), *Everyday memory and aging* (pp. 138–154). New York: Springer-Verlag.

Kemper, S., Kynette, D., Rash, S., O'Brien, K, & Sprott, R. (1989). Life-span changes to adults' language: Effects of memory and genre. *Applied Psycholinguistics, 10,* 49–66.

Kemper, S., & Lyons, K. (1994). The effects of Alzheimer's dementia on language and communication. In M. L. Hummert, J. M. Wiemann, & J. F. Nussbaum (Eds.), *Interpersonal communication in older adulthood: Interdisciplinary theory and research* (pp. 58–82). Thousand Oaks, CA: Sage.

Kemper, S., Rash, S., Kynette, D., & Norman, S. (1990). Telling stories: The structure of older adults' narratives. *European Journal of Cognitive Psychology, 2,* 205–228.

Kiefer, C. W. (1992). Aging in Eastern cultures: A historical overview. In T. R. Cole, D. D. Van Tassel, & R. Kastenbaum (Eds.), *Handbook of the humanities and aging* (pp. 96–123). New York: Springer.

Kiefer, C. W., Kim, S., Choi, K., Kim, L., Kim, B.-L., Shon, S., & Kim, T. (1985). Adjustment problems of Korean American elderly. *The Gerontologist, 25,* 477–482.

Kilman, R., & Thomas, K. (1977). Developing a forced-choice measure of conflict handling behavior: The "MODE" instrument. *Educational and Psychological Measurement, 37,* 309–325.

Kim, C. K., Kim, S., & Hurh, W. M. (1991). Filial piety and intergenerational relationship in Korean immigrant families. *International Journal of Aging and Human Development, 33,* 233–245.

Kim, U. (1994). Individualism and collectivism: Conceptual clarification and elaboration. In U. Kim, H. C. Triandis, C. Kagitcibais, S.-C., Choi, & G. Yoon (Eds.), *Individualism and collectivism: Theory, method, and applications* (pp. 19–40). Thousand Oaks, CA: Sage.

Kim, U., & Yamaguchi, S. (1994). Cross-cultural research methodology and approach: Implications for the advancement of Japanese social psychology. *Research in Social Psychology, 10,* 168–179.

Kite, M. E., & Johnson, B. T. (1988). Attitudes toward older and younger adults: A meta-analysis. *Psychology and Aging, 3,* 233–244.

Kivett, V. R., & Atkinson, M. P. (1984). Filial expectations, association, and helping as a function of number of children among older rural-transition parents. *Journal of Gerontology, 39,* 499–503.

Kogan, N. (1979). Beliefs, attitudes and stereotypes about old people: A new look at some old issues. *Research on Aging, 2,* 11–36.

Kohlberg, L. (1973). Stages and aging in moral development—some speculations. *Gerontologist, 13,* 497–502.

Kohli, M., & Rein, M. (1991). The changing balance of work and retirement. In M. Kohli, M. Rein, A. M. Guillemard, & H. Gunsteren (Eds.). *Time for retirement: Comparative studies of early exit from the labor force* (pp. 1–35). Cambridge, England: Cambridge University Press.

Kornhaber, A. (1996). *Contemporary grandparenting.* Thousand Oaks, CA: Sage.

Kornhaber, A., & Woodward, K. L. (1981). *Grandparents/grandchildren: The vital connection.* Garden City, NY: Doubleday.

Koyano, W. (1989). Japanese attitudes toward the elderly: A review of research findings. *Journal of Cross-Cultural Gerontology, 4,* 335–345.

Kramerae, C. (1981). *Women and men speaking.* Rowley, MA: Newbury House.

Krauss, D. J., & Krauss, H. H. (1990). Conflict in families. In J. B. Gittler (Ed.), *Annual review of conflict knowledge and conflict resolution* (Vol. 1, pp. 1–31). New York: Garland.

Kuypers, J. A., & Bengston, V. L. (1973). Social breakdown and competence: A model of normal aging. *Human Development, 16,* 181–201.

Labov, W., & Waletsky, J. (1967). Narrative analysis: Oral versions of personal experience. In J. Helm (Ed.), *Essay on the verbal and visual arts* (pp. 12–44). Seattle: University of Washington Press.

Ladd, E. C. (1993). The twentysomethings: "Generation myths" revisited. *The Public Perspective, 5,* 14–18.

Lancely, A. (1985). Use of controlling language in the rehabilitation of the elderly. *Journal of Advanced Nursing, 36,* 12–29.

Lawton, L., Silverstein, M., & Bengston, V. L. (1994). Solidarity between generations in families. In V. L. Bengston, R. A. Harootyan, & Contributors (Eds.), *Intergenerational linkages: Hidden connections in American society* (pp. 19–42). New York: Springer.

Lee, Y.-J., Parish, W. L., & Willis, R. J. (1994). Sons, daughters and intergenerational support in Taiwan. *American Journal of Sociology,* 1010–1041.

Leigh, G. K. (1985). Kinship interaction over the family life span. In B. C. Miller & D. H. Olson (Eds.), *Family studies review yearbook* (Vol. 3, pp. 477–486). Beverly Hills, CA: Sage.

Lerner, R., & Busch-Rossnagel, N. (1981). *Individuals as producers of their development: A life span perspective.* New York: Academic Press.

Levin, J., & Levin, W. C. (1980). *Agism: Prejudice and discrimination against the elderly.* Belmont, CA: Wadsworth.

Levinson, D. J., Darrow, D., Klein, E. B., Levinson, M. H., & McKee, B. (1978). *The seasons of a man's life.* New York: Knopf.

Levitt, M., Guacci, N., & Weber, R. A. (1992). Intergenerational support, relationship quality, and well-being: A bicultural analysis. *Journal of Family Issues, 13,* 465–481.

Levy, B., & Langer, E. (1994). Aging free from negative stereotypes: Successful memory in China and among the American deaf. *Journal of Personality and Social Psychology, 66,* 989–997.

Levy, B., & Tsuhako, S. (1994, November). *The status paradox of Japanese elderly.* Paper presented at the annual conference of the Gerontology Society of America, Washington, DC.

Lewis, A. M., & Lewis, S. K. (1985). Intergenerational conflict. Considerations for clergy. *Pastoral Psychology, 35,* 46–49.

Light, L. L. (1988). Language and aging: Competence versus performance. In J. E. Birren & V. L. Bengtson (Eds.), *Emergent theories of aging* (pp. 177–213). New York: Springer.

Light, L. L. (1990). Interactions between memory and language in old age. In J. E. Birren & K. W. Schaie (Eds.), *The handbook of the psychology of aging* (pp. 275–290). San Diego: Academic Press.

Lin, G., & Rogerson, P. A. (1995). Elderly parents and geographic availability of their children. *Research on Aging, 17,* 303–331.

Loomis, L. S., & Booth, A. (1995). Multigenerational caregiving and well being: The myth of the beleaguered sandwich generation. *Journal of Family Issues, 16,* 131–148.

Lubben, J. F., & Becerra, R. M. (1987). Social support among Black, Mexican, and Chinese elderly. In D. F. Gelfand & C. H. Barresi (Eds.), *Ethnic dimensions of aging.* New York: Springer.

Malkin, M. (1994, February 28). Changing times: Generations X's fiscal reality bites. *Dayton News.*

Mangen, D. J., Bengtson, V. L., & Landry, P. H., Jr. (Eds.). (1988). *Measurement of intergenerational relations.* Newbury Park, CA: Sage.

Mannheim, K. (1952). *Essays in the sociology of knowledge.* New York: Oxford University Press.

Mannheim, K. (1972). The problem of generations. In P. G. Altbach & R. S. Laufer (Eds.), *The new pilgrims: Youth protest in transition.* New York: McKay.

Mares, M. -L., & Cantor, J. (1992). Elderly viewer's responses to televised portrayals of old age: Empathy and mood management versus social comparison. *Communication Research, 19*, 459–478.

Markides, K. S., & Coreil, J. (1986). The health of Hispanics in the southwestern United States: An epidemiologic paradox. *Public Health Reports, 101*, 253–265.

Markides, K. S., & Mindel, C. H. (1987). *Aging and ethnicity.* Beverly Hills, CA: Sage.

Markus, H., & Kitayama, S. (1991). Culture and self: Implications for cognition, emotion, and motivation. *Psychological Review, 98*, 224–253.

Markus, H., & Nurius, P. (1986). Possible selves. *American Psychologist, 41*, 954–969.

Martin, L. G. (1988). The aging of Asia. *Journal of Gerontology, 43*, 99–113.

Matthews, S. H., & Sprey, J. (1984). The impact of divorce of grandparenthood: An exploratory study. *The Gerontologist, 24*, 41–47.

Matthews, S. H., & Sprey. J. (1985). Adolescent's relationships with grandparents: An empirical contribution to conceptual clarification. *Journal of Gerontology, 40*, 621–626.

Mazloff, D. C., Shaner, J. L., & Ward, T. D. (1996, May). *Painful self-disclosures in a natural context.* Paper presented at the Third International Conference on Communication, Aging, and Health, Kansas City, MO.

McArthur, L. Z., & Apatow, K. (1983–1984). Impressions of babyfaced adults. *Social Cognition, 2*, 315–318.

McCandless, B. R., & Evans, E. D. (1973). *Children and youth: Psychosocial development.* Hinsdale, IL: Dryden.

McCormick, W. C., lnui, T. S., & Roter, D. L. (1996). Interventions in physician–elderly patient interactions. *Research on Aging, 18*, 103–136.

McGoldrick, J. P, Pearce, J., & Giordona, N. (1982). *Ethnicity and family therapy.* New York: Guilford.

Mead, G. H. (1932). *Philosophy of the present.* LaSalle, IL: Open Court.

Mead, M., & Wofenstein, M. (Eds.). (1955). *Childhood in contemporary cultures.* Chicago: University of Chicago Press.

Mergler, N. L., Faust, M., & Goldstein, M. D. (1985). Storytelling as an age-dependent skill. *International Journal of Aging and Human Development, 20*, 205–228.

Metts, S., & Cupach, W. R. (1990). The influence of relationship beliefs and problem-solving responses on satisfaction in romantic relationships. *Human Communication Research, 17*, 170–185.

Middleton, D., & Edwards, D. (1990). *Collective remembering.* London: Sage.

Miller, A. H., Gurin, P., & Gurin, G. (1980). Age consciousness and political mobilization of older Americans. *The Gerontologist, 20*, 691–700.

Miller, C., & Lelieuvre, R. (1982). A method to reduce chronic pain in elderly nursing home residents. *The Gerontologist, 22*, 314–323.

Miller, G. R. (1983). On various ways of skinning symbolic cats: Recent research on persuasive message strategies. *Journal of Language and Social Psychology, 2*, 123–140.

Milner, D. (1975). *Children and race.* New York: Penguin.

Montemayor, R. (1983). Parents and adolescents in conflict: All families some of the time and some families most of the time. *Journal of Early Adolescence, 3,* 83–103.

Montemayor, R. (1986). Family variation in parent–adolescent storm and stress. *Journal of Adolescent Research, 1,* 15–31.

Montepare, J. U., Steinberg, J., & Rosenberg, B. (1992). Characteristics of vocal communication between young adults and their parents and grandparents. *Communication Research, 19,* 479–492.

Moody, H. R. (1987–1988). Introduction: Why worry about education for older adults? *Generations, 12,* 5–9.

Morgan, D. L., & Zhao, P. Z. (1993). The doctor–caregiver relationship: Managing the care of family members with Alzheimers disease. *Qualitative Health Research, 2,* 133–164.

Mulac, A., & Giles, H. (1996). "You're only as old as you sound:" Chronological, contextual, psychological and perceptual parameters of elderly age attributions. *Health Communication, 8,* 199–216.

Myers, J. E. (1988). The mid-life generation gap: Adult children with aging parents. *Journal of Counseling and Development, 66,* 331–335.

Nagasawa, R. (1980). *The elderly Chinese: A forgotten minority.* Chicago, IL: Pacific Asian American Mental Health Research Center.

Nahemow, L., McCluskey-Fawcett, K. A., & McGhee, P. E. (Eds.). (1986). *Humor and aging.* Orlando, FL: Academic Press.

Nakonezny, P. (1996). *The effect of late life parental divorce on adult child/older parent solidarity.* Unpublished doctoral dissertation, University of Oklahoma, Norman.

Nelson, R., & Cowan, J. (1994). *Revolution X: A survival guide for our generation.* New York: Penguin.

Neugarten, B. L. & Weinstein, K. (1964). The changing American grandparent. *Journal of Marriage and the Family, 26,* 199–204.

Newton, D. A., & Burgoon, J. K. (1990). The use and consequences of verbal influence strategies during interpersonal disagreements. *Human Communication Research, 16,* 477–518.

Ng, S-H. (1998). Social psychology in an ageing world: Ageism and intergenerational relations. *Asian Journal of Social Psychology, 1,* 99–116.

Ng, S-H., & Bradac, J. J. (1993). *Power in language: Verbal communication and social influence.* Newbury Park, CA: Sage.

Ng, S-H., Liu, J. H., Wetherall, A., & Loong, C. S. F. (1997). Younger adult's communication experiences and contact with elders and peers. *Human Communication Research, 24,* 82–108.

Ng, S-H., Moody, J., & Giles, H. (1991). Information-seeking triggered by age. *International Journal of Aging and Human Development, 33,* 269–277.

Noelker, L. S., & Harel, Z. (1978). Predictors of well-being and survival among institutionalized aged. *The Gerontologist, 18,* 562–567.

Noelker, L. S., & Wallace, R. W. (1985). The organization of family care for the impaired elderly. *Journal of Family Issues, 6,* 23–44.

Noels, K., Giles, H., Williams, A., Lim, T-S., Ng, S-H., Ryan, E., & Somera, L. (1997, November). *Intergenerational communication across cultures: Young people's perceptions of conversations with family elders, nonfamily elders, and same-age peers.* Paper presented at the annual meeting of the National Communication Association in Chicago.

Noller, P. (1995). Parent–adolescent relationships. In M. A. Fitzpatrick & A. L. Vangelisti (Eds.), *Explaining family interactions* (pp. 77–111). Thousand Oaks, CA: Sage.

Norman, S., Kemper, S., Kynelte, D., Cheung, H., & Anagnopoulos, C. (1991). Syntactic complexity and adults' running memory span. *Journal of Gerontology: Psychological Sciences, 46,* 346–351.

Notarius, C. I., & Herrick, L. R. (1988). Listener response strategies to a distressed other. *Journal of Social and Personal Relationships, 5,* 97–108.

Nuessel, F. (1982). The language of ageism. *The Gerontologist, 22,* 273–276.

Nuessel, F. (1993). *The semiotics of aging.* Louisville, KY: University of Louisville Press.

Nussbaum, J. F. (1983a). Relational closeness of elderly interaction: Implications for life satisfaction. *The Western Journal of Speech Communication, 47,* 229–243.

Nussbaum, J. F. (1983b). Perceptions of communication content and life satisfaction among the elderly. *Communication Quarterly, 31,* 313–319.

Nussbaum, J. F. (1985). Successful aging: A communicative model. *Communication Quarterly, 33,* 262–269.

Nussbaum, J. F. (1989). *Life-span communication: Normative processes.* Hillsdale, NJ: Lawrence Erlbaum Associates.

Nussbaum, J. F. (1990). Communication within the nursing home: Survivability as a function of resident-staff affinity. In H. Giles, N. Coupland, & J. Wiemann (Eds.), *Communication, health, and the elderly* (pp. 155–171). Manchester, England: Manchester University Press.

Nussbaum, J. F. (1991). Communication, language, and the institutionalized elderly. *Ageing and Society, 11,* 149–166.

Nussbaum, J. F. (1994). Friendship in older adulthood. In M. L. Hummert, J. M. Wiemann, & J. F. Nussbaum (Eds.), *Interpersonal communication in older adulthood: Interdisciplinary theory and research* (pp. 209–225). Thousand Oaks, CA: Sage.

Nussbaum, J. F., Bergstrom, M., & Sparks, L. (1996). The institutionalized elderly: Interactive implications of long-term care. In E. B. Ray (Ed.), *Communication and disenfranchisement* (pp. 219–229). Mahwah, NJ: Lawrence Erlbaum Associates.

Nussbaum, J. F., & Bettini, L. M. (1994). Shared stories of the grandparent–grandchild relationship. *The International Journal of Aging and Human Development, 39* 67–80.

Nussbaum, J. F. & Coupland, J. (1995). *Handbook of communication and aging research.* Mahwah, NJ: Lawrence Erlbaum Associates.

Nussbaum, J. F., Hummert, M. L., Williams, A., & Harwood, J. (1995). Communication and older adults. In B. Burleson (Ed.), *Communication yearbook 19* (pp. 1–47) Thousand Oaks, CA: Sage.

Nussbaum, J.F., Pecchioni, L., Robinson, J. D., & Thompson, T. (2000). *Communication and aging* (2nd ed.). Mahwah, NJ: Lawrence Erlbaum Associates.

Nussbaum, J. F., Robinson, J. D., & Grew, D. J. (1985). Communicative behavior of the long-term health care employee: Implications for the elderly resident. *Communication Research Reports, 2,* 16–22.

Nussbaum, J. F., Thompson, T., & Robinson, J. D. (1989). *Communication and aging.* New York: Harper & Row.

Nye, F. I., & Rushing, W. (1969). Toward family measurement research. In J. Hadden & F. Borgatta (Eds.), *Marriage and family.* Itasca, IL: Peacock.

Nye, I. F., & Bernardo, F. M. (1981). The role of grandparenthood. In L. D. Steinberg (Ed.), *The life cycle: Readings in human development* (pp. 325–330). New York: Columbia University Press.

Obler, L. (1989). Language beyond childhood. In J. B. Gleason (Ed.), *The development of language* (2nd ed., p. 275–302). Columbus, OH: Merrill.

O'Connell, A. N., & Rotter, N. G. (1979). The influence of stimulus age and sex on person perception. *Journal of Gerontology, 34,* 220–228.

Orange, J. B., & Ryan, E. B. (1995). Effective communication. In B. Pickles, A. Compton, J. Simpson, C. A. Cott, & A. Vandervoort (Eds.), *Physiotherapy with older people* (pp. 119–137). London: Saunders.

Ota, H., Giles, H., Harwood, J., Pierson, H. D., Gallois, C., Ng, S. H., Lim, T.-S., Ryan, E. B., Maher, J., & Somera, L. (1996, November). *A neglected dimension of communication and aging: Filial piety across eight nations.* Top paper in the Commission on Communication and Aging in the Speech Communication Association annual conference, San Diego.

Oyer, H. J., & Oyer, E. (1976). *Aging and communication.* Baltimore: University Park Press.

Palmore, E. D. (1975). *The honorable elders: A cross-cultural analysis of aging in Japan.* Durham, NC: Duke University Press.

Palmore, E. D. (1988). *The facts on aging quiz.* New York: Springer.

Palmore, E. D. (1990). *Ageism, negative and positive.* New York: Springer.

Park, M.-S., & Kim, M.-S. (1992). Communication practices in Korea. *Communication Quarterly, 40,* 398–404.

Parsons, T. (1944). The social structure of the family. In R. N. Ashen (Ed.), *The family: Its function and destiny* (pp. 173–201). New York: Harper & Row.

Pasupathi, M., Carstensen, L. L., & Tsai, J. L. (1995). Ageism in interpersonal settings. In B. Lott & D. Maluso (Eds.), *The social psychology of interpersonal discrimination* (pp. 160–182). New York: Guilford.

Perry, J. S., & Varney, T. L. (1978). College student's attitudes toward workers' competence and age. *Psychological Reports, 42,* 1319–1322.

Pett, M. A., Lang, N., & Gander, A. (1992). Late life divorce: Its impact on family rituals. *Journal of Family Issues, 13,* 526–552.

Pettigrew, T. F. (1986). The intergroup contact hypothesis reconsidered. In M. Hewstone & R. Brown (Eds.), *Contact and conflict in intergroup encounters* (pp. 169–195). Oxford, England: Blackwell.

Pichora-Fuller, K., Johnson, C. E., & Roodenburg, K. E. J. (1998). The discrepancy between hearing impairment and handicap in the elderly: Balancing transactions and interaction in conversations. *Journal of Applied Communication Research, 26,* 99–119.

Pittam, J., & Gallois, C. (1998, July). *Negotiating a working consensus in conversations about HIV/AIDS.* Paper presented at the 48th International Communication Association Convention, Jerusalem, Israel.

Poe, L. M. (1991). *Black grandparents as parents.* Unpublished manuscript.

Pollack, R. F. (1988). Serving intergenerational needs, not intergenerational conflict. *Generations, 12,* 14–18.

Poole, M. S., Seibold, D., & McPhee, R. D. (1985). Group decision making as a structurational process. *Quarterly Journal of Speech, 71,* 74–102.

Poon, L. (1987). Learning. In G. Maddox (Ed.), *The encyclopedia of aging.* New York: Springer.

Portrait of the electorate. (1996, November 10). *The New York Times,* p. A16.

Pratt, M. W., & Norris, J. E. (1994). *The social psychology of aging.* Oxford, England: Blackwell.

Pratt, M. W., & Robins, S. (1991). That's the way it was: Age differences in the structure and quality of adult's personal narratives. *Discourse Process, 14,* 73–85.

Prentice, D. A. (1995). Do language reforms change our way of thinking? *Journal of Language and Social Psychology, 13,* 3–19.

Putnam, L. L., & Wilson, C. E. (1982). Communicative strategies in organizational conflicts: Reliability and validity of a measurement scale. In M. Burgoon (Ed.), *Communication yearbook* (Vol. 6, pp. 629–652). New Brunswick, NJ: Transaction.

Quadagno, J. S., & Hardy, M. (1996). Work and retirement. In R. H. Binstock & L. K. George (Eds.), *Handbook of aging and the social sciences* (4th ed., pp. 325–345). San Diego, CA: Academic Press.

Quinn, J. B. (1994, June 6). The luck of the Xers. *Newsweek,* 66–67.

Ramig, L. A. (1986). Aging speech: Physiological and sociological aspects. *Language and Communication, 6,* 25–34.

Rawlins, W. K. (1992). *Friendship matters: Communication, dialectics, and the life course.* New York: de Gruyter.

Rawlins, W. K. (1995). Friendships in later life. In J. F. Nussbaum & J. Coupland (Eds.), *Handbook of communication and aging research* (pp. 227–257). Mahwah, NJ: Lawrence Erlbaum Associates.

Reich, C. (1970). *The greening of America.* New York: Random House.

Reisman, J. M. (1981). Adult friendships. In S. Duck & R. Gilmore (Eds.), *Personal relationships* (Vol. 2, pp. 205–230). London: Academic Press.

Reisman, J. M. (1984). Friendliness and its correlates. *Journal of Social and Clinical Psychology, 2*, 143–155.

Research issues related to physician–elderly patient interactions. (1996). *Research on Aging, 18* (1), 1–136.

Revenson, T. A. (1989). Compassionate stereotyping of elderly patients by physicians: Revising the social contact hypothesis. *Psychology and Aging, 4*, 230–234.

Robinson, J. D. (1989). Mass media and the elderly: A uses and dependency interpretation. In J. F. Nussbaum (Ed.), *Life-span communication: Normative processes* (pp. 319–338). Hillsdale, NJ: Lawrence Erlbaum Associates.

Robinson, J. D., & Skill, T. (November, 1993). *The invisible generation: Portrayals of the elderly on television.* Paper presented at the annual meeting of the Speech Communication Association, Miami, FL.

Robinson, J. D., & Skill, T. (1995). Media usage patterns and portrayals of the elderly. In J. F. Nussbaum & J. Coupland (Eds.), *Handbook of communication and aging research* (pp. 359–391). Mahwah, NJ: Lawrence Erlbaum Associates.

Rodin, J., & Langer, E. J. (1980). Aging labels: The decline of control and the fall of self-esteem. *Journal of Social Issues, 36*, 12–29.

Rosenbaum, W. A., & Button, J. W. (1993). The unquiet future of intergenerational politics. *The Gerontologist, 33*, 481–490.

Rosenfeld, E. T. (1993). When and how old age is relevant in discourse of the elderly: A case study of Georgia O'Keefe. In J. E. Atlatis (Ed.), *Georgetown University round table on languages and linguistics 1992: Language, communication and social meaning.* Washington, DC: Georgetown University Press.

Rosenthal, C. J., Matthews, S. H., & Marshall, V. W. (1989). Is parent care normative? The experiences of a sample of middle-aged women. *Research on Aging, 11*, 244–260.

Rotenberg, K. J., & Hamel, J. (1988). Social interaction and depression in elderly individuals. *International Journal of Aging and Human Development, 27*, 307–320.

Roy, A., & Harwood, J. (1997). Underrepresented, positively portrayed: The representation of older adults in television commercials. *Journal of Applied Communication Research, 25*, 39–56.

Rubin, D. L., Greene, K., & Schneider, D. (1994). Adopting gender-inclusive language reforms: Diachronic and synchronic variation. *Journal of Language and Social Psychology, 13*, 91–114.

Rusbult, C. (1987). Responses to dissatisfaction in romantic involvements: The exit-voice-loyalty-neglect model. In D. Perlman & S. W. Duck (Eds.), *Intimate relationships: Development, dynamics and deterioration* (pp. 209–237). Newbury Park, CA: Sage.

Ryan, E. B. (1991). Language issues in normal aging. In R. Lubinski (Ed.), *Dementia and communication* (pp. 84–97). Philadelphia: Mosby.

Ryan, E. B., Bourhis, R. Y., & Knops, U. (1991). Evaluative perceptions of patronizing speech addressed to elders. *Psychology and Aging, 6*, 442–450.

Ryan, E. B., & Capadano, H. L. (1978). Age-perceptions and evaluative reactions toward adult speakers. *Journal of Gerontology, 33*, 98–102.

Ryan, E. B., & Cole, R. (1990). Evaluative perceptions of interpersonal communication with elders. In H. Giles, N. Coupland, & J. M. Wiemann (Eds.), *Communication, health and the elderly* (pp. 172–190). Manchester, England: Manchester University Press.

Ryan, E. B., & Giles, H. (Eds.). (1982). *Attitudes toward language.* London: Arnold.

Ryan, E. B., Giles, H., Bartolucci, G., & Henwood, K. (1986). Psycholinguistic and social psychological components of communication by and with the elderly. *Language and Communication, 6*(1/2), 1–24.

Ryan, E. B., Giles, H., Harwood, J., & Williams, A. (1993). *Community elders' perceptions and accounts of patronizing speech.* Unpublished manuscript, University of California, Santa Barbara.

Ryan, E. B., & Heaven, R. K. B (1988). The impact of situational context on age-based attitudes. *Social Behaviour, 3*, 105–118.

Ryan, E. B., Hummert, M. L., & Boich, L. H. (1995). Communication predicaments of aging: Patronizing behavior toward older adults. *Journal of Language & Social Psychology, 14*, 144–166.

Ryan, E. B., & Johnston, D. (1987). The influence of communication effectiveness on evaluations of younger and older adult speakers. *Journal of Gerontology, Psychological Sciences, 42*, 163–164.

Ryan, E. B., Kennaley, D., Pratt, M., & Shumovich, M. (1996, May). *Responses in the nursing home: Evaluative perceptions by staff, residents, and community seniors.* Paper presented at Third International conference on Communication, Aging and Health. Kansas City, KS.

Ryan, E. B., & Kwong See, S. (1993). Age-based beliefs about memory change in adulthood. *Journal of Gerontology: Psychological Sciences, 48*, 199–201.

Ryan, E. B., Kwong See, S., Meneer, W. B., & Trovato, D. (1992a). Age-based perceptions of language performance among younger and older adults. *Communication Research, 19*, 311–331.

Ryan, E. B., Kwong See, S., Meneer, W. B., & Trovato, D. (1992b). Age-based perceptions of language performance among younger and older adults. In M. L. Hummert, J. M. Wiemann, & J. F. Nussbaum (Eds.), *Interpersonal communication in older adulthood: Interdisciplinary theory and research* (pp. 15–39). Thousand Oaks, CA: Sage.

Ryan, E. B., & Laurie, S. (1990). Evaluations of older and younger adult speakers: The influence of communication effectiveness and noise. *Psychology and Aging, 5*, 514–519.

Ryan, E. B., Maclean, M., & Orange, J. B. (1994). Inappropriate accommodation in communication to elders: Inferences about nonverbal correlates. *International Journal of Aging and Human Development, 39*, 273–291.

Ryan, E. B., Meredith, S. D., MacLean, M. J., & Orange, J. B. (1995). Changing the way we talk with elders: Promoting health using the Communication Enhancement Model. *International Journal of Aging and Human Development, 41*, 87–105.

Ryan, E. B., Meredith, S. D., & Shantz, G. D. (1994). Evaluative perceptions of patronizing speech addressed to institutionalized elders in varied contexts. *Canadian Journal on Aging, 13*, 236–248.

Sachdev, I., & Bourhis, R. Y. (1993). Ethnolinguistic vitality: Some motivational and cognitive considerations. In M. A. Hogg & D. Abrams (Eds.), *Group motivation: Social psychological perspectives.* New York: Harvester Wheatsheaf.

Sachweh, S. (1998). Granny darling's nappies: Secondary babytalk in German nursing homes for the aged. *Journal of Applied Communication Research, 26*, 52–65.

Salthouse, T. A. (1988). Effects of aging on verbal abilities: Examination of the psychometric literature. In L. L. Light & D. M. Burke (Eds.), *Language memory and aging* (pp. 17–35). New York: Cambridge University Press.

Samuelson, R. J. (1993, July). At issue: Will the generation entering the workforce today have a lower standard of living over their lifetime than their parents enjoyed? No. *CQ Researcher,* 641.

Schaie, K. W. (1990). Intellectual development in adulthood. In J. E. Birren & K. W. Schaie (Eds.), *Handbook of the psychology of aging* (3rd ed., pp. 291–309). San Diego: Academic Press.

Schaie, K. W. (1993). Ageist language in psychological research. *American Psychologist, 48*, 49–51.

Schaie, K. W., & Strother, C. R. (1968). A cross-sequential study of age changes in cognitive behavior. *Psychological Bulletin, 70*, 671–680.

Scheier, M. F., Carver, C. S., Schulz, R., Glass, D. C., & Katz, I. (1978). Sympathy, self-consciousness, and reactions to the stigmatized. *Journal of Applied Social Psychology, 8,* 270–282.

Schlesinger, M., & Kronebusch, K. (1994). Intergenerational tensions and conflict: Attitudes and perceptions about social justice and age-related needs. In V. L. Bengston, R. A. Harootyan, & Contributors (Eds.), *Intergenerational linkages: Hidden connections in American society* (pp. 152–184). New York: Springer.

Schmidt. A., & Padilla, A. M. (1983). Grandparent–grandchild interaction in a Mexican-American group. *Hispanic Journal of Behavioral Sciences, 5,* 181–191.

Schnaiberg, A., & Goldenberg, S. (1989). From empty nest to crowded nest: The dynamics of incompletely launched young adults. *Social Problems, 36,* 251–269.

Schulz, J. H. (1996). Economic security policies. In R. H. Binstock & L. K. George (Eds.), *Handbook of aging and the social sciences* (4th ed., pp. 410–426). San Diego, CA: Academic Press.

Schwalb, S. J., & Sedlacek, W. E. (1990). Have college students' attitudes toward older people changed? *Journal of College Student Development, 31,* 127–132.

Seefeldt, C. (1987). The effect of preschoolers' visits to a nursing home. *The Gerontologist, 27,* 228–232.

Seitzer, M. M., & Ryff, C. D. (1994). Parenting across the life span: The normative and nonnormative cases. In D. L. Featherman, R. M. Lerner, & M. Permutter (Eds.), *Lifespan development and behavior* (Vol. 12, pp. 1–40). Hillsdale, NJ: Lawrence Erlbaum Associates.

Seppa, N. (1996). Wisdom: A quality that may defy age. *The APA Monitor, 28,* 1–9.

Shalit, R. (1994, July 18–25). The kids are alright. *The New Republic,* 23–31.

Shaner, J. L. (1995, November). *"Grumpy old men" vs. life on "Widows peak": A comparison of elderly portrayals.* Paper presented at the annual meeting of the Speech Communication Association, San Antonio, Texas.

Shaner, J. L. (1996). *Painful self-disclosures of older adults in relation to aging stereotypes and perceived motivations.* Unpublished doctoral dissertation, University of Kansas, Lawrence.

Shaner, J. L., Hummert, M. L., Kemper, S., & Vandeputte, D. D. (1994, November). *Elderly self-disclosure: A replication with a new coding scheme.* Poster presented at the annual conference of the Gerontological Society of America, Atlanta, GA.

Sheehy, G. (1976). *Passages: Predictable crises of adult life.* New York: Bantam.

Sher, A. E. (1984). *Aging in post-Mao China: The politics of veneration.* Boulder, CO: Westview.

Shewan, C. M. (1990). The prevalence of hearing impairment. *ASHA, 32,* 62.

Shorter, E. (1977). *The making of the modern family.* New York: Basic Books.

Shotter, J., & Gergen, K. J. (Eds) (1989). *Texts of identity.* London: Sage.

Sillars, A. L. (1980a). Attributions and communication in roommate conflicts. *Communication Monographs, 47,* 180–200.

Sillars, A. L. (1980b). *Communication and attributions in interpersonal conflict.* Unpublished doctoral dissertation, University of Wisconsin, Madison.

Sillars, A. L. (1986). *Procedures for coding interpersonal conflict.* Unpublished manuscript, University of Montana, Missoula.

Sillars, A. L., Coletti, S. F., Parry, D., & Rogers, M. A. (1982). Coding verbal conflict tactics: Nonverbal and perceptual correlates of the "Avoidance-distributive-integrative" distinction. *Human Communication Research, 9,* 83–95.

Sillars, A. L., Pike, G. R., Jones, T. S., & Redmond, K. (1983). Communication and conflict in marriage. In R. Bostrom (Ed.), *Communication yearbook* (Vol. 7, pp. 414–429). Beverly Hills, CA: Sage.

Sillars, A. L., & Weisberg, W. (1987). Conflict as a social skill. In M. E. Roloff & G. R. Miller (Eds.), *Interpersonal processes: New directions in communication research* (pp. 140–171). Newbury Park, CA: Sage.

Sillars, A. L., & Zietlow, P. H. (1993). Investigations of marital communication and lifespan development. In N. Coupland & J. F. Nussbaum (Eds.), *Discourse and lifespan identity.* Newbury Park, CA: Sage.

Silverstein, M., Lawton, L., & Bengtson, V. L. (1994). Types of intergenerational relations. In R. Harootyan, V. L. Bengston, & M. Schlesinger (Eds.), *Hidden connections: Intergenerational linkages in American society* (pp. 43–76). New York: Springer.

Slawinsky, E., Hartel, D., & Kline, D. (1993). Self-reported hearing problems in daily life throughout adulthood. *Psychology and Aging, 8,* 552–561.

Small, J. A., Montoro, J. & Kemper, S., (1996, May). *Discourse styles of conflict resolution in a nursing home setting.* Paper presented at the Third International Conference on Communication, Aging and Health, Kansas City, MO.

Smith, R. M. (1989). *Middle-aged sons' and daughters' resolution of moral conflict with their aging parents.* Unpublished doctoral dissertation, University of North Carolina at Greensboro.

Snyder, M. (1981). On the self-perpetuating nature of social stereotypes. In D. L. Hamilton (Ed.), *Cognitive processes in stereotyping and intergroup behavior* (pp. 183–211). Hillsdale, NJ: Lawrence Erlbaum Associates.

Song, D., & Youn, G. (1989). Characteristics of loneliness for the elderly Korean. *Journal of Korea Gerontological Society, 9,* 64–78.

Sontag, S. (1978). The double standard of ageing. In V. Carver & P. Liddiard (Eds.), *An aging population* (pp. 72–80). Milton Keynes, UK: Open University Press.

Spitze, G., & Logan, J. (1990). More evidence on women (and men) in the middle. *Research on Aging, 12,* 182–198.

Stack, C. B. (1974). Sex roles and survival strategies in an urban Black community. In M. Z. Rosaldo & L. Lamphere (Eds.), *Women, culture, and society* (pp. 113–128). Stanford, CA: Stanford University Press.

Steichen, L., & Arguitt, G. E. (1975). *Intergenerational living: A pilot study in a university setting: Final Report.* Washington, DC: National Science Foundation.

Stewart, M. A., & Ryan, E. B. (1982). Attitudes toward older and younger adult speakers: Effects of varying speech rates. *Journal of Language and Social Psychology, 1,* 91–109.

Stine, E. L., & Wingfield, A. (1987). Process and strategy in memory for speech among younger and older adults. *Psychology and Aging, 2,* 272–279.

Stine, E. L., Wingfield, A., & Poon, L. W. (1986). How much and how fast: Rapid processing of spoken language in later adulthood. *Psychology and Aging, 1,* 303–311.

Stine, E. L., Wingfield, A., & Poon, L. W. (1989). Speech comprehension and memory throughout adulthood: The roles of time and strategy. In L. W. Poon, D. C. Rubin, & B. A. Wilson (Eds.), *Everyday cognition in adulthood and later life* (pp. 195–229). New York: Cambridge University Press.

Stoller, F. P. (1983). Parental caregiving by adult children. *Journal of Marriage and the Family, 45,* 851–858.

Stone, R. I., Cafferata, G. L., & Sangl, J. (1987). Caregivers of the frail elderly: A national profile. *Medical Care, 28,* 513–525.

Strauss, W., Howe, N., & Williams, I. (1993). *Thirteenth generation: Abort, retry, ignore, fail?* New York: Vintage Books.

Stremmel, A. J., Travis, S. S., Kelly-Harrison, P., & Hensley, A. D. (1994). The perceived benefits and problems associated with intergenerational exchanges in day care settings. *The Gerontologist, 34,* 513–519.

Strom, R., Collinsworth, P., Strom, S., & Griswold, D. (1993). Strengths and needs of Black grandparents. *The International Journal of Aging and Human Development, 36,* 255–268.

Sugarman, L. (1986). *Life-span development: Concepts, theories and interventions.* New York: Methuen.

Suitor, J. J., & Pillemer, K. (1988). Explaining intergenerational conflict when adult children and elderly parents live together. *Journal of Marriage and the Family, 50,* 1037–1047.

Suitor, J. J., & Pillemer, K. (1991). Family conflict when adult children and elderly parents share a home. In K. Pillemer & K. McCartney (Eds.), *Parent–child relations throughout life* (pp. 179–199). Hillsdale, NJ: Lawrence Erlbaum Associates.

Sung, Kyu-taik. (1995). Measures and dimensions of filial piety in Korea. *The Gerontologist, 35,* 240–247.

Szapocznik, J., Scopetta, M. A., Kurtines, W., & Aranalde, M. A. (1978). Theory and measurement of acculturation. *Interamerican Journal of Psychology, 12,* 113–130.

Tajfel, H. (Ed.). (1978). *Differentiation between social groups.* London: Academic Press.

Tajfel, H. (1981). *Human groups and social categories.* Cambridge, England: Cambridge University Press.

Tajfel, H., Billig, M. G., Bundy, R. P., & Flament, C. (1971). Social categorization and intergroup behavior. *European Journal of Social Psychology, 1,* 149–178.

Tajfel, H., & Turner, J. C. (1979). An integrative theory of intergroup conflict. In W. C. Austin & S. Worchel (Eds.), *The social psychology of intergroup relations* (pp. 33–53). Monterey, CA: Brooks/Cole.

Tajfel, H., & Turner, J. C. (1986). An integrative theory of intergroup relations. In S. Worchel & W. Austin (Eds.), *The social psychology of intergroup relations* (2nd ed., pp. 7–17). Chicago: Nelson-Hall.

Tajfel, H., & Wilkes, A. (1963). Classification and quantitative judgement. *British Journal of Psychology, 54,* 101–113.

Taylor, B. C. (1992). Elderly identity in conversation: Producing frailty. *Communication Research, 19,* 493–515.

Taylor, B. C. (1994). Frailty, language and elderly identity: Interpretive and critical perspectives on the aging subject. In M. L. Hummert, J. M. Wiemann, & J. F. Nussbaum (Eds.), *Interpersonal communication in older adulthood: Interdisciplinary theory and research* (pp. 185–208). Thousand Oaks, CA: Sage.

Thimm, C., & Kruse, L. (1996, May). *Intergenerational vs. intragenerational discourse: A comparison of speech styles.* Paper presented at the Third International Conference on Communication, Aging, and Health, Kansas City, MO.

Thomas, J. L. (1986). Age and sex differences in perception of grandparenting. *Journal of Gerontology, 41,* 417–423.

Thomas, J. L. (1989). Gender and perceptions of grandparenthood. *The International Journal of Aging and Human Development, 29,* 269–282.

Thomas, J. L. (1994). Older men as fathers and grandfathers. In E. H. Thompson, Jr. (Ed.), *Older men's lives* (Vol. 6). Beverly Hills, CA: Sage.

Thompson, L., & Walker, A. J. (1989). Gender and families in marriage, work, and parenthood. *Journal of Marriage and the Family, 52,* 845–871.

Thornton, A., Orbuch, T. L., & Axinn, W. G. (1995). Parent–child relationships during the transition to adulthood. *Journal of Family Issues, 16,* 538–564.

Thorsheim, H., & Roberts, B. (1990). Empowerment through storysharing: Communication and reciprocal social support among older persons. In H. Giles, N. Coupland, & J. Wiemann (Eds.), *Communication, health and the elderly* (pp. 114–125). Manchester, England: Manchester University Press.

Tien-Hyatt, J. L. (1987). Self-perceptions of aging across cultures: Myth or reality? *International Journal of Aging and Human Development, 24,* 129–148.

Ting-Toomey, S. (1994). Managing conflict in intimate intercultural relationships. In D. Cahn (Ed.), *Intimate conflict in personal relationships.* Hillsdale, NJ: Lawrence Erlbaum Associates.

Tobin, J. J. (1987). The American idealization of old age in Japan. *The Gerontologist, 27,* 53–58.

Townsend, A., Noelker, L., Deimling, G., & Bass, D. (1989). Longitudinal impact of interhousehold caregiving on adult children's mental health. *Psychology and Aging, 4,* 393–401.

Travis, S. S., Stremmel, A. J., & Kelly-Harrison, P. (1995). Intergenerational programming for young children and dependent elders: Current status and future directions. *Activities, Adaptation, and Aging, 20,* 33–50.

Treas, J. (1979). Intergenerational families and social change. In P. K. Ragan (Ed.), *Aging parents* (pp. 58–65). Los Angeles: University of Southern California Press.

Treas, J. (1995). Commentary: Beanpole or beanstalk? Comments on "The demography of changing intergenerational relations." In V. L. Bengston, K. Warner Schaie, & L. M. Burton (Eds.), *Adult intergenerational relations* (pp. 26–29). New York: Springer.

Triandis, H. C., Leung, K., Vallareal, M., & Clack, F. (1985). Allocentric versus Indiocentric tendencies. *Journal of Research in Personality, 19,* 395–415.

Troll, L. E. (1983). Grandparents: The family watchdog. In T. Brubaker (Ed.), *Family relationships in later life* (pp. 63–74). Beverly Hills, CA: Sage.

Turkowski, B. (1975). Growing old in China. *Journal of Gerontological Nursing, 11,* 32–34.

Turner, J. (1982). Towards a cognitive redefinition of the social group. In H. Tajfel (Ed.), *Social identity and intergroup relations* (pp. 15–40). Cambridge, England: Cambridge University Press.

Turner, J., with Hogg, M., Oakes, P., Reicher, S., & Wetherell, M. (1987). *Rediscovering the social group: A self-categorization theory.* Oxford, England: Basil Blackwell.

Turner, J. C. (1986). *Rediscovering the social group: A self-categorization theory.* Oxford, England: Basil Blackwell.

U. S. Bureau of the Census. (1993). *Marital status and living arrangements* (Series p-20, No. 478). Washington, DC: U.S. Government Printing Office.

U.S. Senate Special Committee on Aging. (1991). *Aging America—Trends and projections* (DHHS Publication No. FCoA91-28001). Washington, DC: U.S. Department of Health and Human Services.

Umberson, D. (1992). Relationships between adult children and their parents: Psychological consequences for both generations. *Journal of Marriage and the Family, 54,* 664–674.

Vangelisti, A. (1992). Messages that hurt. In W. Cupach & B. H. Spitzberg (Eds.), *The dark side of interpersonal communication.* Hillsdale, NJ: Lawrence Erlbaum Associates.

Van Nostrand, I. F. (1981). The aged in nursing homes: Baseline data. *Research on Aging, 3,* 403–16.

Van Sant, R. (1993, December 7). Generation X: 20-somethings fear boom years are past. *Cincinnati Post,* p. 1.

Villaume, W. A., Brown, M. H., & Darling, R. (1994). Presbycusis, communication and older adults. In M. L. Hummert, J. M. Wiemann, & J. F. Nussbaum (Eds.), *Interpersonal communication in older adulthood: Interdisciplinary theory and research* (pp. 83–106). Thousand Oaks, CA: Sage

Walker, A. (1990). The economic "burden" of aging and the prospect of intergenerational conflict. *Aging and Society, 10,* 377–396.

Walker, A. J., Acock, A. C., Bowman, S. R., & Li, F. (1996). Amount of care given and caregiving satisfaction: A latent growth curve analysis. *Journal of Gerontology, 51B,* 130–142.

Walker, A. J., Pratt, C. C., & Eddy, L. (1995). Informal caregiving to aging family members: A critical review. *Family Relations, 44,* 402–411.

Ward, R. A., & Spitze, G. (1992). Consequences of parent–child coresidence: A review and research agenda. *Journal of Family Issues, 13,* 553–572.

Werner, C., & Baxter, L. A. (1994). Temporal qualities of relationships: Organismic, transactional and dialectical views. In M. Knapp & G. R. Miller (Eds.), *Handbook of interpersonal communication* (2nd ed., pp. 323–379). Thousand Oaks, CA: Sage.

Wernick, M., & Manaster, G. (1984). Age and perception of age and attractiveness. *Gerontologist, 24,* 593–600.

Wheeler, J. (1984). *Touched with fire: The future of the Vietnam generation.* New York: Avon.

Williams, A. (1992). *Intergenerational communication satisfaction: An intergroup analysis.* Unpublished masters thesis, University of California, Santa Barbara.

Williams, A. (1994). *"Attention, attention. . . I love attention": Younger person's perceptions of satisfying and dissatisfying intergenerational conversations with older people.* Unpublished doctoral thesis, University of California, Santa Barbara.

Williams, A. (1996). Young people's evaluations of intergenerational versus peer underaccommodation: Sometimes older is better? *Journal of Language and Social Psychology, 15,* 291–311.

Williams, A., & Bergstrom, M. J. (1995, May). *Young people's perceptions of intergenerational conflict: Some evaluations and response strategies.* Paper presented at International Communication Association conference, Albuquerque, NM.

Williams, A., & Coupland, J. (1998). The sociopolitical framing of aging and communication research. *Journal of Applied Communication Research, 26,* 139–154.

Williams, A., Coupland, J., Folwell, A., & Sparks, L. (1997). Talking about Generation X: Defining them as they define themselves. *Journal of Language and Social Psychology, 16,* 251–227.

Williams, A., & Giles, H. (1996). Intergenerational conversations: Young adult's retrospective accounts. *Human Communication Research, 23,* 220–250.

Williams, A., & Giles, H. (1998). Communication of ageism. In M. Hecht (Ed.), *Communicating prejudice: Tolerance and intolerance* (pp. 136–160). Thousand Oaks, CA: Sage.

Williams, A., Giles, H., Coupland, N., Dalby, M., & Manasse, H. (1990). The communicative contexts of elderly social support and health: A theoretical model. *Health Communication, 2,* 123–143.

Williams, A., Giles, H., Ota, H., Pierson, H., Gallois, C., Lim, T.-S., Ng, S. H., & Harwood, J. (1997). Young people's beliefs about intergenerational communication: An initial cross-cultural analysis. *Communication Research, 24,* 370–393.

Williamson, J., Evans, L., & Nunley, A. (1980). *Aging and society.* New York: Holt, Rinehart, & Winston.

Wilmot, W. W. (1995). *Relational communication.* New York: McGraw-Hill.

Wingfield, A., Lahar, C. J., & Stine, E. A. L. (1989). Age and decision strategies in running memory for speech: Effects of prosody and linguistic structure. *Journal of Gerontology: Psychological Sciences, 44,* P106–P113.

Wingfield, A, Wayland, S. C., & Stine, E. L. (1992). Adult age differences in the use of prosody for syntactic parsing and recall of spoken sentences. *Journal of Gerontology: Psychological Sciences, 47,* 350–356.

Wober, M., & Gunther, B. (1982). Television and personal threat: Fact or artifact? A British survey. *British Journal of Social Psychology, 21,* 231–248.

Wong, B. P. (1979). *A Chinese American community: Ethnicity and survival strategies.* Singapore: Chopmen Enterprise.

Wood, L. A., & Ryan, E. B. (1991) Talk to elders: Social structure, attitudes, and address. *Ageing and Society, 11,* 167–188.

Wood, V., & Robertson, J. (1976). The significance of grandparenthood. In J. Gubrium (Ed.), *Time, role, and self in old age* (pp. 278–304). New York: Human Sciences.

Wu, F. Y. (1975). Mandarin speaking aged Chinese in the Los Angeles area. *The Gerontologist, 15,* 271–275.

Yeh, J.-H., Williams, A., & Maruyama, M. (1998). Approving and disapproving grandmothers and strangers: Young Taiwanese and American comparisons. *Journal of Asian Pacific Communication, 8,* 125–149.

Ylanne-McEwen, V. (1997). *Relational processes within a transactional setting: An investigation of travel agency discourse.* Unpublished doctoral dissertation, University of Wales, Cardiff.

Youn, G., & Song, D. (1991). Aging Koreans' perceived conflicts in relationships with their offspring as a function of age, gender, cohabitation status and marital status. *The Journal of Social Psychology, 132,* 299–305.

Ytsma, J., & Giles, H. (1997). Reactions to patronizing talk: Some Dutch data. *Journal of Sociolinguistics, 1,* 259–268.

Yuan, M. (1990). Trends in the Chinese family. *Beijing Review, 33,* 30–32.

Yum, J. O. (1988). The impact of Confucianism on interpersonal relations and communication patterns in East Asia. *Communication Monographs, 55,* 374–388.

Zandpour, F., & Sadri, G. (1996). Communication in personal relationships in Iran: A comparative analysis. In W. B. Gudykunst, S. Ting-Toomey, & T. Nishida (Eds.), *Communication in personal relationships across cultures* (pp. 174–196). Thousand Oaks, CA: Sage.

Author Index

Subject Index

A

Accent, 71
Accommodation, 14, 272, 275, 279, 281, 288
  perceived older, 95
  reluctant young, 97
  theory, 234
  see also Age adapted speech; Baby talk; Elderspeak; Overaccommodation; Patronizing speech; Underaccommodation
Activities of daily living (ADLs)
  instrumental activities of daily living (IADLs)
Adolescent–parent relationship, 186–191, see also Family; Parent–child relationship
Adopt-a-grandparent, 217
Adult child–elderly parent relationship, xii, 151–167, 185
  caregiving in, 156–162
  coresidence, 162–164
  divorce, 164–166
  intergenerational solidarity theory, 152–154, 172
  life-span attachment theory, 154–156
  see also Family; Parent–child relationship
Adult day-care, 156, 209–210
Age

categories, 27, 46, 74
categorization, 134–137
discriminations, 294
interactional patronization, 138
prejudice, 46
segregation, 29
structurating in society, 289–293
Age-adapted speech, 137, see also Accommodation; Baby talk; Elderspeak; Overaccommodation; Patronizing speech
Age-decremental, 49
Age-identifying process, 135–137
Age-telling, 180
Age-Wars, see Intergenerational conflict
Aging
  Eastern perspectives on, 265–267
  negative attitudes toward, 205
  and politics, 245–251
  process, x, xii, 205
  social aspects of, 10
Agism, x, 55–59, 71, 205, 294, 296
  toward the young, 59–63
Agist information seeking, 73–74
Alzheimer's Association, 250
Alzheimer's disease (AD), 82–83, 96, 124–125, 285
American Medical Association, 250
Association of Retired People (AARP), 114, 142, 241, 250, 295, 297
  Intergenerational Linkages Survey, 241
Attachment, 166